Praise for *The Only Rule Is It Has to Work*

"*The Only Rule* might be the most important baseball book published this year—though to use the word 'important' detracts from the sheer fun of the situation. . . . You'll never look at a baseball game, from professional down to fantasy, the same way again."
—Allen Barra, *Chicago Tribune*

"A fun lark . . . a terrific book."   —Will Leitch, *Sports on Earth*

"A worthy modern heir to [George] Plimpton's 1950s stunt."
—*Sports Illustrated*

"Ben Lindbergh and Sam Miller have given us a brutally honest but blissfully funny look at where we really stand a decade into the 'analytics revolution.' If you want the insights that statheads and baseball traditionalists still need to learn from one another, start by reading this book.".   —Nate Silver, bestselling author of
The Signal and the Noise and the founder and
editor in chief of *FiveThirtyEight*

"This hilarious, smooth-reading book . . . is a joy not just because it easily finds the humanity in cold data and spreadsheets, but because, like the best baseball books, it's the story of the life of dreams."
—*Maclean's* (Canada)

"In a phenomenal book that is a fun, breezy, and moving read, Ben Lindbergh and Sam Miller invite us into their mad experiment. They show us the trials, travails, and challenges of running an independent league baseball team, and along the way they do something remarkable: They make us care deeply for the players who put their hearts into every point of on-base percentage."   —Jonah Keri, bestselling
author of *Up, Up, & Away* and *The Extra 2%*

"*The Only Rule Is It Has to Work* sounded like it would be a book that would document all the crazy things you could do on a baseball diamond. And while at times it did, it was more a story about loving baseball. As the authors note in the book's acknowledgments, there is no wrong way to love the game, and this book drives that point home thoroughly and unflinchingly." —*The Hardball Times*

"*The Only Rule Is It Has to Work* is the happy, improbable spawn of *Moneyball* and *Bull Durham*—a relentlessly smart and consistently funny journey into the dregs of the minors that proves one thing above all: No matter how many statistics you apply to baseball, you can never kill its heart." —Stefan Fatsis, author of *Word Freak, A Few Seconds of Panic,* and *Wild and Outside*

"Lindbergh and Miller are real storytellers, explaining their strengths and defects as they attempt to field a capable team, using the best stats money can buy. . . . For fantasy baseball junkies and baseball purists alike, this is a vivid, joyful exploration of recruiting and running a team by numbers—and instinct." —*Publishers Weekly*

"*The Only Rule Is It Has to Work* is a terrific read, as Ben Lindbergh and Sam Miller—two of baseball's leading sabermetric writers—put their beliefs on the line by taking over an actual team of actual players and trying to implement their unorthodox theories. The story of their season with the Sonoma Stompers is a fascinating human drama about the give-and-take between the new thinking and the old school." —Ken Rosenthal, MLB on FOX reporter, FOXSports.com senior baseball writer, and MLB Network insider

"*The Only Rule Is It Has to Work* [is] more than a book about using data and objectivity to build a better baseball team. It is an intimately human story. . . . While readers will come for the stats, they'll stay for the story." —*Eephus*

THE ONLY RULE
IS IT HAS TO WORK

THE ONLY RULE
IS IT HAS TO WORK

OUR WILD EXPERIMENT BUILDING A NEW KIND OF BASEBALL TEAM

BEN LINDBERGH + SAM MILLER

ST. MARTIN'S GRIFFIN ☙ NEW YORK

THE ONLY RULE IS IT HAS TO WORK. Copyright © 2016, 2017 by Ben Lindbergh and Sam Miller. All rights reserved. Printed in the United States of America. For information, address St. Martin's Press, 175 Fifth Avenue, New York, N.Y. 10010.

www.stmartins.com

Designed by Kelly S. Too

The Library of Congress has cataloged the Henry Holt edition as follows:

Names: Lindbergh, Ben, author. | Miller, Sam (Sportswriter), author.
Title: The only rule is it has to work : our wild experiment building a new kind of baseball team /
    Ben Lindbergh and Sam Miller.
Description: First Edition. | New York : Henry Holt and Company, [2016]
Identifiers: LCCN 2016005561| ISBN 9781627795647 (hardcover) | ISBN 9781627795654 (e-book)
Subjects: LCSH: Sonoma Stompers (Baseball team) | Baseball teams—California—Sonoma. |
    Baseball—Management. | Baseball—Statistical methods. | Baseball—Mathematical models.
Classification: LCC GV875.S57 L56 2016 | DDC 796.357/640979418—dc23
LC record available at https://lccn.loc.gov/2016005561

ISBN 978-1-250-13090-7 (trade paperback)

Our books may be purchased in bulk for promotional, educational, or business use. Please contact your local bookseller or the Macmillan Corporate and Premium Sales Department at 1-800-221-7945, extension 5442, or by e-mail at MacmillanSpecialMarkets@macmillan.com.

First published by Henry Holt, an imprint of Henry Holt and Company, LLC

First St. Martin's Griffin Edition: May 2017

10 9 8 7 6 5 4 3 2 1

For Jessie,
who didn't think a concert was a dumb first-date idea.

—B.L.

For my dad,
who taught me what to take seriously.

—S.M.

CONTENTS

THE SONOMA STOMPERS
OPENING DAY ROSTER

PITCHERS

No.	Name	Age	Throws	Height	Weight
14	Jeff Conley	22	L	6-2	170
20	Sean Conroy	23	R	6-1	195
33	Jerome Godsey	35	L	5-11	185
12	Erik Gonsalves	26	R	6-0	185
13	Paul Hvozdovic	22	L	6-1	175
19	Mike Jackson Jr.	26	R	6-0	185
27	Gregory Paulino	22	R	6-3	200
28	Jon Rand	23	L	6-3	200
38	Eric Schwieger	25	L	6-8	210
16	Matt Walker	27	R	6-0	185

CATCHERS

No.	Name	Age	Bats/ Throws	Height	Weight
31	Andrew Parker	24	R/R	6-0	215
25	Isaac Wenrich	25	L/R	6-2	230

INFIELDERS

No.	Name	Age	Bats/Throws	Height	Weight
44	Daniel Baptista	24	L/R	6-5	225
7	Joel Carranza	26	R/R	6-2	225
3	T. J. Gavlik	24	L/R	5-11	185
29	Kristian Gayday	23	R/R	6-3	230
10	Sergio Miranda	28	S/R	5-9	190
11	Gered Mochizuki	29	L/R	5-8	170
8	Yuki Yasuda	24	R/R	5-10	170

OUTFIELDERS

No.	Name	Age	Bats/Throws	Height	Weight
1	Matt Hibbert	26	R/R	5-10	180
22	Mark Hurley	22	R/R	6-0	190
24	Fehlandt Lentini	37	R/R	6-0	180

MANAGER/COACHES

No.	Name
24	Fehlandt Lentini
26	Takashi Miyoshi
9	Tommy Lyons
/	Dan Morgan

THE REST OF THE TEAM, IN ORDER OF DEBUT:

- Josh McCauley RHP
- Jose Canseco, DH
- Ryusuke Kikusawa, RHP
- Aritz Garcia, SS
- Taylor Eads, OF
- Santos Saldivar, RHP
- Brennan Metzger, OF
- Dylan Stoops, LHP
- Cole Warren, RHP
- Peter Bowles, OF
- Connor Jones, OF
- Matt Rubino, C
- Eddie Mora-Loera, SS
- Eric Mozeika, RHP
- Chad Bunting, OF
- Keith Kandel, OF

SPRING TRAINING INVITEES

- Kyle Breault, INF
- Collin Forgey, OF
- Jesse Garcia, LHP
- Billy Gonzalez, C
- Marcus Kimura, INF
- Danny Martinez, INF
- Caleb Natov, RHP
- Will Price, OF

THE ONLY RULE
IS IT HAS TO WORK

PROLOGUE

In April 2015, the River City Rascals, a professional baseball team just west of St. Louis in the independent Frontier League, invited six left-handed pitchers to spring training, and entering the last day of intra-squad games Paul Hvozdovic was the only one left. His throwing partner, a lefty who had also been on the team the year before, had been the fifth one cut, and it was clear to them both that nothing remained in Paul's way. He was going to make the team. The throwing partner congratulated him and shook his hand. Paul called his dad, called his girlfriend, told them anything could happen but it sure looked good.

Then he gave up a solo home run in that final scrimmage, and afterward he got a text message from his manager. These texts at the end of spring training, innocuous and inviting on their surface, always had a hidden, ominous meaning. Paul walked down the hall to the manager's office, knowing he was getting cut. The River City Rascals wouldn't carry a left-handed pitcher at all; they wouldn't even carry the full twenty-four-man roster they were allowed, opting to save money by employing just twenty-two players to start the season. Paul's dream was somebody else's unnecessary business expense.

He thanked his manager for the opportunity, then told him he was probably going to hang up his spikes for good and head back home to northern Virginia, where his girlfriend and his future (whatever that might be) were waiting for him. The manager told him to stick around for a couple of weeks—maybe he'd find a spot once the season started— but that was too painful for Paul. He suddenly realized how much he hated baseball, hated the anxiety of standing on the mound knowing that he was always a bad outing away from feeling the rejection he felt now. He stewed about the politics of these decisions, the seemingly arbitrary designs that stoked some guys' careers and smothered the careers of others. He thought about all the time he had invested in something he believed would pay off, and how this manager had probably known all along that it wouldn't. Baseball hurt too much. He was done.

He called his agent, Brian McGinn, and told him that's where he was leaning. Brian didn't pretend Paul was going to be some sort of major league millionaire. He and Paul both knew the reality: Paul had just been cut by an independent minor league that was nine promotions from the majors. But, Brian said, "you're in the prime of your career, and you've never been given the right opportunity. If nothing else, this is the perfect chance to see the world."

The world was a place called Sonoma, two thousand miles west of anywhere Paul had ever walked, somewhere in California in what was exotically described as "wine country." There was a team in Sonoma that had seen something in his college stats and called his agent a month earlier, trying to convince Paul to come to a lower-level club that would give him a bigger role. It would mean a pay cut, from $600 a month to $500; it would mean moving backward, now ten promotions from the majors; it would mean, Paul feared, losing his girlfriend of four years, who was sick of seeing her boyfriend disappear every summer to pursue opportunities that could barely be called such. But it would also mean validation, that the sport hadn't rejected him after all. He chose validation. He felt, just as suddenly, at peace once more. He even went to the Rascals' Opening Night game, and with his execution commuted he was free to enjoy it. His girlfriend dumped him that day, by text message.

The next morning Paul got into his Buick and drove west. He had no navigation, other than some pictures of freeway interchanges printed out from the Internet. He had no motel reservations. He just drove until he had to stop for gas, and then he drove some more. He'd been on long drives on the East Coast, but he'd never seen the world change like this. He finally saw the flat of Kansas, and he finally climbed the mountain ranges in Colorado. He drove 95 mph and watched cars pass him on his left. He detoured only to follow signs for minor league ballparks, just to see them. Eventually he would notice it was 2:00 a.m., and he'd find a motel, collect the Burger King bags and Red Bull cans from his car, sleep a few hours, and hit the road again.

He thought about going back to his girlfriend, but as the Buick went farther the cost of turning back got greater. Eventually, you're halfway through the desert and it feels like the only way out is forward. Or you're halfway over the mountains and the only way out is down. And after the deserts and after the mountains, well, hell, you're already there: The radio stations become Bay Area stations, and just like that you're pulling up to the office of the Sonoma Stompers at 234 West Napa Street, just as they directed you to on the phone, and soon you're in the office shaking hands with the owner, and somebody's telling somebody else about your incredible stats, and they're giving you a card that'll let you eat free at Mary's Pizza Shack, and it turns out the bartender there lets some of the players live with her family every summer. And then you're walking around the downtown square, with its historic city hall and no chain businesses, and there are ducks and two playgrounds and a farmers' market, and this doesn't feel anything like the cold business of rejection that River City was. And now there's no part of you left that wants anything but to be here and pitch and maybe turn into a big deal.

This was our Paul. We knew him as a name on a spreadsheet. We had never seen him, never watched video of him, never held a radar gun for his pitches, never shaken his hand or assessed the swagger in his gait, never looked at his parents and extrapolated what it meant for

the future development of his body, never inspected his elbow liga-
ment through an MRI machine, never studied his temperament on the
mound to deduce whether he was a thrower or a pitcher, whether he
could bear down, whether he'd take it one day at a time. All we knew
about Paul was that the previous season he had struck out one hundred
batters and walked eight for a Division II school called Shepherd University. He had gone 11-1 with a 1.80 ERA. On a spreadsheet of 2014
college seniors, adjusted for level of competition and various other factors,
and sorted by Column R—where we'd devised a metric for overall
performance—Paul Hvozdovic was at the top. Not near the top; *at* the
top. We had a spreadsheet that said Paul Hvozdovic had been the best
senior pitcher at any level of college baseball one year earlier.

At a banquet marking the first day of Sonoma Stompers spring training, we talked to player after player, wondering at each introduction
if this was Paul. He was one of the last players we met. He was sitting
away from the crowd at the end of a long table, talking in short and
patient sentences to a Dominican pitcher who spoke no English. We
told Paul why we'd brought him all the way here from Missouri, why
we'd diverted him from his retirement plans, why he didn't have a girlfriend anymore. We told him about the spreadsheet, and we told him
about what had happened when we'd sorted by Column R. Paul looked
at us doubtfully.

"Your spreadsheet's some shit," he said.

Our trip to Sonoma was no less likely than Paul Hvozdovic's. Since
childhood, we've both loved baseball and searched for deeper under-
standing of the sport through mathematical means. We were fantasy
junkies before our tenth birthdays, the kind of kids who studied minor
league numbers to figure out which rookie cards were the best investments, and the kind of preadolescents who mailed trade suggestions
to our favorite team's general manager. (Note: this was Sam.) That's what
made baseball so different from any other childhood hobby: It came
preloaded with a numerical puzzle. Every cardboard back in a pack of

baseball cards contained a table, and in that table we learned the power of a story told through numbers. Those tables challenged us, as they've challenged baseball fans forever, to be smarter. From a childhood immersed in those tables, we grew up to be details-obsessed calculators who will spend five minutes figuring price-per-ounce at a supermarket to determine the best way to allocate our spreadsheet-ordered food budget. (Also Sam.)

We are apostles of sabermetrics, a term named for the Society for American Baseball Research (SABR) and coined by the discipline's most influential thinker, Bill James, to describe "the search for objective knowledge about baseball." Over the past two decades, the sabermetric movement has plowed across Major League Baseball like a glacier, leaving a strange-looking landscape behind: Ivy League–educated twenty- and thirtysomethings with Wall Street experience replacing weatherbeaten general managers who came up as players and scouts; precise defensive positioning supplanting guesswork and gut feel; strict pitch counts and swelling bullpens crowding out complete games. Every major league franchise has its front-office nerd cave, home to quants with wall-worthy credentials and technical skills that could earn them fortunes in the financial sector.

We loved to play as much as Paul does, but our lack of tools killed our careers early. And yet our lives have still revolved around the game. Each of us has served as editor in chief of *Baseball Prospectus*, the leading media outlet devoted to data-driven baseball analysis. In our writing, we speak this new, analytical language of sports, drawing on advanced statistics to explain the changing game and pass judgment on player acquisitions. The point of baseball management isn't to produce tables and spreadsheets, of course; the point is to make the right decision every time, to give players every resource and advantage available, and to reject "because we've always done it this way" as the answer to any question. And, oh, are there ever questions: Why don't teams try two-man outfields and five-man infields against extreme ground ball/fly ball hitters? Why don't they deploy their best relievers at the most important times, instead of wasting them in low-leverage situations where they're likely to record a "save"? Why don't they have statistically inclined coaches in the dugout who can crunch the numbers before managers make game-changing moves?

The question underlying our entire careers, though, is more personal: Do we really know what we're talking about? It was unanswerable, untestable—until last summer. Through a series of unlikely events, we found ourselves running the baseball operations of the Sonoma Stompers, an independent minor league team north of San Francisco. We were given the latitude to put our theories about baseball to the test in real life, with real players. If we wanted to sign players based on a spreadsheet and arcane calculations, we could. If we wanted to employ unorthodox defensive shifts, we could. If we wanted to use relievers to start the game and starters to finish, we could do that, too. There were no rules, except for one that our players demanded: Whatever we tried had to work.

"Analysis is valuable, certainly," wrote *Baseball Prospectus*'s founder, Gary Huckabay, in 2001. "But there are limits to its utility. . . . Our models are built on enough assumptions about baseball, data, and the world that we need to turn a skeptical eye on them at every opportunity, just like we do to conventional wisdom. What we don't know could fill a book."

This is that book.

Because there are two of us, and because there are some events that happened to only one of us, we've decided to tell our story in alternating chapters. Ben has written chapter 1, Sam has written chapter 2, and so forth. If you can follow the action in a baseball game from the top of the inning to the bottom and back again, you shouldn't have any trouble here, either.

NOT JOKING AT ALL

Sam is sitting in the passenger seat of his 2011 Honda Fit, which is parked inside his garage in Long Beach, California. I'm sitting in my 2005 fading, faux-leather desk chair, which is parked inside the small office in my Manhattan apartment. Sitting between our sound-dampening sanctuaries (where we're trying not to wake Sam's wife or my girlfriend) is former Los Angeles Dodgers general manager Dan Evans, who's in an Arizona hotel on a spring training scouting trip, talking to us on Skype.

It's March 2013, just after midnight my time, and Sam and I are interviewing Evans for the latest episode of *Effectively Wild*, the daily podcast we record for *Baseball Prospectus*. Midway through the call, we ask him about his new job, a side gig as the commissioner of the Northern League, an independent circuit that he's trying to bring back from the dead. Indy leagues are like the minors, except that they're even *more* minor: They employ professional players, but they aren't affiliated with major league organizations. This means they don't take orders from above, but it also means that most of them are in perpetually critical financial condition, one down year away from drowning in debt and leaving only ripples behind. The Northern League, which fielded teams in Minnesota, South Dakota, Iowa, and Ontario, was founded in 1993 and winked out of existence in 2010. Now Evans is trying to wink it back in again. And to do that, he tells us, he needs investors to take on teams.

"If you're asking," I say, "Sam and I will take one team."

Everyone laughs, but cohost telepathy tells Sam I'm serious. I sense the same about him.

"I wonder how many people in this conversation are joking, because at least two of us are not joking at all," Sam says.

Evans responds by extolling the virtues of indy-league life. "Unlike a minor league franchise, where you have no say in the players . . . everything in the independents is under your jurisdiction," he says. "For some people, that's really intimidating. For other people . . . they see that and they go, 'Oh my gosh, this is my real fantasy team.'"

We don't need any additional selling. We spend the rest of the podcast distracted, sending silent text messages to each other and trying to contain our excitement. Once we're off the air, we ask Evans if he was just humoring us or if it's safe for our hopes to be high.

"Down the line, if you guys are really serious, I would actually entertain something like that," he says. We feel as if a real GM has just walked us to the war room where teams talk strategy, flashed his credentials, and assured security that we're with him. After Evans is off the line, Sam and I instant message into the night. We're already playing out all the implications, wondering which ideas we'd test out if we owned a team and could be the bosses of our own baseball sandbox. "I might not sleep again until we have a baseball team," I say to Sam.

Once the sun is up and I can send emails without looking like a vampire, I contact our boss, Joe Hamrahi, the president and CEO of *Baseball Prospectus* and a friend of Dan Evans. *Joe, can we buy a baseball team? Can we? Can we?*

"They want a lot of money," Joe writes back. He keeps me in suspense until the answer to my "How *much* money?" follow-up appears: "$250,000."

I have three minutes to mull over that massive-sounding amount before another email arrives. "By the way, that's just the admission fee," Joe adds. "Then you have to come up with the capital to operate the team, pay the players, the front office, lease the ballpark, run concessions, etc. And you're not talking about real players here. These are has-beens and guys looking for some shot at getting into real baseball."

Well, hell, so are we. Sam and I aren't old enough to be "has-beens" in every respect, but we qualify when it comes to our childhood hopes. Sam was that skinny ten-year-old who pictured himself hitting the World Series–winning home run. Like every amateur hero before him, he sprinted around the imaginary bases as though the earth were crumbling behind him, leaping and skipping, pumping a fist, throwing a helmet, voicing the cheers of each of the thousands of fans who sounded so loud in his head. Over the course of a quarter century, that pretend applause went silent. In the saddest perversion of a sports-movie montage, it became increasingly clear to Sam that he would never hit that home run. He was too shy, then too small, then too distracted, then too old. Finally, he was simply too realistic.

I grew up five years later, after the steroids era had given athletes comic-book bodies. I had no illusions about displacing Alex Rodriguez, but I could see myself as the successor to the New York Yankees' general manager, Brian Cashman. GMs and other team executives look the way we would if we wore more expensive suits. They're the sports heroes of the computer age, and they've instilled in us the oh-so-tantalizing notion that *we could do that.* Thinking along with the GM is the new national pastime. In its most mocked form, this fetish for front offices is known as "rosterbation," a word that captures a fan's sometimes-delusional attempts to engineer the perfect transaction. In its most mainstream form, it's fantasy sports, a multibillion-dollar industry now served by an array of statistical resources so granular and accessible that anyone can retrieve far more data from a home computer than Oakland Athletics GM Billy Beane did in his famous *Moneyball* season.

My mental montage was more sedate than Sam's, but still satisfying: Making the perfect pick on draft day. Swindling a rival team in a trade. Landing the high-priced free agent who lays waste to the league. I

came closer to my dream than Sam did to his: I became a baseball operations intern for the Yankees straight out of college, sitting with other
interns in an office inside Yankee Stadium where every so often Cashman himself would walk by, saying hello (or activating his beloved
handheld fart machine) on his way to continue trade talks or address
the press. He knew, and we knew, that everyone in the room had designs
on his job.

I had good timing: It was 2009, the year the Yankees beat the Phila-
delphia Phillies to win their first World Series since their (most recent)
dynasty team. After Game 6, in which New York's Andy Pettitte outdueled a past-his-prime Pedro Martinez in Pedro's last-ever outing,
I sipped champagne in the clubhouse while CC Sabathia smoked a cigar,
Kate Hudson lounged on A-Rod's lap, and Kurt Russell talked intently
to Mark Teixeira. After the fans had reluctantly cleared out, the players
had hit the town, and the empty stadium was ours again, I did tipsy
cartwheels on the field with the rest of the front office. Later that week,
I rode on a duck boat with the rest of the interns in the ticker-tape
parade as a horde of pinstriped strangers on lower Broadway chanted,
"WHO-ARE-YOU? WHO-ARE-YOU?" and bombarded us with whole
rolls of toilet paper. For the rest of the off-season, I slipped on my lan-
yard and badge as self-importantly as if I were putting on an actual uniform. My MLB.TV account had no blackout restrictions. I felt as if
I belonged in baseball.

But the following spring, my time as an insider ended, almost without warning. On a day like any other, Cashman came in and told us
he'd been ordered to bring in new blood, that the legal department was
worried about interns staying more than a year, and that his hands had
been tied by a hiring freeze. I tried not to be bitter about the news that
the World Series–winning Yankees, who regularly dropped hundreds of
millions on free agents who weren't worth the money, couldn't afford to
convert a few underpaid interns into underpaid full-timers. It stung even
more when the "hiring freeze" turned out to be a comforting fiction:
Two of the senior interns got to stay as full-fledged staffers. My skill set,
it seemed, just wasn't special enough for the team to make an exception.

So what do you do when the guy whose job you grew up wanting to do kicks you (very gently) to the curb? I could have tried to parlay my year with the Yankees into another team internship, eventually ascending to a GM role with another organization and, in my moment of triumph, exacting revenge for my freeze-out by taking Cashman to the cleaners in a lopsided deal. Instead, I steered into the skid and went back to the baseball writing I'd begun in college. In time, I came to believe that the Yankees had done me a favor by pushing me into a role for which I was a far better fit. But now, having spoken to Dan Evans, I see a way to bypass the intern stage and skip directly to running a team. I'm eager to test myself, even in an upstart indy league. Neither Sam nor I had ever completely let go of that one special fantasy, the last lingering what-if: Could we "crack" baseball if we could borrow a GM's job and live it for a single season? How would we be altered? And how would we alter a team?

Unfortunately, we don't know anyone with six figures to throw away on someone else's wish fulfillment. Evidently Dan doesn't either: The new Northern League never gets off the ground. Sam and I don't dismiss our vision of running an indy team, but without an obvious outlet we put it on the back burner. And the longer it sits there, the sillier and less realistic it seems.

It took a podcast conversation to inspire this far-fetched idea; it takes another to make it more real. Sixteen months and hundreds of *Effectively Wild* episodes later, a listener's email prompts us to admit on the air that we've never attended an independent-league game. Some hours after that show ends, a message appears in Sam's inbox. "I hear you're looking for an invite out to an independent league game," writes Tim Livingston, the director of broadcasting and media relations for the Sonoma Stompers, a franchise in the fledgling, four-team Pacific Association of Professional Baseball Clubs, which rose out of the ashes of the North American League (itself a chimera created from the remnants of three earlier leagues). "I think it would be great if you could come by to watch." So does Sam.

SONOMA DREAMING

I fell in love with baseball because it brought me into a world of grown-ups: advertisements for plumbers unions and Budweiser and equipment-rental stores interspersed with fights on the field, $5,000 giveaways for a grand slam in the fifth, the occasional on-field cuss picked up by the broadcasts, and the constant cycling in of ballplayers who had been swapped like trading cards. In this world, I felt as smart and informed as the adults I still had trouble talking to about anything else.

That's what led to my first baseball writing. It was a day game in the summer of 1988. Day games were salvation, three hours in the afternoon when my chores pulling weeds or watering plants could have a dramatic soundtrack. It didn't seem fair that my dad had to miss these games when he went to work, so one afternoon I sat at my desk with a notebook and a pencil and a radio, and I wrote down everything that happened, relying on the broadcasters' selective attention to fill in the details. I took those notes and wrote up a game story so my dad could read about it when he came home. I decided then that after my Hall of Fame playing career was over I would become a baseball writer.

I sort of kept that dream going—"writer" stuck, but "baseball" wandered away, and the Hall of Fame playing career is still waiting. I became a newspaper reporter in Orange County, California, covering everything from a lady's lost cat to the federal education budget. I read *Baseball Prospectus* on my lunch break, printing out each day's articles and hiding under a stairwell so I wouldn't be disturbed, but baseball was just a hobby.

Eventually, the sports section pulled me in to write about "stat stuff," and from there Ben found me and brought me to *Baseball Prospectus*, where I now get an eighteen-hour head start on all the reading that I used to do at lunch.

One perk of the job is that I can do it from anywhere, so, stupidly, I ended up in the most expensive housing market in the country: the San Francisco Bay Area, where my wife had taken a job teaching Mandarin to elementary school students. It's a solid baseball region—two MLB clubs, a high-A team in San Jose, top draft prospects cycling through Stanford's and Cal's spring schedules, but, so far as I knew, no independent-league baseball. When Tim Livingston emailed to invite me to Sonoma, where under the cover of vineyards a self-sustaining league was operating, I made plans to go up and shadow Sonoma's general manager, the too-good-to-be-truly-named Theo Fightmaster. I figured I'd write a piece for BP about how a GM builds a pennant contender at this level, especially in the team's expansion season. A little slice of life for September.

Organized baseball has been played in Sonoma for more than a century, and the locals still brag about the days when Joe DiMaggio played summer ball in Sonoma County. Arnold Field, the Stompers' home park, stands just up the street from Sonoma Plaza, the site of the Bear Flag Revolt, a one-month uprising of American settlers against the Mexican government in 1846, in the opening days of the Mexican-American War. More important (to present-day residents), the plaza allows open containers and houses Town Square and Steiners Tavern, the two bars on opposite sides of the square. Start at the north end of the plaza and stroll past the one-story homes and wine-tasting rooms on First Street West, and you'll soon arrive at Arnold Field, which is shrouded in greenery until you're almost on top of it and can spot the light towers stabbing out of the treetops. The field, which is also home to Babe Ruth baseball in the summer and high school football in the fall, has unusually elongated dimensions: It's Lilliputian down the lines (304 to left, 311 to right), shallow in the alleys (331 and 345), and Brobdingnagian to center (435), where the tallest of the hills surrounding Sonoma serves as a scenic batter's eye.

Arnold is a beautiful ballpark at first glance, although a closer inspection reveals its amateurish quirks. I pace the bases and discover that third base is a foot closer to home than the rest of the bases are to each other—and then I measure again, and again, and again, and once more, because this seems somehow central to the soul of this league. There's a goalpost in right-center, completely in play. The grass lacks that greener-than-green, well-manicured big league look. The PA system is warbly, the lights are dim, and the ads are sometimes misspelled. The anthem singer forgets her words midway through, but instead of powering on she starts over from the beginning, earning twice the applause a perfect rendition would merit. The players' clubhouse is tiny and sweats body heat like dryer exhaust; there's no clubhouse bathroom, just an outdoor Porta Potti protected from public use by a handwritten "Players only!" sign taped to the door. Pregame meals are a tub of peanut butter and Costco-brand white bread, served on a card table. Most players, I learn that night, earn significantly less than $1,000 a month and live off the largesse of local host families, regular folks who let players sleep in a spare room (or two, or three, plus sometimes a couch, a trailer, the garage, or a corner of the kitchen) in exchange for season tickets and nothing else. A player's incentives clause could be a case of beer, and a struggling team might have to slash salary to make its meager payroll in the second half of the season.

The park's official capacity is 1,450, though the Stompers rarely test its limits. On the day I visit, they come pretty close, more because baseball dignitary Dusty Baker is visiting and signing autographs than because of the playoff implications of the game against the Vallejo Admirals. The Pacific Association plays a seventy-eight-game split schedule, with the champion of the first half playing the champion of the second half in a winner-take-all title game. The Stompers and Admirals are trying to prevent the San Rafael Pacifics, the league's flagship franchise and first-half victors, from taking the second half too. It's not looking good, since the Stompers and Admirals have to beat up on each other while the Pacifics face the Pittsburg Mettle, the doormats of the league. Earlier in the month, the Stompers started sixty-seven-year-old former major leaguer Bill "Spaceman" Lee against Pittsburg as a publicity stunt. Lee went 5 1/3 innings in a 6-3 Stompers win, becoming the oldest pitcher ever to win a professional game.

Fightmaster the man is as memorable as Fightmaster the surname. As a big, bad-bodied first baseman, he topped out in junior college, save for the one time when he tried to walk on to Arizona State. He quickly walked off, although he left with a story about getting into an intrasquad game against Dustin Pedroia. He tried coaching and fantasy games, but they didn't scratch his, er, sports itch, so he started writing about baseball for local media outlets. One of those stories was about Mike Shapiro, the man who brought baseball to San Rafael. After he read the story, Shapiro offered Fightmaster a job with the Pacifics as director of operations, and two years later when the Pacifics formed the Stompers to keep an even number of teams in the league, Theo was promoted to Sonoma's GM. Despite his martial name, he's an easygoing guy, thoughtful, quick-witted, and cultured. The Stompers are a family affair for him—his wife is wandering around, sometimes selling concessions; his mom, in a Black Eyed Peas sweatshirt, is here, too—but it's a more-than-full-time job, of which only a few hours a day are spent doing what he wants to do: baseball stuff.

During the hours I spend with him, I see Theo scramble to assign a ceremonial first pitch, clean up litter, tend to ticket and concession sales, keep kids from infiltrating the field, and send a beer (Lagunitas, a Stompers sponsor) to Baker. At most games, he watches an inning or three before he has to grill burgers or replace tapped-out kegs, or go back to the Stompers' office to count tickets and wish they'd sold more. He's always stressed about expenses and looking for ways to recoup costs: Any fan who turns in a foul that falls in the stands gets a snack item for free, because each ball costs the club about five bucks. Once, a visiting manager asked Theo for an on-the-house hot dog. Theo had to turn him down.

This, of course, puts a tremendous strain on his ability to eke out victories. He doesn't have a vast scouting network—he compares his player-acquisition process to Plato's Allegory of the Cave, trying to draw significant information out of brief, flickering shadows.

"What about Moneyball stuff?" I ask. "Is there much opportunity to do that sort of stuff here?"

"You could definitely find inefficiencies," he says. "But if I had another set of hands, I'd have them handing out programs or selling sponsorships, not scouting our opponents."

He wants badly to win—he wants especially to beat the Pacifics, who own the club but give him only two thirds the payroll that San Rafael gets—but he's not selling a winning club. He's selling the small-town experience of being at a ballpark on a mild summer night. "The owners' objective," he tells me, "is basically this vision of a family of four leaving the game, the kids got to high-five the mascot, they got a foul ball, they're walking to their car and saying, 'What a fantastic night at the park. By the way, who won?'"

I watch the Stompers lose. I watch the Colombian starting pitcher get injured, and I see how heartbroken Theo is, knowing that, at this level, the player is responsible for his own, potentially expensive recovery—and that, if it takes too long, the player will likely have to leave the country. I see Theo groan when an important runner is held at third, his emotions getting the better of his business-first spiel. I go home and follow along as the Stompers go 3-5 to finish the season in third place, while the Pacifics end on a 6-2 run to win the second half and the Pacific Association championship. It wasn't a fair fight, I think.

After my trip to Sonoma, I call Ben, and we agree that if we're ever going to pursue our dream of running a team, we'd be hard-pressed to find a better environment than Sonoma, or a more congenial and supportive colleague than Theo Fightmaster. And so, in late October 2014,

I drive to a high-rise office building overlooking San Francisco Bay, where the Pacifics/Stompers owner, Eugene Lupario, runs the professional-staffing company he cofounded. Theo is there, too. I feel like a pitcher with a three-ball count and the bases loaded: I have to be perfect if I'm going to convince them to buy into the plan Ben and I want to put in place, or else I may never get this chance again. I grab a piece of hard candy from the unattended reception desk, tuck it into my cheek for comfort, and throw my pitch: We're legit, experts in the field, constantly surrounded by brilliant baseball minds and ready to put in crazy baseball-exec hours. We can give the Stompers the baseball operations department they lack, expand their player pool, generate publicity, and free up Theo to focus on the business side. We will, we believe, make the Stompers the best independent-league team in the country—or, at least, in the Pacific Association. All we ask for is a pro team to play with.

"So if you took over our baseball operations department," Lupario asks, "what would you *do*?"

In the span of a single intake of breath, I flip through the possibilities. Optimized lineups, with each hitter in his sabermetrics-approved place? Too boring, too small. Social mapping to engineer clubhouse chemistry? Too sinister, sounds like we're Big Brother.

Finally I blurt, "There's no rule that says you have to have three men in the outfield and four in the infield. We'd like to try five-man infields."

Silence. Then Fightmaster, who sees in this proposal the chance to be part of something that changes baseball forever, smiles. Lupario, a businessman through and through, doesn't join him. Too nervous to stop myself, I keep going: "And probably six-man, too."

Fightmaster and Lupario look at each other. Lupario raises his eyebrows. And then, swayed by Theo's what-the-hell look of optimism, he agrees.

We're going to get our opportunity. We're taking our talents, such as they are, to Sonoma.

. . .

Although Ben and I are on the public front lines of baseball's analytical movement, we've fought our battles from the safety of our screens: Our ideas about baseball are academic, theoretical, never exposed to tobacco spit and stray infield pebbles. We talk to pro athletes often, but only to inquire, not to tell them what to do. We pick up and drop players from our fantasy teams, but we don't have to break the bad news in person and look them in the eye as we let them go. We've been armchair GMs, backseat drivers. So as we grip the wheel, we wonder: Can a creative, incisive use of numbers really sharpen the performance of players who've never been able to fulfill their major league dreams? Can we become as proficient at analyzing players' personalities as we are at analyzing their stats? Or will the game's human element build barriers that we'll be too out of *our* element to break down?

After a half decade of writing for a fairly closed circle, we actually want to hear the best arguments against us. One way to encounter those arguments is to read the scolds and the trolls who mock us for our spreadsheets (sure) and our slide rules (never seen one), but they're so scoldy and trolly. Another is to try to anticipate those arguments as best we can, but our personal biases undoubtedly limit our imaginations. No, the best way to find the vulnerabilities in our beliefs is to test them in an uncontrolled, unpredictable, real-world environment.

This is exciting! I'm not nervous at all! After the successful pitch, I celebrate with a hamburger. I eat alone and read a book. I finish my hamburger. I pay. I get to the sidewalk. It hits me. I'm nervous.

There is no reserve clause in the Pacific Association, and there are no multiyear contracts or farm systems. Every season starts with a blank whiteboard. In January, we start filling it with names.

A handful of players from the previous year's team are interested in returning and are good enough for Ben, Theo, and me to agree right away to bring back. Designated hitter Joel Carranza is a former draft pick of the Tampa Bay Rays who never played affiliated ball but did set our league's record with 19 home runs in 2014. (Our season is his off-season—he works at a charter school in Florida the rest of the year.) Andrew Parker is a twenty-four-year-old catcher with the league's quickest "pop" time—the 1.9 seconds between the ball popping his glove and then popping the shortstop's glove on a throw down to second—and a walks-and-power approach at the plate. (He is studying to be an accountant; he's one of the few players in this league who has no dreams of gutting out a career in affiliated ball, and this will be his last summer in the sport regardless of what happens.) Matt Hibbert is a speedy out-fielder who had the Stompers' second-most steals and third-best on-base percentage in 2014. He wants to fight for the leadoff and center field jobs.

That's it. A team of three, with the other nineteen players to be win-nowed down from a list that starts at seven billion. We don't know where to look, we don't know what to look for, and we don't know whom to ask. This puts us at the mercy of what resembles an elaborate ring of email scammers, each promising us huge returns on tiny investments. These emails come from players, parents, college coaches, and amateur "scouts" who produce lists of indy-qualified players as a hobby. Some come from no-rent agents who gather indy-ball clients on the off chance one will someday make the majors, there being absolutely no profit in a 3 percent cut of a Pacific Association wage. They send us emails that have seventy teams cc'd, or emails personally tailored to us and our needs. Some are submitted through the Stompers' general email address, the same way somebody would request directions to the park or ad-buy rates on outfield-wall signs. They contain the grammatical carelessness of a grocery list ("Hope to hear form you soon"). They get sent before spellcheck review ("I strained both my laburnums in shoulders"). They name-drop fringy retired major leaguers (Jamie Brewington! Denny Hocking!) who, we're told, will vouch for these aspirants. They recount personal narratives that give away the players' limitations: the long list of teams that somehow overlooked their talent, the now-famous former teammates who moved up the ladder and left them playing "what if?" on men's league teams, the overdeveloped sense of baseball's unfairness.

"Like at the time of Jackie Robinson, there is something not right with the game we all love, there is too much emphasis on age and not enough emphasis on ability," one tells us.

And they lie. They lie like you can lie only if you believe the lie, like you lie when you *have* to believe the lie, when your career depends on the lie, because the lie is the only thing that keeps you running and lifting and writing emails begging strangers to take a chance on you. One after another promises to run a 6.5 in the 60-yard sprint—a time that would be elite even at the major league level, the time that baseball's fastest man, Billy Hamilton, was once reportedly clocked. One says he runs "approximately" 6.3, but how approximate (plus or minus a second?) isn't specified. One says he ran a 6.6 at a tryout at which (spoiler here) *I was holding the stopwatch*, a tryout at which only one person cracked 7. They say things like "I'm a great kid." They attach a video of a "520+ ft home run," a video that definitely shows a ball being hit—oh, I don't know, pretty far? They elide; they list their .300 college batting average but avoid mentioning the name of their no-name college. ("Hit .171/.237/.228 [batting average / on base / slugging] in senior year of high school, so we can probably rule out UCLA," we note about one.) They list their stats only up to 2013 if the 2014 edition shows too much suck. They blame injuries for every bad stat line but swear they're healthy now, or they blame coaches for tinkering with their swings but swear they're back to form. They promise velocity like online dating profiles promise fifteen-years-ago bodies. (One email bragging of a low-90s fastball came the day before a league tryout. The pitcher sat mid-70s on our radar gun. He knew he was coming to a tryout, knew we'd see the thing itself, and still padded by 15 mph.) These candidates are all flawed, and it rarely takes more than two more minutes online to find that flaw: the suspension for throwing a bat at a pitcher, the disastrous season in a lower indy league, the mean-spirited Twitter account that former team-mates made to parody the guy, the five years of inactivity, the shoulder surgery that preceded a release from affiliated ball.

We give the first fifty or so the respect that a dream deserves, but after a while we skim, mock as appropriate, and file away. The sense of unfairness these guys have? It's not entirely wrong. Even we don't take their abilities seriously, and while some of the mockery is mom-literally-wrote-your-cover-letter-related, much of it comes down to a decision-making shorthand that we start to develop: If you're so good, why are you writing to us? This is a terrible, fallacious bit of reasoning; every player we ultimately sign will be, by definition, available to us, and many of them, we hope, will be valuable parts of a winning team. The question must be asked, but instead of asking it rhetorically—to be answered with a "pfft"—we should be asking it sincerely: What *is* this guy's "why," and does the "why" matter to us? Nobody good will be available to us without a good reason, but good reasons almost certainly exist.

I first heard about Fehlandt Lentini the previous summer, when for an article at *Baseball Prospectus* I went looking for candidates to be designated pinch runners in the majors. Lentini was one of my candidates, having stolen 42 bases in 42 tries for the Long Island Ducks of the independent Atlantic League. (He would reach 46-for-46 by season's end.) It was a tongue-in-cheek article, listing candidates as diverse as Triple-A veterans and Division II college outfielders, and I only went deep enough on Lentini to discover that he had put out a rap album and that he had played in five different independent leagues since the Houston Astros released him from their minor league system twelve years earlier.

Not all indy leagues are created equal. Through natural selection and market forces, the hierarchy of these different levels has become nearly as well defined as the A/Double-A/Triple-A structure of affiliated ball. Lentini's most recent job in the Atlantic League put him at the very top of this collection. It's where released big leaguers go to stay active between job offers; to show they're healthy after rehabbing major injuries; or, more often, to fail one last time in the final days of a long career. The last category has recently included former rookie of the year Dontrelle Willis and Sean Burroughs, who was once the best hitting prospect in the minors. In that 2014 season, Lentini had nine teammates with major league experience, and most of the rest had experience in the affiliated minor leagues. The average age in the league is twenty-nine. The Ducks play their home games in Bethpage Ballpark, with a capacity of 6,000 and an average nightly attendance of 5,067. That's 5,000 fans a night across a 140-game season, more total fans than the average Triple-A team draws. And the level of play is just a tick lower than that Triple-A team's.

Just below the Atlantic League is the American Association, a twelve-team league concentrated in the Midwest that includes the St. Paul Saints, for a while the most famous (and profitable) indy-ball team— its owners include the comedian Bill Murray and Mike Veeck, the son of the legendary baseball owner/GM/showman Bill Veeck. American Association games draw 3,300 fans a night. The Wichita Wing-nuts, one of the more successful franchises, had seven players in 2014 with major league experience. The average player is twenty-seven years old.

Next are the prospect leagues, which have shorter schedules, younger rosters, and a level of play comparable to Single-A. In the Can-Am League, with six permanent teams in New York, New Jersey, and Canada, there is usually a player or two with big league experience—in 2015, that would include the former All-Star relief pitcher Eric Gagne, who would come briefly out of retirement to throw 4 1/3 wild innings. The Frontier League, with clubs in midsize midwestern cities, has strict age requirements to keep it dense with prospects—which, in turn, attract big league scouts, who make this the most attractive league for young players. The average age there is twenty-four and, like the Can-Am League, its per-game attendance hovers at about 2,300.

And then there are the lowest levels, where everything gets *really* far-flung: the Pecos League (where ex-players tell us the $50-per-week paychecks sometimes hinge on whether the GM thinks you played well enough) and the Intercounty Baseball League (where the stats don't even make it onto Baseball-Reference.com) and the start-ups that don't even make it through their first seasons—the Mt. Rainier League and the Ozarks Professional Baseball League and the East Coast Baseball League, all of which canceled their seasons early and sent scores of hopeful players back home without pay.

The Pacific Association is at a level higher than the Pecos League and the fly-by-nights—we pay more, we pay reliably, our stats make Baseball-Reference, and players who come from those dicier leagues tend to see their numbers go down when they join ours. But we're undeniably lower than the Atlantic, the Association, the Can-Am, and the Frontier. That line in *Moneyball*: "There are rich teams, and there are poor teams, and then there's fifty feet of crap, and then there's us." Yeah. That's still six minor league levels and four indy-ball levels ahead of *us*. Every player we sign is aiming to move up to any of those levels.

Which is all to say that a player like Fehlandt Lentini, who in 2014 hit .290 with extra-base power and played center field in the Atlantic League, would absolutely not be available to us without a good reason. In fact, San Rafael, another team in the league, had once tried to sign him by promising to move in the fences so he could hit 60 home runs. Lentini didn't want to hit 60 home runs, and he'd always hated the lights in San Rafael—too high, not enough of them. But we could offer him two things that San Rafael couldn't offer back then: the city of Sonoma, where he had grown up and where he wanted to live to be with his family while his sister was in high school; and a position as player-manager. At thirty-seven years old, Lentini hasn't yet slowed down—he's in remarkable shape and an obsessive student of hitting mechanics—but soon he will. If he wants to stay in baseball, he'll have to make the transition to coaching and managing.

What we don't know is whether he'd be a good manager. In our first conference call, Ben, Theo, and I talk for an hour about what we want in a manager. The previous year, Theo had fired his manager in spring training—the guy had "lost the clubhouse," as they say—and replaced him with Ray Serrano, a former catcher in the Atlanta Braves system and the Stompers' designated hitter/first baseman. Ray was, in

Theo's estimation, worth six or seven wins all by himself. His attributes nicely round up much of what we want in a manager: He was an enforcer, with a sturdy physique and an unpredictable, this-guy-might-deck-me personality. He knew which of his players' excesses to tolerate, and just how much to tolerate them. He spoke Spanish. He wasn't political. He became one of Theo's best friends, so it was never a pain to be hand-cuffed to him for six months. His salary demands were modest. He respected players and they respected him, which, Theo says, "created a chemistry in the clubhouse that I've never seen." His only negatives were his lack of fame or local ties—you couldn't put "Ray Serrano" in a press release—and his in-game tactics, which were conventionally competent but rarely creative.

After that summer he joined the Braves' minor league system as a coach, so we need to replace him. As we talk about candidates on our first day, we have six names:

- The former Blue Jays manager Tim Johnson, who was fired after a short, successful career when it was discovered that his motivational, first-person Vietnam stories were fiction.
- The retired major league catcher Kelly Stinnett, who had managed a team in the now-defunct Freedom Pro Baseball League in 2013.
- Joey Gomes, the brother of big league outfielder Jonny Gomes. Jonny is a local hero from nearby Petaluma and a legendarily good clubhouse presence.
- One of Theo's friends, an assistant coach at Cal Berkeley.
- The longtime coach of the Sonoma State baseball team, John Goelz, who is known for stressing extreme patience at the plate and raising money for his program.
- "Spaceman" Bill Lee, the former major league pitcher/weird guy.

Each brings something—in order: experience; ambition; a clubhouse-ready attitude; an amiable nature we knew we could work with; local ties; and publicity. But none of them seems all that likely to fulfill our vision for what a baseball team can do—not that we even know precisely what that vision will be. We just want somebody who will check off some boxes and show an inclination to listen.

Fehlandt Lentini, who first catches our imagination as an extremely unlikely roster addition, becomes candidate number seven. There are red flags, to be sure: He is a known hothead, a player whose most-viewed YouTube highlight shows him getting in an argument with an umpire during his days in the American Association. That's not so damning, except for the backstory: Fehlandt claims that the umpire already hated him for his constant arguing, so he told the catcher to keep moving outside with his target, farther, farther, farther, pledging he'd call it a strike no matter what. The ump, Fehlandt complains years later, just wanted to piss him off.

During a long lunch interview with me a few weeks later, Fehlandt recounts every manager who ever pissed him off—the guys he thought were phonies, the guys he thought were drunks, the guys he thought were stupid, the guys he never felt had his back, the douchebag cocksuckers and the motherfuckers. He even rips a local junior varsity coach for using unconventional tactics. I leave that lunch worried about his obvious and consistent distrust of authority.

But I'm looking for reasons to say yes to him, rather than reasons to say no. Unlike players, who are mostly in their early twenties, with few expenses in their lives, with delusions that they might still make the majors, and who flood our inboxes with emails and offer to fly themselves out just for a tryout, potential managers are hard to find. They're older, they have families, they have roots, they have perspective, and they have far less interest in going to some short-term summer job just to hang out and get laid by the locals. We can't count on the man of our dreams walking in the door.

As Fehlandt and I keep talking, I keep finding boxes to check off. The first one is the biggest: He'd almost certainly be one of the best players in the league—maybe the best—and because manager salaries are exempt from the league's $15,000-a-month salary cap, his pay would count only as the league minimum. This would be like having a Mike Trout on a rookie's salary. Nobody (except, apparently, Theo) has succeeded yet in quantifying a manager's impact, but it's almost certainly less than one Mike Trout. Not only that, but his skill set would give us tactical leverage: We want fast outfielders, really fast ones, so we can use a two-man outfield and a five-man infield if the right situation comes up. He is undeniably baseball smart: He's a base runner who can exploit a defense without giving up any unnecessary outs, and that requires a kind of baseball genius that statheads love. And if he doesn't know what WAR or wRC+ stands for, he at least seems open-minded. I bring up, for instance, the idea of having a female pitcher. "If there's a solid chick? You ball out, you ball out. I don't care what gender," he replies. He's also willing to take the job even though I've just told him a couple of statheads with no playing experience are going to be his bosses.

He has contacts—he's played with hundreds of guys in leagues higher than ours and in prestigious Latin American winter leagues, and he knows dozens of higher-level managers who could text him if one of their players loses a roster spot. These networks are essential for indy-team construction, and even if Ben and I figure out a way to build a team by spreadsheet, we will need a network like this to fill in blank spaces. He is local, and something of a local celebrity at that, so bringing him on board to be the face of the team would ease pressure from the owner to sign undeserving local players for publicity. And for a manager, he is young. Chris Jaffe, the author of the exhaustive book *Evaluating Baseball's Managers*, has found that managers tend to peak at about age forty-eight, and he has written that managers who get much older lose their ability to personally connect with players. Fehlandt isn't forty-eight, but he would be managing a much younger group than major league managers do. We hope that as a player-manager, and as a young, relatively cool guy, he could be a better liaison between us and the players than an older, more removed manager might be.

Fehlandt is also likable as hell. Shortly after our lunch meeting, we talk for three and a half hours in the Stompers office about how to motivate players—BBQ lunch is better than beer—and about the worst owners he has played for. "They give me a flight, my bags are $60, and they tell me after they'll only reimburse me $50. You serious? You're penny-pinching me over $10? And you knew that when you set the flight up, why you setting me up with that airline?" We also talk about the powerhouse team we might build together. We debate a pitcher he watched throw the day before named Jon Rand, a lefty who came highly recommended by a coach Feh knew, and who showed he could mix five pitches with good command. But when I Google the guy, I find terrible college stats, innings totals that suggest his coach clearly didn't trust him, and a low-80s fastball.

"I don't know about Rand," I say, to see what his response will be as much as anything else.

"Oh, I already saw him, he's legit," Fehlandt says.

"But everywhere he's pitched, he's been bad."

"That all depends. He threw strikes. He made adjustments and put it where he wanted to. His presence on the mound, he knew what he needed to do to get ready. I could see where his four-seamer could get him in trouble, but if he can throw his two-seamer for strikes, it runs all over the place."

"At some point, though, you'd like to see he had success," I respond. "At some point his skills would have shown themselves. Nothing so far says he's been good at pitching. Maybe he looks like a good pitcher, maybe he is a good pitcher, maybe he hasn't even gotten a chance, but—"

"That's what I'm saying: You can't *just* go off numbers," Feh counters. "You're saying he hasn't pitched good, but he might not have been put in a position to get a chance to do what he's capable of."

"But how does he get to this point in his life without anybody else seeing this, you know? How come no better team gave him a chance, no other league gave him a chance?"

That's the question. That's always the question. Why is he available to us? Finding the right "whys" is what is going to separate us from the other teams in the league.

As it turns out, Jon Rand is a charming kid with a pretty good "why." In high school, he threw 75 mph. He went to junior college, threw only four innings, got stronger, went to a summer league in Missouri, and got the attention of a Division I pitching coach. That pitching coach was so impressed he offered him a full scholarship to Division I Central Arkansas.

"And in Arkansas, at least on the team I was on, you had a victory party win or lose," he says when I meet him in person. He shows me his driver's license, where his picture shows a kid who was at least thirty pounds heavier than he is now. He attributes his old weight to beer and McDonald's.

"I was more excited that I was playing D1 baseball than I was actually appreciating the opportunity," he says.

"You were excited to be there because it was a big deal, but you didn't actually realize what a big deal it was," I respond.

"Exactly. I wasn't prepared for how serious they took it," he admits. "And I was mentally checked out and picking fights with coaches. My mom always put it like this: I'm a summer kid. When it came to balancing out school and baseball, I had to be doing well in both, because if I do bad in school then I do bad in baseball, and if I do bad in baseball I do bad in school."

Jon dropped out of Central Arkansas just short of graduating, and declared his retirement on Facebook: "I'm hanging up the cleats. Baseball never brought anything good to me." But his junior college coach saw that post and talked him into driving down to San Jose to pitch in a men's league. He cut the beer from his diet, got into P90x, and struck out 55 batters (and walked 2) in 29 innings for the San Jose Colt 45s. I have no idea what to do with Sunday men's league stats, but I start to see what Fehlandt saw: This is an athlete, he's in shape, he's right in front of me ordering the chicken breast and iced tea instead of the bacon burger and a beer, and he's a nice kid. He's also kind of quirky: His entrance music, he says, is an acoustic ballad by a Swedish sister duo called First Aid Kit—a far cry from the country, hard rock, or hip-hop that most players choose.

"I can't believe you of all people would be picking fights with your coaches," I tell him.

"Never trust the nice guys," he says. "Those are the scariest people. You never know what will set them off."

I can work with this "why." At our first flashpoint, I've come to agree with Fehlandt, and I start to trust him. We hire Fehlandt, and our team, including Jon, is now up to five. And it has a manager.

MODERN BASEBALL

One thing Sam and I don't have to deal with, in our daily lives as baseball analysts, is not knowing what happened in any given baseball game. If anything, we're overloaded with information: At the major league level, every event is almost perfectly preserved. As I write these words, I'm also working on an article about the length of the leads that runners take from first base in major league games. The data I'm drawing on, which was provided by Major League Baseball Advanced Media, tells me the average length of the primary and secondary leads each runner takes and each pitcher allows, both overall and in every individual pitcher/runner matchup, out to three decimal places—as in, Ichiro's average distance from first base before he takes his secondary lead is 13.006 feet, or 13.032 feet against right-handed pitchers. "Down to the millimeter" would be *less* precise than this.

Modern baseball analysis depends on this ever-more-detailed data: As the unexploited advantages available to teams shrink, researchers sift for still smaller ones. Sam and I are spoiled, having had an endless supply of stats at our disposal since we started at *Baseball Prospectus*: the speed, movement, location, and type of each pitch; the approximate angle and landing point of each batted ball; the result of every pitch and play, preserved with perfect accuracy back to before we were born. All of this information is easily retrieved, sorted, and exported, either for free or for a small fee, at websites such as *Baseball Prospectus*, Baseball-Reference, and *FanGraphs*. In seconds, we can dig up estimates of what any player was worth at any point in the past, or how he's projected to do today, for the rest of the season, or over the next decade. We can see spray charts that display the locations of a hitter's batted balls over any span of games, or heat maps that show where a pitcher tends to work, or results for any player on pitches in any part of the strike zone. And anything that doesn't come precalculated can be sliced and diced in minutes, direct from a database, by someone smarter than we are who's usually happy to help. It's an incredibly rich resource that's hard to appreciate until it's taken away.

This is more than most fans want to know, and much more than they *need* to know to appreciate baseball's basic pleasures—the human drama and simple aesthetics that make us obsessed with the sport in the first place. For us, though, the game we learned to love as kids was a gateway drug to baseball's unseen structure, where the interactions of complex forces lead to wins in ways that are often imperceptible to people who've been watching, playing, and even teaching the game for years.

As the information at our fingertips expands at an exponential rate, it's getting tougher to touch bottom, no matter how deep we dive. Lead length is one of many new measurements made possible by Statcast, a system installed in every major league park for the first time in 2015. Statcast combines a Doppler radar array that takes two thousand readings per second with a network of high-definition cameras that capture images thirty times per second, producing a three-dimensional record of every action on the field: every player's position at every instant, as well as the speed, spin, and trajectory of every thrown and batted ball. The system makes it possible to study previously unquantifiable aspects of fielding and base running such as player positioning, speed, acceleration, and route efficiency; to identify pitchers whose stuff seems faster and nastier than its velocity would suggest because of its spin or release-point proximity to the plate; to find hitters whose stats under-sell their abilities because their hard-hit balls have happened to find fielders. Each deep gulp of a game produces terabytes of data, more than generations of statisticians and official scorers generated throughout the sport's first dozen decades.

That gulp is only the beginning. The digestion is more difficult. Sta-tistical studies in sports are plagued by the same problems that pop up in any field's peer-reviewed research: errors in coding and data collec-tion; publication bias; "statistically significant" results that are really random effects masquerading as real ones. Still, when we try to answer questions about big league games, we take it for granted that *some* useful information exists. That's not a safe assumption in the Pacific Associa-tion, where the stats are about twenty-five years behind the bleeding edge.

Pacific Association records are kept by a company called Pointstreak, which handles data entry for many professional, semipro, and amateur leagues across the country. For a seasonal fee of $1,400—it should prob-ably be more, but the Pacific Association cuts costs by buying one account for everyone instead of one per team—Pointstreak keeps track of pitch-level results for every game, compiling full-season stats that are accessible by anyone through a web portal. In theory, these results are accurate and complete. In practice, they're imperfect.

Pointstreak's data is tracked not by a network of cameras, computers, and radar installations, but by a well-meaning (if not completely caring) high school kid working without pay in the unlikely event that Point-streak experience is a prerequisite for his dream job. Sometimes in 2014, the Pointstreak stringer wouldn't show up, or would enter the stats so carelessly that they'd be almost useless. If that high school kid mistak-enly marked a called strike instead of a swinging strike, then as far as the stats are concerned the batter simply didn't swing. The only way to fact-check Pointstreak would be to listen to an archived Internet radio broadcast, and even that might not be available. Video isn't an option: Using my computer, I can call up any major league pitch from the past several seasons, but only one Stompers game in 2015 will be televised.

On top of the accuracy issues, there's the matter of how much infor-mation is missing. Although Pointstreak's software has the capacity to record hit locations, that function is optional, and unpaid operators aren't inclined to do more than the minimum. With no means to track them, pitch speeds and locations are lost to posterity. And while the standard seasonal stats are easily found, something as vital and simple as platoon splits—a player's performance against righties or lefties alone—must be manually calculated with a laborious slog through the game logs. We're not that far removed from Allan Roth, the first full-time statistician in baseball, who was hired by Branch Rickey of the Brooklyn Dodgers in 1947 (the same year Jackie Robinson debuted) to compile and dissect stats by hand.

"Knowledge is power" applies in the Pacific Association, particularly to Sam and me. Information is our sole source of authority, the only handhold we'll have in a dugout environment that might not be hospitable to statheads. Everyone else in the Stompers' sphere will wear uniforms, outward indications that they've earned the right to be there based on baseball skill or coaching experience. But why are *we* here, with our non-baseball backgrounds and nonconforming clothes? We don't get outs or drive in runs, which makes us wastes of space until proven otherwise.

No Stomper has heard of *Baseball Prospectus*, so our writing résumés won't help: In the time it takes to explain what we do, the players' interest will ebb away. And while we have the owner's and the general manager's permission to be backstage, their reflected authority isn't enough: The appeal to a higher power is the last recourse of the flustered substitute teacher, whose only source of respect is the threat of a trip to the principal. We want to be self-made Stompers who aren't just pretending to be part of the team. And that means we have to be baseball oracles with the power to tell players things they don't know, about both themselves and their opponents. So if we want to run the Stompers in a forward-thinking way while cementing our standing in the clubhouse, Pointstreak's level of detail won't do. We will have to close the information gap between the Stompers and the majors, and *widen* the information gap between the Stompers and their Pacific Association competitors. And we'll have to do it fast.

· · ·

Modernizing a throwback baseball team in next to no time and on next to no budget demands some dependence on the kindness of strangers. In our case, two of these strangers have cold, corporate names: Sportvision and Sydex.

Sportvision has done as much as any other entity to drag baseball into the information age. In late 2006, the Bay Area company began installing PITCHf/x in major league parks. The system, which triangulates each pitch's location to within approximately one inch, was tracking every game by 2008, and websites soon sprang up to make the data more manipulable. Before long, one could find a pitcher's release point, average velocity, movement, and pitch-type percentages with a two-second search. Suddenly, anyone with Internet access knew almost as much—or maybe even more—about what happened after the ball left the pitcher's hand as an experienced scout sitting in the stands with a radar gun. In later seasons, Sportvision used its cameras to roll out HITf/x and COMMANDf/x (measurements of batted-ball trajectory and pitch accuracy, respectively) before being supplanted in 2015 by Statcast's combination of cameras and radar.

As accustomed as Sam and I have become to instant feedback on pitcher performance, the prospect of a PITCHf/x-free season is more dismaying than any other information deficit we face. But it doesn't take long for our grief to enter the bargaining phase: Maybe we don't *have* to have a PITCHf/x-free season. Sportvision's main office is in Fremont, only seventy-five miles from Sonoma, and I'm on good terms with the company's staff. Research requests aren't the same as full system installations, but we have little to lose by asking.

In late February, I email Ryan Zander, Sportvision's senior vice president and general manager, to tell him about our plan to take over a team in the nearby Pacific Association (which, we find out later, no one at the company has heard of). Unbeknownst to Zander, I also email someone from TrackMan, the rival company whose tech powers Statcast. Combining two long shots might make for a medium shot, and we'd be thrilled to work with either. We're equal-opportunity moochers.

It takes TrackMan two weeks to respond. Sportvision answers in only two hours, which gives it the inside track on our entirely unremunerative business. Zander's promising reply spawns a multimonth megathread that periodically surfaces in everyone's inbox, punctuated by the occasional conference call. The upshot of the extended exchange is that while Sportvision doesn't typically hand out pitch-tracking systems to anyone who asks—the system costs thousands of dollars, enough that only well-financed teams with the potential for seven-figure insights can afford it—our proximity to Fremont, the potential for publicity, and the ability to offer our data to MLB clients (who are increasingly interested in indy leaguers) might make it worthwhile.

Our slow Sportvision seduction culminates in a conference call with Zander and the company's baseball analytics specialist, Graham Goldbeck, which makes the arrangement official. "We're happy to just participate with you guys without really any sort of monetary contributions," Zander says. "Just being a part of this project is something we're excited about." Jackpot. Not only will we have PITCHf/x, but we'll also have HITf/x and COMMANDf/x—all for free. All we have to do is rent a boom lift to open our eyes in the sky: one on the first-base side, one on the third-base side, and one in center field. We also enlist the aid of Dan Brooks and Harry Pavlidis, two *Baseball Prospectus* colleagues who operate a consulting company called Pitch Info, which enhances and analyzes PITCHf/x and TrackMan data for major league teams. For baseball nerds, this is better than bottle service at an exclusive club, and all it costs us is some Stompers caps and T-shirts. We were worried that the transition to the Pacific Association would mean living with less ball-tracking data than we're used to, but once Sportvision installs our system we'll have even more.

In Arnold Field, at least. At the other three parks, we won't have any high-tech equipment, which means we'll be blind in half of our games. With only seventy-eight games in the season, we'll have to capture as many plate appearances as possible to extract any significance when we sift through the stats, so we need a road solution. It has to be something we can use from the stands, but also something we can collate quickly into reports about player tendencies. In other words, a scorebook won't suffice.

My intern experience is helpful here: A few times during my year with the Yankees, I was asked to fill in for another intern whose primary job was to chart games off of discs that were mailed to the Bronx from the organization's minor league affiliates. To do this, I used a program called BATS (Baseball Analysis and Tracking System), which would import the video and allow the user to set timestamps for each pitch, tag its type and location, and mark the outcome of each at-bat. The result would be a collection of neatly organized clips that could be viewed on command, as well as associated stats that functioned like a low-tech, less-precise PITCHf/x. Theoretically, anyway. I was the *worst* at this—without radar readings, I couldn't reliably recognize pitch types, and I'd spent so little time with the software that I never knew where to click. After my first failed attempt, I tried to be busy with other tasks whenever it looked like I might draw BATS duty (or, failing that, stall until the other intern returned). But I knew BATS would do what we wanted if we could wheedle a license.

Sydex, which distributes BATS, claims that it's used by twenty-nine of the thirty major league organizations. Because the company has virtually cornered the market on charting baseball games via video—an extremely specialized task—it can charge thousands of dollars per license, which would be beyond the Stompers' means. But when I send an exploratory email, I get the same response I received from Sportvision: *Cool project. How can we help?* A couple of calls later, BATS is installed on my laptop, which brings back traumatic memories but also fills one of our most pressing needs. We won't be blowing baseball's collective mind—as innovative as it is in the indy leagues, BATS is old hat in affiliated ball—but we need to catch up on the basics before we can break new ground.

We also need help from humans. To help us straighten up our sloppy Pointstreak stats, we draft John Choiniere, a thirty-year-old research scientist in the Department of Pharmaceutics at the University of Washington. We've never met John, nor even talked to him, but he's been a fixture in our inboxes for almost two years. A regular listener to our podcast, John emailed us out of the blue in 2013 with an offer to track the bets, predictions, and drafts that the two of us make in the course of the show.

We were relieved to have an official podcast scorekeeper, especially once John turned out to be meticulous, pouring far more effort into chronicling our competitions than we did in preparing for them.

In his day job, John says, he uses an "incredibly powerful magnet to strike atoms of carbon and hydrogen with a long series of very short radio wave pulses, tuned in a highly precise way to a very specific power and frequency, in order to change the orientation of how they're spinning in a test tube, so that if I use a special piece of electronics afterwards to listen to them as they return to their normal spin orientation I can learn exactly how they're all connected to each other in the molecule they form." By night, he wastes time working for us, joining a long line of supersmart people who might have cured cancer if they'd never come across a dumb game in which grown-ups hit cowskin with sticks.

John's first self-assigned task is to pull play-by-play logs from Pointstreak and parse the textual descriptions of events into database entries that he can query to answer our questions. This takes two months of sporadic work sandwiched around his other obligations: It's not uncommon for John to send us a lengthy email explaining an attached spreadsheet and then sign off by saying, "My kid just woke up crying," or, "Sorry this took me so long, my daughter was sent home sick from daycare." The process takes longer than we'd like, but that's the bargain we've struck with all of our helpers. Free assistance comes at a cost: We get equipment and brainpower that we wouldn't have access to otherwise, but we're never anyone's top priority, and there's no hotline we can call to demand immediate assistance.

Once John's Pointstreak parsing is complete, we pepper him with research requests. Every query tells us something else about our new ecosystem, like a sortie in a real-time strategy game that reveals a little more of the map. We're relieved to have John as our email lifeline, but once the season starts there will be times when we need answers more quickly than we can count on getting them from a guy who could be bouncing atoms off other atoms at any given time. Ideally, we'd like some of this information to be automated, updated daily, and available online.

If there's one thing we've learned from observing major league teams, it's that every analytically oriented front office needs a fancy private information portal with a tongue-in-cheek name, such as the Astros' "Ground Control," the Pirates' "MITT" (Managing, Information, Tools, and Talent), and the Yankees' "BASE" (Baseball Analytics & Statistics Engine). John calls our web interface "The Grapevine," so named because he hopes it will be how we knew 'bout the Pacifics' plans to make us blue (and also so named because we're in wine country). It's not pretty. It's not even password-protected. But it is a very rich resource, complete with pages for every player and team. On The Grapevine we can instantly compare anyone's performance to that of a league-average player, look up custom stats including pitches per plate appearance, swing rate, and contact rate, and find the batter vs. pitcher splits that are missing from Pointstreak: righty/lefty, home/away, starter/reliever, and time through the order. Best of all, the site is a Ben and Sam exclusive. Managers *love* splits and matchup stats (maybe more than they should), and we just became the Stompers' sole source. That's got to be good for something.

In most ways, we discover, the Pacific Association isn't dramatically different from the baseball we know. "These guys, the difference between them and Tony Gwynn is a hundredth of an inch, a fraction of a second," Theo says. "It's not like they're out there bagging groceries and they miss the bag." Home field advantage, that mysterious force that pervades all sports, is exactly the same: The team with last licks wins 54 percent of the time. But every league has a unique, identifiable fingerprint. Runs are more plentiful in the Pacific Association, largely because balls in play become hits more often than they do in the majors. It's not your kid's Little League, where errors can propagate in an infinite sequence of spiked throws and kicked balls, but almost every player on the field is less sure-handed than the shakiest guy on a big league roster, the player no one wants the ball to be hit to with the tying run on base.

To dig for more differences, John calculates the average value of each event—strikeout, walk, double, and so on—by determining its typical impact on a team's odds of scoring runs. After comparing those values to their big league analogues, he concludes that strikeouts are more costly in the Pacific Association, which confirms our intuition that this would be true in an environment where putting the ball in play is more likely to lead to a runner on base. We make a mental note to give a slight preference to contact hitters.

John also sends us park factors, which tell us how much each park inflates or suppresses certain outcomes for left- and right-handed hitters by comparing players' performance at each venue to the same players' performance elsewhere. We find that Arnold Field is the best place in the Pacific Association to hit homers—not a surprise, in light of its short fences down the line—but that trait doesn't increase scoring. That's probably because it's also the worst place to hit doubles: Like a less pronounced Polo Grounds, it's so deep to center that balls launched straightaway never clear (or even come near) the fence. We're a little disappointed by the league's lack of extreme environments, which might have allowed us to target a certain type of hitter who best suits our park. There doesn't appear to be a Petco Park or a Coors Field—MLB's opposite offensive poles—in the bunch.

With our stats in order, we turn our attention to scouting, another cornerstone of a successful front office. Since the Pacific Association is a four-team league, there will never be more than two games taking place at any one time. We want to be at all of them, at least until we have a handle on the regular players. But we can't do this by ourselves. We need a minimum of one person—but preferably two—at road games, both to set up a camera and to operate BATS. And we need a minimum of two in Arnold Field, where someone has to sit at a computer in the press box and oversee the PITCHf/x software that tells Sportvision's cameras what they're seeing. Sam and I will rotate through these roles, but we want at least one of us in the Stompers' dugout during games. Given those requirements and constraints, we'll have to outsource some of the scouting.

Fortunately, our podcast audience is a farm system for potential Stompers assistants. When we put out a call for NorCal residents—the more baseball experience, the better—with free time to invest in the Stompers, we're swamped with responses, some so impressive that we have to double-check the address line to confirm that they're intended for us. "I currently work as a corporate attorney with a large international law firm but am considering a career change," a fortysomething listener named Zach writes. "Although I don't live in Northern California, if the role sounds interesting (and you are interested in using me), I can handle my own transportation and living arrangements." He attaches a résumé, which informs us that he's a partner at a well-known firm, lives in a sleek Fifth Avenue skyscraper, and has an Ivy League undergrad degree and a JD from a prestigious law school. The résumé wraps up with a two-page "transaction list" that includes several mergers and sales for sums in the billions. He might be history's most overqualified applicant for any position, period.

We're not going to ask Zach to leave his high-powered, high-paid, low-fulfillment life to serve as a summer intern for a low-level independent baseball team. But the fact that a successful professional who's probably billing four figures an hour even entertained the idea of moving across the country to be at our beck and call reminds us of something that we've previously only experienced from the other side of the application process: Millions of people really, *really* want to work for professional sports teams. At our busiest, saddest, and most sleep-deprived moments this summer, we'll still be living the dream.

The applicants we ask to come meet us in spring training—all locals, ranging in age from their early twenties to their midforties—include only one lawyer, as well as one recent law-school graduate who's studying for the bar exam. The latter is Zak Welsh, who grew up in Berkeley and worked as a home clubhouse attendant for the San Francisco Giants for seven seasons, including the 2010 and 2012 championship years. While with the Giants, he regularly logged games with BATS, which immediately makes him my favorite. When we feel the firmness of his handshake and the unwavering weight of his eye contact, we hire him as our advance scouting coordinator. We hope he'll be the point person for the rest of the staff, keeping track of equipment, organizing assignments, and ensuring that the video from each game ends up in some sort of central repository.

The lawyer is Michael Conlan, who's hoping to retire to Hawaii on his online poker profits. He's joined by Mr. Mcllow, Noah Clark, a Sacramento drummer and music teacher with wavy blond hair, sandals, and a scout-approved straw hat; Tom Keown, a biomedical engineering major who's about to start medical school; Kortney Hebert, a Louisianan chef who left Lafayette after Hurricane Katrina and makes a mean gumbo; and a few other volunteers whose enthusiasm outpaces their scouting résumés: Brett Handerson, Leland Bailey, Mark Reynolds, and Spencer Silva.

Some members of our scouting staff are stuck in that aimless after-college period when no one knows what to do. Others are flirting with baseball before committing to a real job that they're about to begin, or using it as an outlet from an established career. One of them is going through a divorce and hoping to use the Stompers as a distraction from an unhappy home life. None of them has any scouting experience. But whatever it is that we're doing, Sam and I couldn't do it without them. We buy them a radar gun for road games so they'll at least *look* legit.

For the blissful few hours between the realization that we're running the Stompers and the onset of abject terror, there's only upside, unsullied by concerns about which tactics we're going to try or whether the players will pick on us. But soon—so soon that it seems almost unfair, as if our brains should lay off and let us enjoy this—the joy of dream fulfillment is tainted by a familiar feeling of self-doubt. We've succeeded in convincing Theo that we're worth working with, but we haven't quite convinced ourselves, let alone a group of professional players.

The best way to ease our anxiety, put our stamp on the Stompers, and ensure that the team can perform functions such as hitting, fielding, and pitching—which our research suggests are all pretty important—is to sign a full complement of players. (We won't be so unorthodox that we can do without those.) The Pacific Association has smaller rosters than the ones we're used to: twenty-two players, as opposed to the typical twenty-five. The smaller roster size will limit our capacity to experiment once the games begin, but for now it gives us the sense that we have a head start, as if we've crossed off the free space on our baseball bingo card. The catch is that we're having a hard time winnowing the pool of potential players from "everyone in the world" to a top ten to fifteen. Everyone who's been in baseball for years has a long list of "his guys," people he's played with or watched play whom he'd recommend for a roster spot if he had the chance. Given our inexperience, that kind of patronage isn't a possibility: Everyone we've played with is roughly as bad at baseball as we are. We're the baseball-operations equivalents of singles milling around a middle-school dance: We know potential partners are out there, but we're neither practiced nor plugged-in enough to pick anyone up.

It's not as if we know *no* players personally. In fact, we're well connected to one: Sam's cousin Pete, a skilled defensive catcher at California State University–Chico, who's recuperating from surgery to fix a fractured glove hand. Sam sounds him out, but Pete tactfully turns him down, explaining that he's waiting for callbacks from contacts in the Frontier League and the American Association. It's an inauspicious start: We're 0-for-1 on persuading blood relatives—and catchers who currently can't catch—to play for our team. Sam chooses this time to tell me, almost as an aside, that his standard response to extreme pressure is to dissociate from whatever he's doing, using withdrawal from the world as a protective shield. This revelation doesn't do wonders for my own mounting anxiety.

TRYOUTS

In the middle of March, Ben and I drive in early-morning silence, imagining a thousand ways to fail. Through an empty city and over a fog-thick bridge and down into Sonoma Valley, where Ben for the first time sees the vineyard-covered hills that barricade wine country from the rest of the Bay Area. It's our first "official" day on the job.

The Stompers and the league's other three teams are holding their annual tryout and draft. It's in Sonoma at the junior varsity practice diamond, across the street from Arnold Field. Nobody expects to find the next Pacific Association All-Star here—more honestly, the front offices need to generate revenue *somehow* during the off-season, and they charge $100 per participant in an *American Idol*–style open call—but for the guys whose emails went unanswered, it's a last, best chance to be more impressive in person than in a choppy highlight reel. A hundred or so ballplayers fly, drive, or bicycle to the one-day event knowing that, at worst, they'll have a story they can impress future girlfriends with ("Yeah, thought about playing pro ball when I was younger. Even tried out for a club once . . .") and, at best, they'll earn an invitation to spring training. Just an invitation. The distinction between the best and the worst, we're led to expect, is between pretenders who have no chance and pretenders who might at least earn the right to hang around for a couple more months. Ben and I dread finding out which category we belong in.

Ballplayers line up for registration, shoulders back, socks high, wearing batting practice T-shirts from their most impressive-sounding former team—in most cases, college. (A Division I school gets your name circled in our notebooks.) Last year, Theo tells us, the turnout looked like "a bunch of dads," but this year it's 85 percent boys, 15 percent men, including the fifty-five-year-old knuckleballer who compared himself to Jackie Robinson. They stretch with purpose and try to make themselves handsome, posing for imagined scouts, not knowing which of the nonathletic thirtysomething dudes circling in sneakers actually has decision-making power. Ben and I, inadvertently matchy-match in rust corduroy pants and black hoodies, grab clipboards and wait for the glow of authority to halo us. Our team's new owner, Eric Gullotta, who bought the team two months earlier and inherited two statheads, delivers our Stompers hats. We're with the team.

It's not just Ben's first day on the job, but also his first day in Sonoma. He quickly gets a feel for its blend of small-town innocence, hippieburnout liberalism, and excess-money eccentrics. It's a place where people keep going to their pediatricians well after they turn eighteen. Where everybody can point out "the sex spot" up on the hill overlooking Arnold Field (and a nearby cemetery). After Ben walks into town to look at a cottage for rent near the ballpark, he comes back like he's under a spell. "I saw a pet pony," he says slowly. "On a leash."

Sure, everybody but us knows the pony guy. They tell us he comes from old Sonoma money—streets are named after his family. The local legend says that the little horse makes him feel safe, and that the city approved a service-animal permit so it could stay by his side. The long knife he straps to his cutoff denim shorts provides further protection.

Ben likes it here.

We move the aspiring ballplayers into right field for the 60-yard dash. There's an extremely good reason we have them run the 60: They expect us to. When they watch the NFL combine, there's always a measured sprint. If they're going to pay $100 to tell their future girlfriends about their pro baseball tryout, there'd better be a combine-style measured sprint to make it real. So even though the grass is drenched with March morning dew, making the runs slow and sloppy, we make them run.

The rest of the coaches all but ignore this formality, which is no more interesting to them than the registration and the stretching. Two teams don't even send a staff member out to the finish line to record times. But Ben and I are as focused as a liquor store owner tracking a group of teenagers in his shop. It's our first day, and we are in full try-hard mode. We're recording *everything*—the way they register and the way they stretch, their handshakes and their undershirts. We're still unsure which data will unlock these players' biographies for us, so we collect it all. We also recall Branch Rickey's philosophy of scouting: The most important tool, in any era or environment, is speed, "the only common denominator of offense and defense, and the best single indicator of major league potential." We load and cock our pro-style stopwatches, and as fast as these kids can skid past us in pairs we record their times.

There are no 6.5s.

There is an 8.8 and there is a 7.3 and there is an 8.1 and there's even a 6.9 and there are a lot in the middle. We lie to kids who ask us for their times, offering them an idealized version of their best self while noting on paper the reality: not fast, not graceful, not controlled, not for us. (Maybe they all think they're 6.5s because no one ever tells them the truth.) Like the big guy standing at the starting point, tryout participant no. 173. He looks like David Ortiz with a few extra pounds, which is not a flattering body type on a kid at this level. "Uh-oh," I say, as the kid readies for a signal. "This could be ugly. This could be a nine." Fehlandt yells "Go!" and the tractor ride begins. . . .

Except the big dude can move. He keeps pace with his race partner, then begins pulling away, picking up speed as he settles into a smooth, symmetrical running stroke. His 250 pounds whoosh past us, and his time is well faster than the median. Ben looks over and smiles. So far as we can tell, no other team at the tryout has just seen this kid run. We have, for the first time this year, in the smallest and subtlest way, built an information advantage.

The boys scatter to their positions, and we migrate to scouting spots thirty feet behind them, where we can see their movements, gauge their arm strength, and hear everything they give away in their small talk. ("Fucking thing took a shit hop on me," one says, and we scratch out his name. There are going to be a lot of bad hops this year, and it's way too early for complaining.) We ignore everybody in left field. There will be no good baseball players who self-identify as left fielders—anybody good will have the range for center, the arm for right, or the self-confidence to pretend one or the other. Ben and I move to center field, marking down our assessments as a crude filter to help us focus our attention. Like typical scouts, we pull the power move of leaving our station and moving onto the next one before each position is finished. Perform for nobody, chum. We've seen enough of you. We've measured you up; nothing you can do now will impress a couple of pros like us. One hour with stopwatches and we're already a couple of assholes.

As during the sprints, we find ourselves the most attentive "scouts" on the field. This is understandable—there's very little chance that a player is going to win a job by the way he flags down a can of corn and hits a cutoff man in a nongame situation—but it once more gives us an edge, as we obsess over the tiniest details. As the shortstops and center fielders flag down fungoes to prove their premium-defender capabilities, we note our surprisingly fast David Ortiz clone fielding throws at first base. His footwork is graceful, his scoops effortless, his arm stroke short, and his throws strong and accurate. And so we have a kid who is 6-foot-5, 250 pounds, looks like David Ortiz, and can field and run. Is there *any* chance this kid can't hit? Is there any player in history who checks off all the "looks like David Ortiz but can field and run" boxes and can't hit? Of course he can hit. He's clearly, unambiguously, the best player on this field.

And we're not going to get him. Earlier in the day, we learned the depressing news that we're probably not going to get any of the players we really want. Pittsburg's owner has accused Theo of tampering. One of the Pittsburg outfielders, furious at how he had been treated during the 2014 season, and ignored all off-season by his club, continually reached out to Theo, asking for a job. Theo ignored him for months but, by January, with Pittsburg apparently uninterested in re-signing the player, and with said player working out regularly with guys from our 2014 team, Theo agreed to sign him to a league-minimum contract. Pittsburg then complained that we had stolen its player—even though it's only a gentleman's agreement that prevents teams from signing one another's players, who are legally independent contractors and have the right to play anywhere they want—and, with the ever-looming threat that the Diamonds (the new name of the Pittsburg team) will simply quit the league if they don't get their way, and with the existential crisis that a three-team league would face, Theo concedes. As restitution, he agrees to pay Pittsburg $500 and give them our first-round pick at the conclusion of this tryout. We did get back one extra pick by trading six doughnuts (three maple, two chocolate, one glazed) for San Rafael's third-round pick. But without a first-rounder, every team will pick twice before we pick once. If that big dude at first base can hit like we think he can hit, he'll certainly be snatched away before our turn comes. As he stands near the batting cage with a bat and a helmet in hand, I do something desperate.

I pull him aside. I ask him two questions.

1. *Why are you here? If you're good, you'd be somewhere else, right?*
   Answer: Seven months earlier, he weighed 325 pounds. He was, by baseball standards, about six standard deviations overweight, at an age when heaviness typically goes from barely tolerable to problematic. (It's hard enough for ballplayers to maintain their mobility as they age out of their late teens or early twenties; harder still when 325 turns into 350.) For that reason, he'd gone unrecruited out of high school and attended a junior college, where he hit nineteen home runs in a two-month season. For that reason, nobody had taken him seriously as a prospect, and for that reason Vallejo, his hometown team, had rejected him at two previous tryouts. For that reason, when he'd

approached Theo in the Vallejo parking lot a year earlier, Theo had
excused himself from the solicitation. For that reason, he'd had to play
in the Pecos League in New Mexico. And for that reason, he'd blown
out his ACL just eight games into his Pecos League career, ending his
lone shot in professional baseball. He was hitting .370 at the time.

And so we have a reason he's here, which was important; without
knowing the "why," we'd only be waiting to discover his weakness,
which would undoubtedly show up at some point. Which leads to question no. 2.

2. *Can you hit?* The kid looks at me and cocks his head, curious at this
   unusual audition. "I'd like to think I can," he says, and I notice he's
   missing a front tooth. I stick out my hand.

   "Sam Miller, Sonoma Stompers. Go home."

   He grips. "Daniel Baptista. What?"

   "Go home. We're signing you. Now let's get you out of here."

I'm not sure how this is going to work. I didn't learn the rules of this
draft all that well before we arrived, but I know that I'm breaking at
least one of them. We have an information advantage, and in about ten
minutes Daniel is going to hit and we're going to lose that advantage
when everybody else sees him. And cheating—was this cheating?—has
never been all that far removed from sabermetrics. Read any profile of
Branch Rickey, perhaps the first sabermetrician (though the word
didn't yet exist) in professional baseball, the Dodgers GM who signed
Jackie Robinson and hired a stathead assistant and built up the first
farm systems and more or less dominated Major League Baseball for
decades, and there's an undercurrent through it all: This dude cheats!
Rickey devised the "desk contract," whereby he would sign a young
player to a contract but file that contract not with the league but to a
desk drawer. The kid would be sent off to play for a farm team, essentially (and unknowingly) still auditioning for a job, and if he didn't pan
out Rickey would simply release him—and disappear the contract.
Rickey's sins, baseball's commissioner once said, were "as big as the
universe."

It's not that cheating is socially acceptable in baseball; the shock and indignation over the steroids era are proof that it is very much not. It's that *certain kinds* of cheating are socially acceptable in baseball, and being competitive means engaging in the ambiguous negotiation of the acceptable vs. the unacceptable. In a twenty-second window, I have to decide which this is. I have to decide whether I am hurting Daniel's negotiating power, and thus exploiting a kid with little leverage. (As only one team would have his rights regardless, and he would have no negotiating power anyway, I decide I am not.) I have to decide whether I am engaging in something like insider trading, where I am taking advantage of information that another team does not have access to. (No. They could have watched the 60-yard dashes as easily as we did. It's not like I am taking Daniel off-site to watch him hit before I sign him—though I briefly consider it.) I have to decide whether there is any other, noncheating way of accomplishing the same goal. (No. Because the Diamonds have screwed us over with their absurd demands. Heck, as I weigh the morality, I conclude that *they* are the ones trying to exploit labor, and *we* are the ones standing up for player mobility and agency. We're the good guys!) In those twenty seconds, I decide that we are definitely going to be in trouble if we get caught and that I definitely am not going to feel guilty if we don't. And we shake. Now if I can just get him off this field without being seen doing it.

Baptista shakes my hand. "Thank you! Thank you!" he says.

"Can you get home?"

"Right now? Actually . . . no. My ride is still trying out."

"I'll give you a ride. You go that way," I say, motioning toward the left-field line, "and I'll meet you in the parking lot in fifteen minutes." He shakes my hand again. He packs his bag, slings it around his shoulder, walks past the chain-link dugout, and begins to walk the 330 feet until he'll be beyond the left-field wall and out of our rivals' sight. He does not make it. We see a man in his early thirties call out to him, and Baptista stops.

"Bleh," I say. "Who is that?"

"That's Matt Kavanaugh," Theo says. The Pacifics' manager, who caught for San Rafael the previous two years. We try not to stare; we know that in a few seconds he's going to look over at us, and we can't be seen paying too much attention. And there it is: He looks over at us, me and Theo and Ben, looking at each other intently and pretending to be talking about something we just saw on the other side of the field.

"Is he looking at us?"

"I think so."

"Is he still looking at us?"

"Yeah."

"Is he still looking at us?"

They talk for a minute, then five. There's no physical contact between them; Kavanaugh looks as if he's trying to talk Baptista into getting his air filter replaced. I move slowly down the right-field line, exaggeratedly jotting down notes about what I'm seeing in the right fielders standing nearby. I reach the outfield wall and survey the area, having transitioned into my needing-to-pee, where's-the-bathroom character. Baptista and Kavanaugh are ninety degrees to my left, and I strain to see separation between them. I dip down a grassy area toward the bathroom, then tuck behind it and find the parking lot. I can no longer see Baptista, and so I stare at my phone, waiting for an update from Ben. And then, suddenly, around a pickup truck, comes Daniel Baptista, his bag still slung, his eyes still wide and hopeful. "Ready to go?" he asks. I am ready to go.

It's a nervous exchange as we drive away, a first-date conversation where your date's ex is sitting at the bar across the restaurant. We're waiting for the reckoning to chime on my phone, and we talk to avoid the tension.

"How'd you lose all the weight?" I ask.

"It was a poor man's college diet. I literally drove to Walmart every morning, bought discounted rotisserie chicken for $4.86, and a bag of iceberg lettuce, and one loaf of French bread. I had to make the bread last the whole week, and after three it would be no carbs. And then work out every day. It was a whole chicken, so it wasn't like I was starving—I was eating well, but it was just good protein, good lean. And seven bucks."

"I don't even want to know how they can sell a chicken that cheap," I say. "You buy a whole chicken raw, it's going to cost you eight, nine bucks. How do they take that, cook it, make it that delicious, put all those spices on it, it's tender, it's slow-cooked, and now it costs half as much?"

"Man, something else gotta be going on behind closed doors to those chickens," he says.

My phone rings. "Okay," I tell him. "Here we go."

"Theo. We're in the car. You're on speakerphone."

"Oh? You and . . . ?"

"Me and Daniel. I'm driving him home."

"Oh. When . . . why did you guys leave?"

"Why'd we leave?" I look at Daniel, confused.

"Yeah," Theo says.

"Uhhhhhh. His . . . grandma was sick?"

"Oh, shit," Theo says, relieved that I'm playing along. "I'm sorry to hear that. Did Kavanaugh ask him why he left?"

"He did ask," Daniel says, "and I told him I was told to go home."

"By who?"

"I said . . . by Sonoma."

"By Sonoma? That's weird. By who with Sonoma?"

I'm now also feigning confusion, unsure whether I'm on speakerphone, too. "Could it have been . . . could Jayce have done it?" "Jayce" is Jayce Ray, the Stompers' star player last year, who has moved up to a higher league but is hanging around the tryout for fun.

"I'm not sure," Theo says. "We'll try to figure it out. I'll see you when you get back here. Tell Daniel we're sorry he had to leave."

The call ends. "Okay," Daniel says. "That scared me a little. What went on right there?"

"I have no idea."

"Hope the contract's still good."

"It'll be good. Either everybody will be cool, or they'll fine us and it'll be worth it."

"I like that," Daniel says. "I'll make it worth it."

• • •

I drop him off and speed back. Ben's calling. Ben's terrified. Everybody is really serious over here, he tells me. He thinks we're in trouble. He and Theo have decided that the best thing to do is blame me, and blame my ignorance: *I didn't know that there was a draft*, we'll say; *I thought we could just sign guys. He told me he wanted to go home, and, like an idiot, I told him he should, because we would definitely like to sign him. Derp.*

I go back, act stupid, say what a dummy I am, say I thought I was just doing a kid a favor, and apologize for my mistake. The compromise is that Daniel will still be available to every team in the draft at the end of this. We still don't pick until every team has picked twice, but at least we've kept anybody else from seeing what we saw. The fear is that, by showing how eager we were to sign him, we've now created an even more attractive player than he otherwise would have been. "They're going to draft him out of spite, aren't they?" I ask Theo as we gather around before our picks. Theo thinks. "Kavanaugh? Yeah, he'd do that."

The rest of the tryout and draft is almost an afterthought now. Fehlandt wants to sign pitchers, particularly a guy named Caleb Natov, who throws in the mid-80s with an easy but unathletic pitching motion. I don't want to fight too hard; it'll be tough enough getting Baptista from the other teams, and I don't want to lose Fehlandt's support by turning our draft into a conflict among ourselves.

"We can draft Natov," I agree, "but we have to draft 173 first if we have him. I promised him. We can't break our promise."

"Pretty sure he's not going to be there anyway," Fehlandt says. "So there's no real point, but okay."

The draft takes place in front of the group of players. They sit there, waiting for us to call their name, and then nine out of ten of them will walk away, shamed.

"This is cruel," I whisper to Ben.

"Like gym class," he says.

Pittsburg is up first; their owner/GM/manager, the former major league reliever Wayne Franklin, has already left, in keeping with the organization's reputation as the league's bad haircut. He has left instructions for his first two picks—his and the one he took from us—and we're confident that, in the half hour he spent at the field today, he didn't see (or hear) enough to take Baptista. He does not. He drafts a good-looking catcher and a slight left-handed pitcher from Hawaii.

Vallejo is next, and this concerns us. They're known for putting a premium on local kids, for the headlines and because host families are harder to find in Vallejo. Baptista is from Vallejo, and he tried out for Vallejo when he was still fat. Their representative, a veteran coach named Mike Samuels, chooses number 146, a pitcher who was on Fehlandt's wish list. I'm impressed; I didn't see anything in the guy, but Fehlandt picked him out, and another team saw it, too. I'm even more impressed when I notice that the Pacifics are mad; they were also going to take him.

San Rafael has the next two picks, and here we're sure we'll lose our guy. The Pacifics are good enough and rich enough that they might not see any two guys on the field they think can crack their lineup; they might take Baptista just to keep him from us. Kavanaugh keeps us in suspense by giving the waiting players a speech: "I just want to say thank you to everyone. As baseball players, we've all been in your shoes. It's a tough place to be." He encourages them all to stay in touch. "With that said, we'll take 144. We got another pick: 60." Two pitchers.

I'm still quietly stressing to Ben and Fehlandt that we need to get Baptista, making it less about how good he is—which might spark debate—but because we promised him, and it's harder to argue against a promise. "Yeah, yeah, we have to," Fehlandt agrees. Vallejo makes its second pick—147—and, as quietly as we can, so nobody sees how desperate we were, we whisper to one another, "We got him."

"Okay," I say calmly, "we'll take 173." I try to act somewhat surprised when nobody stands up—173 apparently isn't here, huh, how about that—and Fehlandt breaks the confusion: "He left." The draft moves on to Pittsburg, who takes . . .

"Hold on, time-out," somebody says. A young man has come over to take his spot on our roster. "I'm 173," he says. And suddenly I panic.

Did I call the wrong number? Hold on. Hold on. Hold on. . . . We look at our sheets, and . . .

"No, you're 174."

"No, I was 173."

"You're Reginald? You're 174."

"Oh."

We got him. We got him. I can't believe we got him. We also got Caleb Natov, the big right-handed pitcher that Fehlandt wanted, and Mark Hurley, a right fielder from nearby Monterey who impressed all of us with his concentration and clean fundamentals. We don't expect much from these two, but at the very least we figure Natov can get outs and Hurley will make plays in the outfield. As Fehlandt puts it, "That's the fun thing about this league: You don't have the money to say there's going to be somebody better coming along."

As we drive home in the dark, back out of Sonoma Valley, back over the fog-thick bridge, back through an empty city, I'm thinking only about Baptista. I scream as loud as I can: "We got him!"

And Ben, quietly, says, "Now let's see if he's any good."

SPREADSHEET GUYS

As proud as we are of our Baptista heist, Sam and I still want to prove that we can find players who wouldn't have been blips on the Stompers' screen without us. What we want is a source of talent that the other teams in the Pacific Association aren't already mining: a good, old-fashioned market inefficiency, like the one the Oakland A's exploited in the *Moneyball* era when they targeted players with high on-base percentages, or the one the Tampa Bay Rays leveraged years later, when they realized that their opponents' emphasis on power bats made it easier to sign players with good gloves at a discount. The problem is that inefficiencies like these are increasingly difficult to find.

What sets us apart from our competitors in the Pacific Association, and theoretically gives us an edge, isn't our meager budget, our nonexistent network of contacts in the indy-league grapevine, or our untested scouting skills. It's our ability to find the significance in statistics, either on our own or through our relationships with the leading lights of the sabermetric community, who can crunch numbers in extremely sophisticated ways. We could search for wrongly released players by sifting through last season's stats from the minors and upper-level indy leagues, but that method wouldn't be the best use of our time. Players who've had any recent success at higher levels won't want to sign with us until they've exhausted all their other options, which might mean waiting until midseason. For now, we need to aim lower. Baseball has a caste system, and at our level we're trafficking in Untouchables.

There's only one level of competition that combines a decent statistical record with players who'd probably be happy to hear from us: college. Every June, the thirty major league teams cull the best college talent in the forty-round amateur draft, leaving only the undesirables behind. But MLB scouting directors work with the far future in mind: Although they know that only a tiny percentage of their selections will work out, every player drafted—aside from a few nepotism picks—has a backer who believes he has some shot, however remote, at developing into a big leaguer. *We* aren't worried about long-term potential; we care only about what players can do this summer. And because our incentives aren't aligned with those of the big league teams that went back for fortieths from this buffet before we were seated, we might unearth a few "one man's trash is another man's treasure" types: guys who can get outs, or avoid making them, *right now*, regardless of whether they have the physical tools that allow teams to dream. Drafting college players instead of riskier high school stars was one of the hallmarks of the *Moneyball* A's, but Oakland owed much of its success to the type of amateur talents who never get near an indy-league team unless their careers take several wrong turns. If the A's were "a collection of misfit toys," as Michael Lewis wrote, then we'll be building a team out of toys that got recalled because they were choke hazards.

Nothing about baseball is as easy as it seems, and finding our statistical standouts isn't as simple as sorting an official NCAA leaderboard. I email an acquaintance named Chris Long, who worked as the San Diego Padres' senior quantitative analyst from 2004 to 2013 and has since consulted for other major league teams. Chris, who had no professional background in baseball when he was hired and occasionally clashed with traditional evaluators, was one of the first quants allowed in a draft room alongside scouts and grizzled special assistants, and his numbers-based evaluations helped dictate the Padres' decisions.

To our relief, Chris loves what we're doing and agrees to help just for fun, even though he charges big league teams sums in the five figures for the same service. "Performance in college has a fairly strong predictive value to how [players] perform in the minors," Chris tells us when Sam and I call to learn at his knee. Better yet, he says, some teams are still overlooking that link. "Probably starting in the late '90s, every year it got a little bit better," he explains. "It's still not great. Even the Chicago Cubs, for example, have a very traditional scouting department in terms of how they approach the draft. It's not like they don't look at performance numbers at all, but they're not analytically evaluating the performances of the players and then combining it in some sophisticated way with their scouting evaluations.

"You're looking for guys that you want to perform immediately," Chris continues, echoing our thoughts. "That actually gives you more freedom, because you can go for guys that have flaws. High strikeouts, but also hit home runs, for example. Those guys tend not to do as well as prospects, but they're certainly going to make contributions to the team. Or the scout's least-favorite player, the short, gritty [batter] that gets hit by a ton of pitches and has a strike zone the size of a postage stamp—those guys are going to be perfect for your team." His voice, normally low-pitched and nasal, takes on the bright timbre of an infomercial. "Win your independent league with this one weird trick!"

Pitchers have a weird trick, too. "I think there's going to be a place for some junkball pitchers, guys that scouts wouldn't touch because their fastball velocity is too low, but they did still strike out guys using a variety of off-speed stuff," Chris says. "Some of those guys are going to do quite well at that level of competition. Put it this way: They did well in college. If your level of competition is at the level of good D1, for example, there's still room for junkball pitching."

College stats are difficult to work with, which explains why, until very recently, major league teams all but ignored them when compiling their predraft rankings. College players face dramatically different levels of competition depending on whether they're in Division I, II, or III, and even within each division there are significant variations from conference to conference. "An average D1 school is going to beat an average D2 baseball team about 70 percent of the time," Chris says. "It's not like 98 percent or anything. There's a bit of luck, and the spread isn't *that* huge." Still, the gap between divisions and schools is large enough that one can get into trouble trying to go on gut feel or surface stats.

On top of the interdivisional differences, there's enormous variability from game to game: Some hitters beat up on bad weekday pitching that would pale in comparison to the Pacific Association's, but look overmatched against stronger weekend starters. There's also unevenness in climate, ballpark dimensions, and playing surfaces. Before players can be compared on an even footing, we have to take into account the diversity in environments that makes raw stats at certain schools far less impressive than the same stats would be elsewhere.

To do his draft work, Chris built a repository of college statistics by "scraping" information from school websites and parsing it into a database-friendly form. By comparing players' production at each park with their production elsewhere, he can isolate the statistical impact of every home field. And by comparing players' performance against each opponent with their performance in all other games, he can also assess the impact of each school's strength of schedule. Apply the appropriate adjustments to each player's actual stats, and the result is a ranking of every player's production on the same scale, independent of division and environment. With the confounding effects of location and competition neutralized, we can compare Division III hitters in good pitchers' parks to Division I hitters in bandboxes, based purely on their play. This should save us from signing a "slugger" who posted gaudy stats against guys throwing garbage in the college equivalent of Coors Field.

"The starting point would be, you really want to identify the best of the seniors that did not get drafted, and also didn't return to college," Chris says. He says he'll send us his adjustments for every school, along with the real prize, rankings of every fourth-year college player from 2013 and 2014. This is our favorite phone call ever.

Listening to Chris, Sam and I realize, much to our relief, that we've found an organizing principle for our Stompers star search. Chris's stats will make the world seem smaller and more manageable, transforming a confusing array of unknown names and unverified claims into objective rankings like the ones we're used to. We'll operate under the theory that a player capable of posting elite stats in college could hold his own in the Pacific Association, one of the lowest rungs on the professional ladder. And if the stats insist that someone can play, we won't rule him out based on body type, facial structure, or fastball speed. We're the Ellis Island of the indy leagues. Give us your small, your soft-throwing, your huddled middle infielders yearning to play for (almost) free.

Although Chris promises results soon, it takes him some time to deliver. That's understandable—we aren't paying him, and plenty of others are—but as the days stretch into weeks, I start torturing myself by checking his Twitter feed a few times a day to see what else he's working on. He's a sports polymath (emphasis on the math), and he's on an NCAA volleyball analytics kick. Thanks to a little light stalking, I learn a lot about the best volleyball schools, but Sam and I are no closer to building a baseball team. I send emails asking for updates at what I deem to be socially acceptable intervals. Finally, one of them works. The long-awaited rankings arrive.

Chris cautions me that "99.9 percent of the talent is sucked away in the draft," but I can almost hear the heavenly choir as my cursor hovers over the file. That remaining 0.1 percent could be the key to the Stompers' season. I open the list of all players, create another spreadsheet of players who *did* get drafted, and filter the latter from the former, leaving only the undrafted guys. (When our story gets made into a movie, the spreadsheet-opening montage will make for an exciting scene.) There are hundreds of rows, each of them containing a name, a school, a division, a position, an at-bats or innings total, and a few columns of hitting or pitching stats, both raw and adjusted. Each player receives an "Index" score, based on adjusted on-base percentage and slugging percentage for hitters and those same stats allowed for pitchers (Column R).

After additional begging by me, Chris also sends us estimates of each catcher's "framing" skill—his ability to catch pitches in a way that makes umpires more likely to call strikes—based on the percentage of taken pitches that are called strikes when he's behind the plate versus the percentage of taken pitches called strikes when the same pitchers are throwing to different catchers. On the phone, Chris suggests that we "find some senior guy who's the best framer in all of the NCAA but wasn't drafted. That would be an interesting guy to invite to a camp."

He's reading my mind. "If you could find one who's left-handed, he might have to get a restraining order against Ben," Sam says. The majors haven't seen a left-hander who played catcher as his primary position since before the birth of the American League, and no left-handed catcher has caught even an inning since 1989. The anti-lefty bias seems based more on superstition than sense, with explanations usually citing theoretical impediments (can't throw to third; trouble applying tags) that don't stand up to scrutiny. Chris agrees. "I think the bias against left-handed-throwing catchers is pretty stupid," he says. He's my statistical spirit animal.

Every rating Chris sends is based on a smaller sample than we'd like—in many cases, a four-year player's entire college career comprises fewer innings or plate appearances than a big leaguer records in a single season—but it's the best we can do. It's clear that we're not the first people to look at a list like this. Scanning the top of our leaderboard of undrafted players, we see a number of players who were signed as free agents *after* the 2014 draft and spent the summer playing for organizations that are known as early adopters of amateur analytics, among them the Cardinals, Astros, and Yankees. This is discouraging in one sense—the college carcass is picked even cleaner than we thought— but encouraging in another: Most of the undrafted free agents played well at minor league levels that are comparable in quality to the Pacific Association. We might be on the right track.

Armed with the names we wanted, our job shifts from ranking to recruiting. Sam and I spend a few hours combing through Google results, YouTube videos, and social-media sites for information on the players with the most impressive stats. At the end of this process, we've created *another* spreadsheet full of players whose coaches we want to call. (Spreadsheet creation is becoming a theme.) Separately, we practice our sales pitches. In our fantasy leagues, it takes us one click to add an available player from the waiver wire, and no one is allowed to turn us down. In reality, we'll have to talk to human beings and try to persuade them to travel to a place they've probably never been, to play for a team that they almost certainly haven't heard of, for a salary that we're embarrassed to say out loud. Aspiring pro athletes expect to lead nomadic lives, but this still isn't the easiest sell.

No matter how persuasive we are as speakers, there's only one aspect of our project that makes this PR campaign possible: We have the power to make these people professional athletes, with all the cultural cachet and appeal to the opposite sex that this occupation confers. With a few words, spoken like a sacrament, we can give a few young men a line on their résumé that they'll never remove, an answer to "What do *you* do?" that makes people perk up. The Stompers are the mangiest mutt of a team imaginable, but a pro team nonetheless. And ballplayers miss being ballplayers: Even two years after graduation, every player's Facebook photo and Twitter bio is a callback to his college career.

As we work our way down our short lists like political candidates calling potential donors, it becomes clear that college coaches—at least the ones we're trying to reach—aren't great at returning calls. I consider trying to catch their attention by claiming to be with a big league team, then decide that misrepresenting myself might not be the best way to persuade players to sign with the Stompers.

Mindful that each passing day might remove someone we want from the market, I bypass coaches who don't call back and contact some players directly, gambling that they won't be bad guys. But ballplayers aren't award-winning communicators, either: Unlike a lot of people in our profession, they aren't constantly connected to email, and they aren't notified when someone sends them a tweet. Whenever possible, I call a player's parents, banking on the fact that if his mother is like mine, he'll know no peace until he replies.

The more players I have trouble tracking down, the more I expand the search, and the longer my short list looks. I form attachments to strangers in our spreadsheet almost instantly: All it takes is a name, a stat line, and a head shot, and I'm mentally penciling a player into our lineup and announcing his name over the public-address system. If you've played fantasy baseball, or even rooted for a real team that's one upgrade away from a well-rounded roster, you know the feeling of fixating on a particular player: refreshing MLB rumor sites until a deal is done or off the table, or sending several permutations of the same trade to a leaguemate and hoping that one of them will land your white whale. This is the same impulse, turned up to 11. I'm perplexed by the players who aren't curious or courteous enough to respond, but the close calls are especially agonizing.

Take Andrew Kelley, a 2014 graduate of Grinnell College, a Division III school known for its "rigorous academics and tradition of social responsibility." (I see nothing about its undervalued athletes, but maybe that means we're ahead of the curve.) Kelley, who's fourth on our pitcher list, is listed at 5-foot-7, which is a concern given the sport's prevailing preference for skyscraping pitchers. But everyone on our list is bound to have some physical flaw. And hey, he was 5-foot-6 as a junior— maybe he's a late bloomer with 5-foot-8 in his future.

In 48 innings, mostly in relief, Kelley struck out 48 batters and walked only 4. His LinkedIn account says he's had a full-time job as an "Integration Engineer" since a few months after his final semester, but I dig up his email and message him anyway, just to make sure. His response, which arrives in under an hour, mentions small samples, machine learning, predictive statistics, a previous internship with an expert on the physics of baseball whose articles I've edited at *Baseball Prospectus*, and the fact that he possesses a "pretty good knuckleball." He can't quit his job to play baseball, but he feels bad about it. "It would have been awesome to have been able to play this summer and chat about all sorts of statistics," he says. I come close to shedding tears. This feels like finding out that your biggest college crush, who met someone else and settled down soon after school, would have wanted to date you if you'd only asked her out sooner. Alas, Andrew is too smart and well compensated to be a baseball player. He's in a better place, and it's time to let go.

Andrew Kelley isn't the only one who gets away. He's not even the only engineer: Our best shortstop option, with the improbable porn-star name Billy Steel, has just joined Northrop Grumman. Then there's George Asmus, a standout pitcher at Sonoma State with hometown-hero potential. Unfortunately for us, he's happy in his current role at Triple-A—as in, the American Automobile Association. There's also Arismendy Nuñez, a well-intentioned but indecisive senior starter at Old Westbury, who strings me along over multiple calls (including a conference call on which Theo makes a passionate appeal) before breaking up with me by text. He says something about family obligations, but odds are he's just not that into us.

And then there's the unicorn, the spreadsheet player who has great stuff. His name is T. J. Fussell, and he's a 6-foot-4, 220-pound right-hander who pitched for Western Carolina, a Division I school. Fussell had a high ERA, but he struck out 81 batters in 64 1/3 innings, and we suspect he got somewhat unlucky. I contact his coach, Bobby Moranda, who gives Fussell as enthusiastic an endorsement as I've heard so far. "He is the best!!!" Moranda writes. "He was up to 94–95 with a plus breaker and change. Really should have been drafted!!!" It's rare enough for us to see any velocity numbers that start with nine, so even after levying the 2–3 mph exaggeration tax, I'm still salivating.

"I'm kind of in a peculiar situation," Fussell says when I call. He explains that while he "hasn't left [his] love of baseball behind," he *has* enlisted in the U.S. Air Force. The good news is that he doesn't have to head to basic training until August 25. The bad news arrives a second later: "I'm supposed to be getting married at the end of May." And there's even worse news than that: "We had a cruise planned right at the start of June, and it's for seven days." He sounds a little uncertain: *Supposed* to be? *Had* a cruise planned? Is the call of the mound so strong that he'd think about being a runaway groom? He says he'll talk to his fiancée and let me know. The next day, he does: Shockingly, she's pretty attached to the whole "honeymoon" thing. There goes my four-pitch flamethrower.

Fortunately for the Stompers (and my sanity), we don't always strike out. Our first "yes" comes from Kristian Gayday. ("He'll be popular on

LGBT night," Theo says.) Gayday, an Indiana native, played shortstop in his final season last spring at Indiana University–Purdue University Fort Wayne, a Division I school where he's still working as a student assistant. Our spreadsheet says he was the best D1 hitter among 2014 fourth-year players. Not the best D1 hitter among *undrafted* fourth-year players; the best D1 hitter, period. (In fairness, most true prospects get drafted after their junior year.) He hit .358/.472/.653 with 12 home runs in 166 at-bats, and Long's adjustments hardly hurt him. And unlike a lot of our targets, he's 6-foot-3 and 220 pounds, blessed with a proto-typical baseball body.

Granted, Gayday's senior season was the exception: In his first three years, he didn't hit for power, never slugging above .327. But it still doesn't make sense that a strapping player with his senior stats and a modicum of defensive ability didn't get drafted. Before talking to him, I email his college coach, Bobby Pierce. I ask him the questions that the spreadsheet can't answer. Why the huge improvement in his senior year? Is he a good guy? Can he play defense? (A big blind spot for us: College fielding locations aren't tracked, so Long's method evaluates only offense.) They're all ways of reframing the indelicate question at the root of all our inquiries: "What's the catch?"

Coach Pierce sets my mind at ease. More than that, he makes me excited, as if we're party to a secret no one else knows. He tells me that Gayday's newfound fourth-year "spray approach allowed him to really handle the breaking ball/off-speed really well," and that he hit at least half of his homers—more than he'd hit *anywhere* in his first three seasons combined—to the opposite field. That change in approach gives us a plausible explanation for the extreme uptick in production.

Even more encouragingly, Pierce says that Gayday *was* drawing interest from scouts and advisers until he suffered "severe lower back issues" for six weeks at midseason, playing one day at 50 percent, resting the next day, and pinch-hitting the day after that. "This middle part of the season was when all our local guys came to see him play, and they either saw him play at 50% with below avg draftable tools/skill/performance/ etc, or they didn't even get to see him play," Pierce writes. But by the end of the season—after his back had blown his chances—he'd recovered and gone deep in each of his last three weekend series.

Despite Gayday's breakout, the Mastodons went 19-34, and for them that was a good year. "We're a small Div I that gets little respect and scouts never come to see us play," Coach Pierce writes. "We haven't been very good and I do understand that scouts are very busy and they can't afford to waste a weekend afternoon on us, but Kristian was plenty good enough to be a 20–30 round guy. If he stayed healthy, he would definitely be in organized baseball." Pierce also reports that Gayday would fit in fine in the clubhouse.

On the phone, Kristian tells me that his back feels fine. I ask about his plans for the summer. "I was just gonna go to a couple tryouts," he says. "And if nothing happened, I was just gonna call it quits." In my eagerness to sign him, I tell him we'll pay for a one-way plane trip, which I'm supposed to use as a bargaining chip in exchange for a lower salary. My unauthorized largesse works: Kristian consults with his family and commits to sign the contract as soon as Theo sends him a copy. I can't believe our luck: We've signed one of our top targets, and he doesn't even look like a runt. It seems as if we've stolen a march on the majors, using stats to take the long view on a player whom others might have missed because of an ill-timed injury.

Sam seems content once we get Kristian to commit—at least we have something to show for our spreadsheet—but the taste of one transaction makes me hungry for more. I turn my attention to pitchers, tag-teaming with Theo on a series of deal-sealing conference calls. Jeff Conley is a skinny, 6-foot-2 lefty out of Alderson Broaddus University, a Division II school in West Virginia so obscure that most scouts haven't heard of it. In eleven starts and six appearances out of the pen, the southpaw recorded a 1.96 ERA with 89 strikeouts and only 15 walks in 78 innings. Moreover, he recorded those stats while also playing outfield for 49 games, batting .345 with 21 walks and 11 hit by pitches against only 22 strikeouts, which helped him post a .446 OBP. His left arm was also an asset in the outfield, where he racked up 17 assists. Conley hit only 3 homers, so his adjusted offense isn't good enough for him to appear on our batter spreadsheet, but even if he's only an emergency outfield option, we're happy to have the flexibility, given our restrictive roster size. Mr. Conley, come on down.

We also recruit Sean Conroy, a 6-foot-1 right-handed pitcher from Rensselaer Polytechnic Institute, an engineering school in upstate New York. In 259 career innings at RPI, Conroy struck out 223, walked 49, and allowed only 4 homers, posting sub-2.00 ERAs in his last three seasons and going the distance in more than a third of his starts. He's also interested in evaluating clubhouse chemistry, an obsession of ours. A psychology major, he's working on a thesis entitled "How Perception of Teammates' Ability Affects Personal Ability," and we envision him as a like-minded mole on the inside who can be our eyes and ears while advising us on avoiding missteps. We also envision him as an effective arm.

"I'm a sidearm pitcher," he says. "Just recently I've added an over-the-top curveball for an out pitch, which is working pretty well for me." He tells me how he dropped down in his senior year of high school, and how he's alternated his arm angle ever since to maximize his deception. "The slider would be the pitch I throw most often, like more than 50 percent of the time," he adds. No wonder the guy didn't get drafted: He uses an atypical repertoire from an unorthodox angle, and according to his coach he tops out at about 85. All of the oddities that make him undraftable endear him to us.

And then, of course, there's Paul Hvozdovic, our on-paper ace and shining spreadsheet star. (The first "v" is silent.) When he signs with us shortly before spring training, I pump my fist, just like Jonah Hill in the *Moneyball* movie when he gets the approval to trade for Ricardo Rincon. I haven't met Hvozdovic—haven't watched him, haven't even talked to him. There's no way I should be this excited about someone I know so little about. But any hidden doubts that might be buried within me will have to talk to the hand, because the limbic system ain't listening.

People who write about prospects often speak disparagingly about "Google scouts," wannabe evaluators who "scout the stat line" instead of seeing players in person or talking to experts who have. Sam and I are guilty of these sins—not because we wouldn't welcome the input of a seasoned on-site observer, but because we have no time, no travel budget, no scouting staff, and next to no video. Stats are our specialty, but they're also our only resort.

Gayday, Conley, Conroy, Hvozdovic. At this point, they're names and numbers, not fully fledged personalities. But they're *our* names and numbers. Thanks to us, they've got golden tickets to spring training. And thanks to them, we won't feel ashamed to show up.

With Opening Day less than a month away, we're trying to cross off the remaining items on our Stompers wish list. Our most acute need is at catcher, where we're looking for someone who hits left-handed and can platoon with righty-batting Andrew Parker. On May 9, a catcher/first baseman named Nick Oddo emails the Stompers, giving us the usual sob story about another indy league folding, leaving him looking for work. Sam puts him through our usual thirty-second screening process—stalk his college stats, see if he's ever played pro ball—and notices that he hit .411/.492/.714 in 65 plate appearances in the Pecos League last summer. (You'd think Oddo might have mentioned that.) Neither of us knows what to make of this: Oddo played for Las Vegas, an offense-first setting in a low-quality, offense-first league, and his hot hitting took place in a sixteen-game span. I'm skeptical—Oddo hit only .273/.315/.365 in his 2014 senior season at Cal State–San Bernardino, a Division II school—but I'm not having a lot of luck wooing *my* catcher crush, Nico Delerme, a 2014 grad from D2 East Stroudsburg who hit .437/.557/.635.

Sam emails Oddo to ask how he went from a middling hitter in college to a .411-batting beast. Oddo responds that he's always been a good hitter who was held back by his bats. "I believe I'm a better hitter with a wood bat because I stay grounded," he writes. "With a metal bat I tend to get big in my swing." In most cases, the transition from metal bats in college to wood bats in pro ball hurts hitters, since they can't get jammed and still expect to hit the ball hard. Oddo is claiming that wood bats made him *better*. We give him points for creativity, but even Sam says he doesn't find the origin story convincing.

Two days later, Chris Long sends us a spreadsheet with framing ratings for college catchers. We don't have to scroll very far from the top before we run into Oddo, who has a comfortably above-average score. Chris quickly follows up to say he's discovered a bug—"We are baby chicks under your stiletto right now," Sam says. "Don't crush us!"—but when he sends an update, Oddo still rates well. By this time, Delerme has decided that playing for the Stompers would endanger his real dream, dentistry, so that option is out. But as soon as I see the spreadsheet, my eye is drawn to two other left-handed-hitting catchers—Victor Romero and Russell Vaughan—who rate even higher than Oddo and who put his college hitting stats to shame. Romero is from Fairfield, only forty minutes from Sonoma, so I track him down first via the "call his mother" method. Sadly, he considers himself retired.

Vaughan, who lives in Arizona, is more tempted, but he's already started a career as a business consultant. Although he's only a year out of college, he's making real money. I hunt him down on Twitter, and Theo and I call to deliver one of our patented two-person pitches. At this point, we're like longtime police partners entering the interrogation room: Each of us has a script that sets up the other, with angles of attack designed to erode the player's resistance. But unlike most of the players we've talked to, Vaughan sounds like he's interviewing us. "Sell this to me," he says. "Why should I play independent ball? Because I know you're not getting paid a lot. Do I have a good chance of getting seen? Do a lot of players get picked up? What's the current catching situation?"

Theo goes silent for a few seconds, weighing possible approaches. "Those are all good questions," he says. "Any of us who are in the game or work around it, you play it because you love it. You play it because it's not golf. It's not something that you can do until you're seventy-five years old. You've got a finite number of at-bats in you—we all do. And you want to get as much out of every pitch that you can see or catch, because that is something that is fleeting and finite. And not to add more emotion to it, but as a guy who's thirty-four, thirty-five years old, it feels like a hundred years ago that I was playing competitive baseball. It's something that I personally miss and wish I could've held on to a little bit longer."

Now he's really rounding into form. He mentions the "approximately eight" players the Stompers have sent to higher levels. He says Sonoma in the summer is "seven hundred degrees cooler" than Phoenix. He talks about building an organization that's worthy of the sport's respect. "This is a real piece of the baseball quilt," he says. "We're a real component of this. It is a small league. It is way on the West Coast. But we do have real baseball people who have real baseball futures."

I mute my mic so I won't be tempted to step on his flow. "I understand where you're at in your life," Theo says. "How old are you, Russell, twenty-four?" Vaughan answers: twenty-three. "Twenty-three. So while it's a big change from your day-to-day life, this very well could be a hundred-day blip on your radar. . . . If there's any bone in your body that says 'I need to give this a shot,' it is gonna fly by like nothing else you've experienced. And I would bet—What's the saying, dollars to doughnuts? I don't even know how that works—but I would bet if you come out here and you play this season for us, that you're going to look back on it, and the idea of not taking this opportunity is going to be something that you're going to regret. Now, if you don't take it, you won't know what you've missed. But it's a very short, brief, quick, amazing summer."

The pitch is a tour de force. I want to give Theo a standing slow clap. When we hang up, I send him a text to tell him he was rolling. "I meant all that," he says. "As a sage thirty-four year-old, ninety days in my twenties feels like a traffic light."

"You left it all on the field," I say, working my baseball clichés. "If he says no, we'll just have to tip our cap to the business consulting industry."

"Per Malcolm Gladwell, we have the upper hand in this battle," Theo says, alluding to Gladwell's book *David and Goliath*.

"Yeah, not sure he's right about that," I respond.

"I didn't say he's right," Theo says.

Two days later, Vaughan texts to tell us that the suits won. Theo delivered a speech worthy of being set to swelling strings, but we couldn't quite persuade a twenty-three-year-old to structure his summer around the Stompers. Between Vaughan and Romero, I have enough material for a Craigslist missed connection. "You were a left-handed-hitting catcher with sexy receiving stats," it might say. "I was an indy-league executive searching for the perfect platoon partner."

Sam and I are still so split on Oddo that we can't even agree on how his surname should sound: Sam pronounces it "ah-doh," while I opt for "oh-doh," like the changeling from *Star Trek: Deep Space Nine*. Sam says the *Star Trek* association is why I'm still not sold. On May 16, our catcher dragnet hits an unexpected snag: Theo emails to tell us that Isaac Wenrich—a twenty-five-year-old, left-handed-hitting catcher who hit .274/.381/.495 for Vallejo in fifty-two games in 2014, and was popular even among opposing players—was just cut from his team's spring-training roster in the American Association, a higher-level league. Our fancy stats say Wenrich was sixteenth-best out of sixty-three Pacific Association hitters with at least fifty plate appearances, and Theo says his glove is serviceable. I want one of "our" guys, but I can't come up with a nonselfish rationale for passing on someone who's already suc-ceeded in the Pacific Association. Fishing for a reason not to sign him, Sam asks John Choiniere for every player's stats against Pittsburg in 2014, figuring that some players with good numbers might be mirages who beat up on the league punching bag, which might be better equipped to retaliate in 2015. Sure enough, Wenrich hit .288/.409/.525 against Pittsburg, but he also held his own against Sonoma and San Rafael, batting .271/.373/.492 against those two teams. When he sees the numbers, Sam concedes. After Theo assures our new consensus backup that he won't be buried behind Parker, Isaac signs with the Stompers.

It's exhausting to consider how much work preceded this single signing. Several spreadsheets produced by two number-crunching con-sultants. A series of online exchanges and conference calls, not to men-tion multiple calls to poor, put-upon Mrs. Romero. The worry that we wouldn't end up with anyone we wanted, plus the emotional suffering inflicted by each rejection. And after all that effort, we've ended up with the most obvious solution—a guy who hit well in the league last year—because he happened to hit the market at the right moment. It's our first lesson in how easily our careful planning can be swept aside, and a reminder of how much legwork major league clubs must do for deals that never get made, let alone the ones we know about.

NO FEEL

We have a friend, Russell Carleton, a clinical psychologist by day and a sabermetric writer on the side. He consulted for the Cleveland Indians for a while, and has since written about clubhouse chemistry for us at *Baseball Prospectus*. Ben writes to him in mid-May: "Our players report to spring training this weekend, and then we have about 10 days before Opening Day. Do you have any recommendations or suggestions? Surveys or personality tests we should administer? Spring training group activities? You name it, we're probably willing to try it."

Russell immediately writes back with some suggestions. "As hokey as they seem, there's evidence that those corporate icebreaker things actually work," he says. "My personal favorite is 'two truths and a lie.' You write two truths and one lie about yourself on an index card and walk around to meet everyone else and vote for which one you think is the lie. Then everyone reveals which things are which. In a group of 25–30 guys, it will get kinda bawdy, but whatever. Everyone gets a turn. Everyone reveals a little bit about themselves, but has control over how much. It's a good, safe, get-to-know-you game.

"I'd recommend water balloons one day. It will be summer. Cheap and so much fun. Guys love them because you can throw them at each other, but it's not an actual thing that will hurt you. If there's a theme to any of this, it's '12-year-old birthday party.' The baseball stuff kinda takes care of itself.

"Start a star sticker chart. 10 stars and you get a burrito. Use food to your advantage. Stars can be given for anything you want to reinforce. Yes, I'm treating them like 4-year-olds. The first rule of child psychology is that it applies throughout all of life. They will scoff at it and three days later be checking out how many stars they have.

"Have an absolute non-sequitur item that is given out to someone each day, by team vote. Funny hats always work. Smith gets the funny hat because he went 3-for-4. A ritual will develop around the presentation of this hat. Go with it. When I worked day care, we had 'The Golden Dustpan' for the cleanest room. The kids went crazy over the Golden Dustpan. You might also try a crazy toilet plunger (spray paint works wonders . . .). The guy who gets it gets to keep it in his locker as a sign that he had the best day, but with the caveat that if the toilet gets clogged up, he's gotta go in there and plunge it out. A little scatological humor. You are both being honored and humiliated.

"Eat together as a team as much as possible. For the first few days, have a 'don't sit with the same person twice' rule. Watch to make sure that everyone has a buddy. Actively approach guys who are friendly, team-leader types and ask them to keep an eye out for loners. Some guys do like to just be by themselves and that's okay, but loneliness might be the most dangerous thing a baseball team has to guard against.

"Accept the fact that there will be a stoner contingent and that one way that guys will bond is going out and getting high together.

"If there is a fight over the music in the clubhouse, it means that there is an issue brewing that you do not know about. Investigate and remediate."

I think about doing any of this and my palms sweat.

The first thing a person needs to do before working in baseball is figure out what he thinks about baseball players. Not his relationship with major league stars—those guys are just as detached from our own world as the Rolling Stones and Billy the Kid and Zeus and Han Solo; they're at best semifictions, built into legends who achieve our greatest ambitions or suffer through our worst fears. Yes, they are as human as we are, but where we struggle to cut dimes from our electric bill, they struggle to add millions to their contracts, and where we worry about this cough that won't go away, they worry about damage to ligaments and tendons that have no practical value in our world. They exist for history, and we take joy from them because we accept that they are superior at an arbitrary assortment of skills that we have collectively decided have value.

Rather, we must come to terms with what we think of the best kid in our first youth league, the one whose dad coached our town's All-Star team, the one with the batting cage in his backyard and a competitive travel team that he cared more about than our everybody-plays weekend Little League squad. For many of us, that kid was our first exposure to celebrity—people in town knew him in a way that people in town never knew us. But he was also our peer, walking alongside us or, more likely, a few steps ahead of us. He was our teammate, but when we both look at the team picture twenty-five years later we fixate on him while he can't quite place our face. And we, who grew at the wrong pace or in the wrong direction, also grew to envy him, or to fear him, or to disregard him, or to admire him, or simply to coexist as equals with him. It's important to know which, because the twenty-two men on our club were all that kid. Whether Ben and I try to be their friends or try to be their bosses, whether we rule as dictators or democrats, our own prejudices will feed subtext into everything we do. They'll notice that subtext, so we must, too.

My answer to the question is revealed by my sweaty palms on this first day of spring training. It terrifies me how terrified I am. It's appropriate to be nervous—the prospect of speaking in front of a group of strangers always puts me on edge—but that I'm *this* nervous tells me I'm not as mature and fully self-actualized as I thought I was. I realize that I never did quit thinking that Adam Ferguson was, by virtue of having the strongest arm in third grade, a better person than I was.

I never did quit thinking that, because other people felt the same way, Adam had a power over me that I couldn't overcome. I never did quit worrying that my own failure to hit .350 like he did was in fact my innate inability to do anything that well, that I was simply mediocre, and now I worry that I will waste this opportunity as surely as I wasted the chance to drive in the winning run against Adam's Rangers when I was thirteen. I am more advanced in my career than these players; I am even more famous than most of them will be; I am paid more than they are; and I am here on this side field in Sonoma not because I failed out of something better but because I succeeded repeatedly, as a writer and as a podcaster and as a baseball analyst. But none of this gives me the swagger that they have. Nobody on this field looks at me as more accomplished than them. If I had any doubts that this social order existed, women at bars around Sonoma would surely erase them.

All of this is to say that, as we walk to the first day of fieldwork on Saturday, May 23, I am aware that at some point this week I will have to stand up in front of these men and explain to them that I, a person they have no built-in respect for, plan to tell them that they, Baseball Stars, will be subject to my charts and tables and crazy ideas. I wear this awareness like a wet patch on the front of my pants.

Meet our team the way we meet them: via a bunch of personal quirks and details that are, in the messy mass of spring training warm-ups and workouts, all we can cling to to remember which guy is which. First are the returnees from the 2014 Stompers. We started with three, but the list has now grown to nine. First-base coach Tommy Lyons is a once and future first baseman recovering from Tommy John surgery; his middle name, amusingly, is John. He carries a wallet made out of duct tape— not wrapped in duct tape, but made of duct tape. "This way nobody will think there's money in it and steal it," he says. "There's not any money in it, actually." He's best friends with our catcher Andrew Parker, who gets somebody in town to buy him a bike, and then asks Theo to pay the guy back in Stompers hats. ("No.") Along with Erik Gonsalves, a right-handed pitcher whose pristine 1978 Firebird enhances his play-boy persona, they make up the club's barhopping cohort. And then there are the rest of the returnees: Eric Schwieger (pronounced "Schweeg," "Schwayg," or "Schwag," depending on the teammate), a 6-foot-8 lefty pitcher who posts pictures of his hunting trophies on Instagram; Jesse Garcia, a lefty who beat cancer and returned to baseball; right-hander Mike Jackson Jr., who sings beautiful snippets of soul music to fill moments of silence; designated hitter Joel Carranza, who set the league's home run record in 2014 and evangelizes for a sports psychology book that he has read fifty times; infielder T. J. Gavlik, the loyal boyfriend that ballplayers can hold up to their girlfriends as proof that not all ballplayers stray; and outfielder Matt Hibbert, who wears a Darth Vader–style breathing mask before he hits the field each day.

Then there's center fielder and manager Fehlandt Lentini, who has worked his connections to bring several players to spring training. His boys are second baseman Sergio Miranda, an affiliated-ball veteran who coaches infield the first day of camp, and shortstop Gered Mochizuki, who screams insults at his friend, our manager. Moch brought with him a former teammate named Matt Walker, a right-handed Canadian pitcher who showed up uninvited by us, but who offers to play the season for free because he doesn't have a work visa. Lefty pitcher Jerome Godsey plays in a Sunday men's league with Fehlandt, where he threw a curveball that Fehlandt said was the first curveball in a long time he could "hear." Godsey, whose day job at a bank separates him from our underpaid players, is our oldest invitee after Feh, and he's ambivalent about his seniority. "Thirty-five," he says when a teammate asks him his age, then waits a few beats and comes clean: "Actually, thirty-six." He'll provide extra leadership, it is hoped, as will "Captain" Dan Morgan, a foul-mouthed local who stays involved at almost every level of Sonoma baseball. Feh has brought him on to be an all-purpose member of the coaching staff, his most visible roles being pregame barbecuer, in-game pitch counter, and postgame Advil supplier. Feh also brought along Marcus Kimura, a squat Hawaiian infielder who played at Sonoma State and then disappeared for a year, as well as the lefty Jon Rand, who is the dude who won't shut up but his teammates don't hate him for it.

Will Price, an outfielder who came recommended by last year's manager, Ray Serrano, is the dude who won't shut up and his teammates do hate him for it. He smokes cigarettes—which is unusual for ballplayers, who mostly smoke weed, and who don't trust cigarette smokers. Price is, via Ray, "Theo's guy," along with infielder Danny Martinez (takes his sandals off and walks barefoot on the field) and catcher Billy Gonzalez (so serious as to avoid any notice at all), whom Theo signed out of the pay-for-play California Winter League. That's also where he found Takashi Miyoshi, our bench coach, who has a career .147 average in independent ball but who plans to manage in the big leagues someday. Yoshi (as he is known) also serves as an agent to several Japanese-born indy ballers, and he brought us undersized infielder Yuki Yasuda, notable mainly for keeping alive the Stompers' streak of seasons with a Yuki on the team—last year's closer was also named Yuki. When he hits in batting practice, the team cheers for "Yuki bombs," fly balls that scrape the top of the shallow left-field fence. Theo also gets credit for our lefty-hitting catcher Isaac Wenrich, who quotes *The Sandlot*, a kids' baseball movie, the way preachers quote Scripture.

Then there are the tryout kids: our first pick, Daniel Baptista, who looks to have lost another ten pounds since March; our second pick, Caleb Natov, a pitcher who tells me with total sincerity that he could hit .180 in the majors right now; and our third pick, Mark Hurley, who went to school at Cal State Monterey and runs face-first into a wall trying to catch a deep fly ball in practice. He's the guy we got for six doughnuts.

Right-handed pitcher Gregory Paulino and outfielder Collin Forgey are the two players we signed off emails. Paulino, a devout Christian who was cut by the Oakland A's after they rehabbed his fragile right arm, is our only Dominican player. Forgey was conference player of the year at a Division I school a year earlier. I pushed for him even though his translated numbers on our spreadsheet don't look great. I buy him a burrito the day before spring training, and we help each other get over our nerves.

Our spreadsheet guys are almost all among the youngest. Paul Hvozdovic set a record for most times thanking Theo for a $25 Mary's Pizza Shack gift card. Kristian Gayday makes a fast friendship with Baps at our kickoff banquet, and the two of them are inseparable during the first week. Jeff Conley's teammates already busted him telling a girl at Town Square that he's the ace of the Sonoma Stompers, and that he's going to start for us on Opening Night. And Sean Conroy shows up to the first day of camp in a bright pink T-shirt—"'80s, minimall pink" is how the Stompers broadcaster, Tim Livingston, describes it. He's the first thing we see when we look at the guys warming up in the outfield.

"That guy," Paul Hvozdovic tells me, "does not pass the eye test." Sean's torso is a little soft by ballplayer standards, his beard is a little ginger by ballplayer standards, his posture is a little stiff by ballplayer standards, and his shirt is tremendously pink by ballplayer standards. This is the sort of thing that makes me fall wildly in love with him—the confidence, the nonchalance, the mature self-actualization. It is also the sort of thing that makes me worry about how he'll fit in. "If he's not good, he's going to be really easy for everybody to marginalize," I tell Ben. "To get kicked off this team."

We are too bashful to try water balloons—it's cold and overcast, anyway—and, still viewing these ballplayers as adversaries, we're really too scared to stand out at all. *They're* not afraid to stand out—*they're* not afraid to carry duct-tape wallets and sing Otis Redding—but it's still junior high in our minds, and we don't want to be the Funny Hat Guys. We don't have the ease of self that Sean Conroy has. And we haven't yet figured out the most important part of sabermetrics: having the courage to act. We're too worried about the imagined insults, about the possibility (which we can't quantify, and thus fearfully treat as near certain) that we'll be ignored and kicked out of the club if we don't play on *their* terms. The shameful truth is that, like a couple of lame Internet writers, we're still willing to discuss building a team according to sabermetrics only as a theoretical idea. This, of course, introduces another imagined stigma—that our stathead friends will judge us for our inaction—but that's a judgment less immediate. "Good ideas," Ben and I agree. "Smart. We should do those things." Instead, we sit quietly, observing, trying to fit in but doing the exact opposite of what would *actually* help us fit in: anything.

Mostly we observe the relationships among our players. We jot down notes about which throwing partner each player chooses and who puts his hands on a teammate's shoulders. Team chemistry is notoriously difficult to measure or engineer, but we believe it's also important—especially at this level, where normal incentives (like million-dollar contracts) don't exist, where winning is secondary to individual promotion, where players constantly move into and out of the league, and where a decent portion of players are here specifically because they haven't shown the makeup or discipline to hang in affiliated ball.

The degree to which a club will get along isn't quite as immeasurable as chemistry's reputation says. At the University of Santa Clara, Katerina Bezrukova, an assistant professor of group dynamics, studied Silicon Valley workplaces to see whether group chemistry could be predicted, and how much it mattered. She found that chemistry was a fairly simple math problem, and that predicting trouble was as easy as identifying what she called "fault lines." Think of fault lines like cliques in high school: If five friends all love cheerleading and five other friends all love marching band, then those ten people are divided into two groups that don't interact—there's the fault line between them. But if a couple of students from each group are also into, say, running the school's canned-food drive, there is now a third, overlapping group. And if there's a conflict between a cheerleader and a clarinetist, there are now networks for resolving it.

For an office, this means you don't want all your twentysomethings to be coders, making similar salaries, coming from similar educational backgrounds, with similar craft beer interests; and all your fortysomethings to be management, hanging out with each other at wine bars. It's better to have both demographics represented in each group.

When Bezrukova applied her research to MLB rosters, breaking teams down into simple demographic groups and modeling the fault lines between old and young players, native-born and Latin players, guys making eight figures and guys making the league minimum, and stars and scrubs, she found a swing of about three wins per year that could be explained (she concluded) by fault lines alone. All teams have diversity, but those with lots of overlap—say, the three Venezuelans on the team who play different positions; the high-priced veterans who speak different languages—outperformed teams with severe fault lines. That would mean that chemistry is not just about the individual personalities, but also about the composition of the group. It would mean chemistry isn't magic but math.

This can take you to some troubling destinations. We realize that, because we hadn't signed our top Latin American target—a pitcher with affiliated experience who was available because of one very bad night involving unpaid prostitutes, a vengeful pimp, and a terrible decision to file a police report—Gregory Paulino will be our only native Spanish speaker. It's hard enough to be Gregory in this league—he's twenty-two, heartbroken by his recent release from the A's, and an unaffordable $900 plane ticket away from his mother and girlfriend. Now add to that that we can't provide him any social support whatsoever and that he'll be on the outside of every clique on the team. We watch closely to see if the club makes time for him, and thankfully some players do: Paul Hvozdovic helps him fill out his paperwork ("this part just says don't post any stupid shit on Facebook") and Joel Carranza sits next to him, puts a hand on his shoulder, and translates some of the trickier parts. But Paulino also stretches alone and jogs alone, a one-man group isolated by fault lines from all the usual sources of support for a young ballplayer. How can that be good for team chemistry? You could make a case that we should simply cut him, whether we think he's good or not.

Or you *could* make a case that a female ballplayer, no matter how good, couldn't fit into a clubhouse. You don't *want* to make this case; what right-thinking person in the twenty-first century would want to make this case? It's an awful case to make! When Ben and I were looking at potential pitchers in the early spring, we talked to Tiffany Brooks, one of the world's best female pitchers. Ultimately, we decided that she wouldn't be quite as good (by talent alone) as our other pitching options. But what if she had been? Would we have risked our precious clubhouse chemistry on her?

I think we would have. I think we're good people, and that we'd have chosen justice (and talent) over comfort. I'm also open to the idea that I'm not nearly as good a person as I think I am. That I'm not as courageous. That the words of Captain Morgan spook me almost as much as they disgust me: "I have no doubt that some girl out there could be good enough to play against men," Captain tells me. "But this is the one place left that these guys have to be themselves. It would be the worst possible thing for chemistry." In some small way, we hope to demonstrate that Captain can't be right. Because Captain, we strongly suspect, is saying exactly the same sort of thing about us.

What we think of as chemistry pervades every action. At the kickoff banquet, Theo—who heard about Jeff Conley and his boast to the girl at the bar—introduces the rookie lefty as our Opening Night starter, and everybody laughs because everybody has already heard about Big League Jeff Conley, even before most of them have met him. What we don't know is whether this faux pas matters. Big League is by far the most common insult at this level of baseball, fired off anytime a guy acts like he's bigger than his stage. But sometimes Big League is amusing. Hvozdovic quickly gets the nickname Big League because of, among other things, his socks, which say "MLB" on them, but Paul is actually humble and self-effacing and carries equipment like a rookie is supposed to (even though he has pitched at a higher level than half of these guys and is, technically speaking, not really a rookie). Big League, in Paul's case, is forgiven. But sometimes Big League is doom. Like when Collin Forgey is assigned a host family room with Sean Conroy, and he starts asking for a new host family assignment on day 1 of spring training, even though he's living in a mansion with a personal chef who cooked him the best breakfast of his life, oblivious to the fact that his host parents are good friends with the owner and that they're hosting him and Sean as a friendly favor—he's Big League and he never recovers. Everything he does this week goes through the Big League filter. He wants to shag balls in center field instead of left? Big League. He smacks his glove angrily when an infielder cuts off his throw home? Big League. He shows a hint of disappointment that a postworkout batting practice is just soft tosses, not live pitching? Big League. He is all but cut by the end of that Opening Night banquet, because you can't have Big League in your clubhouse, bro.

You can't have cancers, either. Fehlandt tells us this over and over—and this often means you can't have rookies. Rookies, he tells us, don't act the right way. They have "no feel"—another fatal insult, the inability to read a room and act right. The infielder who started to throw his glove in frustration after an error. The kid who was showing nude photos of his girlfriend on the first day of camp. The one who asked whether a team dinner was mandatory. No feel.

Veterans have feel, which is why Fehlandt has brought in the two guys he has played with, second baseman Sergio Miranda and shortstop Gered Mochizuki. Both have affiliated experience, Miranda's extensive and recent and Moch's just a blink five years ago. Fehlandt is so adamant that these two friends have roster spots that he actually pays Mochizuki an extra couple hundred bucks a month, out of his own salary and under the table, to entice him to Sonoma for the summer. And it's obvious in spring training that these two do know how to carry themselves on the field. They lead the infield drills, and they give younger guys batting tips. They're well coached, and they turn double plays quicker than anybody. They're also friends with the manager, though, and we realize too late that, in the Bezrukova model of assessing a team, they're creating a demographic cluster that can form fault lines.

But at this point we're so impressed by the complexity of chemistry that we don't put enough faith in Bezrukova's research. We feel like we've discovered a colony of ants that seem to be moving in totally random ways, only to reveal an elaborate and brilliant pattern. Like in the very first moments of spring training, *the first five minutes of the first day*, when there's nearly a fistfight. One of the new players, Isaac Wenrich, with an angry beard and a hard stare, is needling one of our returnees, Eric Schwieger. Isaac's poking his back, telling Eric there's some shit on it. There's no shit on it, and Eric is ignoring him with his head down in intense nonamusement. Finally, our veteran cleanup hitter, Joel Carranza, turns around and tells Isaac to shut it down. Isaac stares in disbelief, torn between saving face and cutting his losses. "Serious," Joel tells him, assuring Isaac that he is very definitely in the wrong here. "He doesn't like it. He doesn't want you to do that. So stop."

The bleachers, having been alive with chatter, are silent. We all stare at Isaac. There's no way out of this situation except escalation, and I expect an overturned table, a shouting match, and a punch or two. But Isaac takes a breath, like a preschooler remembering his mantra: "When you feel so mad that you wanna roar, take a deep breath and count to four." He absorbs the moment of shame. Eventually the chatter comes back.

Our team's chemistry is already a disaster, from five minutes in. Except that I've misread the situation entirely. I saw an extremely petty situation that turned into something tense and serious, where a new player stepped on the toes of the incumbents, who stood up for each other but not for the outsider. I missed the real story: A leader emerged, in Joel; an extremely petty situation was nipped before it could become more; our new catcher chose not to elevate and showed that it was okay to wear a little bit of shame after an overstep. Within an hour, it's clear that Isaac and Eric are also leaders on this team, and as Isaac catches Eric that day there's no lingering tension. Chemistry is complicated, which makes it all the more intimidating to think about how we are going to be part of it.

"Listen up," Fehlandt says, and they do.

"Little bit about myself. Born in San Rafael, moved to Sonoma. I grew up like three blocks away from Albert [where San Rafael plays its home games], lived on a frickin' hill overlooking it. I played there, moved here, went to high school here, graduated in '95, I'm old. I welcome "old" jokes. Moved to Vallejo and happened to live right around the corner from Wilson Park [where Vallejo plays its home games], walked my dogs there every day."

He flips a thumb down and makes a fart noise.

"Played three years in affiliated, and then indy ball came. To be honest, I didn't have much fun in affiliated. It sucks. I felt like my baseball fire was like coals, like little ashes, and then I came to indy ball and . . ."

He pauses, exhales, pauses.

". . . and I had fun again."

He starts again, then stops, and turns around. We see his back as he clenches his fist and tries to slow his emotions.

"This happens every time I talk about baseball. Damn."

"We've got a guy here who you can tell loves the game," Theo says, moving into the speaker's spot. "We all love the game. None of us is here for any reason other than this is baseball. There's way easier jobs, way better pay. Every person is here because we love this stuff."

"Fuck!" Feh says, turning back around. "I love playing ball. I want to have fun, and I definitely want to win.

"Let's talk about this little town we got here. This place is so small. You're not gonna do anything that's not gonna get found out, especially something stupid. I've had to check myself, too. If you're driving and you road rage on somebody, there's a good chance they're gonna know who you are." He's referring, which they don't know, to an incident he had the previous day with the owner's wife. "I already got in trouble for Facebook, guys. I put some political posts on there, and friends in town . . ." Now he's referring, which some know, to a few incendiary Facebook posts he made recently alleging that 9/11 was an inside job, posts that nearly got him fired and shook our faith in his ability to listen to reason. "It's that small. Everyone knows everyone, so you gotta be smart. At the same time, if you do things right, that'll make it a lot of fun, because you'll have a place where you can walk around and get recognized. You don't always get there, definitely not in independent ball or in minor league ball. I mean, shit, makes you feel like you're big league. That's why we do this. So if you do things right and play the game right, I don't know why it's not going to be an awesome summer. But there will be no, pfft, I mean, depending on the fuck-up—I don't have too much tolerance for being an idiot."

"If there's a fuck-up, you're gone," Theo says. "Your job is a commodity; there are hundreds of guys emailing us looking for your job. We will make the hard decisions when we have to. We've made them before in this organization."

Erik Gonsalves picks approximately this moment to show up late. Everyone watches him walk across the field. They clap as he gets close. Half-smiling, he says "Fuck" and sits down.

"Everybody involved in this organization lives in this community," continues Sean Boisson, the assistant general manager. He's the one who wrangles host families and sells sponsorships based as much on civic support as anything else; he's the one who tells me repeatedly that he doesn't care if the Stompers win if we don't have a team of good guys he can sell to the city. "This town has nine thousand people, and we're going to be playing in front of two thousand on Opening Night. That's fucking cool."

For three days, Ben and I stare, hard and serious, left arms bent and resting on the back bars of the turtle-shell-shaped batting cage, trying to get the foul-tip flinches out of our system. "Don't worry, it's spring training for flinchers, too," Tim Livingston reassures us. Our right hands grip stopwatches as we clock catchers' throws to second, second basemen turning the double play, and the flight of each pop-up. We murmur and nod. We're ever present at these spring training workouts. Sean stayed for an hour on the first day, and Theo stayed for a full day, but we're here every day at the same time the players are, with sunscreen and thermoses and afternoon snacks—a plastic bag of mushrooms for Ben, who is increasingly revealed to have unusual tastes. We don't show up late and we don't leave early; we don't take long lunches or long phone calls, even though there's little happening yet. At one point in a preseason meeting with Fehlandt, when the conversation turned to the shittiness of umpires, our manager said something that stuck with me: "I try to explain, dude, this is my résumé. Put yourself in our perspective and understand how important this is. *I need to see you work as hard as me.*" Before we ask the players to trust us, we need them to see how hard we're trying. That's especially true this week, when we'll be forced to make roster cuts based on impossibly short looks at these players. A pitcher might throw two or three times before his dream is litigated; how can we tell him we're making a decision if we haven't shown full effort?

There are immediate happy spots. The spreadsheet third baseman Kristian Gayday turns out to be huge, the one true physical specimen that our method found, and he leads off first-day batting practice with the best show on the club. Better, he's the smoothest third baseman in the group, charging balls well, zipping accurate throws to both bases, and barehanding a hard chopper that takes a terrible hop at his face. Just after we had signed Kristian, Fehlandt had signaled that he was going to make it hard for our guy to win a job, sending me a long text out of nowhere to complain about the glut of infielders crowding out *his* guy. *His* guy, Marcus Kimura, had batted .270/.339/.330 as a senior, at a Division III school, while playing designated hitter; our guy, Kristian, had batted .358/.472/.653 as a senior, at a Division I school, while playing third base. It was not quite 9/11-Facebook-posts troubling, but at least almost-drove-into-the-owner's-wife troubling, that Fehlandt had even invited Marcus to camp, let alone entertained him as a credible candidate over Kristian. "To be honest from what I saw with my own eyes, and from what I've heard, I think Kimura could easily be the guy," he told me. "I am definitely open to one of the young guys forcing me to let them play, but from my experience, knowing what I expect, I feel like other people would have seen it and picked these guys up before we had a shot."

But it's quickly clear that Kristian is good and Marcus, a 5-foot-8 Hawaiian who has muscled up but throws like he's lofting paper airplanes, is not. Fehlandt, perhaps not subtly enough, calls across the field on the first day to tell me with a smile that he's expecting an "I told you so" from me. I tell him I'll never say those words, that we're all just on a search to find the right answer together—but before I finish this fluff, he's turning around and talking to Isaac Wenrich in the cage. Fine. It's our first win, and it's encouraging to see how quickly Fehlandt does respond to a change in the data. He didn't take it personally, and he didn't fight for his first position just to avoid an "I told you so." This is all we want out of a manager.

Sean Conroy throws and looks, at least against rusty, low-effort competition, unhittable, with a low arm slot that has right-handers stepping in the bucket; every so often he comes straight over the top and absolutely blows the hitter's mind. Pink shirt not going to be a problem. And Paul Hvozdovic impresses in his first chance throwing to batters, locating three pitches well with a little pause in his delivery that seems deceptive to the hitter; it reminds us a little bit of Clayton Kershaw's hitch. When we talk later that day, he asks me what we're looking for when we stand behind that cage.

I don't know, man.

But I've got to say something, so I tell him we're looking for anything that'll make him better than his velocity; we know that anybody who can hit 90 from the left side would be getting drafted by a big league club, so we need pitchers who can do things that will approximate that sort of stuff. Pitchers who get good tumble on a deceptive changeup, or who can work inside with the fastball against righties, or who have long pitching strides or who hide the ball well.

"Yeah," he says, and we're quiet for a long time, staring at a field with nobody but a couple of workers building camera hitches on the light poles.

"Were you ever scouted?" I ask him.

"When I was in college, nobody ever really came out and saw us because we were a small school playing against terrible teams. But I had these numbers in my senior year, and I knew I was pitching well. My agent finally asked me if I'd be interested in having him get some scouts out to see me, and I said of course.

"So I show up for my next start and there's ten scouts, all sitting there in a group behind home plate. There is nobody else on either team worth scouting. They're there for me and everybody knows it, my coach knows it, I know it. They follow me around while I'm warming up, standing there writing things down. The game starts, and in the first inning I give up two runs. The second inning I let two guys get on base. And I see them all stand up, almost all at once, and walk out of there.

"That was the worst feeling of my life, seeing these guys who everybody knows are there just to see me, walk out of there. I was great after that, too. I went seven innings, I didn't give up another run, and I struck out seven, but they were all in the last five innings. The Royals scout was the only one who stuck around to see it. He told me I touched 89 and they'd keep looking at me. But when all the scouts were out there, I was at 83. That was that."

On day 3, we scrimmage against San Rafael. As we walk past the Pacifics' manager, Matt Kavanaugh, two months after we saw him at the tryout, we pick up a few words that he's saying to one of his pitchers: ". . . in the corduroy."

The game is ugly. The Pacifics have already had a couple of exhibitions against other teams, so we're not surprised that they're better prepared, but the difference between the teams is obvious before a pitch is thrown: they're big. Their starting pitcher is 6-5; he's relieved by a 6-3, and then a 6-4. They look like grown-ups. Their scrimmage jerseys are sponsored. Their postgame spread has lettuce. We're completely outclassed.

We lose, and Fehlandt tells me he just talked to Theo. "I'm pretty much decided on who the roster's gonna be," he says. "I told Theo and he was on board with everybody." And, as quickly as I got comfortable with Fehlandt because of his open-mindedness regarding Marcus, I get extremely nervous that decisions are being made without our input. Territory is being claimed while Ben and I are still philosophizing about the nature of maps.

Theo rolls his eyes when I tell him what I heard; he says Fehlandt told him he'd made some decisions, but that he, Theo, had told him we should all talk about it. So we call a meeting, the whole brain trust assembling in the Stompers office to assess what we've got. It's Monday, and we've seen our players for three days, including one terribly played scrimmage. Somehow, I'm unreasonably optimistic.

"The more I see, the more I love this team," I say. "We're going 60-18. At least 60-18."

"Oh, we're gonna dominate," Fehlandt says. "The goal is 78-0. Until we lose one, then the goal's 77-1. We'll just go from there."

The problem is that each of us is thinking about our sliver of the team, and we're all bullish on the players we've each brought in, the ones who fit our heuristic for what makes a good ballplayer and a good ball club. I have total faith in our spreadsheet; Fehlandt has total faith in his buddies; Theo has total faith in the returnees. But none of us has total faith in the others' guys—and we'll soon have to cut a quarter of the players in camp.

I speak first. "I was thinking that instead of talking about roster spots right now, we just go down the roster and say what we think of each player. We've seen them for three days. There are guys I have no thoughts on, and guys I have a lot of thoughts on. We can figure out where we agree. So let's start: What do we think of Fehlandt Lentini?"

"Garbage," Fehlandt says.

"He's fucking terrible," Theo says.

"Overran a ball," Ben says.

"No, you look good out there," I tell Fehlandt.

"Yeah, I'm pretty good," he says. "I want to hear Sam's opinions about everybody."

"I like all these guys," I say. "I'm a sucker. I want to hug them all. I want all their dreams to come true. They all have problems and they're all great."

"Some of the things that you don't see, because you're not a baseball guy," Fehlandt says, trying to educate me, "are that some of the guys are doing things, are acting a certain way on the field, that other players are seeing, and those are the guys that are cancers."

"Good, that's what we should share," I say.

We move next to Will Price. Will is an outfielder, a tall and slim kid with thick forearms and a thicker southern accent. He arrived with a backstory: Coming out of high school he was a real prospect, but he and two college teammates were charged in connection with a home burglary, accused of taking $115,000 in jewelry and electronics. He was kicked off his college team, and three years later his mug shot remained the first result on a Google search of his name. Price pled guilty to lesser charges. Ray Serrano told us he was a good kid and that a major league team was interested in signing him but wanted to see him make an indy-ball team first—proof of concept that he could hang in polite society. We hadn't had any problems with him—his host family, who lived in a mansion, loved him, and he was going on three days as the happiest-looking kid in camp. But he had also committed the cardinal sin of ballplayers: He wouldn't shut the fuck up.

"I think he could be a diamond in the rough," Theo says.

I agree: He's got the best natural arm strength in the outfield, and might have the most raw power in batting practice. "There's flaws," I say, "but he's got some tools that are rare in the Pacific Association."

Fehlandt isn't buying it. "It looks like he has a lot of upside, but he's got a lot of ego and a lot of attitude," he says. "That's not necessarily good or bad, but the way he carries himself is bad. For example: He's never played in a league where he wears one-flap helmets. But the first thing he did on the first day was take my helmet and use it. I'm like, 'Where's my fuckin' helmet?' And all of a sudden it comes sliding down the grassy hill and spinning at my feet. And today I see him in another one-flap and I thought it was mine again, and I'm like, this mother-fucker. I say something to him and it ended up being Martinez's, but my point is—I already see how he's all about looks and swag."

"What's the . . . why the one-flap?" I ask.

"It feels sooooo much better. Like the two-flap feels like you're in Little League."

"That . . . doesn't seem like that big a deal, what he did."

"Believe me, I know people, and I know mentalities. He's an overall selfish player."

"We talked about guys having really good instincts in baseball; I don't think there's any proof that Will Price has very good instincts in life," Theo says. "That said, I do think that I've seen a little swagger, a little cockiness, but for the most part I've seen a nice kid who's not really dialed in to the fact that he should be a little quieter and fall in line."

"I don't see him being the guy," Fehlandt says. "I don't think he's coachable. He's not making his own adjustments."

"What did you think about his 3-0 swing in the scrimmage?" I ask.

"Oh, that was a 3-0 swing? See, that goes to everything I was telling you. He's a selfish player. He wanted to hit a tater." (He did hit a tater.) "*I'm* not giving him the 3-0. He took it upon himself. I don't think any of those other guys are swinging on 3-0, but he is, because who he is defines the player he is. And I'm telling you, the ego and the attitude are what got him in trouble and they're obviously still in there.

"Like I said, he's a good player, but if there's a chance to have a team where there's guaranteed not going to be a chance of this, I want that. I've been in a lot of clubhouses and those things matter. These little fucks with the attitude that they think they own everything, they really fucking fire me up. Part of it is I just don't want to be the fucking parent."

"But Feh," I say, "you are! You're the manager!"

"These guys are over eighteen. Yes, I need to be a manager, but I don't have to be a parent. If you come here and can't be a grown-up and carry yourself as a professional, then you're not a professional."

"The things you're talking about," I say, "it just takes more than three days to figure out if they're inherent flaws that can never be fixed. He's a kid. He's clearly gonna be a kid. But we're the Pacific Association. We're gonna have kids. There's gonna be kids that need to be mentored, need to be taught."

"The personality type will tell you. I had that ego. I had that attitude and motherfucking no one could tell me anything. It took such a long road of so much work. He's not there!"

"How long did it take you to get there?"

"It was three years ago. It took me twenty years to realize it, and people I cared about were trying to tell me."

"We don't know if it will take Will twenty years," Theo says. "It might take him thirty years! It might never happen. But I think we can give him six more days."

"The thing is," I tell Fehlandt, "it is your job to coach these guys. I don't want to lose a guy just because a small problem got to be a big problem. If he needs to be pulled aside and talked to, that's your job. And so far nobody has pulled him aside. Look: It's good to have a clubhouse where everybody's awesome. It's even better to have a clubhouse where not only is everybody awesome, but the guys who aren't *become* awesome."

Will Price gets a reprieve, for a few days at least. Whether he makes the team or not isn't that big a deal (though Will would disagree). But territory is being claimed right now, and it already feels as if our strategy—stay quiet and unthreatening, just observe and claim authority by demonstrating a calm and rational approach—is failing. It's becoming clear that power in this sport goes to the one who acts, and while we're observing and taking notes, Fehlandt is writing seventy-eight lineup cards in his head.

So we act. We get our own day of spring training.

The Stompers are going to have something like a scrimmage against the Sonoma Valley High varsity, with each club pitching to its own players. We use this game to practice shift work. We lay out six possible defensive alignments: an infield shift (three men over, corner infielder stays somewhat close to his home); a full overshift (three men over, and the fourth goes nearly all the way); the wall (four men move to one side of second base); a five-man infield; a four-man outfield; and, to keep things light, an eight/ten split, in which eight men defend one batter but ten can defend the next. The last is, of course, absurd; there's no equivalent in a real baseball game. But the point of this whole exercise is, mostly, to see whether batters will try to beat a shift—to aim for the huge chunk of green we've left exposed—and whether they'll succeed. A secondary aim is to see how unnatural our defenders look when they're standing thirty feet from their normal position. The pitcher or catcher gets to choose which alignment he wants to pitch to.

The high schoolers love this idea. Our guys stare blankly while we explain the six options. "So we have to do each one once in the game?" Isaac Wenrich asks me. "No, you have to do one on every player, no matter what," I reply. The point isn't necessarily for it to work; the point is to see where it fails.

And yet, as I stand behind the pitcher—where I'll relay his shift choice to the rest of the defense—I'm terrified. We're asking these players to do something weird, something that all the baseball coaches they've ever had—the guys with credibility and experience, with strong handshakes and refined spitting techniques—have chosen not to do. We're the corduroy boys. What are the odds that the corduroy boys would have discovered something that all those coaches didn't? These shifts, make-believe shifts in a meaningless scrimmage against high school sophomores, are the first time our players have seen our vision. This is our pink warm-up shirt: If it works, we're confident they'll embrace it. If it doesn't, we're not confident we'll have the courage to keep trying. And if it's somewhere in between, it probably counts as a loss for us.

"I don't believe in shifts," Isaac tells me before we take the field. He's going to be choosing the alignment for the first couple of innings, and he's not mad or anything, but he definitely wants me to know it's a bunch of bullshit. Not because players don't hit into certain tendencies, but because "any good hitter only has to adjust. There's no way that a shift should work if you're facing a real hitter."

For two innings, he calls each time for the least extreme option available to him—the basic infield pull shift, three men over, with the corner man staying in the general region of his position to cut off a bunt. Nobody beats the shift, but it's clear they're trying, aiming for the opposite field. But the reason the pull shift works so well is that it's extremely difficult to hit a ground ball to the opposite field. If a hitter aims in that direction, he usually gets under the ball, and in our first two innings we see six balls put in play, five of them fly balls to the opposite field and one a pulled grounder. They're trying like hell to hit the open hole, and not a single one does. The brilliance of the shift dawns on some of them. "It fucks with your head," the lefty-hitting Gered Mochizuki says after his fly ball to left field. "You see all that space and you think you're going to get there, but you're doing something that doesn't feel natural to do." It's hard enough to hit a baseball, and trying to hit a baseball to a specific, tiny sliver of the field is almost impossible. "I love this shit," he concludes.

In the third inning, we pull a fifth man into the infield against Matt Hibbert. He hits a hard ground ball right up the middle—where a defender is standing. Fehlandt bats for the second time, after striking out the first time; he pulls a line drive single into left, the one hitter on the team who refuses to get out of his normal hit-it-hard approach. Then Sergio Miranda lines right to our first baseman, who turns a double play. We bring a five-man infield in for Will Price, betting that he won't change his approach if we leave right field entirely open, and he doesn't—he pulls a ground ball right to our shortstop, playing a few extra steps in the hole. A couple batters try to bunt, but their attempts roll foul. I'm feeling cockier.

So when Isaac Wenrich joins the lineup in the sixth inning, I break out the Wall for the first time. All four infielders are separated from the next guy by about twenty feet, and Isaac has the entire left side of the infield—plus ten feet or so on the right of second base. All he has to do is adjust. Good hitters adjust, and Isaac—who hit well in the Pacific Association a year earlier—is undeniably a good hitter.

But he can't. In his first try he strikes out, after fouling a pop-up the other way for strike two—the telltale sign of a deliberate antishift approach. When he bats again the next inning, he keeps his front side firm and lets the ball get deep, and he manages to hit a ground ball to the left of second base. "Beat that shift!" he yells triumphantly as he busts out of the batter's box—except the ball isn't hit hard, and the farthest defender over (the third baseman) is able to charge it and flip a throw to the shortstop covering second, who tries to turn the double play but airmails his throw. A good throw would have gotten him. Isaac's triumph was actually just a fielder's choice. We learn two things: Baseball is really hard, and Ben and I might be smart.

"I just want to formally introduce us," I say after the game, because it was getting awkward how much we had avoided formally introducing ourselves. The players are all sitting on a grassy berm, done for the day other than this little introduction and a salmon dinner waiting for them in the parking lot. "I know it's been weird that we've just been hanging around in corduroys and acting odd. So in about the next five minutes I want to explain what we're about, what we're gonna do, and how you can help us.

"So what we're about: I know there are things that statheads do that nobody likes. One is looking at you guys not as people but as number generators. We don't feel that way at all. From the first tryout, when we saw Danny Baps, we completely fell in love with this team and with this collection of guys. And we know nothing works if you're not comfortable and we know nothing works if you're not confident. We know you guys have way more wisdom about baseball than we ever will. We're not going to tell you that you know less than us, because you absolutely know more than us. We are very, very, very aware of that. So don't ever think that we're just some assholes who are going to be, 'oh, geez, I played until I was thirteen.' We're not like that. Y'all are good. We think we're pretty smart. Fehlandt is a genius. He will tell you that he has changed my mind about a lot of things. We're out here to learn, not to tell you how smart we are."

"You can talk to 'em," Fehlandt says from his recline.

"The other thing is there's this idea that if we have data, then it's bulletproof and you can't argue with it. That's not true. Data is only a little bit of information. There's context to everything. You can misuse it, you can slant it. We've worked with writers who seemed really smart because they had a lot of data, and then it turned out they were wrong about everything. We're not going to be all certain about anything;

we're just going to be testing things and doing what we can to help you out.

"What we're going to be doing: We're going to be advance scouting. Whatever game is being played that you're not in, we're going to be at, and we've got software to scout it, some stringers to help us scout it, we're going to be videotaping every game out there. At Arnold we're going to have PITCHf/x, which is the cameras that major league parks use to track the pitch from your hand. For every pitch we're going to have the break, the velocity, the location, the speed off the bat, the angle, the trajectory, all this stuff. *You're the only indy league team that's ever going to have this.* There's no way to have this at parks like this, except we called and asked them and they liked the idea a lot and put it in for us.

"I don't know what we're going to do with all that. We're going to be very conservative early on. We're not going to tell you to play five-man infield on day one. We're going to start slow, listen to you guys, hear what you want. We've got access to things if you want information. If you want to know if something would work we can probably run tests on it and answer that. We've got equipment like this—" I hold up a two-inch piece of yellow plastic—"the Zepp sensor, which tracks the speed and the angle of your bat. We're going to try to get these on everybody's bat who is comfortable with it. We're thinking about ways we can use the fans better to help us win. I talked to a director of player development for a major league team and he's like, 'You gotta have naps in the clubhouse, everybody's gotta have naps.' I don't know if we're going to have naps in the clubhouse, but we'll probably talk to you guys about it and see what you think."

"Fuck naps in the clubhouse," Fehlandt says.

"This guy swears by it. I don't know. But mainly we're going to be starting really slow. You're going to look at us and wonder, 'What are they doing, are they doing anything?' We're observing and trying to learn, and not go too fast. You can help us by being patient and recognizing that we're not going to be moving that fast. Our goal is to win the first half and go undefeated in the second half. We want to be unstoppable by the second half. Please be patient, and be open-minded. I know I've worked at a lot of places and when they tell you you're gonna do something new my first reaction is always 'That's a terrible idea, I don't want to do that.' I just ask that you get through that first moment of 'fuck that' and give it, uh, a second moment of 'fuck that,' I guess, before you give up on it. And the third thing is give us a lot of feedback. You guys are experiencing this—you collect way more data in one at-bat than PITCHf/x can ever give us. We want to hear from you and know what makes you uncomfortable, what you think we can do better, what you want from an advance scout, how you want it presented to you. If we're giving you too much detail you can ask."

There are five seconds of silence.

"Sounds great," says T. J. Gavlik, and I walk back to where Ben is. The awkwardest, halfheartedest round of applause carries me along.

The Stompers go to San Quentin for a game against the prisoners. Will Price has been talked to, but his change of behavior is neither subtle nor effective. When a call goes out in the prison parking lot for somebody to carry the equipment bag in, it's Will who quickly volunteers. This can be seen as rookie deference (good) or as eyewash (bad), the practice of looking like you're trying real hard, but doing it just for show. At this stage, either would be an improvement for Will, but after carrying the bag a hundred yards he puts it down momentarily to show his ID at a guard station. Five minutes later, we all notice the abandoned bag, and Will ahead in the distance. "If that guy makes the team, he'll go broke on kangaroo court fines," Andrew Parker predicts.

The San Quentin yard has two teams—the San Quentin A's and the San Quentin Giants—who practice for three hours every weekday and host church groups, men's leagues, college teams, and each other. Against outsiders, they win about 70 percent of their games. It's said they have a huge home field advantage—namely that, for the first couple of innings, the visitors are scared to pitch inside. The Giants and A's have merged to form an All-Star team against us, but their ace, who carried a no-hitter into the fifth inning against San Rafael a year earlier, and who'll supposedly throw 200 pitches in a game to prevent the San Quentin bullpen from blowing his leads, is unavailable due to a disciplinary issue that is unanimously dismissed as "some bullshit" by the players. This is a hard blow for the All-Stars—losing the team's best player without receiving even a compensation pick in return.

Instead, we face a tall left-hander who is rumored on the prison yard to have pitched in the San Francisco Giants' minor league system before he was sent here for killing his wife. (He did not, and he was not.) He's good. Throws in the mid-80s, knows how to spin the ball, and has enough command to get calls from an overeager umpire, who has a strike call—"That's a Rembrandt!"—vigilantly in search of strikes. Our hitters are late on his fastballs and ahead on his curves, shooting foul balls into the basketball courts, where prisoners play, unprotected, under constant threat from these missiles. The chalk lines are pancake flour, supplied by donations. A goose wanders the out-field, which has lost almost all its grass—there's a drought in California, and the first place a state cuts water is to its prisons. "They cut our showers," a prisoner tells me, "so they sure as shit ain't going to water the outfield."

It's a bizarre mix of serious and loose. Serious: They won't let us wear jeans inside, so our assistant GM Sean Boisson, Ben, and I rush off to Target to buy khakis that will make us less likely to be mistaken for a prisoner and shot. Our players are open about how afraid they are—there are signs promising that guards will shoot through us in the event of a hostage situation, and Fehlandt has been making the same rape jokes ("night night, best keep your butthole tight") for days. Loose: Once we're inside, there are no minders; no restricted movement; and, we notice eventually, practically no guards in the yard itself. There are towers, including one just above the field, but for the five hours we spend on this field we are almost always one thousand feet or more away from the nearest guard on the ground. Which means that if a San Quentin prisoner—and, yes, there are murderers among them—wanted to snap our necks, he'd have time to enjoy the experience before anybody could get to us. Of course, the prisoners don't want to snap our necks. This is the biggest game of the year for them, the one time they get to play a real team. Or, for the dozens of fans lined up along the outfield lines, or on a little porch out beyond right field, the one time they get to see real baseball. They get to boo their own guys for screwing up, or yell at the umpires, who themselves get to show off how seriously they take this, talking to each other between pitches to make sure they all rotate in the right direction if a ball is hit into the outfield.

The baseball field is the one place in the yard that is completely desegregated, free of fault lines. Elsewhere, we see guys walking in pairs and groups, and they're always same-race packages; there's an Asian section over by the pull-up bars, there are the Hispanic dudes playing guitar or lifting weights, there are all-black basketball teams running fast breaks and all-white jogging groups doing laps through our outfield. But on the diamond there has been no sorting done at all. It is the loosest scene you can imagine, and within an inning the buttholes untighten, though presumably the guns remain cocked somewhere out of sight.

Will Price scores on a T. J. Gavlik single, the throw rolls unaccounted for toward home plate, and from the dugout a fed-up San Quentin All-Star yells, "Ain't anybody gonna cut that?" Andrew Parker hits a towering home run that looks for a moment like it'll clear Mount Tamalpais off in the distance. "These guys been bragging for a month that they were going to beat you," a prisoner tells us with a laugh and some schadenfreude. Alarms go off every half hour or so, and all the players stop, midplay, and sit down on the ground; we sit, and they tell us, "Y'all don't gotta do that. Just us." Theo puts on a uniform and takes a spot in the lineup. (He fouls out.) Sean Boisson takes a spot in the lineup. ("Mercy! We got a guy in Haggar pants up here!" a fan yells.) I take a spot in the lineup, swinging so wildly on 1-2 that I fall straight backward like the last domino. Ben takes a spot in the lineup, fouling two off before getting punched out on a fastball eight inches outside. "That's a Rembrandt!"

We all shake hands, umps and fans and players, and we all tell each other how we're not that different after all, and we also do the math when they tell us how long they're in here and deduce which ones probably killed somebody. "Beat the shit out of those San Rafael fuckers," they tell us, because *everybody* hates those San Rafael fuckers. We walk out of the yard in twilight, a trumpet in the distance singing sadly, the yard depopulated to just a couple dozen prisoners. Then we go to In-N-Out, where Will Price will get to experience California's main attraction. "I'm ready for this," he says, filling four ketchup cups for one order of fries, and I stare at those ketchups lined up in a row and I finally see the same excesses that Fehlandt sees. Eat fries and be merry, Will, for tomorrow we make cuts.

Everybody takes it a different way. Caleb Natov, the kid Fehlandt fought to draft with our second pick after the tryout, looks like he just woke from a hypnotic trance, like he's wondering how he managed to almost play professional baseball in the first place. "Well," he says slowly, "thanks for having me." We never see him again.

Jesse Garcia, the pitcher who fought back from cancer to keep his pro career going, now fights back tears. "I told myself before I came up here if I don't do it here I'm done," he says, as Theo and Fehlandt choke back their own heaves. "So . . ." he trails off.

Billy Gonzalez, the Puerto Rican catcher signed before Isaac Wenrich fell into our laps, hardly says a word—just agrees with the situation as presented to him. His handshake at departure is almost painfully hard.

And then Will Price. Ultimately, we all agree that Will needs to go. While we haven't seen the same loud tools from Mark Hurley, Mark has outplayed Will with a simple swing, outstanding instincts in drills, and that run-into-the-fence mentality. His teammates like him. We figure Will can perform in this league, but whether it's his fault or Fehlandt's, he has shown no persistent attitude improvement. He told a teammate—one of Fehlandt's best friends on the team, even—that he wanted to punch the manager. Maybe Fehlandt is his own self-fulfilling prophecy, but everything he said Will would do on Monday has come true by Friday. The whole team is against him, and Ben and I aren't big enough believers to insist that he stay.

"It was a tough decision," Theo tells Will, "but we're gonna have to go another direction this season. We think you've got the tools of a baseball player, and there's a spot for you in this game."

"I gotcha."

"Thanks for coming out—"

He's slumped way back in his chair, legs crossed at the ankles, neck cocked back, and he turns to Fehlandt. "Why?"

"From my perspective, I didn't see any adjustments. I'll give this for example: I'm pitching you in BP and I'm pitching you away and you're trying to pull everything. I see you get up on the plate so I bust you in, get up in your kitchen, and then you get off the plate and I go back away and you try to pull it again. Like—"

"So I got cut because of BP?"

"No, that's what—"

"That's what you just—"

"Timeouttimeouttimeout."

"That's what you're saying—"

"Hold on hold on. Why you got such an attitude?"

"Because I just got cut! I'm supposed to be happy?"

"You asked me a question and I'm trying to *share with you* my opinion and that was part of it."

"BP!"

Theo jumps in: "There was a lot of—"

"I made adjustments in the game."

"How'd you make adjustments in the game?" Fehlandt fires back. "Tell me. How many times did I say to the guys, your first at-bat in a game, your first time seeing a pitcher, why would you swing at the first pitch? How many pitches you see in your two at-bats today?"

"Two." One of them he hit for a home run, but he doesn't mention this.

"Two pitches. Exactly. If you're trying to prepare yourself for a season, a good hitter's not gonna swing at the first pitch. You're trying to see as many pitches as possible."

Will growls.

"And on top of that, the attitude. Since you brought it out in this meeting I'm gonna bring it out in this meeting. You're a rookie and you backtalk me. You can't even own up to how you're acting. Everybody on the team is telling me the same thing, and you're in here smiling and laughing—"

"Did everybody on the team say I was not good enough to be on the team?"

"It's not about that, bro. You think I want a cancer?"

"You cut the worst players—"

"DO I WANT A CANCER?"

"Ask them if they would want to be on the field with me."

"I already have; you think I didn't do that?"

"They said no?"

Fehlandt scoffs. "Yeah! They did. You're a rookie. That's just part of knowing your place. You gotta know your role and be quiet. I shouldn't even know you're out there. You gotta bust your ass and you gotta be quiet."

"I did bust my ass!"

"But you gotta be quiet."

"Was I not good enough?"

"I said you have skills but you're raw as shit."

"I'm twenty-one years old!"

"You act like you're twelve," Theo says.

"So the three outfielders you kept were better than me?"

Fehlandt has had enough. "You know what's hilarious, bro?" he says. "I knew exactly to a T what you were gonna say and how this meeting was gonna go, because I played with a million dudes just like you. All right, dude? I'm just being honest with you, dude, your attitude—I could have scripted out this meeting. I knew exactly what this meeting was gonna be. *Oh, those other outfielders are better than me?* They're proven. They played professionally. They know how to act."

Will growls again. "It's cool, though," he says. He walks out of the room, no handshakes for anyone. He walks down the hall toward the main entrance, then abruptly turns around and reenters the conference room.

"How'm I getting home?" he asks.

TAKING THE FIELD

On Sunday, May 31, the evening before Opening Day, the Stompers gather at Rossi's, a combination beer/dance hall in an especially sleepy section of Sonoma with no streetlights or sidewalks, where the frontage on every block looks like it's gone too long without a lawn mower. They're here for the "First Pitch Party," which the event's flyer describes as an opportunity to "Mix and mingle with Sonoma's hometown pro baseball players!" Guests will get autographs, live music, and face time with Rawhide, the bull-like mascot that will always be Theo Fightmaster's finest free-agent signing: Theo picked up the $10,000 mascot costume for free after the local hockey team that commissioned it folded.

Sam and I arrive separately but enter Rossi's side by side. We're still in the "uneasy nod" stage with most of the nonspreadsheet players, who recognize us as emissaries of the team but still aren't sure what part we'll play in their lives, even after Sam's stirring spring training address. If pressed, they could probably identify us as a single entity, "BenandSam," but they'd have a hard time telling which is which. And as of today, the team's unspoken-but-sensed power structure has changed. In camp, the players were only aspiring Stompers, temporary nobodies with the potential to be pros. We were the gatekeepers, wielding the power to decide which wannabes would be baseballers and which would have to return to their girlfriends and families and confess that they hadn't made the cut. But by surviving the spring training wringer, the players have instantly leapfrogged us in Sonoma status. We may be semi-well-known on the Internet, but in person we pale in comparison to the town's only professional athletes, who have almost no chance of making the majors but much *more* of a chance than anyone else in the area. Most of them haven't played a game in Sonoma, but when they're wearing their jerseys, they're instantly local celebrities, catnip for kids with outstretched Sharpies and starstruck, uplifted eyes.

The players are already seated at the restaurant's long tables when we walk in, so Sam and I, accompanied by my girlfriend, Jessie, sit at a table with Theo; Theo's wife, Erin; and the Stompers' new first family, Eric and Lani Gullotta. Eric purchased the Stompers in January from the Marin County outsiders who own the Pacifics (and approved our project, when they still owned the Stompers). He's a tax attorney on the precipice of forty, a large, gradually softening physical presence who's also unabashedly boisterous for a pillar of the local community. A Sonoma native and a graduate of Sonoma Valley High, he became a bro at UC–Santa Barbara and still speaks in a Judd Apatow patois, despite his standing as a board member of the Sonoma Chamber of Commerce. As we settle in, he describes in graphic terms what his wife (still seated alongside him) would do if left alone with Gary Oldman, her Hollywood crush. The conversation grows more colorful, and occasionally uncomfortable, from there.

Behind Eric's frat-boy façade is an ambitious owner who'd like to turn a profit but also cares deeply about the Stompers' ties to Sonoma. "There are two types of owners," Theo told Santa Rosa's *Press Democrat* shortly after the franchise sale. "Owners who don't know anything about their sport and those who realize it." Eric is the latter. A sponsor and season-ticket holder during the Stompers' inaugural season, mostly for business purposes, he didn't buy the team because he loved baseball;

he bought it to burnish his ego, to gaze at a busy ballpark and know that his bank account brought a town together.

When a major league team changes ownership, the new boss talks a big game about signing new players, building a deep farm system, and future-proofing the front office with the latest industry innovations. Indy leagues operate with a smaller scope: When the Stompers changed ownership, Eric told the *Sonoma Index-Tribune* that "improving the bathrooms is one of our top priorities." He turned the vacant office next to his practice into a sleek-looking office and team store, an enormous upgrade from the tiny one-room rental where Theo and Tim had squeezed in the previous summer. Eric also unveiled an aggressive plan to enhance the spectator experience at Arnold Field, proposing several upgrades he's able to implement—a sound system that doesn't make every announcement sound like a squawk; a mesh screen behind home plate that's easier on the eyes (and easier on the baseballs, whose scuffs are a constant expense) than the chain-link fence that preceded it; a canopy over the grandstand that repels some of the sunlight; a 6:05 p.m. start time for home games, an hour earlier than before—and some that have to wait for a future season (such as a working replica of the hand-operated Wrigley Field scoreboard). From our perspective, his most progressive decision is allowing our involvement, ceding some control over his new asset to two carpetbaggers.

He's also surprisingly good at interacting with athletes fifteen years younger, maybe because his sense of humor is still in its twenties. Two nights earlier, I'd heard Eric address the team at a catered, Stompers-only event. His stone-sober speech was a cross between a commencement address and Luke Wilson's wedding toast from *Old School*.

"I just want to say to you guys that Sonoma is so fucking proud to have you," Eric began. "People can look around and see a bunch of ballplayers, and I see a fucking team. And I see a team that Sonoma's ready to get behind. For those of you who don't know, I was born and raised in this town, so I think of Sonoma as my family. And I think of you guys as my family. And I am so excited to see you guys get out there and beat the *shit* out of San Rafael, beat the *shit* out of Vallejo, and beat the *shit* out of Pittsburg. And if anybody needs anything . . . see Theo.

"I was out at the field—it's magic, man. We're putting a ton of dough, a ton of energy, and a ton of love into this season, and this city is ready for an amazing season. There's a ton of buzz. You guys are gonna be gods among these people. You're gonna have a great time after the game. I just don't want to hear the stories, because my wife does not want to hear that shit. So just an email, maybe. If you have pictures, I don't want to see them." He paused. "High-res only, okay?" The team ate up and drank in every word, along with many beers from the open bar.

I limit myself to low-key cringing at Eric's off-color jokes by devoting most of my attention to the players, many of whom have already bonded with the effortless ease of lifelong clubhouse inhabitants. It's "Chicken Fried Sunday" at Rossi's, and our finely tuned athletes swallow pitchers of beer and inhale heaping plates of wings. I guiltily think back to podcast episodes in which Sam and I have discussed the obvious advantage that teams could derive by providing their minor league players with healthy meal options. At the major league level, teams provide players with lavish spreads, and no one is priced out of proper nutrition: The average player makes $4 million a year, the poorest player makes more than half a million, and every player gets a daily meal allowance of more than $100 when the team is on the road. But below the big leagues, many players make less than minimum wage, which has led to lawsuits that have crept through the courts—one of which, we find out, was filed by our current second baseman, Sergio Miranda. Faced with a choice between eating healthy and paying their rent, most players forgo the former and opt for fast food.

In late 2012, our psychologist colleague Russell Carleton estimated in an article for *Baseball Prospectus* that it would take teams $2 million a year to feed all of their players like high-performance machines—a small sum, relative to the value of a major league franchise. If that expense helped one more prospect per decade pan out, or convinced a single budding star to sign a discounted extension, it would pay for itself.

Since Russell's article was published, some teams have adopted his idea, although many still skimp in a shortsighted attempt to cut costs. As I watch our players chow down, I feel frustrated that we have no money to put where our mouths (and, more importantly, our players' mouths) are. The Stompers are sponsored by Sonoma Market, an upscale grocery store, so the postgame spreads at home are high quality. But before and during games, and often on the road, tubs of peanut butter and jelly and a bunch of bananas are as good as it gets. It's worse away from the field: Limiting young adults' junk-food-and-alcohol intake would be a great way to become the bad guys, and even if we wanted to try it, we'd have neither the money nor the manpower to police what players eat. So bring on the beer and fried chicken—the same combination that the *Boston Globe* cited as a cause of the late-season collapse of the 2011 Red Sox.

After everyone gorges, the player introductions begin. Acting as emcee, Tim introduces each player with the aplomb of a part-time pro wrestling announcer (which he is). One by one, he booms out the players' brief bios, and each subject swaggers toward the front of the room, where he high-fives Rawhide, bumps backsides and fists with the rest of the team, and takes his place in a line of clapping players. Stompers seem to outnumber non-Stompers at Rossi's, but the fans and host families who have made the trip sound like a larger crowd, reserving their loudest acclaim for returning players such as Joel Carranza, Eric Schwieger, and Matt Hibbert.

It's the first time we've had a chance to sit back and study the players as a unit, not as names on a whiteboard but as physical beings. "Do we have a good team, Theo?" Sam asks. Theo hems and haws and finally allows that it looks better than last year's model, which finished in third place with a 42-36 record. We can't tell if he's humoring us or truly believes it. And even if he were confident, we wouldn't be. We don't know what a good team *should* look like at this level.

After the introductions are over, the cover band begins. Tim and Theo head over to Arnold Field to make sure the alcohol is in order for Opening Day, while Sam and I are joined by Yoshi, the Stompers' bench coach and the primary helper Feh has on the Stompers' bare-bones staff. Yoshi is thirty-seven and a baseball lifer. A former independent-league player in both the United States and Japan, he spends much of the year away from his wife and young son in Japan's Kanagawa Prefecture, coaching wherever he can. Theo hired him after watching him work in the California Winter League, an eight-team circuit that serves as a showcase for higher-level summer leagues. Yoshi's team, made up mostly of Japanese players, reported to practice earlier and left later than any other club, which explains why he was taken aback by our laid-back spring schedule. He's highly organized, a disciplined gymgoer, and a complete convert to the importance of preparation. Basically, Bizarro Fehlandt Lentini. (The real Fehlandt Lentini will twice send me frantic pregame texts to say he's forgotten half his uniform.)

Everyone in baseball has a résumé, and every résumé has a "Goals" or "Objectives" section that's supposed to tell a potential employer what the person wants to do. The language in these blurbs sounds like a horoscope that's designed to describe every reader: It's wordy and unspecific, just broad enough to make every opening a potential perfect fit. A typical example might say something like, "To obtain a position in the baseball industry that allows me to leverage my skill set in order to further the goals of the organization." (In fewer words: "To get a job in baseball.") The "Objectives" section of Yoshi's résumé doesn't beat around the bush: "To be the first Japanese manager/coach in Major League Baseball history." An indy-league managerial job would be a nice stepping-stone, especially with a winning record; the only previous Japanese-born manager in American pro baseball had washed out after three losing minor league seasons.

Yoshi arrived after spring training started, and we've talked to him only briefly. But on the eve of the season, he seeks us out to ask for intel. He tells us that he's heard what we've said about stats, and he knows he has to be on board if he wants to manage in the modern game. To our delight, he makes this sound more like a learning opportunity than a chore. "Give me all the evidences," he says, using his word for what we do. I look at Sam and see that, like me, he's having a hard time not hugging our unsuspected ally. "Yoshi, you have no idea how happy you just made us," I say. He laughs and jabs me on the chest, which he does whenever he speaks—either affectionately or hard enough to hurt, depending on his mood. Right now he's happy, and his taps barely register over the accelerated beating of our cold, stathead hearts. He walks away and leaves us wondering why we didn't discover this side of him months ago.

"I wish he were the manager," I say to Sam.

"Yup," Sam responds.

It's too late now. The season is starting.

There's nothing Sam and I like less than predicting baseball, a duty we've spent our careers trying and failing to duck. Fans love predictions, in some cases because they genuinely value the perspective of people who are paid to opine about baseball, and in other cases because predictions give them grounds to gloat when those people predict poorly. Stat-averse readers interpret the preseason projections that sites such as *Baseball Prospectus* publish as the embodiment of the hubris of statheads who think they can boil baseball's beauty and complexity down to a few formulas. "The season isn't played in a spreadsheet," these detractors declare. And they're right! But there's no such thing as an analyst who believes the projections are perfect. Although projection systems give the appearance of precision, all they really represent is what each player's past performance—generally a pretty good guide to his future performance—pinpoints as the most likely outcome in a range of possibilities. There are so many *other* potential outcomes, of course, that the odds are in favor of the actual result being one of the less likely ones. And the more we learn about baseball, the better we understand how misguided any sense of certainty is.

If Sam and I had our druthers, we'd predict in probabilities instead of absolutes: Instead of saying "Royals in six," we'd say there was an

X percent chance of Royals in four, and an X percent chance of Royals in five, and an X percent chance of Royals in six, and an X percent chance of Royals in seven. This would be so boring to read that no one would ask us to make more predictions, and better yet, we'd probably be dead before anyone had enough data to decide whether we were good prognosticators or not.

No one makes us predict how each Stomper will play, but against all odds Sam suggests we do so anyway, partly as a historical snapshot and partly so you can look at the misses and laugh at us later. Stompers predictions are impossible: We've never seen these people play outside of spring training, and we don't have enough history to project their performance with any kind of confidence. And because we know there's no way we'll nail any of them, except maybe by accident, we predict with impunity.

You'll notice some similarities between our predictions, probably because we based them on the same limited looks, stat lines, and spring-training discussions. Here are the hitters:

	Sam			Ben		
Player	AVG	OBP	SLG	AVG	OBP	SLG
Daniel Baptista	.230	.290	.440	.250	.340	.470
Joel Carranza	.260	.330	.510	.275	.350	.525
T. J. Gavlik	.265	.320	.375	.260	.320	.350
Kristian Gayday	.305	.375	.490	.285	.390	.480
Matt Hibbert	.290	.400	.440	.300	.410	.415
Mark Hurley	.260	.320	.370	.260	.330	.380
Fehlandt Lentini	.380	.430	.540	.340	.385	.435
Sergio Miranda	.310	.345	.420	.255	.300	.350
Gered Mochizuki	.275	.315	.365	.270	.310	.350
Andrew Parker	.245	.365	.505	.230	.390	.455
Isaac Wenrich	.275	.365	.530	.265	.385	.505

And these are the pitcher predictions:

Name	Sam ERA	Ben ERA
Jeff Conley	3.40	3.70
Sean Conroy	3.35	3.00
Jerome Godsey	3.85	4.20
Erik Gonsalves	5.00	5.10
Paul Hvozdovic	2.65	3.10
Mike Jackson Jr.	3.90	4.30
Gregory Paulino	1.80	3.20
John Rand	4.65	4.40
Eric Schwieger	2.99	3.75
Matt Walker	4.55	4.45

I think the spreadsheet guys (Gayday, Hvozdovic, Conroy, Conley) are going to be good, and I think Feh's patronage players (Mochizuki, Miranda, Walker) are going to be bad. Feel free to use these projections to decide whether we're biased and stupid or biased and smart.

It rains on Opening Day. Just a few drops, hours before first pitch, but a biblical deluge by Sonoma standards, enough to strike superstitious, overstressed minds as an ugly omen. Fortunately, there are no superstitious, overstressed minds on the Stompers. Nope, none at all.

Our opponents are the Pittsburg Diamonds, which would have been better news in 2014. They were the doormats in the Pacific Association's first year, finishing 22-56. The quickest way to convey how bad at baseball they were is to summarize the performance of a Pittsburg pitcher named Chris Nowlin.

Nowlin is a knuckleballer; look him up on YouTube, and you'll find him in what looks like a self-produced proof-of-life video, in which major league pitcher R. A. Dickey delivers a stilted endorsement as Nowlin looks on. The thirty-three-year-old right-hander, who didn't play baseball in high school or college, had four games of pro pitching experience before making his Pacific Association debut. In 2007, he faced four batters in the American Association, allowing three runs without recording an out. In 2009, he faced five batters in the Continental Baseball League, recording one out and surrendering four runs. And in 2010, he got into *two* games for the Sussex Skyhawks of the Canadian-American Association, going a combined 4 1/3 innings and allowing 11 runs. The best one could say is that his ERA was heading in the right direction, falling from "infinite," to 108.00, to 20.77.

In his first start for Pittsburg in 2014—four years after the Skyhawks experience—Nowlin went 2 1/3 innings and allowed 7 runs, walking 6 of the 18 batters he faced. On many teams, in many leagues, that would've been his swan song. But with Pittsburg, he pitched five more times, including one game—not even his last one!—in which he faced 7 batters without earning an out. All told, Nowlin pitched 15 1/3 innings and allowed 24 hits, 4 homers, and *31 walks*, along with 3 hit batters and 4 wild pitches. The good news: Nowlin's ERA decline continued, as the damage dropped to 14.67 (plus 4 unearned runs). He hasn't pitched professionally since, but he's still several years away from his fortieth birthday, which for a knuckleballer means he has time.

Nowlin's game against the Stompers was the only one his team won (thanks to 11 runs of support). But the Stompers still got their share of the spoils in 2014, going 16-8 against Pittsburg despite finishing under .500 (26-28) against the Pacifics and the Admirals. Pittsburg's poor pitching yielded 6.7 runs per game to the Stompers, who scored 5.9 per game against everyone else.

There's no telling how formidable the newly named Diamonds will be. The franchise nearly folded a few months before the season started, which would have forced the remaining clubs to play fewer games or field an always-on-the-road travel team to save the league. These jerry-rigged solutions were avoided when buyers were found between our March tryouts and Opening Day: Pittsburg native Aaron Miles, a former utility man for five major league teams, and Khurram Shah, the owner of a towing company. Miles, who was listed at 5-foot-8, 180 pounds during his playing career, appears to have augmented at least the latter figure substantially: His neck is a nonentity, and his belly protrudes to the point that he walks with a slight backward lean, as if trying to counteract the new ballast before him. But his forearms are still strong, and at thirty-eight he's only three years removed from his last at-bat in affiliated ball. In nineteen games for Pittsburg in 2014 (before he bought into the team), Miles batted .358 with more walks than strikeouts. He'll manage the team in 2015, as he and Shah try to tow the wreck to respectability.

We're still unsure whether the pairing has improved the team's talent, but it's clear that Pittsburg's PR presence remains unpolished. A few hours before first pitch, Sam gleefully emails me a Diamonds press release about Miles becoming the manager, which one glance is enough to identify as a complete copyediting disaster. "Pittsburg's awesome," Sam writes. "This press release abruptly changes from third person to first. So fun." I'm in full lower-expectations mode, so despite my amusement I send back a wet-blanket response: "Anything amateur they do makes it less impressive if we win or more embarrassing if we lose."

The Stompers' Opening Day starting assignment—typically an honor reserved for a team's best pitcher—goes to right-hander Matt Walker, who hails from British Columbia's Bowen Island, a community of thirty-four hundred accessible by ferry from Vancouver. Walker is about to turn twenty-eight, which makes him the second-oldest pitcher and fifth-oldest player on our rookie-packed roster. Ten days ago, Sam and I didn't know he existed; five days ago, we would have had trouble picking him out of a crowd. This is only partly a reflection of our failings as team executives. Mostly, it's a reflection of the fact that he crashed spring training.

Walker isn't a returning player, a spreadsheet guy, or a friend of Feh's: He simply showed up, with the backing of Mochizuki, the *third*-oldest player on the team and Feh's confidant. The two played together in Maui in 2012, as part of the North American League that preceded the Pacific Association. Whatever Moch saw in him doesn't show up in the stats: Walker allowed more than five runs per nine innings and struck out only 10 percent of the hitters he faced. That made him the second-worst of the five pitchers on Maui's staff who got at least ten starts—and the only one less effective was Eri Yoshida, a twenty-year-old female knuckleballer with a 60 mph fastball. More discouraging still, Walker hasn't pitched professionally since that season, devoting most of his time to building up a business as a handyman back in British Columbia.

On the Thursday before Walker's season-opening start against Pittsburg, he received a stay of execution in the conference room at the Stompers' office, where Theo, Feh, and I (with Sam on speakerphone) met to finalize the roster before informing the players the following day. The four of us took turns listing our recommended cuts to the pitching staff, hoping for enough overlap to make the decisions easy. I named Walker and two 2014 Stompers, Jesse Garcia and Erik Gonsalves. Everyone agreed on Garcia, a lefty who'd posted an ERA near 6.00 in his first pro season. No one fought hard for Gonzo, particularly after Theo noted that we could count on him to spend most of his money at Town Square. But Feh was incredulous when I named Walker. "Why do you have Walker at the bottom?" he asked. "What did you not like?"

I had a hard time articulating my objections, partly because I'd watched Walker for only a couple of innings in our entirely-too-short spring training. I didn't *dislike* him. It was more that I hadn't seen him do anything to demand my attention. His surprise arrival wasn't the only reason Sam and I couldn't recognize him until we'd memorized every other player's appearance and learned to identify him by process of elimination. He was built to blend into a crowd, six feet and slender, with friendly but forgettable features. His facial hair was right on the border between blond and red, longer than "stubble" but shorter than "goatee." His accent was only kind of Canadian. He didn't have an odd delivery, he didn't throw hard, and none of his secondary stuff seemed nasty. He just sort of slipped out of our minds, while other players did something to cement themselves. I tried to express this, leaving out the bit about his hair.

"At the end of the day, this is a guy that's already proven himself professionally," Feh answered. (I wasn't sure *what* he'd proven about himself professionally, but I stayed silent.) "And there are some guys on the team who played behind him who would pretty much cosign for him. And even Wenrich has cosigned him too, and I respect Wenrich as a catcher who has a pretty good opinion about pitchers' stuff. I liked his angle. He was hitting all those spots. Obviously it was his first time pitching, but just his demeanor—I really liked the guy. And to be honest, he wants the ball, and no one else has really come at me and said so. Said to *me*—they've went to girls in the bar and said something." We all laugh: Nothing like a little rookie-mocking to lighten the mood.

"But at the end of the day," Feh continued, "I was looking to give him the ball on frickin' Monday. I wasn't sure, but I said that to him and, dude, he was like, 'I want the fucking ball, I'm gonna frickin' get this shit done.' I was like, 'That's what I'm talking about.'"

There was silence for a few seconds as I (and presumably Sam) considered whether wanting the fucking ball was sufficient grounds for getting it. Then Theo spoke up in one of his frequent attempts to appease all parties.

"Walker is really complicated," he said. "He's got no work visa. He's the nicest guy I think we have on the team. He's got some experience. His visa paperwork was submitted today. The other part of the complication with him: We have a volunteer contract in the league, and just to pitch and get a chance to play again, he would be willing to play as a volunteer this year."

Feh piggybacked on the last part. "He already said he'll sleep in his damn truck, he doesn't care," he said. "And he came up to me and said, 'Hey, thanks for having me out.' I want to see what this guy can be. Moch is kind of like me, he doesn't give a lot of people credit. He was all over me from the beginning about this guy: 'Just let him come, just let him come.'"

I didn't fight any further, for a few reasons. For one thing, we didn't have much data: In the absence of a wide slate of statistics or our own extensive scouting, endorsements from veterans and/or former teammates like Feh and Moch were among the most useful info we had. For another, I figured if his first start stunk, we'd send him on his way, assuming a US immigration officer didn't do it for us. For a third thing, there wasn't another pitcher I liked better, and we did need someone to eat innings for ten days, when the major league draft would end and free us to recruit more unsigned spreadsheet standouts. And lastly, hey, he'd play for free. He wouldn't take up any payroll room, and I couldn't question his enthusiasm.

The only thing necessary for the triumph of Feh was for us to do nothing, so when I dropped my objection, the matter was essentially settled. Walker would make the team as long as someone didn't demand the ball even more forcefully before first pitch. Next time someone tries to tell you to "put yourself out there"—join an online dating site after a bad breakup, maybe, or interview for a job whose requirements you can't quite meet—remember Matt Walker, the patron saint of putting oneself out there. Walker went from total stranger to Opening Day starter in the span of ten days, just by being around.

The Stompers open their season at Arnold Field on Monday, June 1, bumped up a day because of a conflict with Tuesday's Sonoma Valley High School graduation ceremony. Monday is the Pacific Association's usual off day, so not only is this the only Monday during the regular season with a game on the schedule, but it's also the only game day without two contests taking place at one time. That makes this the only opportunity to get all our advance scouts together without missing action elsewhere, so we turn it into a crash course with three separate training stations. Graham Goldbeck, who's visiting from Sportvision headquarters in San Francisco, will teach us the ins and outs of operating the PITCHf/x software. Zak Welsh will demonstrate how to log games in BATS. We'll also set up a camera and tripod beyond the left-center-field fence, trained on the pitcher and batter, which will give us a view not unlike the one we're accustomed to on TV. As the game goes on, we'll rotate our assistants from station to station, where we hope they'll absorb everything they need to know to operate on their own.

Hours before first pitch, I walk the few blocks from my rented cottage to Arnold Field. A few of our scouts have beaten me to the ballpark and are floating behind home plate, where they're probably wondering what they've signed up for. Eric spots us standing around and asks us to help complete the park's final preparations by putting up billboards on the outfield fences and bunting behind home plate. It's not a normal game day task for baseball operations employees, but there is no normal in the independent leagues. We put down our laptops and stopwatches and pick up power drills and plastic twist ties. You wouldn't think it would be possible to put up bunting backward, but the four of us find a way.

When we're finished, we watch batting practice. The Stompers swing first, followed by the Diamonds. I stand with our advance scouts down the left-field line, looking over the fence between the visiting dugout and the Leese-Fitch Lounge/Lagunitas Beer Garden, an enclosed area with seating where fans can get their alcohol on while watching the game. Noah Clark, always one to speak his mind, shares his first observation as a scout. "Their guys look better than your guys," he says.

I'm already thinking the same thing. The Diamonds are big, and it looks like they're hitting a lot of line drives that keep carrying. Right fielder Nash Hutter is 6-foot-2, 210, and looks more like a man than most of our players, with the prominent, well-rounded rear that scouts call "baseball butt." Left fielder Brandon Williams is 6-foot-3, 215, and built like a track star. First baseman Mike Taylor is bigger than both of them. When we look at the lineup card posted inside the Diamonds' dugout—their roster, in typical Pittsburg fashion, is the only one in the league that isn't online—we see a surprising name: Nick Oddo, the catcher we came close to signing before Wenrich was an option. The one that got away didn't get very far.

As game time approaches, our scouts congregate at the top of the grandstand, where a small press box overlooks the field. The press box—a barely glorified shack about the width of four Porta Potties—has just enough room for a table and chairs for Tim Livingston, a Pointstreak/scoreboard operator, and Trey Dunia, the PA announcer, who treats the Arnold Field faithful to Billy Squier before games and is quick with a shattered-windshield sound effect when a foul ball flies toward the parking lot. But this year it will also have to hold the PITCHf/x operator, who'll sit at a tiny card table in the corner with a keyboard, monitor, and mouse. The monitor is attached to a desktop computer that sits behind the press box on the roof of the Stompers' clubhouse, protected from the elements (such as they are in Sonoma) by the press-box roof, two pieces of particleboard, and some netting. To turn it on, the operator has to vault over the wall, much to the surprise of the fans sitting in the top rows of the grandstand, who look up with concern whenever they notice one of us executing this seemingly suicidal maneuver.

Sam is spending game one in the dugout, more to establish a foothold in foreign territory than anything else. Right now, we have nothing to add to the players' preparation: We haven't seen Pittsburg play. But at some point in the season, we will want to be in the dugout to discuss tactics and offer information, and we don't want it to be weird when we're there. We also want the players—and perhaps more importantly Feh—to realize that there's nowhere we can't go. Just by standing in the corner or leaning over the railing alongside players in uniform, we're breaking a barrier that still stands strong in the big leagues. In major league front offices, statistical analysts have a much louder voice than they used to, but few of them venture into the clubhouse, and *no one* gets to go in the dugout during games: At most, statheads offer advice or answer questions in pregame meetings before retreating to an office, a luxury box, or a seat in the stands.

This is the way it's always worked, but it's a curious use of resources. In many cases, analysts help determine who plays for a team and for how much money. Why should their influence end when games begin, even though they still have insights to offer? During the Stompers' season, the Denver Broncos of the National Football League announce that the team's director of analytics, Mitch Tanney, will break the front-office fourth wall in their upcoming games, speaking on a headset to head coach Gary Kubiak to offer his input on which plays the probabilities and percentages support. As managers increasingly come from cohorts that tend to be more receptive to sabermetrics, it seems inevitable that something similar will happen in baseball. Although the major leagues still prohibit electronic communications in the dugout, it wouldn't be surprising to see teams hire in-game statistical consultants or recruit bench coaches—who've historically been cronies of the manager with similar philosophies on the sport—with quantitative backgrounds. Maybe Sam and I will serve as the prototypes. Or maybe we'll screw up and set statheads back for another few years.

The two of us will switch off on dugout duty, depending on which of us (and which of our scouts) is with the Stompers on a certain day. Today I'm overseeing the advance-scouting orientation, so I cram into the press box behind Tim and next to Goldbeck, who's going through the pregame setup process for PITCHf/x, entering rosters, lineups, and starting pitchers for both teams. I ask him whether this is the unlikeliest location ever for a Sportvision setup. He doesn't have to mull it over long. "Yeah, I think so," he says. The company installed a system to track fast-pitch softball at the 2011 NCAA Women's College World Series, so that's saying something. Then again, ESPN televised the softball tournament. The Stompers have to settle for Tim's Internet-only radio stream.

As I look at the field over Goldbeck's shoulder, I listen to Tim begin his broadcast. Like Vin Scully, Tim announces solo. Unlike Scully, he carries and sets up his own audio equipment, deals with weak Wi-Fi connections, and does most of the road games at folding tables exposed to the skies, which means that attentive listeners can almost hear his skin sizzle on sunny days. He reads out the Stompers' lineup, which looks like this:

Fehlandt Lentini, CF

Sergio Miranda, 2B

Gered Mochizuki, SS

Joel Carranza, 1B

Isaac Wenrich, C

Kristian Gayday, 3B

Daniel Baptista, DH

Mark Hurley, LF

Matt Hibbert, RF

It's not exactly the way we would've drawn it up. Moch has hit 6 career home runs in 1,292 professional plate appearances, which makes him a slugger compared to Miranda's 9 in 2,655. Power isn't everything—both guys seem selective, and on-base percentage is important. But sabermetric orthodoxy, based on complex run-scoring simulations, says that the number-two batter—who makes almost as many plate appearances as the leadoff man, but bats with more runners on base—should be the club's best hitter, instead of the high-contact, good-bat-control, move-the-runners-over type that teams have been sticking there since time immemorial. In light of that research, we'd rather see someone with pop in that spot. Major league teams are beginning to learn this lesson: The big leaguer with the most plate appearances out of the second slot in 2015 is the Toronto Blue Jays' Josh Donaldson, who will go on to win the American League Most Valuable Player award after tying for third in the AL with 41 home runs.

Hibbert, meanwhile, posted a .408 on-base percentage (with 35 steals in 43 attempts) for the Stompers in 2014, mostly while leading off. Feh likes him at the bottom of the order, where he envisions him serving as a sort of "second leadoff hitter" who gets on base to set up the top of the order. The problem is that the actual leadoff batter comes to the plate far more often than the "second" one. In the Pacific Association in 2014–15, each player after the leadoff batter makes approximately 0.11 fewer plate appearances per game than the hitter ahead of him, which translates to a difference of almost 0.9 plate appearances per game between the leadoff batter and the number-nine guy.

Pacific Association PA Per Game by Lineup Slot, 2014–15								
1	2	3	4	5	6	7	8	9
4.88	4.77	4.68	4.59	4.50	4.37	4.26	4.16	4.02

Hitting Hibbert last would cost him close to seventy plate appearances over a seventy-eight-game season, almost a quarter of the trips to the plate he has the potential to make. Our ideal lineup would have Hibbert at the top, Feh following him, and Miranda and Moch somewhere in the bottom third.

Amid my excitement, I can't help but think that Opening Day is precisely the time when we should take a stand on the batting order, for the same reason that we're trying to lay claim to dugout real estate from the start. If we let Feh bat Miranda and Moch at the top of the order today—based on seniority, favoritism, an inflated belief in their abilities, or some synthesis of the three—we'll give our tacit consent to Feh's sovereignty and also allow him to claim later that we can't make a change because the players are accustomed to where they've been batting.

The arguments against asserting ourselves now are also strong. For one thing, batting order doesn't matter *that* much. Although it's frustrating when managers construct suboptimal batting orders for no reason other than ignorance or distrust of what the stats say—the baseball equivalent of an unforced error—most lineup mistakes don't matter more than a few runs per season. (Although hitting Hibbert last instead of first is about as big a batting-order misstep as a manager can make.) For another, we might be better off broaching the subject delicately. Unless we want Feh to actively undermine us, we have to finesse our relationship. Invading the team's territory during an actual game is adventurous enough; invading and cracking down on the natives might foster an organized resistance. Plus, I'd have to act without the support of my partner: Sam—who doesn't care about the batting order and thinks we have to earn any authority we wield—says he wouldn't be with me if I tried to protest. Reluctantly, I suppress my misgivings. The batting order will wait.

Sonoma is the sort of small town where moments of silence are actually silent, safe from the sound of some big-city guy going "Woooo." I don't hear so much as a murmur from the crowd of more than a thousand fans as the mic cuts in and out during self-billed "soul singer and future Broadway star" Ceilidh Austin's rendition of the national anthem, save for the usual swell of support at the pause after "land of the free." The spectators sustain their applause through a short pregame ceremony, in which Jayce Ray's family accepts the 2014 Pacific Association MVP Award on his behalf. Ray can't be here because he's with the Wichita Wingnuts of the American Association, for whom he's hitting .394/.459/.576 through his first nine games. It's as much a reminder to the players that their performance is appreciated as it is reassurance that there's precedent for escaping from the Pacific Association.

Shadows bisect the field between home plate and the pitcher's mound, a visibility-killing consequence of the six o'clock start time that hitters hate. It's 70 degrees at first pitch, with 70 percent humidity, but the forecast calls for the temperature to drop to 55 in the late innings. That's standard for Sonoma, where one needs a blanket at night even when the temperature touches triple digits during the day.

I've always had to fight the feeling that the first pitch of the season is a powerful portent, as if its outcome might set the tone for the rest of the year. So it's difficult to dismiss the result of Matt Walker's first pitch to Pittsburg leadoff man Brandon Williams: a fastball dribbled to second, which Sergio Miranda gloves and throws too late to retire the speedy left fielder. After that, though, the outs come quickly: Isaac Wenrich catches Williams stealing, and Nick Oddo grounds out. By the time center fielder Tim Battle flies out to Fehlandt for the final out of the inning, I've convinced myself that I'm not superstitious about season-opening singles.

The Diamonds' starter is twenty-five-year-old Dennis Neal, who played for Vallejo in 2014 and was one of the Pacific Association's best pitchers despite a fastball that sits at 84. The lefty, who throws from the stretch even with the bases empty, delivers a fastball to Feh on the inside corner for a called strike, then gets him to swing and miss on a changeup and throws a fastball high for ball one. On the fourth pitch, Feh sends a liner into left-center—our leadoff hitter matching Pittsburg's, single for single. "He's going to be someone that Neal will have to watch very, very closely," Tim says, and Neal does: After strike one to the next batter, Miranda, he throws over and catches Lentini leaning. Feh takes off for second anyway, and slides in safely under the throw—even when he's picked off, Feh can't be caught. Miranda, a switch-hitter batting from the right side, reaches out and bloops a low and away 0-2 pitch down the right-field line. It falls in front of Nash Hutter, and Feh scores the first run of the Stompers' season.

The Diamonds answer in the second. With one out and one on, second baseman Jaylen Harris, a twenty-one-year-old former Dodgers farmhand, lifts a fly ball to left-center, in a part of the park where the wall is roughly 365 feet from home plate. Arnold Field has no warning track—what does this look like, affiliated ball?—and Feh crashes into the barrier at close to full speed. He falls down, but the ball stays up and disappears over the fence. The Diamonds take a 2-1 lead.

This lead doesn't last long, either. It falls in the first highlight of the Stompers' season that's seared into our minds, a moment we immediately know will make the summer montage.

Kristian Gayday comes to the plate to the hook of "Turn Down for What," walking slowly with his head bowed in a way that probably broadcasts calm confidence when he's hitting and bad body language when he's in a slump. "Man alive, what a senior season for him," Tim says, treating his listeners to Kristian's senior stat line at Fort Wayne, which I'm happy to hear again. (Tim is the only person under eighty who still says "man alive.") Hands held high and bat angled forward, Kristian watches a fastball in a way that says *I don't touch first pitches*. He accepts the called strike. The next pitch, a changeup, just misses outside. The 1-1 pitch is bounced foul, where Yoshi barehands it near the third-base coach's box. And the 1-2 is another changeup that misses away to even the count.

The 2-2 is where magic is made. Kristian swings, and his black bat shatters under the combined kinetic force of bat and ball. The shards impale the infield, but the ball keeps going. "Fastball broken bat, down the left-field line," Tim says, abandoning his inside voice as the meters on his soundboard rise into the red. "It's going, and it's GONE! WHAT A DISPLAY OF POWER BY KRISTIAN GAYDAY. A BROKEN-BAT SOLO HOMER, AND IT'S 2-2. AND GOOD WORK, BEN LINDBERGH!" He says my name so I'll stop slamming my palms into his shoulders, carried away by the most exciting solo shot I've seen in person since Aaron Boone beat the Red Sox in 2003.

"Unbelievable," Tim continues, as Kristian rounds the bases. "He's getting a standing ovation, and he should be. That right there is going to wake up some people to Kristian Gayday. Wow, that is an unbelievable display of strength." It's the first professional at-bat and the first professional homer for a twenty-three-year-old who'd probably be back home in Indiana, permanently retired, if Sam and I hadn't trusted Chris Long's conclusions and Kristian hadn't trusted himself. And it's not just any homer, but one that our HITf/x system tells us left a very broken bat at 89 miles per hour.

The score stays tied at 2 until the fourth, when Mark Hurley starts a rally by singling with one out. Matt Hibbert replaces him on a fielder's choice, then steals second, and Feh drives him in with a single. This time, at least, the "second leadoff hitter" approach works. But Pittsburg strikes back in the top of the fifth, evening the score on a hit by pitch, a stolen base, a single, and a wild pitch.

The Stompers go down in order in the bottom of the inning, then manage not to score in the sixth despite a Gayday single—98 mph, HITf/x says, even harder than his homer, and one of the ten hardest-hit balls the system would track all season—and a double by Hurley, his third hit of the day. But in the seventh, Lentini singles again, steals second again, takes third on a throwing error, and scores the go-ahead run on a grounder to third despite a drawn-in infield. One out later, Moch follows with a single, and Carranza goes deep to give the Stompers a 6-3 lead.

Feh has tasked two of our pitching recruits with keeping Pittsburg

off the board once Walker left after five innings, having allowed three
runs on four hits, a walk, and two strikeouts. (It's just the sort of forgettable, undistinguished outing we expected from Walker, but he
kept the Stompers close, which will earn him another chance to
impress us.) Paul Hvozdovic is the first pitcher out of the pen.

Paul leads the Stompers in superstition. His hangup stems from his
freshman year in college, when he was scheduled to start right after a
final exam. A friend drove him from the test to the ballpark, and the
game didn't go well: Paul got a couple of outs, then gave up eight runs.
Since then, he's tried not to take cars to his starts, which is a problem
on the road. (The team van is permissible, but barely, and only if
he sits in the back.) Soon after Opening Day, I make one attempt to
cure him.

"Maybe the bad luck was the test, not the car ride," I suggest. "In that
case, you'll pitch fine as long as you don't take a final first."

For the next twenty seconds, he's silent; his brow knits, but I can't
see his eyes behind his shades. Then he relaxes and smiles, like he's
worked out a complex equation. "I don't see it that way," he says.

Today he's at home, so he has nothing to fear. His delivery doesn't
look fluid, but it's quick and compact, without many moving pieces.
Mike Taylor pinch-hits for Oddo and takes a knee-high fastball for a
called strike, then swings at and misses the next two for the first out.
Paul also strikes out the next batter, Battle, and gets DH Joe Lewis on a
grounder to second. The first successful inning leads to a second, and
the second leads to a third. All told, Hvozdovic fires seventeen four-
seamers at 85, fourteen changeups at 80, and three sliders at 81, almost
all of them in or around the strike zone.

A higher-level team might tee off on Paul's stuff in such enticing
locations, but living in the zone serves him well today, just as it did
during college. The only hint of trouble he encounters comes in the
eighth, his third inning of work, when he allows back-to-back one-out
singles. Facing Taylor for the second time, Paul gets the big righty to fly
out to Hibbert, who guns down Diamonds shortstop Chris DeBiasi try-

ing to tag and advance to third. The final line: three innings, two hits, no walks, and four strikeouts. We wouldn't trade one Hvozdovic for any number of Walkers.

After Paul escapes the jam, Sam suggests that we buy the team beer to celebrate what's looking likely to be an Opening Day win. So as not to spoil the surprise (or give superstitious players any cause to claim that we jinxed the Stompers), we do this in secret, asking Theo to help us ring up a case of Coors and carry it into the clubhouse. We stash it in the freezer next to an old TV, where we'll be able to remove it with a flourish once the players have filled the room.

We make it back to the sidelines in time to watch Sean Conroy, our sidearming, occasionally over-the-top Division III recruit, take the mound. Conroy, a starter in college, enters the game in baseball's easiest save scenario: a three-run lead with no one on and three outs to go. His first pitch, like Paul's, is a swinging strike—a beautiful sight, since no outcome predicts success more reliably than the ability to miss bats. He works quickly, appearing to stick to the same pitching approach he used in spring training: pounding hitters with low sinkers and then spotting sliders on either edge of the plate, using his unusual release point to hide each pitch's true nature until it's too late.

Battle, the leadoff man in the inning, flies out to right, but lefty Joe Lewis—who stands on the side of the plate that allows a longer look at Conroy—singles to center. The Diamonds need base runners—down three runs, Lewis can't tie the game by himself—but Lewis tries to stretch his single into a double. Lentini cuts off the ball and throws on a line to second, where the ball and the tag beat Lewis. Two outs. The Diamonds' last hope is Hutter, the big guy with the baseball butt, who's 0-for-3. Sean starts him with a slider high, followed by a fastball foul, a slider swung on and missed (his tightest breaking ball yet), and another slider that Hutter swings through. "Slider swung on and missed, and that'll do it!" Tim says. "A great first outing for the Stompers. And in this seventy-eight-game season, each one counts a little bit more." The Stompers have a 1 in the win column.

The players form a handshake line on the infield, then sign autographs in front of the first-base dugout, thrilling a cluster of kids who don't understand how far away these uniformed giants are from being big leaguers. Sam and I, our smiles equally wide, shake hands with Feh and walk back to the clubhouse, where we wait for the team to file in. For us, success is usually a solitary experience measured in Twitter mentions. After years of internal, intellectual battles—trying to beat blank pages by filling them with words—it's a real release to triumph (even by proxy) in a physical contest and to celebrate as part of a loud, smelly, sweaty team.

When everyone is inside, Theo calls for the team's attention and gives us the floor. Whatever words I spontaneously say—some brief sentiments to the effect of "You guys are great!"—are forgotten instantly when I add ". . . and we bought you beer." I open the freezer and lift out the actually ice-cold Coors, which earns us a reception as raucous as the one the players got from the satisfied fans. Paul, the winning pitcher, is rubbing up the pristine game ball awarded to him as a memento from his first Pacific Association victory. He sees us and crosses the clubhouse. "Did they get you a game ball?" he asks. "Hang on." He walks over to a bucket, finds another pearl, and brings it back to us. "Nice job." Sam takes it and almost cries.

There's no way Opening Day could have been better. We aren't worried about Walker, or the fact that Hibbert, batting ninth, was the only player not to make four plate appearances, or anything else in the world. We've seen Kristian's bat commit murder-suicide, and we've seen Feh get three hits and steal two bases, making Sam's .380-average projection seem smart. We've seen Hurley, from whom neither of us expected big things, go 3-for-4, and we've seen Carranza show off the power we'd previously seen only in his slugging percentage. We've seen Paul zero in on the strike zone, and we've seen Sean look like slider-spinning Astros closer Luke Gregerson (except 5 mph slower, because this isn't the big leagues). Pittsburg's pitchers threw 147 pitches in eight innings, 59 percent of them strikes; ours threw only 116 pitches in nine innings, 64 percent of them strikes.

Unlike Sam, I'm not a father, so I don't have to pretend that a crying baby's arrival was better than this moment. "Let's walk away now," Sam suggests. It's tempting: Our guys were good, we're in first place, and we're rocking a 1.000 winning percentage. But now that we've taken one hit, we want to chase the high.

TECHNICAL DIFFICULTIES

In the first game of the season, Nick Oddo—"oh-doe," as it turns out; Ben was right—grounded a ball to the second baseman and lined one right to the first baseman. Oddo sat out game two. He's back in the lineup for game three, and I'm back in the dugout, while Ben is in the press box running the PITCHf/x system. Oddo lines a double down the right-field line in the first inning, then lines a double to the wall in right field in the second. In between was a foul ball just wide of first base. It's not just that he's pulling balls, but that three of the four he put in play were pulled at almost identical angles.

There's a reason why Bill James defined sabermetrics as the search not just for knowledge about baseball, but for *objective* knowledge. Months later, I will skim a list of cognitive biases and realize that, at this moment in the dugout, I was suffering from at least a half dozen of them.

Availability heuristic, where we overestimate the likelihood of events that have greater "availability" in our memories. I noticed the landing spots of Oddo's hits largely because I was so focused on Oddo, surprised as I was to see him here and regretful as I was that we hadn't signed him.

Confirmation bias, where we focus mostly on new evidence that supports our existing beliefs. I assumed that Oddo, a left-handed hitter with a long swing, probably pulled the ball a lot. When he pulled the first four, I used that tiny sample to convince myself he was an *extreme* pull hitter.

Clustering illusion, where we underestimate the likelihood of "clusters" of events happening by chance. Even if Oddo directed baseballs with total randomness, the odds of getting four balls pulled in a row by luck alone wouldn't be that long—about one in sixteen. But it didn't occur to me that what I was watching could be a fluke.

Focalism, where we put too much weight on the first piece of information we acquire.

Base rate fallacy, where we ignore universal truths (like "lefties pull a lot of grounders") in favor of narrow, specific data.

And, perhaps, *the Dunning-Kruger effect*, where unskilled individuals overestimate their own abilities.

The point is this: I *know* that it takes about thirty batted balls to draw conclusions about a player's batted-ball tendencies. Russell Carleton has published work demonstrating this, and we cite it regularly when we want to make true and honest points. But after seeing Oddo hit four times, I'm ignoring it completely. I've convinced myself this is the moment when we stop being observers and get into the game. I text Ben.

"We're shifting Oddo."

Ben is excited. We're making an in-game decision and doing something associated with sabermetrics, and we're setting an important precedent before the players forget about our day of defensive drills in spring training. But he's apprehensive, also: We don't have the data. We've always planned to shift, but only once we'd had a chance to see our opponents enough times to learn their habits. We're betting on four ground balls, and the knowledge that most hitters have at least some pull tendencies on ground balls, so the chances are good that Oddo won't embarrass us. Unless . . .

I take my phone back out.

"How worried about a bunt are you?" I text Ben.

"Oddo bunt? Not very," he answers.

The shift is one of Ben's baseball obsessions. He has watched with interest as the frequency of shifts in the major leagues has skyrocketed by 750 percent since 2011, and—even more intriguingly—as most hitters have refused to respond by bunting toward the vacated side of the infield. A fair bunt with the infield overshifted is a free single, if not extra bases. But whether out of pride, the conviction that bunting is counterproductive, or a lack of bunting experience, few hitters attempt it regularly, even though it would dissuade defenses from shifting again.

So when I ask where Ben would put third baseman Kristian Gayday—in the standard shortstop position or in his regular third-base position to protect against the bunt, with only shortstop Gered Mochizuki shifted—he recommends the former.

"Oddo's first time seeing shift, probably isn't going to adjust immediately."

Oddo comes up with two outs in the fourth and a runner on first. The shift is on—Moch moves slightly to the right of second base, and Kristian slides over to the normal shortstop position. And what do you know: Oddo squares around and bunts the first pitch down the third-base line, a perfect bunt, hugging the edge of the infield grass.

"Sheeeeit," Ben texts.

"Worrrrrrrst," I respond.

"Guess we should've signed him," Ben concludes.

I've got nowhere to hide from any accusing eyes in the dugout. I stare straight ahead, and I kick the dugout netting when the next hitter singles, driving in a run that will be charged not to us, but to Jon Rand. When he returns to the dugout, I tell him I'm sorry. That one was on me.

Much later, we will ask Oddo what he was thinking right before he embarrassed us. "Before I step into the box I always look at the defense," he says. "I've never had a shift to that extent played against me. So that was a first for me. When I watch MLB games and see those severe shifts I always tell myself if that ever happens to me I'm going to drop a bunt down. And that's what happened." Just our luck: The first time we try to intervene in an actual game, we run right into the rare hitter who shares our beliefs about bunting to beat the shift.

I spend the fifth inning hiding in the bullpen, where Jerome Godsey is my only company. I'm not sure whether I need advice, reassurance, or a scolding, but I need to hear something from somebody who understands the game from the dugout perspective.

"If it's the right move, you can't worry about it," Godsey says. "You *have* to do it again."

"Have to?"

"Have to. And if I'm out there, I hope he bunts. Because I'm a kitty cat on the mound, and I'll throw him out."

As it turns out, with Oddo due to bat again sometime in the sixth, Godsey *is* in the game. Not only that, but the stakes are suddenly high again—the Stompers scored five runs in the fifth to pull within two. Godsey walks the leadoff man in front of Oddo, and we know that even an accidental squib against the shift would crush our perceived momentum: We might never convince the team to try a shift, or anything else, ever again. So Ben, who's still in the press box, is surprised to see the shortstop, second baseman, and first baseman all move into a shift, playing Oddo to pull. Yes, we're risking our reputations. But I'm more worried about how we'll look if we *don't* do this, if we show so little conviction in our tactics that we flee after one failure. We make one concession: Kristian stays in the vicinity of third base, cutting off the possibility of another gimme bunt. To be extra safe, I yell out to Jerome: "Kitty cat!" which makes me sound like a madman. A few Stompers look at me skeptically.

Oddo, expecting to be pitched inside, has moved way back from the plate so he can slap one the other way. His first swing produces a pop foul to left field. Then he swings at a 1-1 fastball and scorches a grounder straight up the middle. With a normal defensive alignment, the ball would easily scoot into center—for 150 years, that was the surest single in the sport. Instead, Moch gloves it, steps on second, and throws to first to complete a double play. "Fuck!" Oddo yells, and I finally embrace the casual loud profanity of baseball dugouts: "Motherfucking shift!" I yell in Oddo's direction as the batter hauls down the line. Godsey points to me as he returns to the mound.

"!!!!!!!!" I text Ben.

"Score one for sabermetrics," says Tim Livingston, broadcasting in the press box.

For the first week of the season, nothing can stop the Stompers. After sweeping Pittsburg, we head to Vallejo, where we sweep the Admirals for a 6-0 start. But the better things go for the Stompers, the more our advance-scouting efforts unravel. Even the most basic tasks, the ones we assumed would be simple, prove challenging. Our cameras' batteries allegedly last for four hours, but they definitely don't last for four hours of *filming*: They keep cutting out anywhere from the fourth to the sixth inning. We buy bigger batteries, but even those require one midgame switch. We buy long outdoor power cables, and we scout for power outlets within one hundred feet of the league's four fields. We never do find one in San Rafael, so the best place to put the camera is in center field, where there's a small, fenced-in area with a nonworking water fountain. This enclosure can be accessed only by jogging across the outfield, which we do between innings once a game, ignoring the glares from Albert Park officials. The wind in San Rafael is usually a small step below gale force, so at times the tripod topples over for an inning or two.

Even worse, we're unable to import video to our laptops, which means that for the first few weeks of the season we can't show footage to players. That's not great, given that we talked a big game in spring training about all the advantages our know-how would bring to the team. Very quickly, our incompetence—and the time it takes to organize our efforts—takes a toll on our volunteers. On June 3, Zak resigns as advance scouting coordinator. "After reflecting on the last week or so, I have concluded that I've vastly underestimated both the amount of time required to properly study for the bar exam and the amount of time needed to manage this project correctly for you," his email begins. We don't blame him. In fact, we envy his ability to bail out.

Later that night, PITCHf/x compounds our problems. The system is supposed to be easy to operate: The person manning the monitor need only set the lineups, record the outcome of each pitch, and click arrows to advance the software by an at-bat or an inning. But midway through the game, the computer gives us a blue screen of death and can't be resuscitated for more than a few minutes at a time.

"PITCHf/x crashed, everything is awful except that the Stompers won," Ben texts me.

"We aren't going to have it and we are gonna have to make up data so players think we do," I answer. The next day, Sportvision talks Ben and his screwdriver through some *Apollo 13*–esque desktop-tower surgery, which restores partial function, but the computer won't be all the way back until the company can send someone out to replace a part.

There's only one piece of positive news: Ben and I and our scouting staff now have a nickname, which Noah relays by text from Pittsburg on June 5. "I overheard the Pacifics players calling us 'The Corduroy Crew,'" he says. It seems as if we aren't going to live down the unintentionally identical outfits we wore to the tryout in March.

As slow as our own start has been, Ben and I are intoxicated by the Stompers' success. The degree to which the Stompers are dominating the Pacific Association after one week is worth not one table but two. The first one summarizes our offense, which has walked more, struck out less, and hit for more power than every other team, and scored almost twice as many runs as San Rafael. The rightmost column, wRC+, stands for weighted runs created plus, which encapsulates the team's offensive performance in a single stat, relative to a league average of 100. The Stompers' 146 says they've been 46 percent better than the league as a whole.

Team Offense, June 1–7									
Team	PA	R	HR	K%	BB%	AVG	OBP	SLG	wRC+
Sonoma Stompers	273	50	7	15.8	11.4	.315	.403	.451	146
Vallejo Admirals	241	32	5	24.5	7.9	.241	.320	.370	103
Pittsburg Diamonds	265	35	4	19.6	9.4	.226	.309	.319	74
San Rafael Pacifics	261	27	6	23.4	9.2	.228	.310	.339	73

The pitching disparity is just as significant: The Stompers have allowed fewer than half as many runs as San Rafael. It's almost as if we've imported a team from a higher-level league.

Team Pitching, June 1–7										
Team	IP	R	HR	K%	BB%	AVG	OBP	SLG	ERA	FIP
Sonoma Stompers	56.7	21	3	20.7	7.5	.206	.282	.289	2.70	3.41
San Rafael Pacifics	61.0	46	6	22.9	9.7	.255	.341	.389	5.02	3.68
Vallejo Admirals	55.0	36	4	19.3	10.2	.257	.343	.351	3.93	3.90
Pittsburg Diamonds	59.7	41	9	19.6	10.4	.285	.371	.435	4.22	4.66

Through six games, Feh's goal of going 78-0 is still achievable. The Stompers have played 8 percent of their schedule, and thus far they've looked like they can't be beaten. They're the best. We're brilliant. Baseball is easy.

When players ask me during dugout small talk whether Ben and I are having a good time, I shrug. I don't want them thinking we're here for some sort of fantasy camp, pretending for a few weeks that we're real baseball dudes. Yes, technically, I'm having a great time. I'm having the best time of my life. I love the dust, proof of existence in this world, a thick layer of which by game three has ruined my sneakers and Stompers cap for any purpose but dugout wear. I love driving the ninety minutes to Vallejo to scout games with crowds as small as thirty, and then rushing back on silent freeways with the doomed hope that I might get home before every restaurant but In-N-Out is closed. I love cutting across the center field warning track in the fifth inning to change the video camera's batteries, *halfway done*, and I love pulling the mouse cord taut at the end of the game and releasing it with a zzzzzip so that it winds itself back up for storage, *done*. And when Paul Hvozdovic asks to see which socks I'm wearing that day, some shades of argyle having taken on totemic value as luckier than others. And walking out to shut down the stadium lights with Theo, talking about the game the way actual front-office execs get to talk about games, the walk-and-talks that make us feel like we're living an Aaron Sorkin script. And walking past the San Rafael dugout after one game in Pittsburg and hearing somebody call me, under his breath, and not nicely, but inadvertently the most charming compliment I could receive, "big league." And drinking "preworkout," the sickly sweet stimulant-powdered drink mixes the players all carry in their thermoses, "one part caffeine and two parts placebo," which give some guys the itches. And when the Stompers score six in the first inning and Mark Hurley jogs past me to his position and says "nice scouting report." And when Vallejo's manager asks, "You're the stat guy, right? You got any good shit about my players?" And when one of our guys homers deep to left field in San Rafael and I hop the fence and crawl into the space between the tennis courts and the municipal storage bins and find the ball and it's dented, the thing is actually *dented*. And when I go home after games and play Tim saying "Score one for sabermetrics!" over and over. And the spark of *aha!* every time I confidently identify a pitch—for example, as a slider, not a splitter—to input into our software. This, maybe, more than anything, and this, maybe, the weirdest joy I've ever felt: I love logging data. Each pitch feels like our tiny contribution to the eventual organization of the entire world.

But, no, I just shrug. We're here to work, I say. To contribute something and to stay out of the way.

By the time the Stompers roll into San Rafael for the seventh game of the season, we're coming off the first perfect week in our franchise's history. We're beating teams so easily—outscoring our opponents by five runs a game, on average—that I ask Theo whether we're in danger of being too good, whether the league might decide it's not fair and break us up. Baps has hit safely in every game so far, and upon returning to his hometown for a series against Vallejo he scores the winning run in two of our three games there. Fehlandt is batting .357 with speed, power, and elite defense—Mike Trout on a rookie salary, just as we'd envisioned. Our spreadsheet guys are doing great, too. Our bullpen has allowed three runs in thirty innings, and our defense has committed half as many errors as the next-best team.

But Ben and I are consumed by the contradictory pressures of those two mandates—contributing something and staying out of the way. We're not destroying anything, but we're ceding chances to do anything. Like the time we ask Eric Schwieger during an off-day workout whether it would disrupt his routine if, instead of starting and going six innings, he *relieved* and went six innings. Same workload, same eighteen outs, but with just that little twist in the scheduling. We're trying to trick the Pacifics into loading their lineup with left-handed batters, so that when Schwieg comes in he's got the platoon advantage more often. Secretly, we're also trying to make it so our manager can give him a quicker hook (if it makes sense to) without imperiling his deserved win.

To explain: A starting pitcher must complete the fifth inning to qualify for the win. If the starter doesn't make it through five, then the win goes to the reliever who contributed the most, in the judgment of the official scorer. This usually goes to the reliever who pitched the longest. So if Schwieg goes 4 1/3 strong innings as a starter, then comes out of the game because his fastball is starting to lose zip or because we don't want him to face the opposing lineup a third time—and suffer the substantial loss of effectiveness that most starters do in a third trip through the order—then we've cost him the win. But if he throws the same 4 1/3 strong innings after entering the game in the second or third inning, he'll still get the win. This shouldn't matter, but pitchers *love* the win. Taking it from them is like bait-and-switching a kid's dessert at the end of the meal. This turns out to be a substantial obstacle to managers pulling pitchers as early as they should, but it can be avoided by manipulating the starter/reliever roles ever so slightly.

So we bring this up to Schwieg before his first start against San Rafael. It's only the seventh game of the season, and San Rafael is 2-4, but we're still terrified of them—most of the roster is back from last year's championship team, and we fear they're one good inning away from snapping out of this slump. We tell him we figure this plan will give him a little edge, and we'll take any edge we can against such a good lineup. He does a little mental math, just to make sure he'll still be able to warm up on a predictable schedule, and concludes that, yeah, he could do that, he'd give it a try. He relieved much of last season, anyway; there's no reason he has to be locked into an inflexible role that starts with the first pitch of every fifth game. We want this flexibility in our staff; he's flexible. He suggests we run it by Fehlandt.

Who rejects it. Feh downplays the benefit of getting more lefties into the lineup against Schwieg—"Anybody who is any good is playing every day anyway," he says, puzzlingly, since trying to gain lefty-lefty matchups is about as uncontroversial as any strategy in the sport. But what's most worrisome is what he says next: "We don't have to do *anything*. We're so much better than everybody else we don't even have to try."

Winning has become its own obstacle.

We do what we can to contribute without getting in the way. If Fehlandt is uninterested in our scouting observations or unusual strategies, he's at least willing to ask for one thing: a walkie-talkie, so that he can make pitching changes from center field. We order the smallest one we can find, along with an earpiece, and for a few moments we feel like we've earned our keep. "Awesome you're the man," he texts me. Sabermetrics.

We also start packaging our scouting reports for the players. On a whiteboard that we carry to each game, we list the opposing pitcher's repertoire and tendencies and prop it up in the dugout for our hitters to see. Before Schwieg takes the mound against San Rafael, we send him a pregame scouting report on the Pacifics' hitters. The top half of the document is as simple as we can make it, with just one word per batter: In, or Spin. Andrew Parker, our catcher, has explained to us that every hitter is usually bad against one or the other—either he can't pick up breaking pitches away and will chase, or he doesn't have the bat speed or hands to catch up to fastballs inside. Further, each type of pitch requires a different approach to hit, and only elite hitters can "look" for both pitches at the same time. Below this super stupid-simple scouting, I list my observations from San Rafael's first six games, four of which I have personally advance-scouted and all of which have been fed into our pitch-by-pitch data pool.

I'm proud of the report, proud of what we've been able to put together this quickly: The Pacifics' leadoff hitter, Zack Pace, is annoyingly patient but has been rolling over fastballs away, so just pound him with strikes; the cleanup hitter, Jeremy Williams, is squaring every mediocre fastball, but he hasn't adjusted to the steady diet of bendy pitches he's seeing; the seventh hitter, Adrian Martinez, seems almost to have vision problems that keep him from picking up pitches moving away from him and make him chase not just off-speed pitches outside but also two-seamers with tail; the ninth hitter, David Kiriakos, looks uncomfortable in any at-bat in which the pitcher makes him "move his feet" with inside pitches, so just throw him one in and then you can beat him away; and so on. The only batter I'm unsure of is the fifth hitter, Matt Chavez: "Has been late on fastballs, but he homered twice Sunday in the game I didn't see, so I can't really claim to have seen his full output. Don't really have a good read on this guy."

Schwieger is one of the returnees I was initially sure was hostile toward us. He had sniffed at our infield shifts in spring training and razzed me for overreacting to a near-catch on Opening Night. ("Is there some sabermetric value to going 'ooooohhhh'?") But he has asked me for this scouting report, the first player to seek out our help. After I email it to him, he replies in minutes to say thanks. He finds me again before the game to repeat the thanks, and as the game starts he seems to be following the scouting report—and it's working. He carries a no-hitter into the fourth.

Then he starts to lose his mechanics a little, which is the always-there-when-you-need-it explanation for a pitcher's struggles. In this case, even I can see that he's falling off to the side as he drives toward the plate, and his arm isn't able to catch up. There's a run in the fourth, and his pitch count gets higher, and as we go to the fifth he's sitting on a fragile 2-1 lead.

As the inning begins, the ubiquitous Fetty Wap walk-up song "Trap Queen" plays to indicate that Tyger Pederson, the Pacifics' eighth-place hitter, is coming to bat. Schwieger strikes him out, and the even more ubiquitous Fetty Wap walk-up song "Come My Way" tells me David Kiriakos is coming to the plate. He walks, and the top of the lineup comes up for the third time. This is where, if Ben and I were running this team by diktat, we would have a pitcher warming up, where we would consider pulling Schwieger before he can finish the fifth, even though he's in line for the win. I glance down at the bullpen and ... Erik Gonsalves *is* warming up. Feh's on the same page. This arrangement might be working!

I gather Yoshi and Jerome Godsey, who has become our last-second pitching coach (he's the least experienced pitcher on the staff, but he's old!), on the grass between the dugout and the bullpen. We all agree Schwieger looks gassed, and I argue that we should pull him, but it's not my call—is it? Nobody knows. None of us has explicit authority to make a move, other than the blanket power Ben and I hold as everybody's boss. It's Fehlandt's call most of all, but the walkie-talkie, which had come to life when Feh told Godsey to get Gonsalves up, is now silent.

Schwieger allows a stolen base, and the leadoff hitter, Pace, grounds out and pushes Kiriakos to third. Facing the right-handed DH, Johnny Bekakis, for the third time, Schwieger leaves an 88 mph fastball in the middle of the plate and Bekakis bangs it into right field for a double. The game is now tied, and Schwieger can't get a win anyway. Godsey goes out to the mound, his inexperience showing in every step—his gait is way too fast, he forgets to wear his hat, and when he gets there he waffles over whether to take Schwieger out. Even this early in the season, this has been a pattern: There's a fine waiting for him in kangaroo court for his unconvincing pitching-coach walk, and the pitchers have found it disturbingly easy to talk him out of a pitching change. He walks back to the dugout alone, and Schwieg goes to work on Maikel Jova, the Pacifics' right fielder, for the third time. On 1-1, he throws an inside fastball—sticking to the scouting report—that Jova muscles into left field, a flare just past Gered Mochizuki's chase. We're losing.

We fight back to tie it in the top of the sixth, and Gonsalves enters the game to pitch the bottom half. He allows a run, and we're losing again. Then we tie it again in the top of the seventh. Gonzo goes back out to try to hold the line. If he can't, the decision is going to be made by a manager standing 200 feet from where I can reason with him.

Pace walks to lead off the inning. But then, with two strikes, Gonzo hits Bekakis with a sinker up and in. From center field, a staticky voice says, "One more"—as in, Gonzo's leash is one more mistake. If he gives up a hit to Jova, he's gotta come out.

This is a complicated decision. Beginning with Jova, the Pacifics are about to send up three powerful right-handed hitters, and the guy we have warming up is a lefty, Paul Hvozdovic. I have confidence in Paul—he has looked sharp so far, and as a starter his entire career he has always had to retire right-handed hitters. But it would be an unusual move to bring in a lefty to face a string of righties.

Our only other available right-hander, Sean Conroy, isn't warming, partly because we have only one bullpen catcher and partly because closers don't come into the game in the seventh inning. But I'm trying to convince somebody that Sean, our best reliever, the guy with the release point and repertoire that has stupefied every right-hander he has faced this year, is an option here. Not even trying to convince them he must come in, but that *he's an option*, and that, for him to really be an option, somebody had better start warming him up.

Godsey walks to the mound to talk to Gonsalves. Again he walks back alone. He shakes his head. "I asked Gonzo how he was and he didn't say anything," Godsey reports. "His eyes were dead."

This does not make me confident. Neither does Gonzo's first pitch, a wild one that goes to the backstop. Pace, the lead runner, doesn't pick it up and, to our shock, stays put; meanwhile, Bekakis is watching the ball, not Pace, so he tries to take second. Soon two runners are standing on the same bag. Isaac Wenrich makes a strong throw there and we get a gift out.

Jova hits a hard grounder to shortstop, and Mochizuki gets the second out of the inning. Gonsalves then walks left fielder Jeremy Williams on four pitches. "He looks like shit," I tell Godsey. "*Terrible*," Yoshi says. The walkie-talkie makes a noise that we can't decode: "frrrsheefeer-grrrr." Godsey finally goes out to replace Gonsalves with Hvozdovic, then walks back to where Yoshi and I are, watching the game not in the dugout or in the bullpen but in the grassy space between, where none of our players can hear how dysfunctional we sound.

We've been throwing inside fastballs all game to these right-handed batters, partly because it's the scouting report and partly because Fehlandt is convinced that only two (or maybe three) hitters in the entire league can hit an inside fastball. But after seeing Eric Schwieger's high-80s inside fastballs all game, they now get to see Paul Hvozdovic's low-mid-80s inside fastballs.

Paul's third pitch, to Matt Chavez, is a fastball, 83 mph, medium-in. Chavez hits a three-run homer to center field. As he circles the bases, Godsey and I walk back to the dugout, stunned. When the players see us approaching, their chatter stops. I hear Gonsalves say one last word: "fucking." Then, silence.

Sean Conroy never gets into the game, and our winning streak dies a 10-6 death. There's an unwritten rule some managers enforce that nobody can appear too happy after a loss, but as everybody packs up and slumps into the visitors' clubhouse it doesn't feel like anybody is posturing. What makes losing so bad for clubhouse chemistry is immediately clear: It's not just that it makes people less happy, but also that a defeat requires blame be distributed. Not everybody lost that game equally, and nobody wants to go home with more than his fair share of it. So, sometimes silently and sometimes not, they make sure the record is clear: *That* guy fucked up. *That* guy lost it more than I did. There's no way all-for-one-one-for-all can survive forensic blame accounting.

There is a feeling that we lost this game because the organizers were disorganized. Nobody knew who was making the decisions—especially after Fehlandt ran into the dugout and scolded Godsey for putting in Hvozdovic. *You can't put a lefty in to face righties*, he says. Even if it's the better pitcher—even if the lefty is better against righties than the righty, you can't do it, because (as I follow it) the righties *want* to face lefties, and when they see a lefty come in their mouths water in anticipation. The platoon-advantages-don't-matter argument he made to me one day earlier is forgotten; the fact that we had no problem letting Schwieger, a lefty, face all those right-handers three times doesn't matter. Hell, if Paul had come into the game to face a lefty, he could have *stayed in* to face the righties, but you can't bring him *in* to face righties. I try not to dwell too long on the logic.

Because that's what I learn in the seventh inning: The game happens too fast for logical discussions. This is why I couldn't win the argument to get Schwieger out earlier, or to put Paul in earlier, or to have Conroy up in a seventh-inning nonsave situation. While I'm trying to put together a logical argument, batters are hitting and pitchers are warming up and base runners are getting thrown out and Fehlandt is thinking about his next at-bat and Godsey is trying to figure out what "dead eyes" mean for a pitcher. It happens too fast to have a manager trying to make decisions from center field, and it happens too fast to have just one bullpen catcher, and it happens too fast for me to stand by passively, hoping the right decisions will get made if I just scatter bread crumbs between all of us and the obviously right decision.

"I thought you said one more," Godsey says, alluding to the walk of Jeremy Williams as the "one more." Fehlandt looks exasperated. "Gonzo was pitching *around* Williams," he says. We saw a wild pitcher lose a batter; Fehlandt saw a plan, executed. "He's not going to give some cookie to Williams in that situation."

At the Pacific Association tryout in March, Daniel Baptista runs a speedy 60-yard dash, unseen by Sonoma Stompers general manager Theo Fightmaster and San Rafael Pacifics GM Mike Shapiro in the blurry background.

Third baseman Kristian Gayday crushes the ball and breaks his bat in the Stompers' Opening Day game.

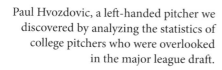

Paul Hvozdovic, a left-handed pitcher we discovered by analyzing the statistics of college pitchers who were overlooked in the major league draft.

Isaac Wenrich, one of our catchers, quickly became a team leader. Here he is hugging and hydrating outfielder Mark Hurley.

Theo (with cap) watches a practice with a stopwatch-wearing Ben Lindbergh.

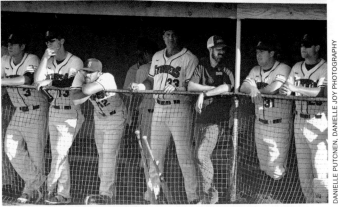

To bring fans to the ballpark, Theo invited former major league star Jose Canseco to join the Stompers' roster for one weekend in June. From left to right: T. J. Gavlik, Paul Hvozdovic, Erik Gonsalves, Jose Canseco, Sam Miller (in blue shirt), Andrew Parker, Jon Rand.

Managers Matt Kavanaugh of the San Rafael Pacifics and Fehlandt Lentini of the Stompers exchange lineups before a game at Arnold Field. Note the football goalposts in the field of play in right-center field.

Bench coach Takashi Miyoshi (universally known as Yoshi) was surprisingly open to using advanced statistics to devise strategy.

Sean Conroy, the first openly gay player in professional baseball, was the starting pitcher on Pride Night on June 25.

Many of the players wore rainbow sleeves to support Sean on Pride Night. Here Joel Carranza bumps arms with Isaac Wenrich as Mark Hurley looks on.

Sean does a TV interview after the Pride Night game, with second baseman Sergio Miranda standing beside him.

Isaac and Sean pose in Cooperstown in front of a Hall of Fame display case containing the scorecard from the Stompers' Pride Night game.

Player/manager
Fehlandt Lentini
pleads his case to an
unsympathetic umpire.

Daniel Baptista
watches the flight of
the ball he's just hit.

Shortstop Gered Mochizuki
was one of "Fehlandt's guys,"
and his attitude sometimes
rubbed teammates
the wrong way.

The Stompers (and an unsmiling Fehlandt Lentini) celebrate clinching the Pacific Association's first-half championship. Front row (from left to right): Tommy Lyons, Andrew Parker, Gered Mochizuki, Matt Hibbert, Kristian Gayday, Mike Jackson Jr., Jeff Conley. Middle row: Yuki Yasuda, Joel Carranza, Takashi Miyoshi, Erik Gonsalves, Mark Hurley, T. J. Gavlik, Matt Walker, Mac Sweeney, Paul Hvozdovic. Back row: Ryusuke Kikusawa, Daniel Baptista, Jon Rand, Gregory Paulino, Sean Conroy, Fehlandt Lentini, Eric Schwieger, Isaac Wenrich, Aritz Garcia.

Outfielder Taylor Eads, another player unearthed from our spreadsheet, hits a ball to the opposite field.

EMILY RUTHERFORD

The big bat of San Rafael Pacifics first baseman Matt Chavez put the Stompers' scouting to the test. Here he admires another deep drive as Isaac Wenrich watches.

JAMES TOY III, STOMPERS BASEBALL CLUB

The grind of the summer wore on Sam, seen here capturing Stompers hitters with a camera perched above the home dugout at Arnold Field.

BEN LINDBERGH

The Stompers deploy a five-man infield against Scott David of the Pittsburg Diamonds.

Andrew Parker connects for the Stompers' biggest hit in the championship game against San Rafael.

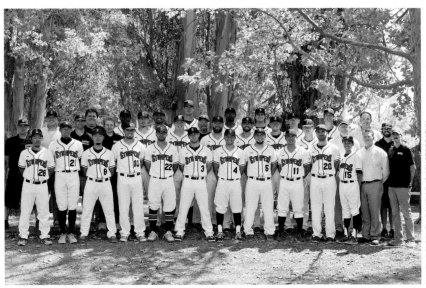

The official team photo, taken during the last week of the season. Front row (from left to right): Takashi Miyoshi, Ryusuke Kikusawa, Yuki Yasuda, Taylor Eads, Mark Hurley, Matt Rubino, Eddie Mora-Loera, Santos Saldivar, Gered Mochizuki, Sean Conroy, Dax Adams, Dr. Laurence Adams, Sam Miller. Middle: Marley Miller, Jason Masciorini, Ben Lindbergh, Kristian Gayday, Andrew Parker, Dan Morgan, Tommy Lyons, Erik Gonsalves, Matt Walker, Peter Bowles, Jack Burkam, Mac Sweeney. Back row: Theo Fightmaster, Tim Livingston, Gregory Paulino, Daniel Baptista, Eric Schwieger, Mike Jackson Jr., Cole Warren, Connor Jones, Dylan Stoops, Eric Gullotta.

Fehlandt walks away, and Godsey looks at me. "You heard him say one more, too, right?"

Our walkie-talkie is a disaster.

As the players eat from the postgame spread, Fehlandt hops into the stands to go find somebody with the Pacifics. He's pissed, because early in the game, when Schwieg had a no-hitter going, somebody put a hit up on the scoreboard. "That's so *fucking* bush league," he says.

I follow him so that, away from everybody else, we can talk about the loss. So we can talk about why bad decisions were made, why communication broke down, what I can do to help, and why I expect better. Patiently, peacefully—I think—I ask why he thinks we lost.

"You can't bring the lefty in there to face the righties," he says again. "If I'm a batter, and you bring a lefty in to face me there, I'm like, these guys are fucking stupid."

"It's tough with that bullpen," I say, "because we don't have a lot of righties ready to go. Was Sean an option there?"

"What? In the seventh?"

"Yeah."

"Nah, Sean's the closer."

"But he was our best pitcher available and those were the biggest outs of the game. He's right-handed, he's—"

"If it were the eighth, maybe, but I'm not going to leave him out there to finish three innings."

"But you could get him to pitch those huge at-bats, then pull him when you need to."

"But then I don't have a closer."

"Sure. But if you don't go to him, you lose the game."

"But I need to have a closer. If I don't have a closer, I can't count on anybody else to get those last outs."

"But the outs in the seventh were just as important."

"Dude," he says, breaking eye contact completely, "if you tried that in the majors you would get laughed out of the game."

"But we lost because we didn't get to use him at all."

"No, dude. The closer's the closer because he's the closer."

And then he leaves.

As I walk to my car, Theo calls me.

"Feh just ran over to me and told me that you're insane. He just kept saying, 'The closer's the closer because he's the closer.'"

Losing, it turns out, is just as much an obstacle as winning.

Two days after that distressing defeat, the Stompers sign Jose Canseco, the almost-fifty-one-year-old 1988 American League MVP who hit 462 major league homers and wrote two postretirement tell-all books about steroid abuse in baseball. Canseco isn't the cavalry. He's a sideshow, a temporary rent-a-draw for teams without their own gate attractions. Fueled by three of his passions—hitting home runs, making money, and maintaining his famous physique—Canseco makes occasional cameos in the lower levels of pro baseball, doing home run derbies and DHing in games. The Stompers sign him for one derby, two games, and two postgame autograph-signing sessions over the second weekend in June, hoping to realize a 2-to-1 return on his appearance fee. While Ben and I are stressing out about winning, Eric and Theo are worrying more about making ends meet, which reminds us that from the organization's perspective batting orders and bullpen moves are secondary concerns.

I drive to the airport to pick up Canseco and his unresponsive fiancée and am treated to the spectacle of an absurdly large and muscular man cramming himself into my car. I ask him if there's anything he wants to listen to on the ride to Sonoma—Golden State Warriors game, sports talk, take your pick. He looks at me like I'm the world's simplest intern and says, with the gentle condescension of a kid talking to a doll, "The hits of the day?" When we arrive in Sonoma, the team isn't sure how to treat him. Fehlandt, who's suddenly not nearly the oldest or most experienced player in the Stompers' clubhouse, is annoyed by the intrusion, while the younger players, most of whom weren't alive during Canseco's prime, are curious to see this PED Paul Bunyan up close.

In the Friday game, Canseco's timing is off and he looks as old as he is, going 0-for-4 and giving the spectators only one ephemeral thrill on a fly to the deep part of the park. But after he loses to Isaac Wenrich in the Saturday derby (despite drilling the facing of the Veterans Memorial Building well beyond the Arnold Field fence), Canseco's swing seems to be back. Setting up in the box with the same imposing physical presence and open stance he had decades earlier, he rips a single off the wall in left-center—he can't really run—and then leads off the sixth with a solo shot that Tim Livingston estimates at 410 feet, starting a Stompers comeback that culminates in a one-run win. Canseco can still catch up to a fastball, provided it's centered and flat: We clock the pitch he hits out, off Pacifics starter Max Beatty, at 90 mph. The team draws 680 fans on Friday and 872 on Saturday—big numbers by Stompers standards, not to mention the extra proceeds from the Canseco Stompers shirts that Theo will be trying to sell out of until approximately the end of time. It's also the only time all season that the team is on local TV.

A little over a week after Canseco leaves Sonoma, his agent emails Theo to ask if we're interested in signing him permanently at a "decent" rate. "He found a new love for the game after playing with u guys," the agent writes.

"We should tell him to play for his newfound love of the game," Ben says.

"Ask him what he runs a 60 in," I joke. And then, on the off chance that Theo is actually intrigued, I make it clear that I'm strongly against bringing him back.

"I'm doing my due diligence," Theo answers. "From a pure baseball standpoint, where you get to comfortably reside, it is a for sure no. But as far as selling tickets, having an attraction and league visibility, we have to at least ponder this." The next day, he texts me that he's beyond pondering: He's signing Canseco for the rest of the season.

I text Ben to tell him I'm infuriated. "I want to quit this stupid project now," I write. It feels like all our authority, and our ability to represent ourselves as a team that's really trying to win and has the best interests of its young players at heart, has been wiped away with one move. Ben is already trying to figure out how we'll squeeze Canseco onto the roster, which has less room for him than my compact car. Will we platoon him with Baps? Could we trade Carranza for an ace starter? Whom will we drop? Theo's ducking my calls, so I start fomenting rebellion: I text the roster news to Fehlandt, who is as "hell naw" about it as I am. There's a real chance that he'll refuse to play or manage if the front office foists Canseco on him. I'm egging him on, trying to get him to issue an ultimatum. Finally, seven hours after I woke up to the news, Theo picks up my call. Laughing, he admits that it was all a joke. Not only are we not re-signing Canseco, but Theo never seriously considered it.

Sheepishly, I tell Fehlandt that I wound him up for no reason. "I've never been more got than I just got got," I text Ben. At least I've learned something from this embarrassing experience: It is possible for me to find common ground with Feh. All it takes to force us into an uneasy alliance is a false alarm about a fifty-year-old former Bash Brother. I guess we'll have to hope that exact scenario arises again.

BREAKING BARRIERS

There's an ad from my childhood that I saw so often it's stuck with me, even though I no longer know who paid to put it on TV. It was like a lighthearted cover of a Sally Struthers commercial, which made poverty seem almost pleasant: Instead of starving children in squalid surroundings, it showed a well-fed but apparently poor boy playing with a puppy, backed by the boy's grateful voice reading a letter to the man whose donation made the puppy possible. "I've never met you, but I love you," the voice-over said. The ad was supposed to put parents in a giving mood, but it made me envy the boy. I couldn't convince my mom to get me a dog before fifth grade.

I think of this ad for the first time in years thanks to Taylor Eads, an outfielder from Spring Hill College in Mobile, Alabama. In my mind, he's both the boy in the ad and the man who supplies the puppy: I want to help him, and I want him to help me. And I love him (in a purely statistical sense) long before we meet.

I see Taylor's name for the first time on June 12—the day before his twenty-third birthday and two days after the final round of the MLB amateur draft—when Chris Long sends us a spreadsheet of 2015 senior position players, ranked using the same statistical method that guided our preseason signings. The top rows look like this:

Division	Name	Team	Pos.	PA	Adj_OBP	SLG	Adj_SLG	Index
D2	Ryan Uhl	Indiana (PA)	OF	180	0.513	1.085	1.032	2.057
D2	Nick Sell	Seton Hill	INF	223	0.503	1.032	0.973	1.980
D2	Taylor Eads	Spring Hill	OF	164	0.568	0.846	0.758	1.895
D1	Kevin Kaczmarski	Evansville	OF	219	0.559	0.746	0.761	1.878
D2	Dylan Tice	West Chester	INF	188	0.524	0.827	0.792	1.841
D2	Collins Cuthrell	UNC Pembroke	3B	245	0.493	0.904	0.853	1.838
D2	Tanner Rainey	West Alabama	INF	209	0.493	0.842	0.834	1.819

Just as I did months earlier, I filter Chris's spreadsheet, resentfully removing the drafted players who are already negotiating with the major league teams that took them. Uhl was selected in the seventh round (215th overall) by the Seattle Mariners; he eventually signs for a $50,000 bonus. Kaczmarski went to the New York Mets in the ninth round; he settles for $5,000. Tice was a thirty-sixth-round pick by the St. Louis Cardinals, who have previously struck gold by using stats to pan for prospects at the tail end of the draft. Rainey is a serious prospect: He was taken in the second round by the Reds, for a bonus of $432,950. He was near the top of our list as a hitter, but he was drafted as a pitcher, which gives you some sense of how good at baseball one has to be to catch a team's eye early on. Rainey, we learn later, once struck out Eads on a 97 mph fastball, the hardest pitch Eads had ever seen (and harder than any he might see with the Stompers).

My first fixation from the spreadsheet isn't Eads, but Nick Sell, a senior from Seton Hill, a strong Division II team outside of Pittsburgh. In a pitcher's park, Sell batted .444/.520/1.032, with 28 homers and way more walks than strikeouts. He finished first or second in Division II in virtually every offensive category, and he won the Tino Martinez Award, D2's equivalent of the MVP. Somehow, he wasn't one of the 1,215 players picked during the draft's forty rounds. "I'd jump on that guy like a hobo on a ham sandwich," Chris tells us.

Our infatuation doesn't last long. The next day, while trawling Twitter for info on our top targets, I discover that the Los Angeles Dodgers have signed Sell as an undrafted free agent. According to a newspaper report, the team's assistant director of player development called him two minutes after the draft ended, pouncing just after Sell's spirits had sunk. No one else offered a contract, so Sell now belongs to L.A. "I'd be throwing furniture if I still worked for the Padres," Chris says. "That's the kind of stuff that literally gave me ulcers."

On June 17, Collins Cuthrell—the third-ranked undrafted hitter— signs with the Florence (Kentucky) Freedom of the Frontier League, a higher-level circuit that's also close to his home in North Carolina. It's a week after the draft, and Eads is the only one of those seven leaders who's still on the board. This makes him my precious.

Eads, a right-handed outfielder from Slidell, Louisiana, batted .538 for the Spring Hill Badgers, with a .623 on-base percentage and an .846 slugging percentage. (All three of those numbers have implied exclamation points.) He walked or was hit by a pitch twice as often as he struck out, and his team went 16-0 against Southern Intercollegiate Athletic Conference competition. Unlike Kristian Gayday, our first spreadsheet signee, Eads wasn't a one-year wonder. In high school, he homered in five straight at-bats and was disciplined enough to take a walk between the fourth and fifth dingers. As a junior in college, he batted .423 with an OBP over .500 and a slugging percentage well over .700. Because of Spring Hill's provisional status in 2015—a consequence of switching from the NAIA to Division II—Eads was ineligible for league awards, but he was a second-team NAIA All-American in 2014, which speaks to some all-around skills. He's a fifth-year senior, which makes him less projectable (and less appealing to MLB teams) than a younger player with the same stats, but we aren't ageists. "Eads has the OBP skills to really push up your scoring," Chris tells me. "He'd grind opposing pitchers into dust. He's the guy if you can sign him."

I'm less worried about persuading Eads to sign with the Stompers than I am about persuading Feh that the team needs another rookie. I know the stats alone won't sell him, so I have to paint a more complete picture, preferably one that appeals to Feh's old-school sensibilities. A few days after receiving Chris's spreadsheet, I email Frank Sims, the head coach at Spring Hill. Unlike a lot of college coaches, who seem to log in to their email accounts on a quarterly basis, Sims sends me a lengthy response almost immediately, which seems like either an indicator that he cares about Eads or a sign that he's sick of Spring Hill being passed over by major league teams. (The most recent Spring Hill draftee was selected in 1994.)

> Yes I think Taylor would be very interested in playing some independent baseball. He is working out for the White Sox today in Birmingham so I know he has a strong interest in wanting to play more baseball. Taylor comes from a very poor family, they lived in a FEMA trailer after Hurricane Katrina (he is from the New Orleans area). His mom left the family a few years ago leaving his dad to raise three kids with one special needs child! His character and work ethic are very strong and he also loves the fitness end of athletics. He was voted Captain his two years at Spring Hill and did a nice job in that role. The other players knew he worked hard and played hard every play!! He was our team leader!
>
> His outfield play is very solid. Runs a 6.9, gets good jumps on balls and is not afraid of the wall. His arm to me is a left fielder's arm in pro ball. It is an average arm in college baseball. He played right field for us and a little center. He is very strong at the plate, hits the ball consistently on the barrel and has a pretty good eye at the plate. Would have been the player of the year in our conference and would have had a great chance to have been player of the year in all of NCAA II if we had not been on provisional status. To be honest we had several teams contact us about Taylor, but no one drafted him! I thought he should have gotten a shot to play somewhere! He is a very respectful young man (the yes sir no sir type kid).

It's hard to imagine a more encouraging recommendation, or a more sympathetic player. Not only is Eads a statistical standout, he's a fitness freak, a team leader, and a genuine Southern gentleman—the anti–Will Price. And his hardscrabble backstory is a documentarian's dream, the perfect companion for his Twitter bio, which is pulled from an inspirational poster: "The ONLY disability in life is a bad attitude."

Later that day, I get a call from Spring Hill assistant coach Andy McCall, who works with the hitters and outfielders and oversees the strength-and-conditioning program. He also sings Eads's praises. Most coaches don't call me back; this is the first call I've received unsolicited. These sellers seem so motivated that I'm almost suspicious, but they're mainly motivated by an attachment to Eads, which I already share. McCall sends me video from the White Sox workout. It's a little more than a minute of footage, shot from a phone in the first-base dugout, in standard definition. The video is vertical, with big black bars on both sides, and Eads is standing inside a turtle-shell batting cage, partially obscured by its support bars. He watches one pitch, takes eleven swings, and connects eleven times, with a large stride, good bat speed, and a one-handed, helicoptering follow-through. I have now confirmed that he can make contact with batting-practice pitches. McCall also shares video of two outfield throws, shot from so far away that I can barely see the ball. With that, I have everything: stats, a story, two testimonials, and some low-quality, inconclusive video. It's time to talk to Feh.

The Stompers are rolling, having won eleven of our first thirteen games, so I know this will be a tough case to make. But I also know it would be a mistake to buy our own bullshit, like a monarch who convinces himself he's a god. We're good, but we aren't unbeatable. And the stats say that our pitchers, in particular, have been lucky, succeeding in a way that almost certainly isn't sustainable. Here's where the league's pitching staffs stand through our first thirteen games:

Team	IP	Runs	HR	Opp wOBA	Opp BABIP	K%	BB%	FIP
Pacifics	121 2/3	98	11	.348	.358	21.4	9.1	3.70
Diamonds	139	93	14	.356	.339	21.5	11.5	4.04
Admirals	136	91	13	.344	.326	17.9	9.0	4.13
Stompers	117	53	10	.302	.276	18.4	8.6	4.03

On June 16, with his family in attendance and a small Pittsburg crowd buzzing about the Warriors' win in the NBA finals, Matt Walker (of all pitchers) comes within two outs of a no-hitter before Diamonds third baseman Rich Mejia breaks it up with a single to center on a 1-2 slider. Walker's complete-game one-hitter is all the more improbable because, as usual, he doesn't have no-hit stuff: Walker whiffs only four batters but walks five, plunks two, and gets an assist from Isaac on a caught-stealing. The start is a microcosm of our staff's season.

No one has hit us hard: Our pitchers have allowed the league's lowest Weighted On-Base Average (wOBA), an offensive statistic that measures the entirety of a batter's contributions on the same scale as on-base percentage. But our strikeout rate isn't impressive, and our walk and home run rates aren't far out of line with the rest of the Pacific Association's. As a result, our Fielding Independent Pitching, or FIP—an ERA estimator that filters out the effect of the defense by focusing on the "three true outcomes" (walks, strikeouts, and homers) that the pitcher largely controls—is actually higher than the Pacifics', which suggests that our staff isn't more skilled, even though San Rafael has allowed the most runs in the league. The big difference between the Stompers and everyone else is opponent batting average on balls in play, or BABIP: Ours is .276, while everyone else's is at least 50 points higher.

One of the sabermetric movement's most counterintuitive, game-changing insights is that there's little variation in most pitchers' ability to prevent hits on balls in play. In 1999, at the peak of his powers, Pedro Martinez allowed a .323 BABIP, in a league where the average BABIP allowed was .301. The next year, Martinez's BABIP allowed dropped to .236, even though he was slightly less dominant overall. Most variations in BABIP from one season to the next are noise, driven by bloopers and bleeders that fall in or evade fielders one year and not the next. Good pitchers are good mostly because they keep balls *out* of play (by striking batters out), while also limiting walks and suppressing home runs. There's no sign that we'll excel enough in those areas to keep throwing shut-outs, and while we may be better than our opponents at defense, we can't keep our BABIP below the major league average in an environment where both the fields and the fielders are bumpier than in the big leagues. Although I don't admit we've been lucky when Tim asks me for a progress report in a Q&A on the Stompers' website—knowing that the players might see what I say, I've already learned how to dissemble like a seasoned front-office exec—I know this won't last. I want to build an ark to help the Stompers stay afloat during the flood of runs I foresee.

Eads can't help our pitching staff, but runs are runs, whether they're scored or saved. If we can upgrade our offense, it will offset some of the regression in store on the defensive side. "Really, the moment you're satisfied with your team you're done," Chris Long tells me.

Left field looks like our weakest link. On June 17, Mark Hurley goes 1-for-5 with an error and fails to execute a sacrifice bunt. "If you're having your LF sac bunt, yeah, he's not the guy you want in LF," Chris observes. The next day, the Stompers lose 3-2 to Pittsburg, and Hurley goes 0-for-3 with 3 strikeouts. This seems like my moment. Hurley is hitting .245/.310/.359 through 58 plate appearances, with 12 strikeouts and only 4 walks. His line sits just slightly below our Opening Day estimates: .260/.320/.370 (Sam's) and .260/.330/.380 (mine). This was roughly how we thought he'd hit, and nothing we've seen has made us change our minds. "I don't think your LF is going to do much better," Chris says. "That's unacceptable for that position." Hurley is well liked, but he's also a rookie, which keeps him outside of the clubhouse inner circle. Nor does it seem as if the team views him as a budding superstar: Although our players have taken to calling him "Baby Bulldog," the nickname owes as much to his age and his underbite as to his mentality. In the dugout one day, as Hurley went down swinging, I heard the Stompers' starting pitcher say, "Hurley's like clockwork. Takes a first-pitch fastball and swings through a second-pitch breaking ball, every time." He sounded disappointed that he wouldn't get to face Hurley himself.

The morning after the loss on June 18, I put together a Taylor Eads primer for Feh, including the stats, the character reference from Coach Sims, and the batting-practice video. "I'm hesitant to suggest any changes

because I know we don't want to mess with what we have going," my
email begins, an attempt to defang Feh's response. "On the other hand,
we don't want to get complacent because we're off to a good start." I
also mention that while Mark is a good guy who gives a great effort, his
bat seems a little light for a left fielder's.

The reply, which comes later that day, doesn't even mention Mark.

> As good as Taylor sounds, there is no way I'm replacing an
> outfielder that we have with him. If we release TJ the chemistry will
> easily take a shit because he is close with everyone on the team.
> And Yuki as well has earned everyone's respect and admiration. It
> has nothing to do with complacency, it has to do with guys doing
> their jobs. If changes are made when guys are doing their jobs,
> then every single person in there starts feeling the pressure
> because if guys doing the job get released than anyone can.
> I understand what you are saying, but until we need to make a
> change im not going to be for making one. . . . We have the best
> team and we are playing baseball the best. Now is not the time for
> changes.

I see what Feh is saying, even if I'm not sure whether "take a shit" is a
typo or something he intended to write. As an actual baseball player,
he's much better qualified to assess the impact of a move on team
morale. I just wonder whether there's a point at which it's worth risking a decline in chemistry to improve a position. I respond to clarify
that I'm not talking about T. J. or Yuki, which is how I learn that Feh is
much higher on Hurley than we are.

> I don't see Mark as a weak link at all. And honestly he is just
> learning the swing that will allow him to hit for power. Yesterday
> was his best batting practice yet. And I know he is getting the
> swing because he has driven two balls to the wall in left/ left center
> in the last few games. He hasn't scratched the surface yet and he
> is getting the job done. And he has a level of knowing the nuances
> of the game that I know comes from the same coach that taught
> me. The instincts he has already shown me show that his baseball
> IQ and instincts are far beyond his level of experience and I know

that is why. I have seriously no doubts about how he is going to perform we are only 13 games in and he has earned my confidence.

Five minutes later, Feh emails again.

One thing you will learn is when a guy has already shown you what he can do with your own eyes, it's a big chance to go off numbers, and someone's recommendation especially when I don't really know the persons accountability on judging talent. I've seen plenty of guys that had great numbers and potential come and not be what they were supposed to be.

The frustrating thing is that Feh isn't wrong. Taylor is still an unknown, to a certain extent, and thirteen games is too small a sample to prove that Hurley is hopeless. In such abbreviated time frames, scouts see talent that stats might miss, and Feh is a more experienced in-person evaluator than I am. He has promised, since the day Sam first interviewed him, to make each hitter on the team the best hitter on the team. He has spent years studying hitting mechanics, and he invests hours drilling and adjusting our young players. Early returns validate his coaching: Daniel Baptista is in the middle of a franchise-record 16-game hitting streak to start the season, and he swears by Feh's advice and drills—especially one where a pitcher sets up a few feet to the side of the mound and throws batting practice from "behind" the batter, forcing the batter to keep his hands back and maintain a firm front side. There's only one hitter on the team who laps up Feh's hitting instructions more studiously than Baps: Mark Hurley.

All I can do is stay in touch with Coach McCall, sending him texts to see if anything is imminent, assuring him that Eads is the first person we'll call when we have a vacancy, and dreading a message that says the White Sox have signed him. At one point, Kristian—my first crush, a player I'm pulling for as hard as anyone on the roster—rolls an ankle, and even with his health at stake, I think unclean thoughts: If Kristian is out for a while, we could move Baps to third, and Carranza could play first, and DH would be open for Eads. I'm like a starving cartoon character who pictures basting turkeys in place of people. Every occupied roster spot starts to look like Taylor Eads.

Well, every roster spot save one. Even at the height of my Eads-mania, there's a special place in my psyche for the stats-based signee who's not only exceeded our highest hopes for his on-field performance, but also made the Stompers national news: Sean Conroy.

When he left his hometown of Clifton Park, New York, to spend the summer with the Stompers, in response to a phone call from a stranger who had sorted a spreadsheet and seen his name near the top, Sean Conroy wasn't worried about making his first-ever trip to California, or being away from his family for longer than ever before, or whether he'd have trouble retiring professional hitters. Nor did he lose sleep over an unknown that no previous player had dared to confront: what his teammates would say when he told them (and team management, and probably the press) that he was gay, which would make him the first openly, publicly gay player in professional baseball.

The only thing Sean was "just a little bit apprehensive about," his mother, Terry, recalls, was how he was going to get from San Francisco International Airport to Sonoma, the last sixty-five miles of his cross-country trip.

"I told him to take a bus to Petaluma, and he was reading online how to get to the bus, and then he texted me when he got there and he said, 'My ride's here,'" Terry Conroy says. "And then the next text was, 'My ride left without me, so I took the bus anyway.' It was a good experience for him, figuring it out on his own."

How could a just-turned-twenty-three-year-old who was about to become a trailblazer be worried about a bus? "He was so busy, I don't think he had time to think about [anything else]," Terry says. Sean had unfinished baseball business. Less than a week earlier, he had been on the mound at Falcon Park in Auburn, New York, trying to take the Rensselaer Engineers to a title. On May 8, he started for RPI in the

Liberty League Tournament and beat the University of Rochester, throwing 106 pitches over 7 1/3 innings. On May 9—the *next day*—he came out of the bullpen to close out a 10-5 win over the Rochester Institute of Technology in the second game of a doubleheader sweep, throwing 20 pitches in 1 2/3 scoreless innings to send the Engineers to the NCAA Division III Regional Tournament. In RPI's next game, on May 13, he earned a four-out save in a 2-0 victory over Keystone College. And two days later, he started against SUNY Cortland—the number-one team in all of Division III baseball—and took a tough-luck loss, allowing two earned runs over seven innings but exiting with a 6-5 deficit after his defense committed three errors behind him. A few days later, he moved out of the Phi Kappa Tau frat house and set off for Sonoma. He was three credits short of a degree, but baseball wouldn't wait.

Some aspects of Sean's baseball background are the same as every other professional player's. He remembers swinging one of those short plastic bats with the big barrels when he was barely old enough to stand, and he grew up going to his father's rec-league softball games. By the time Jack Conroy stopped playing, Sean was old enough to start, and his father coached him in tee-ball. "When I was five I got my name in the newspaper because I actually hit the ball off the tee," Sean says. "That was the big story." For an engineering-school student with a tax-analyst father, he has enviable athletic bloodlines, including his cousins Ethan and Owen Pochman, converted soccer players who placekicked for Brigham Young. Owen Pochman played two seasons in the NFL, completing eight of seventeen field-goal attempts. He wrote a memoir called *I'm Just a Kicker* and dated a Playmate of the Year.

Backyards are a common component of athlete origin stories, which abound with batters who learned to hit lefty or to aim toward the opposite field because pulling a pitch might have meant breaking a window. The Conroys' backyard was long but narrow—more than 100 feet long, and about 20 feet wide—which made it perfect for pitching and long toss. When Sean was seven, one of his father's friends taught him to throw a curveball. That's younger than kids are supposed to be when they start snapping off breaking balls, but it never hurt his arm.

An all-star in almost every league he belonged to, he never counted on becoming a big leaguer, but he was determined to try until the competition convinced him to quit. "I remember in fifth grade a teacher telling us to pay attention because none of us are going to be professional athletes, and I remember disagreeing with her," he says. "She said statistically speaking, it's not likely." To be fair, she hadn't seen our spreadsheet.

Sean's fastball tops out at 85 mph, so he never overpowered his opponents. "There were always people throwing harder than me," he says. "I never considered myself a power pitcher. I was always control and spin." Finesse doesn't turn heads at tryouts, and Sean didn't make his high school team as a sophomore. "Everyone I was playing with knew how I pitched in games, but it just didn't come through in tryouts." Even high school sophomores are supposed to throw hard.

He made the team as a junior, and as a senior he started dropping down to give right-handed hitters less of a look at his stuff. He adjusts his arm angle and pitch selection by the outing, depending on what he has in his arsenal. "When I have the 82 mph fastball, I try to drop my arm slot a little lower so it'll drop more, so it still looks fast," he says. Ninety-five percent of his pitches are fastballs or sliders, split about evenly. Naturally, he has a knuckleball, which he's saving for a free strike against someone who doesn't expect it.

To us, Sean seems cerebral, maybe because it suits our self-image; we serve the Stompers in an intellectual capacity, and we want to see something of ourselves in the players we sign. It's not because he's a bookworm: The lone book in the clubhouse belongs to T. J. Gavlik, who carries a round-cornered copy of Buzz Bissinger's *Three Nights in August* that our sources say he started in the summer of 2014. ("Those three nights in August sure are taking a lot longer than expected," one veteran remarks to me.) Textbooks excluded, the only book Sean has read in the past several years is *The Secret*, the self-help best seller about the mystical power of positive thinking. Sam and I haven't discovered *The Secret*, which might explain why our fastballs are slow and the universe hasn't seen fit to reward us with an unbeatable team or a manager who values what we say.

When we ask Sean questions, he pauses for a few seconds to construct a thoughtful response—just long enough that we worry he won't answer at all. (He's the same way with texts.) He questions baseball beliefs about bunting and pitcher usage, although he's not a student of sabermetrics per se. And he's a master of the metagame, the highest level of strategy in any competition that pits people against other people. It's the part of a head-to-head sport that develops in and around the actual rules, that tests not how fast you can run or how hard you can throw but how well you can anticipate what your opponent thinks you're thinking.

I discover Sean's interest in tactics when we bond over Super Smash Bros., the 1999 Nintendo 64 game that's spawned three sequels and a fierce professional Smash circuit. It's a four-player brawler that pits well-known Nintendo characters against one another in a battle to knock everyone else off the edges of an arena suspended in the sky. Every successful attack drives up an opponent's damage counter, and the higher the damage counter climbs, the farther a character flies after subsequent attacks—not unlike pitchers, who get hit harder the deeper they go into games. The Stompers' N64 is always on, from the moment the clubhouse opens to the time when the players start to toss in foul territory before first pitch. Sean is the best of the Stompers at Smash—pro gaming is his backup plan if baseball doesn't pan out—but I'm a match for him, thanks to the countless hours I logged as a kid instead of practicing sports. He likes playing me, he says, because he can't tell what my next move will be. After one white-knuckle game, he tells me that he tries to bring the intensity of our Smash showdowns out to the mound.

Sean approaches pitching with the same studious desire to stay one step ahead. No one else on the Stompers' staff shakes off signs as often. "I always know what I want to throw, and it's difficult for the catcher to be thinking along the same lines as me," he says. ("The slider's the one I like," I hear him remind Parker, semi-sarcastically, before a game.) But he still wants his catchers to call pitches, because he can learn from their suggestions even if he rejects them. "My line that I told my catcher last year is, 'I like when you call pitches, because you confirm to me what the hitter's thinking I'm going to throw,'" Sean says. In other words, Sean considers the catcher a proxy for the hitter: The catcher is trying to outthink the batter, but the batter is alert to the danger of being outthought. Even if the batter reads the catcher's mind, he'll still be surprised when Sean does something different. On one pitch during spring training with the Stompers, Sean shakes off the catcher three times, but he keeps putting down the same sign. The fourth time, Sean acquiesces and throws what the receiver wants. It results in the only hit he allows all spring.

Sean stopped watching Major League Baseball when he was ten or twelve, bored because he "didn't get everything going on." But when he got my call in April and realized that his career didn't have to die in Division III, he tuned in again to pick up tips from the pros, the way he watches Smash matches on YouTube and Twitch. "I just love watching pitchers pitch," he says. "I don't care [which team] wins. I want the pitcher to win." This goes triple for his own outings. The first time I set up my laptop to show Sean the pitches from his previous start, he's as glued to the screen as a four-year-old watching weekend cartoons, silent and motionless except for an occasional smile or soft snort when he paints a corner with a sinker or induces an ugly chase with his slider. After that, he's hooked. The day after he gets into a game, I can count on a tap on my arm or a conspiratorial question: "Do you have my video?"

Compared to his complex approach to pitching, Sean's openness about his sexual orientation seems simple. But his transparency as a person makes him as tough to anticipate as his deceptive pitch selection. Thanks to the lack of public precedents, no one expects a pro baseball player to be gay. And if a pro baseball player *is* gay, no one expects him to say so: Previous players who've come out have either been driven from the game despite their private lives not appearing in the public eye (Glenn Burke) or waited until long after retirement to disclose their orientation (Billy Bean). So Sean does the opposite of what everyone expects, just as he does on the mound: He hides nothing. When he came out to his parents, they embraced him immediately but worried about whether others would. "I think it was in tenth grade,"

Terry Conroy recalls. "I said, 'I think you should kinda keep it in your back pocket until you get through high school. It's just a better life, because I know what life was like when I was in school.' And he said, 'No, I'm not doing that.'"

He didn't. Sean's high school teammates knew he was gay. His college teammates knew he was gay. And he went west knowing that soon the Stompers would, too. "I learned in the newspaper that he was hoping to be the first player to come out," Terry says. "But he thought he'd have to be at a higher level for it to matter."

On June 10, the night of the Stompers' first loss, Eric Gullotta drives Sean and a few other players back to Sonoma from San Rafael, so that Theo—Sean's usual chauffeur—can take a more direct route to his home in Santa Rosa. Prolonged exposure to Eric's raunchy humor in a confined space can make a man do desperate things to change the subject, which might explain why Sean picks this time to let Eric in on his non-secret. "We were just talking about life after he dropped everyone else off," Sean says. "So when it was just me and him in the car it just felt like the right time. I had already told a few players and I wanted him to hear it from me so he didn't think I was trying to hide it from anyone."

The news trickles down to Theo, and then to me and Sam. Our first reaction is excitement: Our small-time team has a chance to help a player make history, thanks to a spreadsheet that discriminates based only on stats. Not only has our statistical scouting method yielded an impressive pitcher, proving that a pair of writers with scant baseball experience could contribute to a team, but it's also given one player an opportunity to break a barrier that matters much more. And even more serendipitously, that player is a psychology student who's as intrigued as we are by the sport's interpersonal puzzles.

Our second reaction is uncertainty: What can we do to make Sean's experience easier? The country has come a long way since Burke and Bean, but the prevailing beliefs of pro baseball's conservative clubhouses are still inscrutable. In March, New York Mets infielder Daniel Murphy responded to a spring-training visit from Bean (now serving as MLB's Ambassador for Inclusion) by telling reporters, "I disagree with his lifestyle," and "I disagree with the fact he is homosexual." Will there be similar "disagreements" between Stompers? And even if no players object to Sean's presence, might the extra attention trained on the team impair its performance? For years, we've seen insinuations that a gay player would be "a distraction." Those fears have always seemed flimsy, a way to whitewash bigotry, but until now we've never had the chance to provide proof.

There was only one ugly incident in Sean's amateur career, which occurred in the Albany Twilight League. "Sean struck a kid out," Terry says. "I was sitting there, and I believe he said, 'I can't believe that faggot struck me out.' So then the next time he came up, Sean struck him out again. That was it. He didn't say another word." Considering Sonoma's proximity to San Francisco, one would expect the community to give an openly gay player a warm welcome, but our players' attitudes are unknown. The first time Sam talks to Theo after we learn about Sean, they agree that any player who makes trouble for Sean won't have a home with us. "We'll cut all twenty-one if we have to," Sam says.

Theo sees Sean's revelation as a way for everyone to get what they want. The Stompers have a Pride Night scheduled for June 25, just before Sonoma County's Pride Weekend. If the team structures the game around the rookie, then Sean gets to set an example, and the team gets to make its Pride Night—as Theo puts it—"a more genuine event, rather than just, 'Hey LGBT people, come watch baseball.'" And the best way to make Sean the centerpiece of Pride Night is to have him start, which we want him to do anyway. It's a crafty move by Theo, who wants to see Sean's role expanded just as much as we do. This is a way to use his role as the head of the Stompers' business side to compel Feh to give him what he wants on the baseball side: It's easy for Feh to complain about losing his closer for competitive reasons, but this night will be bigger than baseball.

On June 19, the Stompers put out the press release. As soon as I see it, I scramble to the clubhouse, not knowing what I'll witness. A prepared address to the team? Torches and pitchforks? A Sister Sledge sing-along?

Instead, I find nothing out of the ordinary. It's still early, and players are ambling in one by one or in little one-car-capacity clumps. Sean is sitting outside the clubhouse, fiddling with his phone. I ask him to take a walk, and we stroll down the concourse toward third base, stopping when the concrete bulk of the visitors' clubhouse blocks us from the view of the rest of the team. I ask him if he's had any problems. He says no. I ask if he's planning to talk to the team. He says probably not in any formal meeting. I tell him that we'd love to spread his story, and that we hope he'll tell us if there's any way we can help. He says he will. Then we walk back to the clubhouse. All told, the interaction takes two or three minutes. I can't tell what I am when I talk to him: a team official, a reporter, or just a guy who got him into this situation and wants his experience to go smoothly. I feel a little nosy, as if I'm trying to horn in on his moment. We're new to knowing Sean is gay, but Sean is not new to *being* gay, nor is he new to having everyone around him aware of it. He can handle things from here.

The backlash, such as it is, is confined to online comment sections. "You just lost a supporter," the first comment on the Stompers' Facebook post about Pride Night says. "See ya!" Pressed by other users, the lost supporter explains himself, saying, "when has Sonoma or the stompers celebrated Straight identity, Straight couples, or Straight pride? Never!!! Don't sit there and tell me I'm being hateful. I'm just saying the truth!" He's not the only commenter who speaks up for the straights. "Hmmmm, wonder if there's gonna be a Heterosexual night for the rest of the players on this team Not being recognized," muses one woman, who notes that she's "definitely not homophobic." She continues, "My reaction is to management & how they are trying to promote one individual player to try & line their own pockets!! This year has definitely been disappointing with a few aspects on the field as well as management decisions. If this year ends with the current disappointment, its sad that I will no longer be a supporter."

Using the official Stompers account, Theo responds, "We celebrated heterosexual night with 6-STRAIGHT wins to start the season." The Stompers, at this point, are 15-3, having followed up the 6-1 start with another impressive 9-2 run. We've averaged 7 runs per game and allowed barely half that many. Our starters have thrown the first two complete-game shutouts in our franchise's history, our bullpen has a 2.27 ERA, and Feh, Daniel Baptista, and Matt Hibbert have been the three most productive hitters in the league. I feel the frustration of Phillies GM Ruben Amaro, who weeks earlier whined about fans who "bitch and complain" and "don't understand the game." At least Amaro had earned it: The Phillies were in last place. We're setting records here, and people are worried about whether we're properly honoring our other twenty-one players for wanting to have sex with women.

In the days before Pride Night, many local and even national outlets pick up Sean's story. More coverage means more comments. "I found myself reading the comments and then answering those hateful comments the next time I had an interview," Sean tells Sam. "When that question got asked to me I answered it in a way that would answer it to them. Like, people that would say that I was just looking for my fifteen minutes of fame, that I just wanted to come out to get the attention, which is wrong in a couple different ways. I don't want the attention, nor is the coming-out part new." Angry Internet commenters rarely respond to reason, which makes them immune to Sean's tactical thinking. But most strangers are supportive, like the man in Minnesota who mails Sean a custom Stompers baseball card.

If anyone on the Stompers objects to not having their own night, they keep their complaints to themselves, or far away from either our ears or Sean's. The clubhouse conversation becomes cleaner, more sanitized. The baseline level of homophobic language—from off-color comments to unthinking adjectives—recedes. In a game against the Pacifics a few days before Sean came out, San Rafael's designated hitter/third baseman Adrian Martinez was pressed into service as a catcher and inelegantly squatted behind home plate. "This catcher's going down to one knee," Isaac Wenrich said in the dugout. "He's getting ready for tonight. He must be from the rainbow district of San Fran." Jon Rand, the cheerful San Franciscan, responded, "Hey, what's wrong with that?"

Sean's announcement stops this sort of exchange. "I definitely heard homophobic things every day before I came out," he tells Sam. "I pretty much just assumed that it was all in jest, just habits. It just made me come out sooner so that I could start teaching people. That stuff only bothers me because it bothers other people." What bothered him more was having to hold back during clubhouse bull sessions—a more acute version of the personality-sapping politeness that accompanies any new relationship. As an unproven rookie, Sean didn't want to police what other players said from his first day in uniform. Nor did he want to adapt his own identity to the team's. "I just stayed quiet a lot more of the time," he says. After he goes public, his mood improves "immediately, like day one," he says. "I just feel better when everyone knows the truth."

Sam asks if Sean has noticed any subtle signs of disapproval after the announcement: players going out of their way to walk around him, anyone averting their eyes. But Sean isn't gregarious, which makes the answer less obvious. "*I* avert my eyes," Sean says. "If someone wants to come talk to me, then I'll pay attention, but I'm not one to go out of my way to talk to people. So it's just hard to tell."

Like any clique composed of mostly unsupervised people whose prefrontal cortexes haven't fully matured, the Stompers joke and jockey for social status by mocking each other's most salient surface-level traits. The players pile on Andrew Parker for being a meathead. Gered Mochizuki, the short Hawaiian, gets called "coconut head" and "midget." T. J. Gavlik, who's half Asian, hears a steady stream of slurs and stereotypes. Players tell him to "hit it to Hong Kong" or promise to reward his hits by buying him a cat for dinner. They call him "supple leopard" and "crouching tiger, hidden T. J." They make jokes about how he's afraid of dishonoring the umpire. All of these words would be offensive in other environments—maybe even in this environment, given a different group of guys, or the wrong mix of moods, or less shared history. In the clubhouse, though, they're mostly seen as signs of acceptance, routine shit tests that every pro player has passed (and administered) since Little League. Although there's no telling whether every insult is really shrugged off as easily as the players make it appear, the intention isn't to hurt. It might hurt more *not* to be mocked, which would mean being beneath the team's notice.

In the immediate aftermath of the announcement, the team's conversational tone around Sean takes on an almost Victorian propriety. No one wants to say something inappropriate and become the bigot of Sean's story. This is mildly uncomfortable for all involved: The players feel they have to watch their words, and Sean says he feels self-conscious because he senses their restraint and knows "that people might not be completely open with me, just because I'm always talking to reporters and they always ask me about my relationship with my teammates." The clubhouse is usually a place where players can be their most unrestrained selves. Now it's a place where they feel obligated to be on their best behavior, a possible drag on morale.

Gradually, though, the language loosens. During a pregame Smash Bros. session about a week after the announcement, Jon Rand, who's one of Sean's closest friends on the team, makes a joke about "playing Smash with fairy boy." He's talking about Link, the hero of the Legend of Zelda and the character he's controlling in the game, but he's also talking about Sean, who's seated beside him. By the time everyone turns toward Sean to gauge his reaction, he's already smiling.

That smile seems to open the offensive floodgates. In the dugout one day, Rand brags about how his butt looks in baseball pants, and someone else says Sean's looks better. "Hey, buy me dinner first," Sean responds. On another night, Sean is pitching against San Rafael and working so quickly that he can't wait to return to the mound after a half inning off. "Sean, slow down and let me put a dip in my mouth," Isaac says. "That wasn't a gay reference. I said *dip*." On still another night, Feh yells, "At least lube us up, at least give us some K-Y" at one of the many umpires he thinks is squeezing the Stompers.

And during a cold, windy game in Vallejo, I sit in the bullpen, listening in on a conversation in which the other relievers ask Sean about "signals," or ways to tell whether someone is gay. Erik Gonsalves suggests the silliest signals he can think of—flight attendants with crooked name tags, or drivers with their side mirrors fully extended. Isaac, serving as the bullpen catcher on a scheduled rest day, observes that the right fielder is wearing sunglasses on his hat even though the sun has long since set. He asks if that's a signal. I look at Sean and see that he has multiple sunglasses on his hat—his own, and also Rand's, since the lefty left his with his friend when he entered the game. "*That's* the signal," I say, pointing at Sean's hat. "*Two* pairs of sunglasses." He laughs. Now even I'm doing it.

In a normal workplace, these comments would be grounds for a lawsuit, or at the very least a sensitivity seminar. In baseball, they represent a strange sort of progress. "You can kinda tell when people are holding back from jokes they would make, so the more days that go by, the more every once in a while people start to be okay with it," Sean says. "And I'm trying to jump right on and be like, 'Okay, yeah, yeah, that's fine. Keep doing that.' It's what makes me feel comfortable."

The integration has gone as well as we could have imagined. For years, ballplayers and sportswriters have said baseball clubhouses weren't ready for a gay ballplayer—but that just turned out to be its own hurtful stereotype, a presumption that the jocks wouldn't act the way any decent people do toward a friend. It was an excuse, and the fear it engendered may have delayed this moment for years. Professional baseball, we've discovered, is no less enlightened than the rest of society: Sean is prepared for the Pacific Association, and the Pacific Association is prepared for Sean. "I don't know if people thought [it wouldn't be] because of the culture cop that baseball is in the locker rooms, just all the different backgrounds that people come from," Sean says. "You can never know how many people are going to be hard core, set in their ways." Sam and I weren't seriously concerned, but even we underestimated the Stompers. Sean was right not to fear anything but the bus to Petaluma.

Back in Clifton Park, Sean's parents discover that they have one more gay relation than they had thought.

"I have a relative who was gay also, and had never come out," Jack Conroy tells me. "He was almost seventy years old. And because of

Sean, he was able to come out. He felt so good about what was going on that he really felt compelled to."

"[Jack's relative] called me and he said, 'I don't know if you've figured this out or not, but if Sean can do it, I can do it,'" Terry Conroy recounts. She also tells me that Sean's story has made her a magnet for anyone in Clifton Park with a gay family member.

"I've had a lot of people come to me," Terry says. "Like our hair-dresser said, 'My older brother's gay,' and a guy at work told me that his oldest son is. Everybody just feels the need to tell me now." She smiles. "But can they pitch?"

One day fairly early in the season I bought a heavy steel safe and put it in the clubhouse, right by the Wonder Bread and peanut butter and below the whiteboard that tells ballplayers what time they have to be at batting practice. The same day, I distributed a survey to each of the players, asking two questions: "How 'locked-in' are you?" and "How's your mood?" We intend to test the reasonable hypothesis that happy ballplayers play better (as opposed to the even more reasonable but not mutually exclusive hypothesis that ballplayers who play better get happier), and to see whether we can find some evidence that hot streaks are real by, in essence, asking players to predict their own. The lockbox is to put the players' minds at ease, to reassure them that we're not going to use their happiness levels as a way of making roster or lineup decisions. They can stuff their responses into the safe, and we won't look at them until after the season.

Which means we didn't know what response Sean gave on June 25, the day that the first openly gay baseball player would start in a professional baseball game. We didn't know whether reading articles by national baseball writers praising him for his courage and strength would make him feel courageous and strong—or whether his inability to avoid hateful comments at the bottom of those articles would make him feel persecuted and alone. We didn't know what it meant to him that, on the day of the game, Sergio Miranda and Jon Rand arranged for every player's locker to have a pair of rainbow socks, and that nearly all the players would wear those socks—or, as many modified them, armbands—as a show of support for him.

Nor did we know what it was like to see teammates who had previously been so casual about insensitive speech—one of our veterans once told us he had opted to sign with us, not San Rafael, because "they're too faggy over there"—respond with such positive nonchalance to his announcement. Or what it was like that at least a couple of season-ticket holders and host families are boycotting this game. Or how it feels to have the world picking over his relationship with his teammates, wanting to know what it's like for them in the locker room, not knowing that the relationship between him and his teammates developed over a month of intimacy, of accidental moments like the time he got drunk downtown and tried to walk three miles home but got so lost he eventually had to turn right back around and walk downtown again, by which point it was so late and he was so disoriented that all he could do was find Arnold Field and hop the fence and sleep in a huddle on the dugout bench, and how everybody found out about this so that's why they all call him "Sleepy," and is that relevant to the gay thing? We don't know what it was like to watch his catcher, Isaac Wenrich, get ambushed by a TV interviewer right in the middle of his pregame preparation and answer questions so beautifully, talking about how Sean on the mound is just a pitcher and an athlete and how not one guy on the team sees him as anything but a teammate, completely equal, nothing complicated about it, and we sort of look at each other shocked, like *Isaac? Isaac said that?*

"Theo, don't you ever ambush me with a fucking camera again," Isaac complains afterward. "I don't know how to answer gay questions. The guy's like, 'What's it like playing with gay Sean?' I don't know. Shit. He's Sean. He's awesome at Mario. He Smashes me."

Then Isaac walks out of the dugout to go warm up Sean in the bullpen, and calls out to some teammates in a bored monotone, "Hey everybody, Sean's gay."

Before the game, Sam stands in the batter's box in the bullpen, giving

Sean a dummy to pitch against so that he can replicate the feeling of facing a real batter. The slider is sharp today; Sam bails out of the way. The fastball whistles. The command is tight. Sam asks him, "So hey, you nervous?" And Sean answers, "No more than any other day."

We're nervous. Not the gay thing. The starting pitching thing. For three weeks Sam and I have been agitating with Feh for Sean to get more innings—our most effective pitcher has thrown the fewest innings of anyone on the staff. In those few innings he has been the league's best pitcher, allowing only two hits and no earned runs, with just one walk. He also plays great defense and has a swell pickoff move. He's clearly way too good to use exclusively in protection of three-run leads in the ninth inning. But we have concerns about Sean as a starter. He basically uses only two pitches, so batters will have seen everything he throws by the end of the first at-bat. (A slight wrinkle is his over-the-top surprise, which is usually good for one strike per game per batter.) He succeeds partly because of a deceptive motion, which will get less deceptive the more a batter sees it. He is less dominant against lefties, who pick up the ball out of his hand better and lay off his slider. And he hasn't thrown more than two innings in a month, so we have no idea how much stamina he'll have as a starter. In a way, Sean being gay has called our bluff: We were like third-party candidates whose positions could never be proven wrong, until by fluke of circumstance we accidentally got elected.

"We win when we hug," Joel Carranza announces in the dugout. "We win when we hug." He goes from teammate to teammate, hugging them all, hugging Sean. Isaac and Mike Jackson join in, hugging, hugging, hugging, hugging. "Brothers don't shake hands. Brothers hug."

Sean takes the field to more applause than usual, but it's a pretty typical weeknight crowd—478 is the official paid attendance. This is not Jose Canseco appearing for two games and a home run derby; to most Stompers fans, it's just baseball. "Why are they wearing those socks?" one young fan wonders aloud, and nobody answers. Sean takes a deep breath on the mound, then throws his first pitch: a swinging strike.

He gets another swinging strike, then tries to get Vallejo's leadoff hitter, Jaylen Harris, to chase a ball out of the zone. After Sean's third wayward attempt, Harris jogs down to first base. "We play four in this league," Eric Schwieger calls from the dugout, and everybody laughs at Harris's goof. "You know what's embarrassing?" Jon Rand asks. "That." Harris digs back in, and Conroy fires his 3-2 pitch: strike three looking.

"Well, the changeup's working," Jon says. "I taught him that pitch." He turns to a reporter and points to the notepad. "Put that in there." A voice calls out from the stands, "Wake up, Sleepy!" which makes all of us insiders laugh.

From there, it's dominance. Sean calmly walks off the mound after the first inning and asks Sam for a pen; he keeps a broken-bat tally on the bill of his cap, and he just got one. Vallejo will never get two men on in an inning, will never get a runner past second base. The Stompers score a run in the third to get Sean a lead, then a pair of runs in each of the next three innings, and the closest thing to a contest comes when Harris gets forced out at second base in the sixth and gets up jawing at second baseman Sergio Miranda. Feh nearly runs in from center field to fight him—"Don't try to be a gangster!" he's yelling—and Carranza takes a step out of the dugout, hollering, "We could do this right here, bro." There's some discussion in the dugout about whether Isaac should put down the sign for a beanball, which, apparently, is a middle finger. The decision is no.

That decision is one of two we have to make. The other is whether to let Sean keep pitching deep into the game. He's not, in baseball lingo, stretched out for such a start, but he's insistent. Feh, who's unhappy that a Sean start has been forced on him and mutters that Sean is "fucking himself" by wanting to stay in, tries to remove him. Sean pleads his case. A week earlier, in an attempt to get more innings, Sean had gone into Feh's office and asked to be removed from the closer's role. He told Feh he was having trouble recovering quickly from his outings, so it didn't make sense to use him in a role that might require back-to-back appearances. This was, basically, a lie, anything to get Feh to loosen up the "only in save situations" limitation, and Feh rebuffed him in an unsatisfying conversation that lasted less than a minute. Now, having temporarily lost the right to use his pitcher as he pleases, Feh is sour that Sean isn't letting him take his closer out of a game in which he's dominating as a starter.

But this time Sean wins the argument. And on his 140th pitch—a potentially harmful total that we, like many managers before us, find easier to rationalize while emotions are high and history is happening— he gets the final out, just as he had done six times previously as a reliever. "Goddamn, starting is easy," Gonsalves says. Sean pumps his fist. Isaac hugs him in front of the mound, the rest of Sean's teammates surround him, and then the local TV news crews replace them. Sam grabs Feh and tells him to dump a water-cooler ice bath on Sean, and Feh says it's a great idea, and Sam beams because he had a great idea and the manager agreed to follow it! A few players sneak around the back of the dugout, then cut through the bullpen and soak Sean, and he gasps as he struggles to continue the interviews. He gets his breath back and says he hopes kids out there are inspired by his performance. He says it was just a game like any other, that he's not sure what his future holds but he's starting to think he'd like to do some sort of activism. As the cameras roll, Isaac Wenrich walks past, and with a mug he gratuitously slaps Sean Conroy's gay ass.

That night, we're at the bar. Every night at least some of the Stompers start drinking at Town Square (where a host mom bartends, and whence free drink tokens have a habit of collecting in the players' pockets throughout the week) before walking across the town plaza to Steiners, where one of the bartenders lets each player put down a $20 bill and drink the rest of the night on that. But tonight Sean and Sam and I go straight to Steiners, where Thursdays are called "Thursgays," and where a couple of radio hosts who came to report on the game for a local LGBT program offer to buy Sean drinks. Amid it all, Sean tells Sam he has to admit something.

"I lied," he says.

About?

"On my happiness survey today. I lied. I wrote 7 for 'locked-in,'" the highest rating on our scale. "I was probably really a 5. I just didn't think there was any point in admitting that to myself." He wants us to know so that when the season ends and we try to make the numbers mean something, our data won't be skewed.

In August, Billy Bean will ask Sean to talk to David Denson, a twenty-year-old first baseman in the Milwaukee Brewers system who's about to become the first openly gay player in affiliated ball. Denson will ask Sean about the media attention and the effect coming out has had on team chemistry. "I basically told him it was worth it," Sean will say.

But before that, not long after the first pitch on Pride Night, the National Baseball Hall of Fame and Museum requests that the Stompers send the scorecard from Sean's start to Cooperstown. Everyone signs it, even me: We know it's the only way we're ever going to get there. Five months later and almost three thousand miles east of Sonoma, on a nothing-special Saturday, Isaac makes a pilgrimage from his home in Pennsylvania to see the scorecard on display. He texts Sean to ask him if he's seen it, and Sean texts him back to say, *I'm standing at the exhibit right now.* It's a complete coincidence, the latest in a long line of unlikely events that had to happen for a Sean Conroy relic to end up in a baseball museum next to the bat Alex Rodriguez used to drive in his two thousandth run and the cap Cole Hamels was wearing when he no-hit the Cubs. Standing in their off-season Stompers attire, Sean and Isaac pose for pictures in front of a glass case labeled "TODAY'S GAME," where the historic scorecard sits front and center. They're hugging again.

Sam and I have helped put Sean in the Hall of Fame, but we can't keep him in the Stompers' starting rotation. The first time I talk to him after

Pride Night, he tells me he's back to being a closer. For me, it's a mouth-agape moment: It hadn't even entered my mind that Feh would want Sean back in the bullpen after he'd proved beyond any doubt that he could handle a larger role. But Sean says Feh made it clear to him in the week leading up to the start that because of his lack of confidence in the team's alternate closer candidates, the outing would be a one-off, no matter how he did. "I was always in relief in his mind," Sean tells me.

On June 28, three days after Sean's Pride Night gem and his immediate demotion/forced relocation back to relief, our indy-league drama intersects with the big leagues in a way that reminds us that our conflict with Feh echoes a larger debate within baseball. Los Angeles Angels closer Huston Street makes headlines when he's asked about the possibility of entering the game whenever high-leverage situations arise, like relievers used to in the 1980s and earlier, instead of being used strictly in save situations (which may or may not be particularly tight).

"I'll retire if that ever happens," Street says. "If they ever tell me, 'Oh, we're gonna start using you in these high-leverage situations.' . . . All right, good. You now can go find someone else to do that, because I'm going home."

Street doesn't stop there. "It's a ridiculous idea," he continues. "It really is. The fact is, a bullpen functions best when you have roles. If you want to have a good pen, you need three or four guys that you trust. And if you trust them, give them roles, so they know what they have to do every day."

Is it possible that Feh put Street up to this? It sounds as if Street is speaking to us, reaching down from his privileged place at the back of a big league bullpen to say that Sam and I were silly to think we could topple an entrenched system. "There's too many holes in the theory for me personally," he concludes. "I can't stand it. I think it's an idea that's built on paper but doesn't work in real life. That's really what it is to me."

That last comment really rankles, because it cuts to the heart of why we've come to Sonoma: to put "on paper" ideas like this into practice. Thus far, it seems as if those who side with Street are right. Not because the idea of less restrictive roles doesn't work—it *did* work, before big league bullpens became hyperspecialized—but because everyone is so convinced it *wouldn't* work now that they aren't even willing to try it. The idea is disqualified because it can't pass a test that no one will allow it to take.

The irony is that we're not trying to transport a kicking, screaming, Street-style closer back to the days before bullpens grew rigid. Street was always a closer, even at the University of Texas at Austin, where he set a record for the most saves in a College World Series. He's been conditioned for more than a decade to come in at the end of games, and he's clearly more comfortable doing so. Sean Conroy is the anti-Street: He has extensive starting experience, and he has no qualms about coming in early. Yet we're using Sean as if the Angels closer's comments had come from him.

Street is still on my mind in the hours before Sonoma's next game, on June 30. The Stompers are in San Rafael, and I'm scouting in Pittsburg, where the Diamonds are facing Vallejo's slow-motion southpaw, Demetrius Banks. Banks moves so slowly that when he's facing the Stompers, our team narrates his trips back to the dugout by announcing the surface he steps on with each excruciating stride: "GRASS, GRASS, GRASS, DIRT, DIRT, GRASS." (He smiles in response, but he doesn't speed up.) In need of distraction, I pull up the Stompers' stream on my phone and listen to Tim Livingston with one earbud. The second-place Pacifics are riding a three-series winning streak, so for the first time since the first week of the season our games have something approaching playoff implications.

Eric Schwieger is starting for the Stompers, in his third outing after the game we lost when Erik Gonsalves and Paul Hvozdovic relieved him instead of closer-because-he's-the-closer Sean Conroy. He and Pacifics starter Ryan DeJesus put up zeroes for four innings, and then each works into and out of trouble. It's 4-2 Sonoma after six innings.

Disaster *starts* to strike in the seventh, that dangerous, in-between inning when the hitters are often facing the starter for the third time in the game, but the manager might not be ready to bring in his big bullpen guns. Two men reach, which brings up short, pesky center fielder

Zack Pace—already one of the opponents whose name I most dread, thanks to his willingness to work the count and his extra-small strike zone. He takes a called strike and fouls off the second pitch, then shortens up his already compact swing and grounds to Moch . . . who takes his time while Pace busts it down the line and beats the lackadaisical throw. "That doesn't go down as an error, but that is most definitely a mental mistake by Mochizuki," Tim says. Frickin' Pace. Frickin' Moch. Frickin' baseball.

With runners at first and second, the Stompers up by one, and a right-handed hitter due up, Schwieg's day is done at 102 pitches. Godsey walks to the mound, takes the ball, and signals for . . . Jon Rand.

It's not the move I would make. Rand has a 1.56 ERA through his first six games, but we know he's not that good, both because we have eyes and because the stats say so: His FIP is 3.64, and FIP predicts future ERA more accurately than ERA itself. He's struck out only 7 batters in 17 1/3 innings. This smacks of a move made because it's the seventh, which modern managerial law says is too soon to use an elite reliever— the same situation we faced two weeks earlier, and effectively the same response, with Rand replacing Hvozdovic in the script. Yet the game could be decided here. If the batter makes an out, the sport's actuarial tables say that the Stompers will have a 75.4 percent chance of winning. But if he singles and Martinez scores, the Stompers' win expectancy will drop to 38.1 percent. For that reason, this plate appearance has a Leverage Index of 4.08—which means it "matters" more than four times as much as the average plate appearance. Sitting in Pittsburg's sparsely populated stands, I'm a mechanical man, performing my functions on autopilot with most of my consciousness centered on the game in San Rafael. "Wish Sean were pitching," I text Sam.

The Stompers get a break: Pacifics manager Matt Kavanaugh pinch-hits with lefty Tyger Pederson, who's three years older, two inches (and forty pounds) smaller, and way worse at baseball than his brother Joc, who's already hit 20 homers in 257 at-bats for the Dodgers in his first full season. Tyger (not a nickname) is slugging .233. Rand strikes him out swinging. I remind myself that managerial moves usually don't make or break games: In many cases, the worse choice works out, and in some cases, the better choice backfires.

In the top of the eighth, the broadcast gives me good news. "Sean Conroy has gotten up in the Stompers' bullpen, starting to toss the ball a little bit," Tim says. I exhale. We dodged one bullet, and it looks like we won't have to dodge another. But after two outs, Tim delivers another report on the pen. "Conroy, who got up and threw just a little bit, maybe to get the arm loose, has come off the hill," he says. "He'll probably be called upon in the eighth inning if Rand gets into trouble." Instead of using Sean to forestall a rally, we're waiting until he'll have to escape one. That's like deciding to treat the symptoms of a disease instead of using an available vaccine. The top of the eighth ends, and Rand returns to the mound to face Matt Chavez, Maikel Jova, and Jeremy Williams, the Pacifics' 3-4-5 hitters, all righties.

Chavez works the count full, then lines a changeup into left for a single. Rand is officially in trouble. Where's Sean? Not up yet, but no rush.

Sean finally gets up again after a fouled-off first pitch to Jova, but the second pitch is smacked down the right-field line for a double. "And you wonder now, leaving in Rand to face the three right-handed hitters in the eighth might be coming back to bite the Stompers here," Tim says. Oh, I wondered a while ago.

Isaac stalls with a mound visit, but Sean needs more than one pitch to warm up, so Rand stays in to face Williams. Rand needs a strikeout here, but he's the last guy we want pitching in a strikeout situation. On 1-1, Williams singles through the right side. The game is tied. And Tim's next words pour gas on the fire that's burning in my brain: "Now Gonsalves will get up in the bullpen, and Conroy will sit down. And it's not a save situation."

I text Theo, who's listening at home.

"This bullpen usage is driving me crazy," I say.

"Me too," he answers. "How do we let Rand face possibly the three best righties in the league?"

On the broadcast, Tim is singing the same tune. "This has been an issue for the Stompers, in the sense that Lentini's out in center and technically the manager," he says. "Jerome Godsey has kind of been the de facto pitching coach. But this is a situation that the Stompers should've prepared for, with three right-handed hitters coming up, and the three best hitters that the Pacifics have, as they leave Rand out there. Conroy's someone who can go two innings if they need him to."

At last, the Stompers summon a right-handed reliever—the *wrong* right-handed reliever, Gonsalves, who's in there not because he's the pitcher most likely to get an out, but because Conroy's the closer, and the closer's the closer because he's the closer, bro. On his second pitch, Danny Gonzalez commits Gonzo-on-Gonzo crime, singling into right to score Jova and give the Pacifics a 5-4 win. It's a 5-4 final in Pittsburg, too, in favor of the Admirals, but I can tell I'll remember the game I didn't go to much more clearly than the one I actually saw. As I'm packing up the camera, I get a text from Theo. "I was sick to my stomach listening to that," he says.

The Stompers just made another stupid mistake attributable to the type of illogical, by-the-book thinking sabermetricians disparage. Worse, we're supposed to be the team that doesn't make stupid mistakes—not necessarily the biggest or the fastest or the strongest, and certainly not the most experienced, but the smartest. Every fan knows the feeling of listening or watching while his or her team self-destructs, but this was worse. Not just because we have some skin in the game, but because, to some extent, we're responsible. We're not fans far away from the action, whose only recourse is to yell at the TV or send a snarky tweet. This happened not *while* we watched, but *on* our watch. We could have done something to stop it.

I'm fed up with Feh, but I'm just as annoyed by our own inaction, which puts me at odds with Sam. Before the Stompers' season started we were so often in accordance that we could have called our podcast *Two Guys Agreeing*. But now there's a noticeable tension, which comes out in colder communication. (We both dread confrontation, which might be contributing to our trouble with Feh.) We're in a bad mood because of the loss, and our postgame text exchange sounds like band-mates squabbling on *Behind the Music*. I suggest that Sam, Theo, and I meet with Feh about Sean. "Be real," Sam says. The rest of us already agree, I say. Isn't Feh the one we need to talk to? "If you want nothing to happen, yes, go ahead and rush into a conversation that will lead nowhere," he says. "Get kicked out of the dugout. Etc. So on." He tells me to skip scouting in Pittsburg, to come to San Rafael and discuss what to do. I ask if we can call Theo tomorrow—I don't need to skip scouting for us to talk. "Yes you do," he responds. "The plan is going to come out of the conversation Theo and I have. You can be there or not, but that's where the plan is coming from." The fact that I think this is a matter for a brief phone call, he adds, is the "biggest problem. Bigger problem than Feh."

Sam is being too tentative: He's so unwilling to get in anyone's way that he even objects when I thread an extension cord through the stands to power our camera in Vallejo, because he's worried someone might trip. (No one ever does.) I can't figure out why we're fighting when we're on the same side. This dispute over saves vs. leverage is a predictable clash, something we saw coming from the second we signed up. We've tried the subtle suggestion route, and while we haven't been black-balled, we're dangerously close to becoming bystanders, which would be just as bad. If we were building a foundation for the future—trying to set up a system, a Stompers Way that would stand the test of time— I'd be all for more baby steps and buy-in and building consensus. But it's not clear to me that our manager is interested in diplomatic discussions, and we're a third of the way through a three-month season, after which we won't see the guy again. This, it seems to me, is the time to stop tiptoeing, and if someone stubs a toe—well, we never thought this experiment would be completely painless. If we want to do things differently, we're almost certain to ruffle a few feathers.

As a player, Feh has honed instincts that we'll never develop. As a manager, though, he hasn't earned our deference. We don't work for Feh, we're backed by his boss, and we found Sean. We matter as much to the franchise as Feh does, and he was warned about what we'd be doing before he took the job. The worst thing we can do is do nothing and let Feh feel secure in his fiefdom while needless losses add up. We can continue to be tactful, cajoling instead of pushing or pulling or provoking a fight, but we have to state our case clearly. I'm not so naïve that I think Feh will roll right over if we ask him politely, but one way or another it would pop the pimple.

Early the next morning I email Feh, needing to do *something* to assuage my anxiety. The subject isn't Sean—that will wait until after the San Rafael summit—but the batting order. I crib some stats from The Grapevine and do my best to sound ecumenical, unthreatening, and almost unconcerned, as if the order hasn't been bugging me since Opening Day. I even sprinkle in a little light flattery.

"Hey Feh," I begin.

> I was just looking over some numbers about our batting order, and I wanted to run something by you. This table shows the average number of runners that have been on base when each of our regular hitters has come to the plate this season:

Name	Average # of Runners on Base
Gered Mochizuki	0.948
Sergio Miranda	0.887
Mark Hurley	0.877
Matt Hibbert	0.871
Feh Lentini	0.849
Joel Carranza	0.833
Daniel Baptista	0.735
Isaac Wenrich	0.679
Kristian Gayday	0.649

> The way the lineup is set up now, Moch is coming up with the most runners on, because he's batting third with the combo of Hibbert, Serge, and you hitting in front of him. I was thinking that since you're tied for the team lead in homers, it might make sense

to get you into a spot where you'd have more of those opportunities to drive guys in.

Have you considered batting Hibb leadoff, with Serge second, you in the 3 hole, and Moch somewhere in the bottom third? I'm thinking that might help us in a couple ways:

1) It would get Hibb more plate appearances. Right now, he comes up less often than everyone else, because he's batting ninth. He's one of our best overall hitters and on-base guys, so the more he gets to bat, the more we pack the basepaths. We'd still keep the Hibb-Serge-you sequence in order, and Hibb led off last season, so he's comfortable in that role.

2) It would help us make the most of your power by putting you in the best RBI spot. Right now you're more likely to come up with the bases empty, in which case the best you can do is hit a solo shot (like you did last night). It would also mean more runners on for Joel and Isaac.

Thought it might be worth trying, at least temporarily until Moch heats up again. Let me know what you think.

While I'm waiting for a response, I scan the news and see that the statistically oriented general manager of the Angels, Jerry Dipoto, has resigned after clashing with manager Mike Scioscia, who after the season will tell a reporter, in a Lentini-esque turn of phrase, "I think the manager is the manager." I wonder whether I should start drafting my own farewell. Then Feh's answer arrives, in a big block of text.

What's up Ben. I hear what you're saying but it's never a good idea to make changes just because a few games don't go our way. The message it sends are that I am panicking, and I am not because I know there are stretches where things go your way, and there are stretches where they don't. You can't give up on a guy cause he has a rough week. Maybe a little later. Plus I already debated this before the season. I am not a middle of the order guy, I am a lead off hitter. And Hibby is a 9 hole guy. That's why he is succeeding the way he is. And that's why I am too because of the opportunities he is creating for me. He will get pitched differently in the 1 hole and there is a lot more pressure to set the table. I also don't have the confidence to put anyone else in 3 hole in terms of

experience because that is where you get pitched the toughest. I
will get Moch dialed back in. It's not like he is getting dominated.

There's so much I want to say. Such as: I didn't suggest this because
we lost a few games, I suggested this because it's made sense from the
start. And: If you can't make changes when you're winning *or* when
you're losing, when *is* it safe to make them? Or: Doesn't which kind of
hitter you are depend on where and with whom you're playing? Maybe
you're a leadoff hitter in the Atlantic League, but look around: In the
Pacific Association, you're one of the best power hitters we have. Or: If
Hibby is succeeding only because he's hitting ninth, how do you explain
his success in the leadoff slot last season (and the fact that he told me
he was just as happy hitting there)? Plus: What does experience have to
do with batting third? In April, Cubs rookie Kris Bryant made his
major league debut in the cleanup spot, because Bryant is a cleanup
kind of hitter, twenty-three years old or not. Why can't you be more
like Cubs manager Joe Maddon?

Instead, I say, "OK, thanks for thinking about it." My email didn't
work wonders. All in all, it went worse than when T. J. Gavlik tried to
explain the concept of "blue balls" to Yuki Yasuda using obscene hand
gestures alone. But: Feh read, he responded, and he didn't blow up about
it. Maybe he'll mull it over. Maybe I'm in his head.

In the evening, I go back to Pittsburg as planned. The Diamonds take
an early lead, but the Admirals come back to force extra innings, perhaps inspired by a Pittsburg sound-system mistake that results in rally
music playing with the visitors up. Behind me, an older Vallejo fan—
probably a player's relative, like almost *every* Vallejo fan—relays a litany
of loud, extremely simplistic advice. "Make him come to you," he says
when the Admirals are up. "Sit on the fastball, wait on the curve." With
the Admirals in the field, he's even more vocal. "Be ready, defense. Look
it into your glove. Don't stand flat-footed. Step and throw." As the game
goes on, his advice grows more granular: "Get the ball first, and *then*
make the play," is one sentence he says, out loud, to a team of professional
players. He's two innings away from telling them which base they can

throw to for a force play, four innings away from reminding them to breathe and circulate blood through their bodies. But the Diamonds walk off in the tenth, in part because the defense disobeys him: A ball gets by catcher Tyler Nordgren, allowing the winning run to reach second and then score on a single. The Admirals supporter gets up slowly and walks off, aggrieved. I feel for him. Sam and I are learning the same lesson: Knowing what we *want* a team to do isn't nearly enough.

While I'm half-stewing, half-scouting in Pittsburg, Sam and Theo have the promised meeting in San Rafael, pulling Yoshi into the grandstand before batting practice. Theo points out that "approximately 100 percent of our losses" can be pinned on bullpen mismanagement and asks why we're still acting as if it's spring training and making moves based mostly on whose turn it is to throw. To Theo's relief, Yoshi agrees with every critique: He tells Theo that the pitchers are tired of being neglected by Feh in favor of the hitters, and of being mishandled by Godsey. Theo and Sam ask Yoshi if he would be interested in taking over the pitching-coach duties, including the power to make pitching changes. The surprise reveal is that Feh has already talked to Yoshi about assuming more responsibility for relievers, since the walkie-talkie way isn't working. Theo goes down to the dugout to tell Feh he endorses the idea and, easy as that, Jerome's reign is over.

Six days later, Feh tells me that he's finally looked at some statistics, which he "[doesn't] like to do as a player." When I look at the lineup, I see Hibbert leading off and Lentini listed third.

10

FEHBALL

On a drizzly off-day in June, the team opens the cardboard "Bang Box," where over the past month the players have deposited handwritten kangaroo-court charges levied against each other for lack-of-feel faux pas. For instance: "Gonzo left his open Parkpoint water bottle on top of stereo amp. Would you rather us not have a stereo? #sabotage." Or: "Sleepy: Overslept. $2.50." These charges will be litigated and fines will be assessed. I've been led to believe that I will be among those fined, for tattling (inadvertently) to Theo about one of the players' claims to having put down twenty-five alcoholic drinks a night during the season.

As court comes to order, Fehlandt sees me across the clubhouse and calls out that I have to go. "No stat guys allowed," he orders. I redden, and I dig in. I have no real way of knowing whether he is serious—he used almost the exact same language on the first day of the season when he saw me in the clubhouse before the game, and when I asked him then whether he meant it, he laughed and said that, no, of course not, he was joking, he loved having me there. So I stay. Yoshi, the bench coach, reassures me that I am part of the team and thus welcome.

There are other nonplayers in the room—including the clubhouse attendant, Mac, and Captain Morgan. And it isn't as if I am some exec who is never around the team; Ben or I have been in the dugout every game, bench coaches in corduroys. A number of players know I intend to be at the kangaroo court and haven't indicated any surprise—and, yeah, I fully expect to be fined. Two minutes pass and Fehlandt sees me again, and again he calls out that I have to leave.

"I'm not leaving, Feh," I tell him.

"Players only," he says, "you gotta go."

"I've got to be here to defend myself."

Joel Carranza jumps in, incredulous. "Defend yourself *from what*?"

Aw, hell. Now it isn't just me and Feh. Now there are going to be players, at least a few, telling me to get out. I know this battle is lost, and I know I'm going to lose face.

"I might be in there," I say, motioning toward the Bang Box.

Carranza laughs. "You ain't going to be in there!"

Tommy Lyons, the first-base coach, raises his eyebrows. "Actually . . . I think he might be."

But I know that no player will stand up for me if any players are against my being there. And when somebody from the veterans' side of the room yells "Get the fuck out!" well, I grab my bag and go.

I'm furious. Fehlandt kicking me out feels like a microcosm of everything he's done wrong this season: Instead of seeing us as part of the team, he sees us as outsiders, as the other. And instead of looking for ways to bring the other into the circle and make us part of the team, he protects his territory and makes life much, much harder. He could have made a statement by saying that I could stay for court. Barring that, he could have quietly pulled me aside and said that it's probably not the right place for a guy with a tape recorder to be. Instead, he's widened the divide.

I pace outside the clubhouse, hearing muffled crashes of laughter from inside, and for the first time I think that I'd like to fire Fehlandt. Not that I would fire a manager for kicking me out of kangaroo court, where, heck, maybe I really shouldn't be. But my disgust at how closed-circled he is summons the possibility to mind for the first time, and brings into focus how doomed this collaboration is. Ben and I can either dictate to him exactly what to do, or we can concede the season to his traditional style of play, or we can fire him. The anger I feel makes the last option seem the most satisfying.

At the kangaroo court, Fehlandt gets a max fine of five bucks for wearing the wrong jersey on Jose Canseco night, a gaffe that Canseco himself pointed at just as a photographer snapped. He will pin the citation and the photo outside the doorway to his office. Meanwhile, I will stew.

We're a first-place team, running away with the first-half crown, 18-4 after twenty-two games, and all we can do is worry. Ben is terrified that we've been lucky on batted balls—that our pitchers aren't as good as they have looked—and frustrated that our manager doesn't want to listen to advice on tactics, lineup decisions, or the virtues of Taylor Eads. I'm also troubled by the slow realization that not all ballplayers are the socially flexible and tribally generous individuals I'd convinced myself they were. The clique-free clubhouse we were so proud of early is now—and, in retrospect, always was—clearly cliquey.

The most troubling clique is the one at the top, formed by our manager and his boys, the veterans Sergio Miranda and Gered Mochizuki. Serge and Moch are skilled ballplayers who see themselves as mentors and leaders, but the rest of the club sees them as nonhustlers who are a little too up-front about their desire to leave this team for something better. Neither quite fits in with the younger ones—"Everybody Feh brought to this team is a fuck," one player tells me at Steiners one night, referring not just to Miranda and Mochizuki but also to pitcher/coach Jerome Godsey. (Jon Rand, another guy Feh brought to this team, seems to be exempt from this, as most of the team is unaware of where he came from.)

That game against San Rafael when Schwieger, again left in too long against the heart of the Pacifics' order, was trying to work out of a seventh-inning jam with a one-run lead? When he got what looked to be the final out of the inning, a weak grounder toward Gered Mochizuki, except Mochizuki's throw was late? Not an automatic play, not an error, but a play that was easy to notice because of a number of other moments in that game—when Miranda, for instance, tried to take second on what he thought was a wild pitch, but jogged so slowly that he was gunned down easily. (The pitch hit the umpire and fell right at the catcher's feet.) Or when Schwieger allowed a deep fly ball to center field that Fehlandt fielded off the wall and fired in to second base—in time, it appeared, to challenge the batter going for a double, except that Miranda was unaccountably far from the bag and couldn't make the tag. Or when Mochizuki struck out on a pitch that got to the backstop but didn't bother to run to first—especially galling because, with Fehlandt running in to score on the wild pitch, there would have been no attempted throw to first to retire Moch. Or when Miranda grounded out and loped toward first, a potentially close play losing all suspense.

"Wouldn't . . ." I begin, but then pause, hesitant to assume too much about how baseball players play ten levels higher than I ever reached. "Wouldn't Serge have had a pretty good chance of beating that?"

"Yeah," Gonzo says, "but we don't play baseball around here. We play Fehball."

Fehball: Where your boys don't have to do what everybody else has to do. Where one day Moch carelessly wears Fehlandt's pants, and Feh runs around in pants way too small for him and can't figure out why he feels off his game. Where one day Miranda shows up late to a game because he'd slipped away for a quick Vegas trip that ended up being not so quick. Where Miranda misses a subsequent game entirely, and also asks a ballpark employee to fill his water bottle with beer while another game (which he's exited early) is still going.

So that was the frustration in the air when Mochizuki failed to convert the third out of the inning, and that was part of the frustration Schwieger felt when he walked toward the dugout after being removed from the game immediately afterward, and when he did what he always does when he allows a hit: He yelled profanity into his glove, mad at himself, mad at bad luck, mad at the other team, and a little bit mad at Moch.

That's what Matt Kavanaugh was in a position to overhear from the Pacifics' third-base coach's box, and that's what Kavanaugh made sure to tell Moch about after the game, which is why I arrive the next day and hear screaming in the clubhouse, so exaggerated and over the top I assume I'm hearing horseplay or video games. But what I see upon taking one step into (and immediately one step back out of) the clubhouse is actually Mochizuki bent down and screaming at Schwieger. He calls him a bitch, he tells him to fight him right here and right now, he picks up a chair, and for a second I think he's going to assault his teammate with it in front of everybody. Mercifully, the chair is just for emphasis, and he lifts it up over his head to slam it into the ceiling and then onto the ground. Schwieg, meanwhile, stares blankly at the floor, refusing to escalate against a player who, by now, some of the team considers a cancer.

When Fehlandt addresses the team after the game—a loss, our third in a row—he makes it clear to everybody that, no, you should not be starting fights with your teammates, so cut that out. "If we're fighting in here, we're not fighting them out there," he says, as twenty pairs of eyes focus on him. There's one pair of eyes that doesn't. Mochizuki has his back to the manager and is leaning on a knee and shoveling spaghetti and salad into his mouth. It looks—to me—like blatant disrespect. If it looks like that to me, then I know it looks that way to much of the team.

Fehball.

Ben, Theo, and I wonder what can be done. I vote that Moch has to go; he scares me. Theo and Ben prefer to release Miranda, because we don't have another shortstop but we do have another second baseman, Yuki Yasuda. Yasuda, who records every pitch he sees in a spreadsheet, never gives away an at-bat, and only swings at strikes, has played extremely well but rarely gets to start, partly out of veteran deference, partly because Fehlandt doesn't like to change his lineup, and partly perhaps because Fehlandt never trusted him. ("Do I really have to keep the Japanese guy?" he asked us after *the first day* of spring training.) Yuki is frustrated. He's been talking quietly with Yoshi about finding another opportunity in that great big world of shitty baseball teams.

Ultimately, we decide that Theo has to tell Fehlandt what the perception is; even he will see the problem if he realizes that he's losing the team because of this perceived favoritism. When Theo talks to him, Fehlandt agrees. He calls Sergio in for a meeting and releases him, and our Opening Day lineup is down by one man. San Rafael immediately signs him. ("That's just a classic San Rafael move," Tommy Lyons says.)

Five days later, Sean starts again. Nobody's quite sure why; Sean got a call saying he'd start, so he did. He pitches brilliantly. We're leading 3-1 going to the ninth. Because Sean is our closer—and thus today we don't *have* a closer—he goes back out for the ninth. The first batter reaches on an error, and everything unravels, first against Sean and then against Paul Hvozdovic, who relieves but is not the closer (because the closer is the closer). We lose 7-3: proof, Feh insists, that we need a closer more than a starter. So Sean's back in the bullpen. Now we're 20-10, with a three-game lead and just nine games left in the first half, but it feels as if we might never win again.

Meetings get called. Fehlandt brings the team together in the clubhouse to remind everybody to hit their spots and have a plan at the plate and just trust their talent. Mochizuki interrupts.

"Can I say one quick thing?" he says. "You know before we started in spring training like I didn't think we were gonna go fucking—our record? Did you guys think that, no? I, we fucking were kind of nervous, okay, and then we started winning games and winning games when that built us to how we think we are, when in reality we aren't shit. The reason why we fucking got this record was (1) lucky, (2) we put ourselves in good position, and (3) we fucking with this you know just trying to do our best. We got lucky, we won a couple games as a team, and that's why we got our record."

As Fehlandt and Isaac try to wrestle the floor away from this, Moch persists—"We need to just fuck what we did like fuck it and just be like I'm just saying and go about it like it's a brand-new season that just . . ."

And that's that meeting.

Then Eric Gullotta calls Theo and Ben into his law office to find out why his team is collapsing. "The best team doesn't always win," Theo tries to explain. "Right now we're not the best team. We're not playing like a good team."

"What about Feh?" Eric asks. "At what point do you draw the line in the sand, if not for Feh, for yourself? Because I hold you accountable for Feh's decisions."

"If I hadn't seen any growth or progress in how he's coming to conclusions this would be a much direr situation," Theo says. But he also adds, "It could not work. He could just not be cut out to manage. I don't think that's off the table."

It doesn't help that Fehlandt, whose former teammates in the Mexican League called him "Ferrari Lamborghini," hasn't lost his high-performance temper, which still goes 0–60 in seconds. "Don't tell me where I got touched on my body!" he shouts at one umpire who calls him out on a pickoff attempt. "There's no guessing in baseball." The next day, he leaps off the bench in San Rafael to argue a call, kicking the dirt the ump has just kicked off the plate right back onto it, then detouring to argue with the field ump before returning to the plate and taking a 360-degree crab walk around it, using his hands to pile dirt onto the dish from every direction. When the ump runs him, he complains about how awkward it is to get ejected in the Pacific Association: With no showers and cramped clubhouses, there's nowhere to go let off steam. Worse, when he gets ejected it leaves a hole in our lineup and forces one of our backup infielders to play the outfield.

In fairness to Fehlandt, some Pacific Association umpires are awful: One guy holds his chest protector in front of him like a shield when he's behind home plate, and another stands well behind the catcher and steps *back* as the pitch approaches. (The latter once called ball four on a two-strike pitch Kristian Gayday actually swung at and tipped, as our whole bench said "Foul!" in unison.) Few of the umps make an effort to defuse conflicts. But Feh's explosions are impotent and pointless, raising the team's temperature without a corresponding rise in morale. Even when his anger is directed inward, it's a distraction. During another game in Pittsburg, Feh makes a weak out, comes back to the dugout, and pounds his bat on the bench. Moch, one of the few players with the edge required to talk to Feh when he's hulking out, calls out from the on-deck circle, "Someone doing carpentry over there?"

Feh turns that temper on me, Ben, and Theo in a meeting in the dugout during batting practice shortly after the conversation in Eric's office. We've reached a deadlock on how to use Sean. We're going to try one last time to make it clear how much we, Feh's bosses, want to see him do something different.

"But you're asking me to go against something that my whole career has taught me," Feh says. "I'm in a damned manager role right now. I've almost fucking died out there a million times as a player, and now I get to have a say, and you're trying to tell me that it's not that important. You can't not have a lights-out guy in the closer role."

"I know the value of the closer is obvious," I say, "and that every coach has told you that—"

"It's what *the game* has taught me."

"And that's fair. But no time in history has the team's best starter been the closer. Nobody tried to make Roger Clemens the closer."

"Everything was great and then one bad week and all of a sudden we have to take the closer out of his role," Feh says.

Ben jumps in. "It's not a response to—"

"But that's what it looks like!"

Ben lets out a sickly groan: *Eeeohgggh.*

"Whatever you think it looks like, to everyone out there it's not a good move," Fehlandt continues. "Guys, listen: I'm not going to fucking take the closer out. Every game this week has shown me that you need a fucking closer. We lost one and then they just lost one and I feel like those games happened to make the fucking point. How demoralizing it is for the fucking starter to give it up because he doesn't have somebody shut the fucking door. You guys don't fucking—I can't have this talk anymore." He walks away, yelling at the sky. "This is Baseball 101. This is just Baseball 101 because you haven't fucking played it."

In the game later that evening, Fehlandt lasts three pitches into his first-inning at-bat. After a first-pitch ball, he takes a strike on a reasonable call that he's convinced is a crime. Fuming, he chases the 1-1 and then says something to the umpire that ends his day. The ump ejects him, and Feh gives him hell at home plate, treating the grandstand to the full extent of his profane firepower. Eventually he returns to the dugout, grabs his gear, and heads for the clubhouse. Just like we had hours earlier, we watch him walk away, yelling even louder than the last time.

PULLING THE TRIGGER

After the failed dugout meeting, the early Lentini ejection, and the Stompers' third straight loss, Theo and I are restless. Normally, we would grimace and go our separate ways: I would walk home, and he would drive home to Santa Rosa or go back to the office to count tickets sold. ("Not enough" is the usual total.) But tonight we want to talk, so we drive to La Casa, a Mexican restaurant just off the town square. This eventful day isn't done.

We like La Casa because it's open late (by Sonoma standards), the staff is friendly, and the food comes quickly. We're also fond of the painting in the corner farthest from the door. A young Mexican girl in colorful clothes sits on a blanket, barefoot, gazing out at the viewer. Behind her is a pile of unshelled peas and two older women, maybe her mother and grandmother. The grandmother looks forlorn; the mother holds out a hand, palm up, as if asking for aid. The girl is supposed to seem similarly sad and beseeching. But the slight tilt of her head and the purse of her lips, and the way her left eyebrow lifts up, make her seem exasperated, disappointed that we haven't done better. It's an expression we've gotten used to seeing this summer, so we feel at ease while she sits in silent judgment, an instant away from an eye roll.

Jessie and a few friends are on their way out when Theo and I arrive. We're too late to eat, but we stay for a drink—green tea for me and a Diet Coke for Theo, because that's the way we roll. My only agenda is to blow off some steam, so I tell Jessie how things went with Feh while she makes sympathetic sounds. I'm glad we talked to Feh, I explain, but also discouraged because I can't see a way to work things out. A willingness to talk is the minimum we want from our manager, and Feh failed that test. Even a civil discussion made him flustered enough to exit dugout left.

"I wish you were the manager," I tell Theo. It's a frequent first-half refrain, at this point more pie in the sky than real request. But to my surprise, Theo doesn't dismiss the idea with his usual smile and self-deprecating comment. Instead he says, "Me too," and starts listing logistical concerns: Would he have time? Would the players support him? Would Erin leave him for a less baseball-obsessed spouse? And in that moment, my motivation changes, the way it did at the moment all of this started, when Sam and I told Dan Evans that we would take a team, and he actually considered it.

This is my second chance to get Feh fired. The first came in March, when the soon-to-be-manager was on thin ice for his inflammatory Facebook posts. Instead of lying low, he created another account under an alias, Franklin Fettuccini, whose profile picture was a naked boy swinging a bat with a helmet on his head and nothing below that blurred out. It occurred to me then that a guy who couldn't abide by his boss's orders about Facebook probably wouldn't welcome our input about baseball. When Theo set up a conference call to ask Sam and me whether we thought Feh deserved to be fired, I was tempted to drop the hammer. But I'd met him only once, and I'd found him friendly, and I didn't know enough about him to put him out of a job, even if he'd have no trouble finding another in a higher league. Instead, I said something wishy-washy, and Feh escaped the ax.

This time, I'm coming at the king. The dugout fight and the latest early ejection have cleared my conscience. For one thing, our failure to communicate clearly isn't all our fault. Negotiations have failed, but only because Feh walked away from the table. For another, firing Feh no longer feels like a self-serving power play. He's always been in *our* way, but, before, the franchise was fine. Now, though, he's the distraction that Sean never came close to becoming, terrorizing umpires, putting his temper ahead of the team, and disturbing the peace at family-friendly Arnold Field with salvos of highly audible swear words. Lastly, either age or the demands of managing have made Feh's on-field performance more dispensable than we expected. He's hitting .289/.345/.459: very good, but far from the transcendent slash lines in our preseason predictions. He's been worse than our average hitter. We could live without that bat, and Hibb could handle center.

Like a captive hero held at gunpoint, stalling until he can turn the tables, I try to keep Theo talking. On the way to his car, we take a detour to see the Stompers' old office from the pre-Eric, even-more-microscopic-payroll days; Theo tries the door and discovers it's locked. I suggest a nightcap, so we drive to Safeway, buy a bottle of wine, and bring it back to my house. When we get there, Theo takes out a tin of dip, a guilty pleasure from his ball-playing days, and grabs an empty can of garbanzo beans from the kitchen counter to use as a juice receptacle. "You're not allowed to tell Erin about this," he says. (If Erin is reading, the statute of limitations has expired.)

We light a Duraflame log on the stove and bring it to the backyard, where we gather around a small circular table. I carry a speaker outside and DJ while we talk; my first song selection is "Mr. Manager" by Badfinger. (Subtlety isn't my strong suit.) On-the-nose song aside, I don't push too hard, because I don't want to make Theo more stressed than he already is. He's juggling a number of competing pressures, on top of the usual conflict between his personal life and baseball's all-consuming summer schedule. Eric is upset with him because the Stompers aren't undefeated. Feh is upset with him because two statheads are meddling in managerial business. I'm upset because our meddling hasn't made more of a difference. Theo is no more fond of confrontation than we are, and thus far he's been more of a mediator than a manager. It's not in his nature to lay down the law.

I'm elated at the thought of having a manager who'll go along with (and actually agree with) what we advise. Theo says he's simultaneously thrilled and terrified. I try to tamp down his terror by pointing out that there's precedent for gaps in the wall separating front office from field staff. Manager/GMs were once common in the majors, lingering into the early 1980s, when Whitey Herzog served in both capacities for the St. Louis Cardinals. And in mid-May of *this season*, the Miami Marlins moved GM Dan Jennings into the manager's office. Granted, the Marlins are far from a model franchise, and the move made them an object of (even more) ridicule. But the players went about their business and, instead of cratering, the team's winning percentage rose slightly, from .421 under their ex-manager, former major leaguer Mike Redmond, to .444 under the intruder from upstairs. Theo is well liked by most members of the team, and even if some of the Stompers aren't pleased with the switch, what's the worst that could happen in six weeks?

We touch on other subjects, but the conversation keeps circling back to Feh, each time coming closer to a real resolution. Theo says he's sick of his own insecurity. He's been depriving himself all summer—he's on a diet, and I've yet to see him consume a solid calorie—and now he's tempted to treat himself, to take a chance despite his misgivings. Eventually, hours after we left La Casa, he acquiesces: If Eric approves, he'll take over for Feh. I wish I could ask for a sworn statement: I'm afraid that if I don't pin him down, he'll come to his senses once his tobacco high wears off. Instead, I ask him for Eric's number and tell him I'm going to get the Gullotta blessing in the morning. It's still a few days away from Perseid season, but before Theo leaves we see a shooting star, which primitive cultures would have interpreted as an omen of upheaval. I'm hoping they would have been right.

In the morning, I call Sam and fill him in on the La Casa coup. He has no objections to a transfer of power. After we hang up, he sends me a text: "This idea excites me to the point that now I will be devastated if it doesn't happen." I forward it to Theo to fend off cold feet. "At the end of the year, I'm going to lie and tell Feh he was fired for kicking me out of kangaroo court," Sam adds. He also points out that, if possible, we should trade Feh to another league; if we release him, the Pacifics will sign him in a second, the way they did with Sergio Miranda. We don't want Feh with us, but we don't want him against us, either.

A little after nine, I text Eric and ask if he has time to talk. "Of course," he says, after an agonizing wait. "Call me in 30 min?" I spend the time mentally polishing my script, adding imaginary bullet points in favor of firing Feh. Lack of discipline. Double standards. Quick temper. Doesn't work well with others. Makes scenes. Not fan-friendly. And the big finish: Theo and Sam and I have discussed it, and we're all agreed. I decide that I don't need to remind him about the bad Facebook behavior, the near-collision with his wife's car, or the suspicious odor that wafts from the team van whenever Feh is inside.

Thirty seconds and two bullet points into the call, it's clear that I hardly had to rehearse. Getting Eric's assent is by far the easiest part of the process. He's no fan of Feh, and he says he'll support whatever we want to do. The only caveat is that he'll have to talk to Theo about how the team's tiny staff would handle the business side of the Stompers if the GM is in the dugout for hours a day.

I call Theo to tell him Eric is on board, and he reveals that his wife has endorsed the idea. Then, a day later, he backs out, as I'd worried he would. He's thought about what it would mean for his family if he were the manager: all the road games in Vallejo and Pittsburg, the hours even longer and more stressful than those he already logs. He can't do it. But Yoshi, the coach Kristian Gayday once described as "our baseball Yoda," who was so enthusiastic about our "evidences" before Opening Day, can do the job. Yoshi represents progress: We'll have a manager who (we hope) will actually want to hear what we can add. This wasn't our first choice, but it's a victory.

The only remaining impediment is the fact that Feh is still a Stomper. With Theo's blessing, I email Arizona Diamondbacks scout Chris Carminucci, whose travels around the independent leagues give him an encyclopedic knowledge of team needs, making him the perfect facilitator. "I will pass this along to a few teams," Chris says. "I know Ricky VanAsselberg in the Atlantic League may be looking for an offensive type guy." This sounds like a fit; Feh is a recent Atlantic Leaguer, and he's offensive in more ways than one. Sixteen minutes later, I get a text from Theo. "Ricky wants him," he says.

Holy hell, this is happening. We're in first place, a few days away from a first-half title, and we're firing Feh.

Before the home game against Vallejo that night, Eric and Theo huddle with the Stompers' dead manager walking in Feh's office. When the meeting breaks up, Feh storms out of the clubhouse without a word, and Theo addresses the team, looking sterner than I've ever seen him. In a brief speech, he tells the Stompers that Feh has been suspended because of his conduct toward umpires, and that Yoshi will take over in his absence. Theo doesn't mention that he's using the suspension to stall while he puts the finishing touches on a trade with VanAsselberg's team, the Bridgeport Bluefish.

The game must go on. Hibbert slides over to center and goes 3-for-4. Baps crushes a line-drive home run, lifting his average to .339, fourth-best in the league. Schwieger makes his best start of the season, striking out nine over eight innings. We win, 9-2. It's the most runs the Stompers have scored in nine days, and multiple players remark that the mood in the dugout is looser than they've felt it in weeks. No one makes any inspiring speeches about winning this one for Feh. If anyone minds that the manager is missing, they keep their complaints quiet.

The next day, Sunday, is the Stompers' first chance to clinch the first half. By the fifth inning, both the game and the title seem well in hand. Gregory Paulino is throwing a shutout, we've scored a few runs, and we're rallying for more. Meanwhile, our manager is serving out his suspension in a white utility truck on the far side of the center-field wall. Sam, in the dugout, takes out the binoculars that we bought for still-unspecified scouting purposes and sees two guys standing on the bed of the truck—Feh and his old rap partner. "He was there yesterday, too," Paul Hvozdovic tells him. Sam grabs his notebook and walks out to see the suspended manager.

"Whoa, bad timing," Feh says when he sees Sam, who suspects that he's just taken a hit. (Our team smokes *so* much weed.) Sam asks him how he feels about the summer so far, and Feh confides that he's been in some miserable leagues. He's been in clubhouses that weren't this loose, he's dealt with asshole team veterans and asshole ornery coaches, and he's stayed in cities where teams told their players it was too dangerous to walk the four blocks back home after the games. He's been in leagues whose seasons were twice as long as this one, but that had so few teams that he'd end up playing the same team a dozen games in a row. Once in the Atlantic League his team was out of the pennant race and had to spend the entire last month of the season playing Bridgeport—the same Bridgeport where we're currently trying to trade him.

"And that's the worst place to play," he says. "We're just in hell for the whole month of September, just there playing at the worst place over and over. Bridgeport's the hood. And the port, where the ferry comes in, in right-center field and center field it's just that whole industrial center that's the backdrop. It's just a shithole. No fans come."

Sonoma has been better than that. He's been back at home, been a mentor to a number of players who have thrived under his hitting advice, been a friend to players who go over to his house and (we're told) smoke weed with him between batting practice and the game. His sister got a job with the Stompers. His mom sometimes sat in the front row behind home plate. We started 18-3, and everybody left him alone, but since then—man, he doesn't know. He's not even sure if he's going to run out there and dogpile with the players if we win this game, which seems all but certain. (The score is now 6-0.)

One thing Feh says to Sam is revealing: "The only person who can back me up and support me is Theo." He never understood that Sam and I could have been the support. That we were making decisions, that we were vacuuming up information to make those decisions, and that we could have been his allies, with actual power that could have augmented his own. I remember a scene from the second game of the season, when Feh dropped his glasses in the dirt and then wiped them, without asking, on my sleeve. I had hoped in that moment that the gesture would symbolize a symbiotic relationship: Feh, on the field, getting dirty and doing the actual work, and Sam and me as sideline resources, helping him see clearly. And now I know what Feh was thinking: *Hey, look, somebody's sleeve.*

"So we've had an issue here financially," Theo tells Feh in Theo's office, two hours and seven runs later and forty-five minutes after we all dog-piled (and yes, Feh did dogpile with us) and drank champagne from the bottle. "We need to unload payroll, you're the most valuable guy."

"Sweet."

"You're gonna go to Bridgeport. VanAsselberg wants you. They need an outfielder."

"No, I'm not going to Bridgeport."

"You're not going to Bridgeport?"

"No, I'm not going to Bridgeport. No chance. I get to choose where I can go. There's no way I'm going to Bridgeport. That's the worst place in the league, there's no chance."

"I thought you'd appreciate the opportunity—"

"I can get my own opportunities. Yeah. I'm outta here. I don't even want to . . ."

He picks up his check and walks out. We hear him walking farther down the hallway, and then Fehlandt gets the final word:

"Hi-*LAR*-ious."

We're happy to let him have it. After struggling to make small changes for half a season, we're making the biggest change of all.

Feh's firing removes the two obstacles preventing me from telling Taylor Eads, my still-unsigned crush from Spring Hill College, to come west: the manager's resistance to change and the lack of room on the roster. Not only is there now room on the roster, there's also room in the outfield, where Eads plays. For me, the prospect of Taylor taking Feh's roster spot is deliciously sweet, although the perception that he's filling Feh's role on the roster will put extra pressure on him to perform.

By this time, the other undrafted gems from the class of 2015 have given me more reason to trust Taylor's ranking. Nick Sell homers in his first pro at-bat, makes the Pioneer League all-star team, and posts a .347/.401/.629 line at that level before earning a promotion to A ball, where he goes 5-for-5 with a homer in his third game. Collins Cuthrell carries an OPS over 1.000 into July; he'll finish second on his team in homers, one bomb behind a twenty-five-year-old with affiliated experience. Eads was sandwiched between the two of them on our spreadsheet, but he's still languishing on the proverbial waiver wire.

Late on July 11—the night before the Stompers clinch the first-half title and Feh finds out he's been traded—I send a cathartic text to Eads, which marks the first direct contact between us. "This is Ben Lindbergh from the Sonoma Stompers," I type, my fingers stroking the keyboard as seductively as possible. "Could you give me a call when you get this?" The next morning, the response arrives. "Yes sir I'll call you in about a hour or so after breakfast," he says. Coach Sims wasn't kidding when he called Taylor "the yes sir no sir type."

Each of us has imagined this moment for a month, but our actual conversation is quick. I say I'm sorry to have strung him along. In his sped-up drawl, he says he's happy to have the opportunity. I say he'll be starting as soon as he gets to Sonoma. He says he'll look at flights. Not long after we express our mutual excitement and hang up, he texts again to say, "Just booked my flight sir and I'll be in San Francisco at 11:30 tomorrow morning." Another "sir": This is what it would look like if Marcie texted Peppermint Patty. Most players ask if the Stompers pay for transportation, or confirm their flight details before they book to make sure someone will meet them at the airport. Money is tight for Taylor—his family is just getting back on its feet after Hurricane Katrina and his parents' divorce, and he's on scholarship at Spring Hill, where he's struggled to buy his books—but he isn't going to ask about specifics and give me a chance to change my mind. At this point, he's probably willing to walk from SFO to Sonoma.

The next day, Tim Livingston and I drive to San Francisco to pick him up. He's a quarter of an inch under six feet but powerfully built, with Andrew Parker–sized forearms. He says the flight was smooth, although he has no frame of reference: This was his first time in an airplane, and it's also his first time west of San Antonio. Like any tourist on an inaugural visit to the Bay Area, he leans forward to take pictures when we cross the Golden Gate Bridge and reflexively defends his hometown burgers when we stop for In-N-Out.

Taylor hasn't played since Spring Hill's last game on April 21, which means he has to shake off almost two months of atrophy from virtual retirement. When the White Sox workout didn't lead to an offer, he says, he "kinda just shut it down." He dropped weight, thinking there was "no reason to be heavy anymore." He worked construction and went a month without hitting, until Coach McCall told him to expect a text from me. Then he spent some time at a batting cage, a poor substitute for live pitching. He has three games to get his groove back before the second half starts and the wins and losses once again count toward the standings.

My anticipation of Taylor's debut is tempered by my embarrassment about being way off on Mark Hurley. The day after my email exchange with Feh about Eads, in which Feh predicted that Hurley was about to break out, Hurley hit a two-run homer—his first of the season—in a game against Vallejo that the Stompers won 8-7. I was in the dugout, and as Hurley crossed the plate I turned to make eye contact with Feh, prepared to take my medicine. He cackled and came over to give me a pound.

By July 14, the day Taylor debuts in the six hole, Hurley is hitting cleanup. He's earned it: A 3-for-6 showing in the previous game has raised his seasonal line to .315/.382/.438. And he's about to embark on his hottest streak of the season. From July 16 to July 18, Hurley has the following sequence of twelve plate appearances:

Single, hit by pitch, single, strikeout, reach on error, single, double, single, single, single, single, double

That's eleven of twelve trips to the plate without making an out, including eight in a row. For a few hours on the eighteenth, I think there may be a way to restore some of my pride by claiming partial credit for

Hurley's hot streak. Before the game, he asks to see video of Vallejo's
starter, and I joke that he doesn't need the help, since he's coming off a
5-for-5 night. "This is why," he says, pointing to my laptop. Those three
words justify all the hours of game logging and video editing: Our hottest hitter attributes his hotness to us! I show Hurley video of Admirals
righty Scott Weinschenk, who Sam says is starting. But when I get to
the game, I discover that southpaw Devon Ramirez is starting instead.
(We would pay a small fortune for an accurate "probable starters" page
for the Pacific Association.) Hurley goes 2-for-5 with a double anyway.
Maybe my laptop is overrated. (Weinschenk starts the next day, and
Hurley singles and doubles in two at-bats against him. I am taking credit
for those.)

   With that two-hit game—one month to the day that I tried to tell Feh
that Hurley was our weak point—Hurley reaches his high-water mark
for the season, riding a fifteen-game hitting streak with nine multihit
games in his last thirteen. His slash line stands at .350/.410/.497, good
for a 174 wRC+, which makes him the third-best hitter in the Pacific
Association on a per-plate-appearance basis.

   This is persuasive evidence that I'm stupid. After a sixth of the season, I wanted to bench the guy who's been the best hitter on our team
in the first half. I've spent weeks bemoaning Feh's interference, but
in this case, deferring to Feh saved me from making a major mistake.
Lately, I've been thinking of trading Feh as our *Moneyball* moment, a
cousin to the scene in Michael Lewis's book in which GM Billy Beane,
irked by manager Art Howe's insistence on starting the scout-certified
prospect Carlos Peña instead of the undervalued on-base machine
Scott Hatteberg in 2002, trades Peña to the Tigers so that Howe's
hands will be tied. (We did Billy one better: In our version, he would
have traded *Howe* to the Tigers.) What *Moneyball* omits is that Peña hit
almost as well as Hatteberg down the stretch in '02, then outplayed
him in each of Hatteberg's three subsequent seasons in Oakland and
eventually blossomed into an all-star, a Gold Glover, a home run king,
and a two-time top-ten MVP finisher. Sometimes the scouts are right.
Either I lacked the experience to see what Feh saw in Hurley or I was

blinded by confirmation bias, duped by my preconceived notions into believing the small-sample stats.

I've also overlooked some nonstatistical factors. Even before his debut, Taylor's presence has become a clubhouse flash point. He's more obviously "our guy" than the spreadsheet recruits who've been here since spring training, and there's some grumbling about his signing that we didn't foresee. Every veteran, it seems, knows someone they'd rather we'd signed than an unproven rookie from Louisiana with gaudy college stats. Matt Hibbert has a friend from Cal State Long Beach, Brennan Metzger, who was recently released from San Jose, the Giants' high-A affiliate. Isaac Wenrich has a friend from San Diego who was released from the Indians' high-A affiliate in 2012 and hasn't played professionally since 2013. Both of them wonder why we signed an unknown when we could have brought in one of their buddies instead. I feel like a frustrated father, who, tormented by backtalk from his kids, loses his cool and declares, "This isn't a democracy."

Outside the sports industry, it's not the norm for employees to dictate hiring decisions: CEOs don't distribute company-wide surveys when they want to replace a sales rep, and editors in chief don't get the go-ahead from everyone on the masthead before bringing in a contributing writer. But "pro athlete" is different from most jobs, in that players see each other naked, cope with pressure from fans, and depend to a greater degree on complementary skills and communication styles (although that's debatable in baseball, compared to more free-flowing sports). It makes sense to give players some say in vetoing potential problems like Will Price, particularly if the potential problem tries to pull every pitch. But the spreadsheet is impartial, whereas a player may care more about doing a favor for a friend (or gaining a good drinking buddy) than scouring the country for the best option available.

One would think that our team would be more receptive to rookies, since we wouldn't be where we are without them. In fact, they're our defining feature. Halfway through the season, each club's identity has crystallized in my mind. The San Rafael Pacifics, who have the most former members of higher-level leagues, are the oldest, biggest, and most balding. Led by Matt Kavanaugh, who's never not rocking his wrap-around Oakleys, they're the better-equipped bullies from an '80s ski comedy, baseball meets *Better Off Dead*. They live and breathe big league, from their fancy pullovers to their midgame celebrity autograph signings. The Pittsburg Diamonds are the most ragtag, the team with the worst website, the most typos on Facebook, and the latest-posted lineup cards; their best hitter, Scott David, wears three different numbers on the front of his jersey, back of his jersey, and batting helmet, and they shamelessly copy the Stompers' Jose Canseco publicity stunt by signing Canseco themselves. The Admirals are aggressive, attempting to steal and bunt the most often. They're also the team with the most off-brand MLB bloodlines: Their manager is Garry Templeton Jr., and their roster features the brothers of Brandon Phillips and Javier Baez (P. J. and Gadiel), and the son of Lloyd Moseby (Lydell). Naturally, they trade for Tyger Pederson, too. We're the team with the Corduroy Crew, and our roster takes after our inexperience. Weighted by playing time, the Stompers have the league's lowest average age and the highest percentage of players in their first professional season.

Team	Age	% 1st-Year Players
Pacifics	26.2	16.0
Diamonds	25.7	17.3
Admirals	25.3	30.3
Stompers	25.2	30.8

Yet despite our rookies' valuable contributions, the Stompers' elders tend to focus on their flaws. It's a mental block they almost can't be blamed for, a condition neither Sam nor I can correct. As talented as our young players are, they inevitably make mistakes—by definition, the most damning kind, *rookie* mistakes. And whenever one of these errors occurs, a veteran is waiting with an "I told you so," either spoken or strongly implied. It's the latest skirmish in the longest-running battle in baseball, a Darwinian struggle for roster spots in which each rookie's rise comes at an older player's expense.

Before he meets Taylor, Captain Morgan—who never misses a chance to badmouth the Stompers' front office—asks Sam the question we've grappled with from the start: "If Eads is so good, why is he available to us?" While Sam and I ask (and attempt to answer) that question about all our recruits, Captain sees it as an argument ender. By that standard, we might as well cut our entire team. At this level, we have to take other leagues' leavings and like it.

We know it will take time to determine Taylor's true talent level, but our lives will be easier if he impresses right away. Sadly, his mechanics are the wrong kind of eye-catching, which means he's most convincing as a slugger when he's standing still. "The showcases don't really help me out too much," he says, echoing what we heard from Sean Conroy. "I don't have the blazing speed or the cannon of an arm, so I don't stand out at those. I have to play the game." We can testify to his unimpressive appearance. In BP, he doesn't drive the ball or even look as if he could. His swing, with its one-handed release, is all upper body, with none of the separation that leads to torque and power. His warm-up hacks are worse: He starts his slowed-down practice swings at shoulder height, then angles them upward, as if he's trying to meet a piñata or a ball being thrown by someone standing on Randy Johnson's shoulders. His throws are equally inelegant: His windup has a hitch unlike any other I've seen, a weird wasted movement that robs his arm of momentum and makes my shoulder sore when I try to mimic it in a mirror. I'm hoping he's the Stompers' Millennium Falcon, an apparent piece of junk with concealed capabilities. He hit .538 somehow.

"I felt like through college, I put everything in that I had to do to get a draft call, or get this call, and it paid off," he says. "I've always needed one shot, and I feel like I'm gonna take advantage of it." If he doesn't, it's our asses.

Eads couldn't have asked for a softer landing. In his first game, he faces the worst starter on the worst team in the league, Admirals lefty Nick Flory, who enters the game with a league-leading ten homers allowed, three more than anyone else. He acquits himself adequately at the plate, whiffing twice, walking twice, and scoring a run. No one expects his timing to be perfect, but his patience is as advertised. He sees twenty-one pitches, backing up Chris Long's claim that he'd wear out opposing pitchers.

Unfortunately, Eads's offense is an afterthought, overshadowed by a few frantic seconds in right field. He has no trouble with his first fielding chance, a low liner right at him for the first out of the fifth, but three batters later, with two outs and a runner on first, his rust is exposed. He breaks in on a fly ball, then realizes that it's caught in the wind. He backpedals furiously but drops the ball, looking incredibly uncoordinated. It's a two-base error, and an Admirals run scores. Taylor seems completely out of his element. Watching the play, I want to slip out of the stadium; I can't imagine how *he* feels. When he gets back to the dugout, head down, Sam tries to comfort him with some words about the wind, but he barely responds. "Oh, God, that was bad," he tells us days later at lunch. "I don't know if I ever really played a game where it was that windy. It doesn't get windy like that back at home."

The next day, Eads goes 0-for-3, and his outfield issues recur, this time in left. In the second inning, Admirals third baseman Josh Wong sends a catchable ball toward Taylor. Shortstop Yuki Yasuda goes out, and tentatively, Taylor runs in, but the ball drops. He doesn't get a glove on it, so it's scored a hit, but it's an E-7 in the minds of everyone watching. "I'm not used to playing with these players, and I was playing deep, and on that one I figured the shortstop was going to get back," he explains at lunch. In isolation, it's an understandable screwup between a Japanese-speaker and a guy in his second game after a long layoff, the way the first mistake was an understandable screwup caused by a swirling wind. But two understandable screwups in quick succession start to look like a pattern, particularly when the skeptics are watching for weakness.

The next afternoon, I get a text from Feh, whom I haven't talked to in a week. "Way to not listen to a lifetime of baseball knowledge!" he says. "Nice decision with the Eads pickup! I heard he can't even catch a fly ball!"

Over the next two hours, he sends me literally twenty more texts, most of them variations on this theme. The digitized I-told-you-sos march down my screen, mocking my naïveté.

"I've been planning a book on my career for years now and you have given me one of the best chapters ever! Hahahaha."

"When people want to sell their guys they are going to sell the shit out of them. Very rarely is what you hear actually what you get."

"The scouting report you gave me sounded way too good to be true."

"If those numbers were really that related to his ability he would have gotten a job somewhere else."

"Pitchers have a far greater chance of success than a position player because there is so much more to being a position player."

"When you see numbers like his and nothing came of it, then something is off."

"Usually guys that haven't played in that long don't get picked up midseason because in indy ball people don't get that kind of time outside of spring training."

(Forty-three minutes elapse.)

"You should ask the other players and manager what they think so far I heard it wasn't good."

(Fifty-four more minutes elapse.)

"Just remember, you wanted me to dump Hurley for that guy when we were 11-2."

He wraps up by comping Eads to Chris Burke, a former teammate of his in the Astros' system who was drafted tenth overall but never amounted to much in the majors, thanks to what Feh says was a swing built for aluminum bats. I take the high road, knowing he has every right to rub it in now but hoping I'll get to gloat later.

For me, every Eads fielding opportunity and plate appearance after the text barrage from Feh is like a mini–*Breaking Bad* finale. The stakes are so high that the rest of the game feels like filler. Taylor strikes out swinging in his first at-bat of game three, but he tells me he's seeing the ball well and hopes to hit a couple hard. He snaps his 0-for-6 streak his next time up, swinging at the first pitch and bouncing a grounder through the middle to score Hurley from second. My smile is wider than his.

There's little time to enjoy the hit before the next defensive crisis. The first batter in the bottom of the inning lifts a fly to left that tails toward the corner. The ball bounces off the palm of Taylor's glove, then off and finally into the palm of his bare right hand as he slides feet-first. He's greeted good-naturedly when he gets back to the dugout, but I'm aware of how disastrous a different ricochet could've been.

In the top of the fifth, Taylor makes up for the scare with a two-out, bases-loaded ground rule double to the right-center-field gap, scoring two runs. I will the ball not to be hit to him for the final few innings, and Vallejo's hitters comply. His third game ends on a high note, and the Stompers' first half ends with a sweep. Eads's error, misplay, and bobble did no damage, and he's shown he can hit. And the Stompers are now 26-11 with a +72 run differential, the only team in the league with a record over .500.

By game 4 of the Eads era, some players are starting to come around. During one of Taylor's at-bats, Sam and Andrew Parker are at the dugout railing, discussing Collin Forgey, Sean Conroy's spring-training roommate, who was one of our first cuts because he rubbed Feh and Theo the wrong way. Parker had been a believer that Forgey could play. "But he wasn't as good as this guy is," Parker says, pointing to Taylor, whose outfield misplays still outnumber his hits.

Erik Gonsalves chimes in. "I sense a bit of sarcasm there?"

"No way, this guy is super legit," Parker says. "That guy is such a ballplayer, he doesn't even dip. He just eats the tin." Gonzo still can't tell if he's serious.

"Look," Parker continues, "if it looks like a duck and it quacks like a duck, it's a duck, right? So this guy looks like a ballplayer, he's a ballplayer."

Taylor doubles again that day, one of twenty Stompers hits in a strange 16-5 loss. (No major league team has ever scored so few runs despite so many hits.) I'm in San Rafael, and Sam texts me Eads's slash line, presented without comment: ".272/.429/.454." The next day, Yoshi calls a team meeting before the players leave for Vallejo. He tells the rookies to talk to the veterans, and reminds them that they should be putting in extra practice and asking for advice. Isaac, Hibbert, Moch,

Walker, and Carranza chime in to say the same thing. Yoshi tells Sam that Eads didn't display enough remorse for his misplays, which strikes us as silly. Essentially, he's asking for eyewash, a more public display of penitence. We know Taylor felt terrible, and he always shows up early to take flies and hit buckets of balls.

If the criticism was intended for him, Taylor responds, going 2-for-2 with three walks and three steals—more than he had in his whole senior season at Spring Hill, where Coach Sims wouldn't give him the green light. This time, Sam texts ".500 obp." On the nineteenth, as Taylor goes 3-for-3 with three doubles, a walk, and a sacrifice fly, Sam texts ".353/.521/.588," then ".388/.520/.611," then ".421/.538/.684," and finally ".421/.555/.684." Sam has a limited texting plan and uses his messages sparingly, so this onslaught is a sign that he's as excited as I am. The doubles are sprayed to all fields—line drive to right-center, grounder down the right-field line, liner to left-center—and the resulting stats are Spring Hill–esque. Nothing Taylor does before games looks good, but at the moment he makes contact off live pitching, we can see the hitter who produced eye-popping numbers. His calloused bare hands blur—he doesn't wear batting gloves, because he "got tired of buying them"—and his wrists flick, and the ball soars somewhere, harder than anything he hits in batting practice.

Each time Eads gets on base or makes a catch (which he now does without incident), Parker looks at Sam and says, "Quaaack."

"It's tough joining the team halfway through their year, and it's like, 'Oh, here's a new guy,' and the next thing you know I dropped a fly ball and I'm like, 'Oh, now they really hate me,'" Eads says before his first home game. "The last few games I've been getting a few more high fives in the dugout, people starting to talk a little more. You gotta earn it. It's not given. Everything is earned."

I've already noted that Hurley is the third-best hitter in the Pacific Association with at least thirty plate appearances through July 19. If we indulge ourselves and drop that threshold to twenty-five, though, the best hitter in the Pacific Association through July 19 is Taylor Eads. One game after that—his seventh with the Stompers—he draws his eighth walk, tying Feh's full-season total.

It's a small sample, but as Sam says to me, "It was also a small sample when people were burying him. They were trying to get rid of him. They were legitimately trying to get rid of him."

Somehow I resist the urge to text Feh.

For every list of undrafted position players, there's also a list of undrafted pitchers. And for every Taylor Eads, there's a Santos Saldivar, the right-handed pitcher who debuts for the Stompers a day after Eads's error, when I'm desperate for a spreadsheet signee to make a strong first impression.

Santos is fifth on the 2015 seniors leaderboard for adjusted FIP, behind four drafted pitchers: eighth-rounder, seventh-rounder, eighth-rounder, sixth-rounder, Santos. In 87 senior-year innings at Baton Rouge's Southern University, the Division I alma mater of Lou Brock and Vida Blue, he struck out 115; in 143 2/3 combined innings as a junior and senior, he posted a 2.63 ERA, with no homers allowed. He was passed over anyway, punishment for the sin of being a small righty.

By the time I come across him, Santos has already made his pro pitching debut for the River City Rascals of the Frontier League, the team Paul Hvozdovic pitched for in 2014. He lasted only 3 1/3 innings, allowing three runs on four hits and four walks. The Rascals released him shortly thereafter. I do my due diligence despite that inauspicious start, calling Roger Cador, Southern's longtime baseball coach, who vouches for Santos and gets his assistant to send me Santos's cell. Cador confirms that Santos is bilingual, which is a plus, since Gregory Paulino—whose English gets better by the day, uncovering a quirky sense of humor—is still the only native Spanish-speaker on the Stompers' roster.

Next, I ask for a scouting report from Steve Brook, River City's manager and director of baseball operations.

"Santos had one decent start for us against a pretty solid hitting club," Brook says. "He's a good guy . . . just didn't showcase the strike-out stuff that we anticipated based upon his college numbers. FB in the mid to upper 80s with limited movement. Decent SL. Not much of a CH. Hope this helps."

It hurts, actually, since it almost makes me cross Santos off my list. It's one thing to sign players who make major league teams turn up their noses. It's another to sign an indy club castoff. The Frontier League is more competitive than our league, but not by so much that a guy who went one and done there would normally be a big Pacific Association prospect. As I see it, there are four possibilities:

1. Santos wasn't at his best because of a nineteen-day layoff after Southern's conference-title game.
2. Santos is good, but Brook is a bad evaluator.
3. Santos isn't good enough for the Frontier League, but he is good enough for the Pacific Association.
4. Santos sucks, and he somehow struck out twelve D1 batters per nine innings without any transferable skills.

I decide to take a chance on the answer not being behind door number four. For one thing, my other undrafted pitching targets, Taylor Thurber and Matt Fraudin, have signed with Frontier League teams despite my most persuasive tweets, texts, and voice mails. More importantly, Santos can't be worse than Jeff Conley, who's struggling, or Ryusuke Kikusawa, a righty Yoshi recruited, who has an 8.44 ERA through his first three games. Even if he's not suited to starting, he might make a shutdown reliever who'd give us more leeway to use Sean Conroy the way we want.

When I reach him, Santos is home in Houston. Like Taylor Eads, he considers himself retired, and like Andrew Parker, he's planning to be an accountant. I ask him to explain the River City saga. When he signed with the Rascals, Santos says, he was told he'd be taking the place of starter Clint Wright, who had a torn labrum. But after his sloppy start, the team told him Wright was going to try to pitch through the injury. I offer him a chance to show Brook that he'd made a mistake.

Santos is wary because of the way things went in River City, but after taking a weekend to weigh his options, he tells me he can't pass up the opportunity. "Just need a one-way ticket up there and we have a deal," he says. I book his flight for the next morning, and he joins us in time to see Sean get a save on July 14. "You guys are going to like me," he says, with endearing immodesty. "I pitch like him."

Santos set Southern's record for strikeouts, which is all the more impressive because he was a teammate of Jose De Leon, who was drafted by the Dodgers. Statistically speaking, Santos's senior season is probably better than any De Leon had at Southern, but De Leon didn't *have* a senior season: The Puerto Rican right-hander, who stands 6-foot-2, was drafted in 2013, after his junior year. Shortly before Santos's start for River City, De Leon rose from Rancho Cucamonga in the Cal League to Tulsa in the Texas League, where he posted a Santos-esque strikeout rate, fanning 105 batters in 76 2/3 Double-A innings. After the season, MLB.com will list him as the second-best minor league prospect in what might be baseball's best farm system. When Sam asks Santos who was better, Santos says, "Probably me."

Santos's debut out of the bullpen is scheduled for the next day. He'll follow Paul Hvozdovic's first start of the season, another hurdle for a "Ben and Sam" signee. Paul has the league's second-best walk rate, and we want to try him in a more prominent role. Our experiment works: Paul throws six scoreless innings, allowing no walks and only four hits (one of which was the ball that fell in front of Taylor). Now he has the lowest walk rate in the league.

The seventh inning belongs to Santos. The shortest pitcher on the shortest team, he's listed, very charitably, at 5-foot-10: He's grown a fake inch since his fake 5-foot-9 at Southern, an egregious stretch even by the standards of baseball's notoriously flattering measurement system. In the footage we shoot from behind home plate, he looks like an eighth grader from the goatee down, an effect enhanced by his baggy pants, which billow in the wind. Normally, the pitcher's head comes close to touching the top of the frame, but there's a lot of sky above Santos.

This would be the time for a tortured transition sentence about how Santos's stuff is as big as his body is small. Compared to most of our staff, it seems as if Santos throws *everything*: He has, in descending order of usage, a four-seam fastball, a slider, a sinker, a curve, and a changeup. His four-seamer sits 89–90, spiking as high as 93; his curve comes in at about 70 but often dips into the 60s. (One of his curveballs sinks to 61, one tick above the minimum speed that BATS can record.) When he finishes, he corkscrews off to the first-base side, using all of his inches to generate pace and spin. He has too many weapons, at too many speeds, to be predictable, and nothing he throws stays straight. Going from facing Paul—who has great control but throws three pitches in a narrow velocity band—to facing Santos is like switching from an acoustic act to the Wall of Sound. The Frontier League must be special if this is "decent" stuff there.

Like every visitor to Vallejo, Santos has trouble transitioning from the nearly flat ground in the bullpen to Mound Everest, our name for the Admirals' nonregulation, Aggro Crag–esque pitcher's surface. (The first time we see its steep slope, we complain to the league. When we get no response, we drop the matter, figuring the mound must hurt the Admirals on the road as much it helps them at home.) He hasn't pitched in a real game since his start for the Rascals six weeks earlier, so his velocity is off its peak. He's cold: "I thought it was warm in California," he told us in a betrayed tone on his first night with the team, after borrowing Sam's sweatshirt, which he can't take to the mound. And he also has trouble seeing Isaac's signs, so Isaac switches to hand signals. None of it matters. Santos is dominant, striking out five of the six batters he faces. A weak grounder to second is the only ball put in play, and he never reaches a three-ball count. I watch from the dugout, Taylor's second miscue temporarily forgotten, trying to hide how giddy I'm getting. "You look like a little kid right now," Paul says, starting to smile because I can't stop. No one will grumble about how we signed Santos instead of someone on the veteran-approved players list.

"Absolutely sensational performance," Tim says on the radio stream. "Unbelievable stuff." Santos was right. We've found a second Conroy.

At worst, we've clinched a spot in the title game by winning the season's first half, and I've managed to transfuse new and better blood, on both the roster and the coaching staff. But my relationship with Yoshi, which was cordial early on, grows rocky as he gains greater responsibility and his authority comes into conflict with mine.

The trouble starts during the waning days of Feh's tenure, when Feh agrees to cede some control of bullpen management to Yoshi after Sam, Theo, and Yoshi meet in San Rafael to discuss the excruciating (and easily avoidable) June 30 loss to the Pacifics in which Jon Rand was forced to face the middle of the order. On July 4, Yoshi's first game as bullpen boss, Matt Walker goes four scoreless innings against San Rafael but runs into trouble in the fifth, getting two quick outs but then loading the bases with walks and allowing a two-run single to Zack Pace. In the midst of the walkfest, Walker jogs to the dugout to superglue a cut on his right hand, which is bleeding and killing his control of the changeup. I assume his outing is over when he gets Johnny Bekakis for the final out of the fifth, but bloody hand and all, he comes back out for the sixth and allows a leadoff single to Matt Chavez and a two-run homer to Jeremy Williams, which wins the game. Later, Yoshi admits he was too tentative—that because he was new to his role, he was reluctant to assert himself (Sam and I can commiserate) and allowed Walker, whom he dismayingly describes as our "ace," to try to gut it out and get a win. It's a mistake, but at least he admits it instead of doubling down and insisting that "the ace is the ace."

Three days later, though, Yoshi fails his second test on the same material. Sean starts and gets through the eighth with a 2-1 lead. He's been extremely economical—his pitch count is at 80—but the times-through-the-order penalty is more about familiarity than fatigue, and he's about to face the heart of Pittsburg's order for the fourth time in the game. "Pull him," Sam texts me from San Rafael, where he's scouting and following along online. Before Yoshi returns to the third-base coach's box, I sidle up and ask, "New arm for the ninth?" It's supposed to sound more like a helpful suggestion than an instruction, but he doesn't seem to take it well. "No," he says, and walks away. In the ninth, Sean loads the bases without getting an out. Paul, a longtime starter who doesn't seem as comfortable entering games mid-inning, relieves him and allows all three runs to score, then coughs up three of his own, all in fourteen pitches—an impressive pitch-to-run ratio. The Stompers lose 7-5.

The next day, Mike Jackson holds Pittsburg to one run over seven, striking out nine. "They'll never pull a starter again," Sam texts from San Rafael. This time I ask Yoshi what I hope is an even more innocent question—"Is Jackson done?"—and he almost *sprints* away, muttering, "Don't ask me, it's bad luck, we lost yesterday." Apparently his takeaway from the previous game isn't that I might've had a point about pulling the starter, but that I jinx the Stompers when I ask questions. On the plus side, Jackson *is* done for the day: Yoshi takes him out, and the Stompers win 4-3.

After that I lie low until the day after Taylor Eads's first game, when I knock on the door to the manager's office, which by then belongs to Yoshi. Like the rest of the clubhouse, it's far neater than it was when Feh was in charge. Yoshi sits at the desk directly in front of me, facing the wall, while Captain manspreads in a folding chair. I ask Yoshi if he has a second.

"I was thinking that since Taylor doesn't have a strong arm, it might make sense for him and Hurley to switch in left and right," I say. "If they're comfortable playing those positions, of course."

Yoshi considers. "Taylor's arm is *terrible*," he says. (To Yoshi, almost every rookie is *terrible* and in dire need of discipline.) "We'll have to talk to him and Mark."

I'm already withdrawing, my limited mission accomplished. "Okay, thanks," I say. "Should I ask, or do you want to talk to them?"

When he answers, Yoshi suddenly sounds cold. "No," he says. "You don't talk to players."

I'm so taken aback by his curt response that I can't come up with one of my own. I head back to my laptop and hard drive, which are set up on the clubhouse freezer for anyone who wants to watch video. I wonder whether he was trying to say he'd prefer to talk to Taylor and Hurley himself, or whether he was actually telling me not to talk to players, period.

A few minutes later, I get my answer. Captain sticks his head out and asks me to come back in. "You can't do that," Yoshi says when the door is closed. "It's not your job to talk to players." I'm still so surprised that I can only stammer something about how I've been talking to players all season. "You know what I mean," he says. "You're not stupid. You just don't know how to behave."

It's true that on a typical team, posing questions to players would be the exclusive domain of the manager. But on a typical team, I wouldn't be signing players, picking them up at the airport, playing Super Smash Bros. with them, giving them dap in the dugout, filming their games, and showing them their video. The point of my presence, and Sam's presence, is that this isn't a typical team. To this point, I've been Taylor's contact with the Stompers, the guy he texts when he wants to know what time to get to the clubhouse, or who has the key to the Arnold Field entrance, or whether he can come over while he waits for his host family to take him home. It doesn't seem like a stretch for me to ask how he feels about playing left field. Moreover, I was just trying to be helpful. I didn't care who talked to the players, and I asked Yoshi which way he preferred. This seems like a disproportionate response, as if I'd walked up to the whiteboard without talking to anyone and switched their assignments myself.

But it's not disproportionate, because it's not a response to a single incident. He also brings up my impertinent in-game pitcher advice. "I'm here to offer information and recommend moves," I say. "How would you like me to do that?" Captain butts in to tell me how *he* thinks I should treat Yoshi, which sounds like an aristocrat telling a debutante how to approach the queen at cotillion: Walk forward when announced, curtsy, and don't speak unless spoken to. "Sam knows what to do," Yoshi says. Of course he prefers Sam, since Sam wants to take it so slow the season might end before anyone knows why we were here.

If I had an attack mode, this would be a good time to enter it. Yoshi is marking his territory, so I should mark mine. Maybe this is the time to push, to point out that in a very real sense I outrank him. But the prospect of turning Yoshi against me for good, so soon after resolving the conflict with Feh, is too terrible to risk. I can't take another six weeks of cold war, so I try to be conciliatory. I say that I meant no offense, that I respect his opinion, and that I hope we can collaborate. We shake hands. Hurley starts in right and Taylor plays left.

The drama subsides for six days, until another arrival forces us back into the ring. Theo tells Brennan Metzger, Matt Hibbert's outfielder friend from Long Beach, that he can come work out with the team, and once he takes fungoes everyone wants him on the roster. He's a little smaller than Eads, but much more athletic: In the minors with the Giants, who took him in the twenty-second round of the 2012 draft, he played four positions, stole a few bases, and took enough walks to offset some of the damage done by his low batting average and paltry power. He reeks of recent affiliated experience, a perfume that's intoxicating to Yoshi. We sign him, but we don't have an empty place to play him.

After batting practice, Sam, Theo, Yoshi, and I walk down the right-field line, out of earshot of anyone else. I'd hoped that Taylor's doubles streak would have endeared him to the doubters, but Yoshi wants to bench him to make room for Metzger. Sam and I strenuously object. This is a Tuesday, and the team was off Monday, so I say I'm concerned that we'll disrupt Taylor's rhythm if he doesn't start until Wednesday.

Yoshi complains about Taylor's *terrible* defense and *terrible* reaction to his first dropped-ball blunder. Sam says he told Taylor in the dugout not to get too down. Yoshi gives him the same "don't talk to players" scolding I've already received, and Sam says it was a human reaction, that he was just trying to comfort a kid who clearly felt awful. Yoshi says that isn't his job. Now that Sam is trying to give Yoshi orders, he's apparently no longer the model of preferred front-office behavior.

"Hurley and Hibbert have been here all year," Yoshi says. "How can I tell them that they're not going to play?"

"What does it say to Taylor if right after he gets going we bench him and bring in *another* guy?" I ask. Sam points out that Hurley and Hibbert have hardly had any days off. They were already due for a rest.

"Sam, you don't understand," Yoshi says. "You don't know baseball." He punctuates each sentence with a chest jab—not the friendly kind, but a display of dominance designed to put Sam in his place.

Sam's stiffening posture says he's had enough jabs. Nor is he happy about being told he doesn't understand baseball. Yoshi says he's already implied that Hurley and Hibbert will play, and that if he flip-flops now, after talking to us, it will undermine his authority. "Blame it on us," Sam says. "Make us the bad guys." Yoshi scoffs, exasperated by our ignorance of clubhouse dynamics. Sam sighs and plays his trump card: "Taylor isn't losing his job, so I guess we won't sign Brennan." Yoshi stares back in shock.

After that, we reach an agreement: Taylor will get this game off, but Yoshi will tell Hurley and Hibbert, today, that each of them will take a different day off this week—and Brennan will join the team. We're all slightly dissatisfied with the outcome, the sign of a successful compromise. The argument got heated, but it led us to a productive place. And unlike Feh, Yoshi didn't walk away.

In June, during one of our earliest, daydreaming discussions about replacing Feh with Yoshi, Theo pointed out that Sam and I were probably overestimating how much better life with Yoshi would be. "Yoshi is probably 95 percent the same as Feh," Theo said. "I'm probably 92 percent the same."

"Ben and I are probably about 87 percent the same," Sam said. "It's good DNA."

Eight imaginary percentage points doesn't sound like that big a barrier. We just have to work on whittling it away.

EVIDENCES

Memo to: Yoshi et al.
From: Sam

There's been a lot of evidence that, in the major leagues, pitchers perform significantly worse the third time through the batting order. This was first reported in 2004 by the noted sabermetricians Tom Tango (a consultant to the Cubs) and Mitchel Lichtman (a consultant to many teams, most notably the Cardinals). The so-called times-through-the-order penalty is likely a combination of two factors: pitcher fatigue, and batters' increasing familiarity with the pitcher. This is a brief rundown of the evidence for this, factors to consider when we make our in-game decisions, and whether the same thing is true for Pacific Association pitchers.

Evidence

First, the evidence at the major league level, where we have the most data and the cleanest data. These are the splits for all batters against starting pitchers this year, for each time they've seen the pitcher in a game:

- First time: .248/.305/.388, .693 OPS
- Second time: .261/.317/.405, .722 OPS
- Third time: .268/.326/.434, .760 OPS

The difference primarily comes in lowered strikeout rates. Pitchers strike out 21 percent of batters the first time they see them, then 19 percent the second time, then 17 percent the third. Walk rates and home runs also go up, mostly from the second time to the third. Here are the pitchers' FIPs each time through:

- First time: 3.74
- Second time: 3.94
- Third time: 4.54

FIP is fielding-independent pitching; it creates an ERA-like number based on a pitcher's strikeouts, home runs, and walks, and it "predicts" what the pitcher's ERA would be. As with ERA, a FIP below 3.00 is very good, above 4.00 is bad, 2.00 is elite.

In other words, an average pitcher at the start of the game turns into a fringy pitcher by the end. A no. 1 starter becomes a no. 3, and a no. 3 becomes a no. 5, and a no. 5 becomes outright awful.

There are MLB teams who are using this knowledge to make their pitching decisions. The Tampa Bay Rays in particular have taken to pulling some starting pitchers once they've faced 18 batters. Their starters have faced the fewest batters per game of any team in the American League. The Kansas City Royals are second. The Rays and Royals have something else in common: They also have the two best pitching staffs in the American League this year.

We don't think this is a coincidence.

Pacific Association

But would it work in the Pacific Association? To answer this, let's see whether the same thing happens to our pitchers.

These are the team's strikeout and walk rates each trip through:

- First: 19.5%, 7.3%
- Second: 17.1%, 7.4%
- Third: 17.4%, 11.1%

As you see, our pitchers strike out fewer and walk more the deeper into a game they get. In five of our nine losses, it has been *this very trip through the order* in which the game has changed from a Stompers lead to a Stompers deficit.

> Loss 1: Leading 2-1 in the fifth; starter (Schwieger) allowed two in the fifth. Both runs driven in by hitters seeing him for the third time.
>
> Loss 3: Leading 1-0 in the sixth; starter (Conley) allowed two in the sixth. Both runs driven in by hitters seeing him for the third time.
>
> Loss 4: Leading 4-3 in the sixth; starter (Walker) allowed four in the sixth. All batters in the inning saw him for the third time.
>
> Loss 5: Leading 4-2 in the seventh; starter (Schwieger) allowed one in the seventh. The run and the RBI were both by hitters seeing him for the third time.
>
> Loss 7: Leading 2-0 in the fifth. Starter (Walker) allows two in the fifth, two in the sixth. All runs driven in by batters seeing him a third time.

Challenges

The most obvious challenge is that starting pitchers don't want to come out of games, particularly before completing five innings when a potential W is on the line. It's up to the pitching coach or the manager to assess how disruptive it would be; however, at this level pitchers generally don't have the same set patterns or the same financial incentives that a major leaguer does. Most of our pitchers have pitched in various roles in their careers, and should be accustomed to adjusting their routines depending on where they are and what the team needs. The value of a win to their career seems very low—teams in higher indy leagues would, I imagine, be much more interested in the pitchers' ERAs and strikeout totals than win totals, especially because so many pitchers are shuffling between leagues and because league schedules are of differing lengths; there is no equivalent of a 20-game winner at this level. Affiliated-ball scouts are going to be entirely uninterested in a pitcher's win totals.

Regardless, in close games the benefit to using our pitchers in shorter stints would potentially be great.

. . .

Forty-one months before all of this started, my wife and I put our eight-month-old daughter to sleep on a cold December night, poured champagne into paper cups, and went outside to walk tight laps in front of our Southern California home. We talked about our favorite moments of 2011, and declared our resolutions for 2012. This was a lifetime ago; I didn't work for *Baseball Prospectus* yet, I hadn't moved to the Bay Area, I'd never heard of the Stompers. My resolution was inspired mainly by my bosses, whom I hated, and whom I had increasingly found myself arguing with. These arguments never made them like me more, I had found. Further, I never won these arguments. (Even though I was always right!) So my resolution was simple: Never try to win an argument.

It wasn't just my bosses. I'd grown tired of arguing, with my wife, with people on the Internet, with friends who thought that the Notorious B.I.G. was a better rapper than Ghostface Killah. Once I started trying to win an argument, I found myself rotating every fact to suit my position. This was true of the facts that came out of my mouth and also of facts that went into my ears, which I heard only deeply enough to deflate or reposition. Conversation became an exercise in bullshit.

A few months after this resolution, I read an article in the *New Yorker* that made me intensely happy to be argument-free. Its premise, based on the work of political scientists, was that the worst thing a president can do to advance his positions is to state them; as soon as he does, a huge number of people will position themselves in opposition, and they will lose the ability to be swayed by any contradictory evidence.

That's in politics, of course, where partisanship separates people into intractable opposition against each other. But after three years of writing about baseball and two years on Twitter I had come to feel that nearly everything was a partisan struggle—at least, once it had turned into an argument that people attached themselves to. This was the ugly part of the stats-vs.-tradition debate in baseball: Rather than a conversation about the best way to make baseball decisions, it had become an argument, in which it increasingly felt as if the purpose was to score points by humiliating one's opponent. So far as I could tell, nobody had ever changed his mind about anything in an argument. Dale Carnegie was way ahead of me: "If you tell them they are wrong," he wrote, "do you make them want to agree with you? Never! For you have struck a direct blow at their intelligence, judgment, pride and self-respect. That will make them want to strike back. But it will never make them want to change their minds. If you are going to prove anything, do it so subtly that no one will feel that you are doing it."

Indeed, I'd become convinced that the only way our minds are changed is by slow absorption, the feeling that other people we respect all believe different things than we do. The best argument is, essentially, peer pressure.

Of course, this is a problem when taking over a baseball team filled with players and coaches who need to be persuaded. Ben and I (and Theo) clashed over whether we should rule as tyrants. The deeper into the season we went, the more I appreciated Ben's chagrin about my reluctance to dictate terms. But I was less interested in the question of what would happen if we quit sacrifice bunting and more interested in the question of whether we could persuade people to do it because it's good and right and rational. Hence the speech in spring training: *We're going to go slow, so be patient with us.* We wanted to win them over, not overwhelm them or argue them into submission.

But that came with risks.

Back before this started, when our roster was a blank whiteboard, we weren't worried about losing; everybody loses. We weren't worried about our ideas failing; that's how science happens. We had one worry, which was that two months into the season a friend or colleague or podcast listener would come out to watch the Stompers and it would look like . . . just baseball. That they'd watch a few innings and ask us, with a bit of disappointment, which part was ours. That it wouldn't be obvious. Or even that there wouldn't be a part that was ours at all.

A few hours after Yoshi poked my chest and asked why I was so hostile—when I was trying so hard not to argue at all—I watch Paul

Hvozdovic start against San Rafael, and I struggle to answer the question even to myself. Which part is ours? I scribble a list of ways the Stompers are different because Ben and I had been born: There are scouting reports in the dugout, and we've been able to provide players with the sort of pregame preparation that only major leaguers typically have access to. There are a handful of players—some who were essentially retired before we called them—who have become stars in this little Galápagos, thanks to our spreadsheet and faith. That spreadsheet has turned out to be surprisingly progressive and has helped make baseball (and cultural) history. We have a Japanese-born manager who is (in theory) statistically enlightened, and we have the first openly gay player in American professional baseball. There are some defensive shifts, otherwise unheard of in this league. These are all things we're proud of—but they are more about helping the team reach basic levels of competence than they are helping the team to be visionary.

We'd dreamed of pushing baseball twenty years forward. We'd envisioned, for instance, a system of calling pitches from the dugout using a computerized random-number generator. The way we (and Sean Conroy) see it, most pitchers are fairly predictable; hitters have a pretty good idea what's coming because the game theory of pitch sequencing (*I know he's looking for* this, *so I'll throw him* this) has become predictable. Rather than try to outsmart the hitter using this game theory—and following the same predictable routine—we wanted to have a computer select pitches using a random-number generator. It would be extremely difficult to set up. For one thing, just because the pitch-calling would be random doesn't mean that we would want the pitcher to throw all of his pitches at identical rates. Sean's slider, for instance, is much better than his changeup, so he should throw his slider about ten times as often, and in certain counts (where a swinging strike is more valuable, or a pitch in the dirt less dangerous) maybe even more than that. But even if the slider is going to be 70 percent of his pitches, the decision about when to throw the exceptions should be decided using complete unpredictability. (I, too, understand how much this paragraph makes me sound like a philosophizing stoner.) In short: We would have had to figure out how often to throw each pitch, for each pitcher, in each game situation, and how to relay that call to the catcher and/or the pitcher in just a few seconds, and how to convince the pitcher to throw a pitch that he doesn't want to throw—the basic concept of this whole thing being that sometimes the wrong pitch is the right pitch, especially if the wrong pitch makes future right pitches even more right. (Whooooa.)

You are not reading about the success of our random-number-generated pitch-calling, though, because of course we hadn't implemented it—hadn't even gotten close. We also hadn't implemented our plan for making pitching changes based on arm-fatigue metrics that would be relayed to our iPhones via a futuristic wearable sensor called the mThrow. In the lead-up to spring training, Ben envisioned us as Ivan Drago's training team from *Rocky IV*, studying readouts and graphs as our sensor-equipped players pummeled their opponents. We talked to a lengthy list of cutting-edge companies—brain-training, eye-training, bat-tracking, motion-sensing, injury-preventing—but have little to show for it, only partly because most of this stuff is still in its infancy and very much unsettled science at the dawn of the wearable-technology era. We hadn't reimagined batting practice in a way that would give our guys more focused preparation while conserving their energy for the game. There are no naps in our clubhouse, and our guys are eating boring peanut butter on white bread before games, and if they are bunting less than the typical team and stealing bases at a higher success rate and drawing more walks and hit-by-pitches (all things we have encouraged), it's not because of us. It's because of them. Our most direct contributions have been limited to a pretty phenomenal gumbo night prepared by Kortney from our scouting staff, a Culinary Institute of America graduate who specializes in Cajun food; Sean's ice bath during his TV interviews; and the one time we used PITCHf/x to determine balls and strikes in an exhibition game, which went well except that the players who made the calls from our computer made deliberate mistakes to mess with their friends on the field. Our dreams have become small. Our lives feel small.

The problem, as I explain sheepishly when friends, colleagues, and podcast listeners come to games, is bandwidth. We hadn't imagined how time-consuming writing prescrics scouting reports would be. We hadn't anticipated how many hours we would spend with tech support so that our pitch databases would be complete. Mostly, though, we hadn't expected the entire season to be hijacked by a six-week struggle over the way we use our damned closer. And yet, here I am, in the middle of our forty-third game, furious with our second handpicked manager over the way he is using our damned closer.

It's the seventh inning, and Paul has been absolutely cruising with an 8-2 lead. He has thrown thirteen balls through six innings and has retired sixteen of the previous eighteen batters. But in the seventh the Pacifics get to him. He walks a pair, then allows a hit, then another. Matt Chavez, the best hitter in the league, owner and occupant of every pitch Paul Hvozdovic can throw, is allowed to face Paul with two men on and one out, the tying run on deck. Paul's mechanics, after a tutorial with Isaac Wenrich before the game, had been wonderful all night but are completely lost in this inning. Chavez singles, and now with a right-handed-hitting cleanup man representing the tying run, Paul is *still* out there. Yoshi goes to the mound not to ask but to tell Paul that this is his inning. Paul is shocked. Paul would have pulled himself three batters ago, he later tells me. He glances at the scoreboard, glances at the batter, and thinks, "Shit, this is crazy."

It is. He gets out of the inning on a base-running blunder by San Rafael, but by this point Yoshi has lost me completely. I'd been his ally, trying to convince Ben that Yoshi was listening to us but that we had to accept that sometimes he would still make decisions we didn't agree with. After this game—a win—I am furious at myself for believing all that. Ben, Theo, and Tim Livingston fume with me at Yoshi's inability to bring Sean into that seventh-inning situation, despite a week of us explaining to him that that is exactly when to bring Sean in. After frustrating Ben with my unwillingness to order Yoshi around, I am finally on Ben's side. Ben has won the argument.

"My instinct," I tell the brain trust in the half-lit bleachers, "would be to say to Yoshi, 'You fucked that up. We're not washing over that.

That was very badly managed. If you want to have the power to make decisions you have to make good decisions. You failed, and if you fail like this you're not going to have the privilege of making decisions.'"

It's a little embarrassing to read those words. To remember how much I wanted to win. To recall how single-minded we had become, ignoring every other aspect of the team until we could get Sean into the expanded role we envisioned. This monomania is arguably why so little else got done. But it's also why, in the next two days, we finally got what we wanted.

Ben Lindbergh

emailing yoshi?

Sam Miller

I am now, just made a couple tweaks to the language and sending it along

Ben Lindbergh

oh, you're sending him the thing I wrote?

Sam Miller

yes

sending it + we want to talk to you

I'm almost hoping he argues; I want to bust out my "you've misunderstood this relationship entirely" speech and make it clear that he's going to work for us

If he doesn't argue, then we're stuck in diplomacy land

Ben Lindbergh

yessss

love the new you

From: Ben and Sam
To: Yoshi
CC: Theo

Yoshi,

Ben and I have been thinking a lot about the best way to get the most out of our pitchers, and we have written up some recommendations. We would like to talk to you as well.

As you know, Sean has been our most effective pitcher this season, and one of the best pitchers in the Pacific Association. He's leading the Stompers in strikeout rate (27 percent of all plate appearances) and ground-ball rate (73 percent of balls in play), and he's tied with Paul in walk rate (3 percent). Our goal is to get the most value we can out of his arm.

Earlier in the season, we recommended using Sean as a starting pitcher, while Feh preferred to use him as a reliever who could pitch one inning at a time in save situations. We believe a compromise between those two positions would most suit our club: using Sean as a "fireman," a throwback reliever who comes in whenever trouble arises from roughly the sixth inning on, stays in to pitch multiple innings, and often finishes the game. In this role, Sean would truly be "saving" games—not just by the rulebook definition of a "save," which includes relatively routine one-inning outings with a three-run lead, but by *any* definition.

Although it can be comforting for teams to know that they can call upon their closer in the ninth, we believe it often backfires when they wait that long, since many potential save situations never materialize because the lead is lost before the ball gets to the bullpen's best pitcher. In other words, by worrying so much about losing leads in the ninth—which, admittedly, is especially demoralizing—teams lose more leads in the sixth, seventh, and eighth, or ensure that they never gain the lead by falling further behind. We'd like to avoid this problem by being more flexible, summoning Sean whenever we need him to protect leads, preserve ties, and keep deficits small enough that our offense can come back.

We acknowledge that some pitchers prefer (and probably pitch better in) predetermined roles, because they know when they'll be coming into the game and can prepare accordingly. For example, Angels closer Huston Street recently threatened to retire if he were used before the ninth inning. If Sean felt the same way, we wouldn't suggest that he be used in a fashion that might make him uncomfortable. However, Sean isn't the typical closer: He was a starter in college (which for him was only a few months ago), and we've seen him succeed as a starter with the Stompers. He doesn't have the long-term closing experience that conditions a pitcher to prefer a ninth-inning-only role. Based on our conversations with him throughout the season, we believe he prefers to get more work than he could if he came in for only one inning a couple times a week. In fact, at times he's been frustrated to see leads slip away before he could come in to stop the bleeding. He wants to be the one on the mound when the game is on the line, whether it's in the ninth inning or not.

There is plenty of precedent for pitchers succeeding in the sort of role we're describing: In the 1970s and 1980s, it was common for relievers to be used in this way, and many of them—Goose Gossage, Bruce Sutter, Rollie Fingers—made the Hall of Fame as a result of the value that pitching so many innings allowed them to contribute. Here are the top ten seasons ever by relievers, ranked by Wins Above Replacement Player, a statistic that accounts for the number of innings they pitched, and the quality and importance of those innings:

Name	Year	Team	G	IP	WAR
Bruce Sutter	1977	Cubs	62	107 1/3	5.2
Mark Eichhorn	1986	Blue Jays	69	157	4.9
Bruce Sutter	1979	Cubs	62	101 1/3	4.8
Jim Kern	1979	Rangers	71	143	4.7
Eric Gagne	2003	Dodgers	77	82 1/3	4.5
Rob Dibble	1990	Reds	68	98	4.3
Mariano Rivera	1996	Yankees	61	107 2/3	4.3
Goose Gossage	1977	Pirates	72	133	4.2
Mike Marshall	1974	Dodgers	106	208 1/3	4.1
Rollie Fingers	1976	Athletics	70	134 2/3	4.1

You'll notice that no relief seasons from the past decade make the list; only one, Eric Gagne's 2003, came in the past 15 seasons (and Gagne was taking tons of steroids). It's no accident that Mariano Rivera makes the list for his 1996 season, the year *before* he became a closer. When Rivera was a setup man, his usage wasn't governed by the save rule, and his manager, Joe Torre, felt free to use him for multiple innings, allowing him to help the Yankees even more.

No recent seasons appear on the list because major league bullpens have become increasingly specialized, with relievers averaging shorter and shorter outings and therefore having fewer opportunities to add value. In 2014, Royals closer Greg Holland never entered a game earlier than the ninth or pitched more than one inning. Compare that to Gossage's 1977 season: forty-eight of his seventy-two outings lasted longer than one inning, thirty-seven lasted at least two innings, and thirteen lasted at least three innings, with several relief appearances of four innings or more. Both pitchers finished their seasons with ERAs of about 1.50, but Gossage was worth much more.

Big league teams, with twenty-five-man rosters and seven- or eight-man bullpens, have the luxury of restricting great relievers to an inning at a time. The Royals had a lights-out reliever for every late inning, so they could afford to use Holland to get three outs. With a twenty-two-man roster, though, we think we are beating ourselves if we don't maximize the weapon we have and use Sean to pitch important innings that would otherwise fall to less reliable pitchers.

We don't necessarily need pages of numbers to support this plan: It's pretty intuitive that we would want our best pitcher on the mound more often, particularly with our roster-size restrictions. Consider an example from this season: One of our most painful losses came on June 30 in San Rafael, when we went into the bottom of the eighth with a 4-3 lead and the right-handed heart of the Pacifics' lineup (Chavez, Jova, and Williams) due up. Because it wasn't the ninth inning, we stuck with Jon Rand instead of Sean. Five batters later, the Pacifics had scored the game-winning run, and we still hadn't used our most effective arm. We can't say for sure that we would have won if we'd called on Sean, but we can say that we would have forced our opponent to beat our *best* pitcher.

One common objection to the idea of bringing in one's best reliever in the sixth or seventh is that there wouldn't be a trustworthy option available for the ninth. In our case, though, that wouldn't be a problem. We've seen Sean go through opposing lineups two or three times with ease, and we know he has a rubber arm and always wants to throw (to the point that if he *doesn't* get into the game, he throws on his own anyway). As a result, we won't have to worry that if we use Sean in, say, the seventh, we wouldn't have a good pitcher to finish the game or go in the next day. Sean could come in, pitch a few innings, and still be available for an inning in the following game. Further, with Santos on the roster, we have another pitcher we feel comfortable using in the ninth inning if Sean has been used up by that point and the game remains close. Simply put, Sean is an unusual pitcher who gives us a chance to gain an unusual edge. He has both the mind-set and the skill-set to flourish as a fireman, and the Stompers would benefit from having him on the mound when it matters the most.

Sam Miller

> Sent it

> It's our job to train rookies, like Yoshi.

Going to just start acting like his boss. Going to threaten him with discipline.

Thought about what that discipline would be, and it will make you *very* happy

(unless he reads this, agrees with it, and we stay stuck in diplomacyland)

Ben Lindbergh

what would it be

Sam Miller

We write the lineup

Walk into the clubhouse, write that motherfucker on the board, walk out.

Ben Lindbergh

dream come true

The thing that gets us madder than anything, actually, is that Matt Chavez is still here. The Pacifics' first baseman, the guy I had struggled to come up with a scouting report against earlier in the year, is homering in almost every game against us. That's barely an exaggeration; he's homering once every two games against the league overall and doing more damage against us than against anybody else. At one point, his OPS is *four hundred* points higher than anybody else's in the league—equivalent to the gap between Babe Ruth's career OPS and mediocre Kansas City Royals third baseman Joe Randa's career OPS. Chavez is an adult playing in a kids' league, and we're mystified that no higher power has picked him up.

"He'll be gone soon," Isaac tells me. He's heard that a manager in the American Association had called Yoshi to ask about Chavez. Our hopes are raised; our hopes are dashed when we find out that Yoshi, improbably, gave Matt Chavez a negative review, telling the manager that Chavez is a poor fielder who can't hit breaking balls and would bat .250 in the Association. We admire his integrity in giving an honest assessment, considering that Chavez is costing us game after game. We admire the integrity, but we're aghast at it all the same.

I obsess over all of this for the next eighteen hours, driving home and then lying awake and then kicking around my apartment the next morning and, finally, sitting in traffic on my drive back up to Sonoma. Alone in my car, I have conversations in my head with an imaginary Yoshi, who says everything I need him to say to fuel my resolve. By the time I pull into the Arnold Field parking lot, I've spent two hours rehearsing a conversation that gets progressively more hostile.

I walk into Yoshi's office and say I want to talk. Yes, he says, that's great, because he wants to get my help on some things. I'm stunned. I'm losing my angry face. He pulls out that night's lineup and asks what I think. I stare at it. Uhhhhhhhh. I say I'd rather see Taylor Eads that night instead of Daniel Baptista, with a lefty on the mound. He agrees, scratches out Baps, and writes in Eads at DH, batting eighth. I say I don't think Moch should be batting third anymore, especially against lefties. He nods and asks whether I have Moch's numbers against lefties, and I pull them up on my little laptop. "Good evidences," he says, and moves Moch down. I recommend dropping Isaac Wenrich down against the lefty; I show him the evidences; done. I want Matt Hibbert back leading off; evidences; done.

Then I tell him I think he has been missing chances to pinch-hit, especially with Isaac and Andrew Parker, who are now in a platoon and yet rarely replace each other when relievers come in. He agrees!

I say it seems like it's hard for him to anticipate those sorts of midgame opportunities when he's coaching third base, so I suggest that Tommy Lyons, our forward-thinking first-base coach, should be bumped up to bench coach to help Yoshi out. He agrees! I tell him it's time to get Matt Chavez out of this league, and that Ben and I are going to put together a statistical report that we can send to the inquiring American Association manager. I say it's going to show how great he's been against breaking balls, among other things. He says that's a great idea. He says, and I almost choke on my tongue, that the manager "will appreciate that. He's the smartest coach I know. He's like you."

I'm . . .

I'm touched. I just spent a day demonizing this wonderful man. I'm a monster.

But the most important thing is not where Isaac Wenrich is batting. I tell Yoshi that in last night's game, when he didn't have a reliever ready to replace Paul, when he didn't go to Sean—that was a mistake. That was a failure. He looks at me like he's surprised I don't realize he already knows that. Of course it was. He's already told Theo that he had fucked up.

So today, I say. Matt Walker is pitching. Walker has been our worst pitcher. I tell Yoshi that when I used to cover the Los Angeles Angels as a reporter, their manager, Mike Scioscia, had a trick for how to handle struggling starting pitchers. He'd tell them ahead of time they were only going to throw five innings. Even if it was a perfect game, they were coming out early. Yoshi nods. It helps them to know they don't have to pace themselves, I say. And it makes it much easier for us to go out there and pull him after he's gone through the lineup twice. I say that if Matt Walker faces Matt Chavez three times tonight, I'm going to be extremely unhappy, and Yoshi nods.

Fade into . . . a ball game that is as picaresque as the rest. From my spot on the dugout rail, bits of conversation reach me out of context, and I try to stitch them back together. Andrew Parker is hungover, having spent the previous evening drinking with the Pacifics' Maikel Jova, and he fights through the pain by focusing on the even greater pain he hopes Jova is in. "Swing at the middle one!" he yells when Jova bats. Maybe Jova does exactly that; he lines out to third base, takes a step toward first base, and pivots back to his dugout. "Exactly what Jova wanted," Parker says. "Hard-hit ball, doesn't have to run." Santos Saldivar ignores criticism of his smooth arms; "I'm Mexican." *So? Mexicans don't grow arm hair?* "No." *Oh.* Taylor Eads bats with runners at the corners and nobody out in the second inning and drives home a run with a weak groundout. "Attaboy, do a job!" his teammates yell, raining high fives and helmet pats upon him, the recurring proof that respect doesn't come from doubles but from jobs getting done, to which Parker—Eads's number-one supporter, and a big believer in doubles— can't help but reply sardonically, "Our DH just did that. A grown man just hit that." To which Taylor, aware that he's riding a wave of popularity that comes from a 4-3 dribbler, tells him, "Shut up." To which Kristian Gayday, joining in, then tells Taylor, "Just gotta take the tampon out next time," to which I think, *Good heavens, the world is so different without the moderating effect of women.*

Or maybe boys just talk like this no matter who else is around. The moderating effect of Sean Conroy, after all, has worn off: One veteran walks back to the dugout after a strikeout and says, loud enough for the pitcher to hear, "Better hold on to that last strikeout, because it's never gonna happen again." Then, muttering, "Fucking faggot." Somebody recounts the time a San Quentin prisoner walked over to our chain-link dugout, grabbed on with both hands, and told our guys sternly that we'd better beat San Rafael because "they're a bunch of homosexuals." "Nmf," Isaac says after a pickoff throw, which draws quizzical looks that require Isaac to explain—but Isaac is hesitant. "Nmf," he says again. "Sean, you know Nmf, right?" Sean nods, but offers Isaac no lifesaver. Isaac: "Like when a guy makes a throw to first, and you yell Nice Move . . . Friend. Nice Move . . . uhhh, Fella. Nice Move, word we're not allowed to say anymore. NMF."

The opposing pitcher does not have a nice move, friend. This is an opportunity. The Pacifics have their backup catcher playing tonight, and I tip off Yoshi before the bottom of the first that this guy can't throw. His "pop" times, in our scouting, average roughly 2.3. The math of stealing bases goes like this:

- The pitcher takes a certain amount of time to deliver the ball home. Call that X.
- The catcher then takes a certain amount of time to redirect the ball to the second baseman or shortstop covering. Call that Y.
- The base runner takes a certain amount of time to cover the seventy-nine feet from his lead off first base to the tip of the second-base bag. So long as that time is less than X + Y, he'll be safe practically every time. Otherwise, he needs the throw to be wild, dropped, etc.

A pitcher aims to deliver the ball in about 1.2 to 1.3 seconds. This turns out to be one skill where Pacific Association pitchers can more or less match their big league role models. Some skills are like this. We've observed, for instance, that pitchers in our league often have MLB-quality pickoff moves—even better than MLB-quality, in some cases, because they can balk with near impunity. (We have only two umpires on the field, restricting their view of illegal moves, and umps at this level seem hesitant to make any unusual call.) There are other examples: Hitters tend to be skilled at leaning in and getting hit by pitches; pitchers are about as capable as big leaguers when they *have* to throw a strike—on 3-0, for instance. But in nearly all other facets of the game, our guys are just worse. It's like exceptionalism doesn't just manifest in certain areas of major leaguers' bodies, but also in every atom in every cell of their bodies, to the degree that one wonders whether major leaguers are also more resistant to headaches and have more acute taste buds and know when a sneeze is coming before the rest of us do.

So they run faster—a *lot* faster. This shocked us. There are, of course, plenty of fast major league players, but there are also plenty of other athletes who are fast, and because being fast isn't enough to get a player to the majors all on its own, we figured there must be loads of superspeed guys with the sort of mediocre baseball skills that would banish them to indy ball. In fact, there was exactly one superfast guy in the league, a Vallejo Admiral named Darian Sandford, who would sometimes steal home on the catcher's throw back to the pitcher. He played a fourth of the Pacific Association season before he got a job in a higher league, and he still ends up second in our league in steals. He can make it from home to first (from the right side) in 4.0 seconds, which is elite even at the major league level. But nobody else in the league is close to that. Our fastest guy, Matt Hibbert, who leads the league in steals, is 4.3 to first, which is major league average. I've clocked just about every player in the league running to first, and that is pretty much the high end: average. Meanwhile, guys who are considered fairly fast in our league are 4.5 to first, which is about the third percentile of major league runners. "Slow" players in our league will chase 5.0, which is unheard of in the majors—even the famously slow Molina brothers can beat that.

This mediocrity, as I said, surprised me, but I came to understand it better. One day, Gered Mochizuki was tutoring Mark Hurley in our dugout before the game, and out of the fog of Moch-speech came the most insightful—and depressing—explanation of the gap between indy ballers and minor leaguers. Hurley was inside the dugout; Moch was outside it, leaning over the rail, and he stepped back and pointed at the fishnet, a series of small squares that protected all our shins from foul balls. "You think that you're this whole big screen, like a big rectangle," he said. "But you're actually a collection of all these little squares in here. And each one is a part of the game that you have to learn and polish. In affiliated ball, they start with the first square and they polish it until it's perfect. Then they go on to the next square, and they polish that one. Eventually you've polished every spot and you're a complete ballplayer, you know how to play the game. But nobody does that for you here. If you don't do it yourself, you never learn all these little ways that you should be better."

This is profoundly sad if you're the guy who is signing twenty-two-year-old ballplayers who dream of reaching the big leagues, because it means that just by being here they're falling behind their peers. Mark Hurley and some dude who was drafted in the thirty-ninth round last year might have started this season at the same talent level, more or less. But that other guy, by luck of having been seen by a scout, or having a slightly more promising frame or repertoire or profile, or a dad who played minor league ball, gets the benefit of dozens of the world's best coaches, who are dedicated to spending sixty hours a week training him, teaching him, polishing him, and compelling him to spend sixty hours a week on the same. But Mark was here. For most of the season Mark essentially had one coach, and that one coach had no experience coaching, and a full-time job on the side playing center field. Every day that Mark spends here, impressing the hell out of us, blowing our minds at how much better he is than we expected, maybe even catching a scout's eye or producing stats good enough to move up to the Association, is a day that he's falling further behind Mr. Thirty-Ninth-Round Pick. Nothing he can do at this level can overwhelm the toxic fact that he is *at this level*.

So, yes, the players here don't hit as well. They don't throw as hard. They don't catch as many balls. But their flaws are smaller and pervasive: If a slow-hit grounder forces the shortstop to move in and to his right, it's probably going to be a hit (despite the slow-ass runners), because shortstops at this level don't have the quick transfers and the strong arms to throw across their bodies. It's an infield-hits league, really. And if a left-handed pitcher with a camouflaged balk move picks a runner off, and that runner can run even a little bit, and if instead of diving back or freezing in his tracks that runner just turns and sprints to second, he's quite often going to be safe because the first basemen are so slow to get the ball out of their gloves, so clumsy stepping over to get a clear throwing lane, and so unable to throw a good, crisp strike to a target that (if the shortstop is still moving over to cover) isn't even there yet. And if the backup catcher is starting that day, and you want to steal a bunch of bases against him, you probably can.

So we do. Remember our math: Pitcher Time + Catcher Time > Runner Time = Stolen Base. This pitcher, a big lefty with a high leg kick, usually comes in at 1.4 seconds. Catchers aim for 1.8; most in the pros are 1.9 to 2.0; most here are 2.0 to 2.1. (Ours, Isaac and Parker, are 1.9, which might be the most undermentioned reason that our team is so good.) This kid for San Rafael is 2.3. Which puts the Pacifics' pitcher-catcher combo at 3.7 seconds, not counting the few microseconds it takes for the fielder to lay the tag on. At 3.7 seconds, the only reason not to go is if you're worried about the other team's feelings. By Matt Hibbert's fourth steal of the game—and our team's ninth—I'm starting to be.

This gives us a nice cushion, as we go ahead 4-0 in the first three innings. Walker is pitching . . . better. He normally throws about 80 mph, with a weird habit of throwing in the high-70s early in games and building up, as though he's pacing himself for the ninth inning. But today he comes out throwing harder, 82, 83, the fastest we've clocked him at in at least a month, if still the slowest of any of our starters. I'm actually relieved when he allows a bases-empty double in the second, because I feared Yoshi wouldn't stick to our plan if Walker were throwing a no-hitter.

In the fourth, though, Walker's second time through the order, he's not throwing as hard and he puts the first two men on. He gets the next two outs, but throws his one inarguably awful pitch of the night—a hanging curveball to the Pacifics' massive new third baseman, Jake Taylor—and nineteen seconds later, Taylor touches home plate with the lead cut to 4-3. We answer back, and as Walker takes the hill in the fifth, he has a 7-3 lead and is facing the bottom of the Pacifics' order for the second time. The no. 8 hitter singles. The no. 9 hitter singles. The top of the order is coming up. We don't lose often, but when we do it is almost always right here. This spot, over and over and over again.

But this time the mouse is going to turn left.

Of all the pitchers who've been left out to face lineups for a third time, Walker's extended outings have been the most galling. For one thing, he's been our worst starter overall—maybe our worst pitcher overall, going by our metrics—so trying to squeeze extra innings out of him makes the least sense of all. For another, he's been by far our worst starter the third time through the order. Entering this game, he had a 4.55 FIP the first time through the order; 4.94 the second time; and 6.80 the third time. The league as a whole had hit about as well against him the third time through as Hank Aaron hit in his best season.

But perhaps most annoying is that our managers have justified leaving him out there by noting that he is our no. 1 starter. Because he started Opening Day. Which, you'll recall, he did only because he'd asked. In his second start of the season, Walker was removed when he was one out away from a win. Even though he left with a lead, he was livid when he got back to the dugout. But this time, Yoshi told Walker before the game that exiting early was the plan, and Yoshi follows through. Walker calmly hands the ball to his manager and walks to the dugout as Sean Conroy trots in. "The ol' bring-in-the-closer-for-the-five-inning-save," Eric Schwieger deadpans in the dugout, and hearing that reminds me that this is going to be *our* game: Everybody on the team knows that Yoshi would never have made this move on his own, that he's now following our lead. Ben and I are going to wear this one like a crown or like skunk, depending. When Sean's first pitch to Zack Pace is a line drive just foul down the first-base line, I feel, for the first time since our first shift against Nick Oddo, that everything rides on this. That's the downside to taking action: results matter. We've finally quit hiding, and now we're going to be judged. Walker, especially, will want to kill us if this doesn't work.

Ahead 0-1, Sean gets Pace to pop out to second base. Then he gets ahead of Danny Gonzalez and induces a pop-up to shallow center field. Now Sean can get out of this without allowing a run. Naturally, he'll have to get past Matt Chavez.

Chavez reminds me most of all of Albert Pujols. He has a sort of stiff-necked posture that makes it look like he's built out of Legos, but that hides a fairly easy athleticism. He enters this game hitting .371/.444/.743 with 18 home runs in forty-three games, but against us he is batting .481 and *slugging* 1.077. He has played thirteen games against us and homered in nine of them. At twenty-six, he's too old to be a big prospect; the Giants signed him after a tryout in 2014, but they cut him when he failed to tear up A ball in his first ten games. After that setback, he flitted through the Frontier League and the United League before landing in San Rafael, where he became a beast right away. On his bio page at the University of San Francisco, Chavez wrote that he "would like to be Superman for a day." Now he's getting to be Superman for a season.

Our catchers have figured out that he's unpitchable, but our pitchers all continue to insist that *they* can get him out. Even those who have allowed homers (which includes most of them) insist everybody else is just being stupid, or gutless, or reckless, or they just suck; we're told anytime we give a scouting report on Chavez that somebody just needs to bean him (yet only twice all year has he been hit by a pitch) or throw him breaking balls away or fastballs inside or pitches down and in. Meanwhile, everybody else on the team gets pissed off and asks why we're still trying to pitch to him at all—just intentionally walk the dude. (Oddly, he hasn't been walked intentionally all year; his overall walk rate is lower than our team's as a whole.)

I'd been promoting the idea that, with every team in the league obsessed with getting an inside fastball past him, he is sitting on that pitch. I tell everybody about the time I saw him get a fastball right at his hands and hit it about 450 feet, just foul down the left-field line. But because he's looking for that pitch, he is occasionally made to look silly on breaking stuff. At least it was a plan. I talk up this plan. He goes 5-for-11 with a homer in the first two games of this series.

So this is who is coming up to face Sean now. "Come on, Sleepy," a fan calls as Chavez comes to the plate, and the Pacifics' dugout gets noticeably more alert for the matchup. The two have never faced each other. Sean and I have talked about how he'll get Chavez out when they meet, but Sean's plan is no different than against any other hitter: Throw him what he's not expecting and keep the ball down. I recommend he finally break out the knuckleball.

Sean's first pitch is a slider, up and in—and Wenrich frames it beautifully, for a strike. "Here we go, be smart here, kid!" Walker calls to

Sean, and then, to himself, "Bottom of the zone." Conroy fires another slider and it is in the bottom of the zone, but Chavez gets good wood on it and sends a fly ball to right field. We've seen the Pacifics' strong right-handers homer on cheap fly balls down the 310-foot line, and for a moment I'm sure this is another one; I groan loudly, losing for the moment my disciplined, dugout-approved nonchalance. But Brennan Metzger moves back and stops under it for an easy third out. Walker is the first one out of the dugout. "Attaboy, Sean, good job!" He approves. We all, for the moment, approve.

Sean leans against the railing next to me. "I just ruined my ground-ball rate," he says.

"Keeping Chavez in the park counts as a ground ball," I answer.

It's not easy, this game. Sean gets through the sixth smoothly and strikes out the first two in the seventh. Then he gets squeezed by the umpire and walks a pair, and Chavez is up again. Our infield shifts way over to the pull side, almost begging him to cut down his swing and poke a single the other way. But he won't: After a slider for a strike, Sean throws him another slider, and Chavez hits one into the first row of the left-field bleachers, cutting the Stompers' lead to 7-6. (The home run ties the league's all-time home run record, and we're only a week past the halfway point in the season.) Then Sean gets through the eighth easily, and as Yoshi jogs out to the third-base coach's box for the bottom of the eighth, I flag him down.

"Do you want Gonzo to get ready?" I ask.

"Ready, yeah," Yoshi says. But only in case Sean gets in trouble. Otherwise, our closer is going to close this.

The math is obnoxious: The Stompers go into the ninth with a two-run lead, having tacked on a run in the eighth. Chavez is the fifth batter due up. If two guys get on base, he'll bat as the go-ahead run.

Of course, two guys get on base, with two men out. Tyger Pederson, a left-handed hitter, singles on a ground ball to right field. Then Pace, another lefty, nubs a grounder down the third-base line; T. J. Gavlik fields it but has no play. Gonsalves is warm in the bullpen.

"What do you do here?" I ask Matt Walker.

"He's leaving him in," he says.

"Yeah?"

"Yeah. Sean's our best guy. He's our closer. This is why you've got him."

Yoshi does leave him in, for what Tim Livingston tells his listeners is "the most high-leverage situation in a ball game at Arnold Field this year." Sean throws a fastball at Chavez's shins for a called strike one. He throws a slider low and away and gets a pop-up into our bullpen, just out of Joel Carranza's leaping reach. Chavez still hasn't seen Sean's overhand pitch, so on 0-2 Sean tries it—a fastball at the letters freezes Chavez, but it's just inside for a ball. Then, on 1-2, he throws a fastball at the knees, inside corner, for a called strike three. Game over. I'm almost crying. I'm almost crying *right now*, months later. It's the most I've ever felt at a baseball game, because it worked. It's a hell of a thing to care.

The team goes through its own high-five line, as with any other victory, but when they wheel around to return to the dugout I'm no longer just the leftover equipment.

"Good job, guys," Matt Hibbert tells Ben and me and gives us high fives.

"Samwise—well done," Tommy Lyons says.

Yoshi comes to shake my hand, pats my shoulder, and says, "Good game."

"How fucking tight was your butthole?" Isaac asks Ben. "I look over and I see Sam and Ben—" and here he mimes a puckered butthole.

There's much laughter. Sean's host family hugs him. I hug him. Then I go find Matt Walker and tell him he pitched a helluva game, and I couldn't be prouder of him.

After that, there's a thaw between the statheads and the manager. Three days later, Sean again comes into the game in the fifth against San Rafael, this time to relieve Paul Hvozdovic. His first pitch—to

Matt Chavez—is a slider down the middle, and Chavez homers. But Sean allows only one more hit the rest of the way. In the ninth, he walks the leadoff man, but with Chavez on deck in a one-run game, Matt Kavanaugh makes the unthinkable decision to have Danny Gonzalez bunt the runner over. It works, opening up first base, and Sean issues the first intentional walk of Chavez all year. He then gets Pacifics cleanup man Maikel Jova to fly out and strikes out Jeremy Williams on nine pitches. After the game I tweet: "Another huge performance from Sean Conroy, professional baseball's only openly five-inning closer."

Yoshi starts coming to us, asking for information—often information we consider less than useful, like how a certain pitcher has done against a certain hitter (usually too small a sample to be helpful), or how each of the day's lineup options has done against lefties (it takes hundreds or thousands of at-bats before a player's "true" platoon split emerges; safer to assume all batters will have typical platoon advantages), or how that day's starting pitcher does the third time through the order (when the default should be to remove all but the very best pitchers the third time through if the bullpen is rested enough to handle it). We're happy to help. We drill ever deeper into Matt Chavez's numbers and realize that he has hit every fastball Gregory Paulino has thrown him this year, but whiffed on, fouled off, or made weak contact with every slider; all we have to do is throw sliders. Yoshi is impressed: "Evidences," he says, encouraging Andrew Parker to listen to us. We give Yoshi guidelines on when it would make sense to intentionally walk Chavez, using research done during Barry Bonds's PED heyday. Now that Sean has broken the seal, we're all less scared to do it again. At one point our pitchers walk Chavez six times in a row, as the Pacifics and their fans taunt us.

And we really start to shift. Not once in a while; not timidly; but constantly, every game, for multiple batters in each lineup. We keep waiting for it to backfire, for some hitter to take what we give him and single the other way. But it never happens. We put on scores of shifts, maybe hundreds, and though they don't always work—sometimes a guy hits one right through the teeth of it, or is late on a fastball and pokes one through the undefended part, or bombs a towering homer over the top of it—they never look "beatable." We've been so worried that the other teams would just flip a switch and start trying to beat it, would successfully beat it, and would reveal the vulnerabilities in our plan. They don't; they can't; we're invincible. There are only four obstacles to shifting even more at this point.

1. There are hardly any left-handed batters in this league, so we're shifting mostly against righties. Lefty shifts are so much easier—we're moving for every left-hander in the league at this point, except for one guy, Scott David of the Pittsburg Diamonds, who seems immune to our fancy defenses. The philosophical premise of the shift is that positions are irrelevant, that behind the pitcher are just seven guys with seven gloves trying to catch the ball and standing wherever makes that outcome most likely. But one of those seven does have a nonnegotiable role, covering first base. This one tether is a huge inconvenience against right-handers. Even so, we do shift against righties. A lot.

2. At this level, errors happen. We're all used to them, and we're all happy to blame the lousy infield grass (which gets worse throughout the year). But when a second baseman is standing forty feet over from his normal position and makes an error, it's easy for everybody to blame the error on his being unaccustomed to that angle, or that throw, which by extension means blaming us. Or at least it's easy for me to *assume* they're blaming us.

3. A lot of dudes at this level just aren't good enough to be pull hitters. They want to be: They swing like pull hitters and have the approach of pull hitters, but against good fastballs they're just slow. It's like playing poker against somebody who is just learning the rules: They're too unpredictable to feel comfortable against.

4. The big one: Mochizuki, our veteran second baseman/shortstop, who is supposed to be guiding the rest of the infielders, can't remember the plans we deliver to him before the game. So we yell out to him and wave

our arms at him, which increasingly seems to peeve him—partly my fault, I fear, because of the time that I (with absolutely no feel) yelled "Moch!" just as the pitcher was delivering his pitch. He's nice as hell about it and acts really into the concept of the shifts, but when he's out on the field he simply begins to ignore us. We're thwarted by simple churlishness.

The greatest feeling isn't when a shift works perfectly—when a guy grounds one right at the shortstop pulled way over into the hole, or lines one right at the second baseman standing behind the bag. The greatest is when a shifted-against guy hits one where we're most exposed—a right-hander grounds to the right side, or even lines one— but our lone remaining defender is there. When we were nervous about the shift, we focused on that big empty space on the underdefended side of the infield. But once we implemented it, we realized things could go totally wrong and still work out totally right. Once, a right-hander crushed a line drive between where the first and second basemen usually play. It's a hit a hundred times out of a hundred in a normal alignment, but it went right into first baseman Kristian Gayday's glove. We didn't exactly want Gayday there—if we could have, he'd have been fifty feet farther from the line—but we needed him there to cover the bag. That limitation forced him to stand exactly where the ball went. It was a total accident, and we looked so smart. It's reassuring to be reminded that, yes, even our dumb plans have some margin for error.

But back to the unshiftable one, Scott David. The Pittsburg second baseman arrived midseason from a Canadian circuit called the Intercounty Baseball League, where he was hitting .435/.500/.652. His numbers took a hit coming to our league, but .435 can take a lot of hits before it stops being awesome, and David is contending for our league's batting title. (He is, in fact, the only thing between Matt Chavez and a Triple Crown.) We're determined to find something that we can offer our pitchers heading into a series against the Diamonds, but David hits everything, everywhere. For two hours on Ben's hardwood living-room floor, I parse David's results finer and finer, hoping to find *something* I can give to the team.

But it's only when Ben and I start joking about outlandish solutions that we realize Scott David is exactly the sort of hitter they invented the five-man infield for. Except, nobody has invented the five-man infield. We're inventing it, right now. And he's the hitter we're inventing it for.

Up to now, we've been stealing from major league teams, trying to bring the twentieth-century world of indy ball into the twenty-first. This is the first time we're going to try something that *nobody* does. There are two steps to this: We have to make the case to our team (manager, fielders, pitchers) that this makes sense; and we have to figure out the right way to do it. If we get those two done, we go to step three: observing how David handles it and adjusting as needed.

The case is easy enough to make, on paper. David is a left-handed batter, and he'll be facing our right-handed pitchers. Against right-handed pitchers, he has a .440 batting average when he hits a ground ball. That's the highest success rate on his team, more than double the league's average. He also hits ground balls more frequently than anybody on his team, and he sprays those ground balls all over the field, so we can't possibly defend every hole. Further, his signature hit is a shallow grounder that the shortstop or third baseman charges but can't transfer fast enough to beat him to first. If we had five men in the infield, we'd plug more of those infield holes, while also allowing everybody to play a couple of steps in and field his choppers more quickly.

Ground balls are only part of it, though. He's hitting .923 on line drives, about half of which are low enough that an infielder could snag them if properly positioned. (They also follow no directional tendency.) Meanwhile—our closing argument, the truly captivating spray chart: *He never pulls fly balls*. Not rarely. Never. He has hit seven fly balls all year: four to straightaway left field, two to shallow left-center, and one pop-up to deep shortstop.

Clearly, playing a five-man infield—with the ambition of cutting off singles and turning them into outs—will leave us vulnerable to doubles and triples. But turning a single into an out is far more important— about 2.5 times more important—than letting a single turn into a double; even the difference between a single and a triple is smaller, on average, than the change from a single to an out. And in certain situations, the benefits of the out are even greater. For instance, runners on second and third with two outs: A single does very nearly as much damage as a triple does, while an out ends the inning, saves the game, changes the world. So we make up some numbers:

a. If Scott David hits 55 percent grounders, and converts 44 percent of those grounders to hits (i.e., he hits .440 on grounders), and

b. if he hits 30 percent line drives at a .900 batting average, and

c. if he hits 15 percent fly balls at a .286 batting average,

and we shift so that he now hits .300 on grounders, .800 on line drives, and .400 on fly balls, then over the course of 100 batted balls we'll turn about nine hits into outs. Even assuming all those nine hits would have been singles, he would have to turn nearly thirty singles into doubles to make up the difference in value. Basically, every hit would have to be a double.

This vastly oversimplifies things, of course. For one thing, we wouldn't put the shift on in situations where a double or triple is especially harmful (relative to a single), such as with two outs and a runner on first. This means that our average "values" of singles, doubles, and outs are skewed against us. For another, some of those doubles might come from "outs," if David proves capable of hitting routine cans of corn to right field that suddenly become extra bases. But we've found that vastly oversimplifying things is the best way to make these cases. Most of our players aren't like the commenters on our articles, picking apart our data and arguments. Thank goodness.

Actually, they also don't necessarily read or care about the arguments at all, which is the problem: A good case on paper promises nothing with our team. We need them to want to be on our side. We need them to feel like we've been listening to them all year, that we don't come at them with bullshit, that we're not trying to make them guinea pigs, and that whatever we're suggesting isn't some sort of slippery slope that leads to extra practice tomorrow morning. Maybe we just need them to feel like this is all fun.

Which makes this a test not just of our data but also of our labor this whole season. We're reminding them, with our spray charts, that we have been working as hard as they have. We're showing them, in the manner in which we approach them, that we're always learning and listening to their concerns. We're also underscoring, by the outrageousness of our idea, that we aren't afraid; that we have authority, and that we're using it now. We promised way back in spring training that we were going to go slow, because we believe not just in using data but also in using data right; our patience was our pledge, and it was the proof that we were true to our principles. Now here we are, two months in, and if you can't trust us today then you're really telling us that we will never have a place on your team. And we *do* have a place on your team. We didn't sit in the bullpen all those hours listening to you describe your dicks for nothing.

Before the first game of the series, I gather the whole team in the dugout to discuss the five-man infield we're going to deploy against Scott David. Nervous to speak for the first time since spring, I explain it all in the span of one hundred seconds. Connor Jones, our new right fielder who's making his first start as a Stomper, will run in to play a deep second base; I texted him earlier in the day to advise that he take grounders in batting practice, and I hope he listened. The second baseman, Gered Mochizuki, will play right up the middle; new shortstop Peter Bowles and third baseman Yuki Yasuda will pinch in a few steps so they can charge the slow rollers, and first baseman Kristian Gayday will play on the line but a bit deeper than usual so nothing gets past him. Center fielder Matt Hibbert will pull way over into the right-center-field gap; anything that gets over Jones or Gayday will be his to chase down. Left fielder Mark Hurley, meanwhile, won't move at all. He's going to be straight away, where David tends to hit fly balls. To David, it's going to look as if right field—where he never hits fly balls—is the wide open space, but really we're far more worried that he'll go to dead center, where the 435 feet between home plate and the fence give him a potential inside-the-park home run on any well-struck fly ball. "If he does that," I say, "we'll adjust. Okay. Okay?"

It's silent for a second, and then Moch says, "Fuck yeah, awesome. Let's fuckin' do it."

We don't put the shift on in the first inning—we want to give our pitcher, Gregory Paulino, a chance to get settled in—and David grounds a single past our shortstop for a hit that an extra infielder might have prevented. When he bats in the fourth, I step outside the dugout and wave at Connor Jones. Everyone on the field moves, except Hurley.

David brushes the dirt in the batter's box smooth, then looks toward his dugout, as if somebody is saying something to him. He steps out and turns to survey the field, freezing for a moment when he looks to the right side. He grimaces, spits, then digs into the box. The first pitch he sees is a fastball, just below the knees, on the inside part of the plate. It's supposed to be on the outer half, but targets are only suggestions at this level. David flies open, a dead-pull swing, his belt buckle pointing at the vacant right field as his arms extend to wrap around the inside pitch. He hits it square and drives a low line drive toward right field. Connor Jones takes a step and dives to his right—and misses it by inches. Matt Hibbert jogs in to field the ball. About thirty feet down the line, David flips his bat at least twenty feet in the air and screams "Yargh!" as he passes our dugout. The five-man infield didn't work. It also didn't hurt, and it actually makes our case stronger: That's exactly the sort of ball that we're defending against, a certain base hit that, with a fifth man closing holes, we very nearly turned into an out. Somebody pats my shoulder, recognition that the plan "worked."

We keep working at it. The next at-bat, David grounds one right down the first-base line; Gayday, hugging the line and playing deep, doesn't even have to move to field it. "Now flip the bat!" I say, loud enough to *sound* like I want David to hear me as he jogs it out, though not loud enough that he actually will. In his third and final at-bat into the shift, he taps a grounder up the middle, and Paulino tips it with his glove, slowing it down even more. Mochizuki is playing right behind Paulino, in perfect position to make the play. He fields it so casually, though, that David beats the throw. Everybody on the team is sick of Mochizuki's lack of effort on plays like this one, so this one gets me another backslap. In four plate appearances today, David hit three grounders and a low line drive inches away from our repositioned infield.

He also went 3-for-4.

But we consider this a huge success. With everybody watching David's approach closely, he did exactly what we said he would do. We put the same shift on the next day with Sean Conroy, the league's most extreme ground-ball pitcher, on the mound. David grounds right to the shortstop in his first at-bat, then back to Conroy in his second, then lines one to right-center field, where Matt Hibbert is playing. A single streak of sunlight through the trees to the west of Arnold Field turns this routine play into a difficult one, and it deflects off Hibbert's glove. "You have to feel good about this," I tell Theo. "David is trying to pull the ball. He's getting out of his natural swing. And he's hitting balls more or less right at defenders. That's six times he has put the ball in play with that five-man infield, and he has basically hit it at fielders all six times."

David goes 1-for-3 in the next game, then 0-for-3, then sits out the next two games he plays against us. He's hurt, we hear, and we have no real reason to doubt it. But he's chasing a batting title, and I flatter myself by believing that he's avoiding our defense. He went 4-for-12 against the shift, all singles, and at least two (and maybe three) of those hits were due to our fielders' awkwardness at their new "positions." We were getting better at it. David—who admitted to one of our catchers that it bugged him to see the defense like that, and that he was trying like hell to hit the open expanses in the outfield—was not. "Hit it in the air one goddamn time," one of his teammates groaned in exasperation, after watching him ground out again.

13

SANDS OF TIME

There's a sentiment I've grown used to expressing, a lame little cop-out that cushions the blow when I have to tell a hopeful player that the Stompers don't have room on the roster. "There's a ton of turnover at this level, so stay in touch," I say, or, "Guys get signed all the time, so we'll let you know if we have a need," or, "Not right now, but things can change overnight." The sentiment isn't always sincere—in some cases, I know there's no way we'll sign the player I'm talking to unless our whole roster gets raptured—but from what I've been told, the statement is technically true. Based on the Stompers' long list of transactions in 2014, Theo and Tim have warned us since spring training that players leave with almost no notice, that we shouldn't get too attached, that we can't count on keeping anyone who impresses enough to attract attention from higher-level leagues. But for the first two-thirds of the season, the only departures we've had to deal with were players we weren't sorry to see go.

In the Stompers' clubhouse, there's a memorial wall where the players post the names and numbers of their former teammates. At the top, there's a piece of tape on which someone has written "RIP" in big blue letters, the top of an adhesive headstone. When we clinched the first

half, there were only three names beneath. The first was Danny Martinez, who started the season with the Stompers as infield insurance on
the inactive list but never got into a game. His tape strip, like the littlest
angel's crooked halo, is the saddest of all: It says "XX" next to his name,
since he never had a number. Below Martinez were Josh McCauley, a
right-hander who pitched two games for the Stompers in June, and Sergio Miranda. The next day, Feh's name became the fourth.

Anyone who's been through a breakup knows that who does the
dumping makes all the difference. Both sides are sad to see most relationships end, but the dumpee's disappointment is compounded by the
burden of being deemed disposable. For several weeks, Sam and Theo
and I have done all the dumping, excluding Andrew Parker, who one
day in the dugout bragged about taking "at least four dumps a day."

Just before the second half started, I got a reminder that most of our
players see the Stompers as a stepping-stone to . . . something. With
a southpaw starter on the mound for the Admirals, our lefty-hitting
catcher Isaac Wenrich got the evening off. As I sat on a bench in the
bullpen while Isaac waited to warm up a pitcher in the late innings,
I heard him complain about being out of the lineup, telling everyone
within earshot that he hoped to get out of the Pacific Association in
the next couple of days, as teams in the Can-Am League, the Frontier
League, and the American Association replaced their struggling starters
or lost their stars to even *more* desirable leagues. For Isaac, serving time
in his third Pacific Association season at twenty-five, a day off wasn't a
welcome respite; it was another sunset added to the end of his sentence,
a day when he couldn't do anything to show he deserved to be somewhere else. No one criticized his lack of team spirit, since almost every
Stomper was thinking the same thing.

If pressed, I would have acknowledged on Opening Day that all our
players had agreed to go out with us only to make better teams jealous.
But as the season settled into a comfortable routine and we watched
strangers become companions, their emotional states ebbing and flow-
ing with our wins and losses, it was easy to convince ourselves that our
players were happy to be here and that they were as invested as Sam and

I in the Stompers' success. Everyone we love eventually leaves us, if we don't leave them first, but we've evolved to be good at forgetting painful facts. Hearing Isaac declare his ambition out loud was like discovering that your girlfriend has an active OkCupid profile or a malignant mole.

Unlike Sean Conroy, I don't believe in the "law of attraction," as I reminded myself when I pictured Isaac's declaration magically drawing a GM's eye, like Sauron swiveling on his tower when Frodo puts on the ring. But as much as I'd hate to lose Isaac or Sean, or Baps or Hibbert or Hurley, part of me actually hopes it will happen. For one thing, I'm insulted that no one wants what we have: Can't they see that we've built the best baseball team, with the best baseball players? For another, I want our players to get what they want, even if what they want makes us worse. A promotion to a midlevel indy league would barely improve their minuscule salaries and even more minuscule odds of making the majors, but it would still be a sign that someone is watching. It might also pay dividends down the line, if it led to the briefest of minor league looks. Some of our players plan to start batting cages, become baseball instructors at sports academies, or give private lessons to local kids. Even a day of affiliated experience would help them recruit clients and charge higher rates, as well as give them better stories to tell at the bar when they're trying to get girls (or guys!) to go home with them.

Access to casual sex aside, signings fulfill the Stompers' social contract: Prostrate yourself before baseball, and baseball will lift you up. If other teams start taking our talent, the franchise will have held up its end of the bargain, and Theo will be able to boast about all the guys who got out of the league when he's recruiting next spring. ("If you play for us, you might not have to *keep* playing for us.") Lastly, there's the selfish reason: If one of our spreadsheet guys gets signed, it would make us seem supersmart. Not only would we get to see someone we like flourish, but we'd also get to take credit for finding a gem that the baseball establishment missed.

Isaac's hopes don't pan out immediately: Days, and then weeks, pass without any defections. The Stompers win their first three series of the second half, two of them against the Pacifics, including a 17-5 blowout in which Joel Carranza goes 5-for-6 with two homers and seven runs driven in, wiping away the inevitable Matt Chavez solo shot. Meanwhile, we've pulled off our détente with Yoshi: Not only have we settled the long-standing disagreement about how to use Sean Conroy, but there's a clear sense that we're all on the same side. The same guy who told me weeks earlier that I didn't know how to behave now gives me friendly backslaps when I see him at the field. We've had the old-school, obstructionist-skipper experience, and now we're finding out what the new model looks like, reaping the benefits of collaboration between front office and field staff. Most of our first-half stressors—staking our claim to dugout real estate, fighting (or worse, not fighting) with Feh, longing for Taylor and Santos, struggling to set up our scouting network and overcoming a comical sequence of technical setbacks—have been removed or defused. We no longer have to steel ourselves for any awkward confrontations. The clubhouse feels like home.

Naturally, this idyllic interlude doesn't last. It's almost a relief when our first player gets poached, as it is when a hide-and-seek game goes on for so long that the hider looks forward to being found. At the end of July, Joel Carranza gets a call from the Trois-Rivières Aigles, a Québécois team in the Can-Am League part owned by Eric Gagne and former NHL defenseman Marc-André Bergeron. Because of a connection with Feh, the Aigles have been sniffing around the Stompers all season. They were reputed to have interest in Carranza early in the year, and for a few days in mid-July we were convinced they were about to sign Sean Conroy. Both were false alarms, so we don't believe this scare will be any different until Carranza tells us the Aigles have bought him a plane ticket, something indy-league teams don't do lightly. On July 30, he goes 1-for-3 and comes out early, taking in the final few innings from a folding chair next to the visitors' dugout, a Stomper emeritus. The next day, he takes off for Québec; two days after that, he's DHing for the Aigles.

Joel's ascension reassures the rest of the Stompers that there's hope for them. But it's still a big blow to morale, because Carranza has carried our team for most of the month. Joel isn't much of a fielder: When he makes a diving stop down the line in early July, our bench gets on him, asking, "When did we pick that guy up?" just loud enough for him to hear. He's not much of a base runner, either: In another game, he looks so winded crossing home plate that someone asks him if he's tired, to which he responds, "I just ran from first to third, so yeah." But he's also our most potent run producer. Carranza has hit safely in seventeen of his last eighteen games for the Stompers, posting a .405/.460/.618 July slash line in 100 plate appearances and producing about 60 percent more offensive value over that span than the next-hottest Stomper, Yuki Yasuda.

Joel was one of the few Stompers with whom we were never at ease, although he hit so well that we were happy to have him. He was the closest thing on the team to a star: In Sonoma, a high-pitched, synchronized scream of "We love you, Joel!" accompanied his every at-bat, as he sauntered to the plate holding the barrel of his bat, the length of it angled upward under his armpit such that the handle would pat him on the back every time he took a step. Like all the holdovers from 2014, he predated our arrival, so he knew we weren't a permanent part of the scenery. And while he wasn't outright unfriendly, we didn't get the sense that he was happy we were there.

Feh considered Carranza a confidant, but Joel was also one of the first to announce that the mood seemed improved when Feh was suspended. In an earlier game, I'd heard him commiserating with Isaac about Feh's umpire harassment an inning after commiserating with Feh about Isaac's pitch selection. Upon hearing that Feh had been fired, he told Theo, "Feh was a great ballplayer. I'll leave it at that."

The way he treated us also seemed to depend on the day and the audience. In a game in mid-July, Sam wrote out a report on Pacifics starter Max Beatty, a twenty-four-year-old former Padres farmhand who entered the outing with the league's lowest FIP among pitchers with at least 30 innings. In addition to the usual breakdown of pitch types, patterns, and velocities, Sam wrote, "He's good," which was intended to put our hitters on high alert but inadvertently violated an unwritten rule against complimenting opponents. Joel erased the line, and later grumbled to teammates about Sam's description of Beatty's breaking ball. Sam sought out Joel in the clubhouse after the game and asked whether the report had been wrong, looking to avoid making the same mistake the next time. "It was nails, thanks," Joel said, ending the exchange with an unconvincing smile. (At Sam's suggestion, I wrote "He's horseshit" on our next Beatty report, just to make amends. It went over well.)

Our camerawork may have helped Joel get a job—at Yoshi's request, I patched some clips together to send to the Aigles' manager, just before Joel was signed—but he rarely watched video before games, even when we offered to queue it up. When we open our safeful of happiness surveys after the season, we discover that he didn't take that exercise seriously, either. Even when he did deposit a slip, he rarely filled it out honestly; instead he'd write, "I don't know. How happy are you?" or circle all seven ratings. Except, that is, for his last slip of the season, on which he wrote, "Thanks for everything guys," either a masterful troll or an odd attempt at sincerity that assumed we wouldn't see all the earlier, insincere responses when we unlocked the box. It's as confusing a sign-off as the hug he gives me the last time he leaves the clubhouse, the only indication that I've brought him happiness since I handed him an ice pack after he suffered a groin strain and told him to enjoy the shrinkage. (He laughed and told me to shut up.) In twenty-eight games for Trois-Rivières, Joel hits .267/.362/.433, a comedown from his Stompers stats, but he helps the Aigles qualify for the postseason (a first for the franchise), and after two playoff rounds the team wins the Can-Am title. It's a storybook end to his season but, from the Stompers' perspective, it plays out offscreen.

Joel's departure seems to break the seal on the Stompers. Ten days later, Brennan Metzger is signed by the RailCats, an American Association team in Gary, Indiana. Both the Stompers and the RailCats are professional teams, but the RailCats are much *more* professional, with a real radio station and real video broadcasts and a real ballpark built just for them. Metzger slugged only .389 for Sonoma, but he stole five bases, played a solid right field, and drew enough walks to put up a .407

on-base percentage. We're sorry to see him go. So is Yoshi, since it might mean more *terrible* Taylor Eads in the outfield.

Six days after Metzger goes, it's finally Isaac's turn. He joins the Florence Freedom of the Frontier League, and his absence hurts even more than the others. In addition to being the best power hitter on our post-Carranza roster, Isaac was an adept defender (leading the league's catchers with a 43.5 percent caught-stealing rate) and a vocal leader, the guy who during the first week of the season told Feh to "Keep your ass in center" when Feh spoke semi-seriously about pitching part-time. The dugout gets quiet without him incongruously singing "Jeepers Creepers" when someone takes a close pitch, or telling Jeff Conley *"Fuck* the first inning" when Jeff gives up a few early runs, or saying, "Sounds like a library in here, and I don't like studying" when the relievers move to the bullpen and the dugout chatter dies down. He was also a big, bearded symbol of assimilation—both ours and Sean's. At first we found him intimidating, for no better reason than a primitive, instinctive response to someone large and loud and hairy whom we assumed wouldn't welcome outsiders. Before long, he made us feel more at home than almost anyone else. And not only us. "I'll tell you what, national exposure for the Stompers," Isaac said soon after Pride Night. "That makes me happy. Hey, Sean, thanks for being gay, man."

Isaac hits .250/.304/.438 in eighteen games for the Freedom, who lose in the wild card round to River City, Paul and Santos's old team. Like Joel, he posts pictures of his playoff run on Facebook. In the images, both players wear their new uniforms, celebrate with their new bands of brothers, and show no signs of missing Sonoma. Isaac's other life makes me much more jealous than Joel's. Months after the season, Isaac posts a video that shows him on an empty field, doing a four-way drill that covers every catcher movement: leap up and lunge for an invisible ball on its way to the backstop; block an invisible dirt-ball down the middle; block to the right; block to the left; repeat. The first comment, a "Good luck bro," comes from a former player, a late-round pick in 2011 who washed out of affiliated after six games and played part of a season in indy ball. He's Isaac's age, but he's left baseball behind. "Just still chasing it," Isaac answers, adding that he's in the Frontier League and hoping to move up. "Is this gonna be your last year if u don't get picked up?" the ex-player asks. Isaac says no: He loves it, he's getting better every year, he can't consider quitting because he continues to progress. There's no reason why this exchange, or a dozen others like it from my other Stompers Facebook friends, should make me sad. Yes, the implacable aging curves say that Isaac has probably come close to peaking, and he's almost impossibly far from the "it" he's chasing. But baseball makes him happy, and there are worse ways to spend one's twenties than happily failing to become one of the best 750 players in pro ball. Offices and cubicles can wait.

I still feel sad, in spite of myself.

Counting Feh's reassignment to the Atlantic League, we've now sent talent to all four higher-level indy leagues. On the Pacific Association's online transactions page, the entry for each loss says, "traded to outside league." "Traded" implies a two-way exchange, but most of these moves don't bring back compensation. Officially, Carranza and Metzger are traded for "future considerations," which in practice translates to "In the future, we'll consider raiding your roster again." When the Freedom ask for Isaac, I tell Theo to counter by asking for my old crush Collins Cuthrell, who ranked just below Eads on the 2015 seniors spreadsheet but signed with Florence right after the draft. Cuthrell is slumping, and Florence just activated an injured outfielder, so I figure there may be a chance to profit from a roster crunch. There isn't. Florence declines our request for Cuthrell but kindly offers to send us rookie catcher Matt Rubino, who's batting .053 after eight games and is about to be bumped by Isaac. We accept, because Florence has the hand and we have no hand at all. It's getting crowded on the clubhouse memorial wall.

"Prom season started when Joel [got signed]," Theo texts to Sam. "All of these guys are used to being homecoming kings. Now the guys still here are looking around wondering why they don't have dates. Metzger got a date? Isaac's getting a date? Joel's been getting laid for

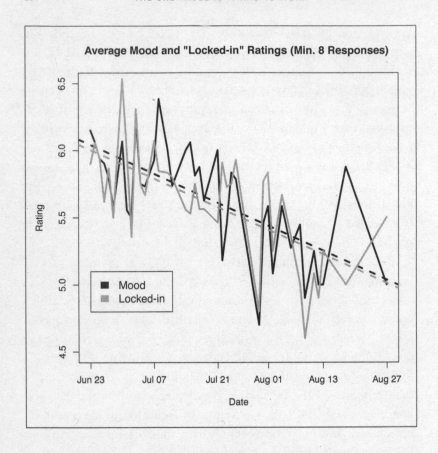

three weeks by his date. Fuck, even Serge and Feh are going to the dance! What about me?!" That wallflower feeling coincides with a steady decline in the team's self-reported mood and self-confidence ratings, which we discover when we unlock the survey safe at the end of the season.

For most of the season, the bench has been such a strength for the Stompers that we've worried about where to find playing time for second stringers who could have been starters in Vallejo or Pittsburg. Very rarely does such depth survive a season. When fans fret about having more players than positions, the solution is always simple: Wait for the surplus to resolve itself. Now, Yoshi has to siphon from that strength just to fill out a lineup card. Parker, the best backup catcher in the league, becomes the best starting catcher in the league. An amorphous combination of Baps, Kristian Gayday, and T. J. Gavlik covers first, third, and DH. Taylor fills in for Metzger.

Rearranging our remaining assets plugs the holes, but it doesn't replace the production. Not only have we lost players, we've also watched some remaining guys get worse. Kristian, who had five multihit games in his first eight starts of the season, followed that up by going eight games without one, and then another eight games before the next. Over that stretch of sixteen games and 60 plate appearances, he hit .157/.267/.177. "I might lead the nation in most cockshots not hit anywhere," he said. Mechanically, he was a mess that everyone thought they could fix, the way armchair scouts always do when guys inexplicably suck. In the midst of that stretch, I heard Baps tell Kristian it looked like he was trying to hit homers, and I saw Feh reposition his hands during practice and declare a breakthrough when Kristian homered on the next batting-practice pitch. "He has the load and the timing, he just needs swing control," Feh said. "The load is the hard part." The swing control must have been pretty tough, too, because Kristian continued to struggle. When Diamondbacks scout Chris Carminucci came to see the Stompers, he told me Gayday wasn't getting his foot down early enough, so I filmed Kristian from the roof of the first-base dugout, showed him how he looked from the side, and passed on the tip, hoping in vain that it would help. For a time, we contemplated cutting him, especially since his offensive struggles seemed to cause (or at least coincide with) a breakdown in his defense. Eventually he pulled out of the nosedive, maybe because the suggestions helped or maybe because he was so sick of hearing them that he decided to make them stop. From his nadir on July 10 through the end of the season, Kristian hits .236/.344/.364, posting a 98 wRC+—almost exactly league average. Average is useful, but it isn't exciting. The guy who made us delirious when he broken-bat homered on his second swing as a professional goes deep only two more times in his remaining 364 swings.

The only thing that saved Kristian's job during his deep dry spell was that Gavlik hit even worse. T. J. made the team because he looked slick in spring training at several positions, but it's bad news when your utility guy gets regular at-bats. After his first few starts, T. J.'s OPS fluctuates within a mediocre range, peaking at .709 and bottoming out at .567. Sam and I don't try to replace him, because we suspect he's the victim of bad luck: T. J. ranks fifth on the Stompers with an average HITf/x exit velocity of 72.6 mph at Arnold Field, and he leads the team with a 37 percent overall "hard-hit rate," based on subjective hit-hardness ratings entered into BATS by the Corduroy Crew. Despite his hard contact and encouraging batted-ball profile—he ties for fourth on the team in line-drive rate—he finishes with a .261 batting average on balls in play, the third-lowest figure among Pacific Association players with at least 80 plate appearances. If the season lasted six months, T. J.'s luck might have changed, and more of his squarely struck balls might have fallen in. But it stops after three months, freezing the stats forever at a time when T. J. is the least-productive Pacific Association hitter who never played for Vallejo.

Taylor Eads, too, tanks when we need him to deliver. From the day that we argued with Yoshi about benching him through the end of the year, his slash line is in freefall: His seasonal OPS declines in all but three of his remaining twenty-three games. Yet what we like about Eads still stands out in the stats. Among Stompers hitters, only Andrew Parker has a higher average exit velocity at Arnold Field than Taylor's 76.5 mph, and Parker is the closest a human can get to The Hulk without turning green and ruining a perfectly good pair of purple pants. Taylor also leads all hitters with at least 70 plate appearances in pitches per plate appearance (5.15) and walk rate (17.7 percent). He does grind opposing pitchers into dust, as Chris Long predicted. He just doesn't make much contact, and while he hits the ball hard, he doesn't elevate.

If Sam and I were inclined to attribute players' on-field performance to their psychological states, we'd consider it highly significant that Taylor's downfall began right after the move we feared—and warned Yoshi—would shatter his fragile confidence. Maybe it *is* significant. Or maybe Yoshi was the prescient one: Maybe Taylor really was too good to be true, and those mechanics really were too awkward to work, as any scout who'd seen him at Spring Hill had evidently decided. Either way, we bought Taylor "as is," and we have to live with his flaws: A team can't rebuild a bad swing with weeks left in a season, especially when it doesn't have a hitting coach and the player won't cooperate. During our mid-July victory-lap lunch with Taylor, when we were convinced we'd signed a superstar, he told us about a friend of his from home, Ryan Eades, a pitcher taken by the Twins in the second round of the 2013 draft. According to Taylor, the Twins tried to change Ryan's mechanics in his first full season, and he never felt comfortable, posting a 5.14 ERA. In his second season, they let him go back to throwing the way he had at LSU, and his ERA shrank by more than two runs. Taylor told us that changing his mechanics is "the only thing that I wouldn't want. I'd rather stick with what got me here." He takes the failure of what got him here hard. I root for him to put the bat on the ball just so I won't have to see him shaking his head and talking to himself on the way back to the bench after another strikeout. "He was a guy who hadn't batted below like .500 since he was a kid," Tommy Lyons tells me. "Never knew how to slump."

Taylor does make one change: After he breaks his bat in a game in Vallejo, he's forced to switch to a lighter model, which he uses to crush a ball that's caught at the wall. After the game, he tells me that he can't wait to try it again, because he knows now that his old bat was too big. Feeling unreasonably optimistic about how Taylor will look with a lighter bat, I email Yoshi to tell him what Taylor told me. When I get to the clubhouse the next day, Yoshi pulls me aside and says he knew this all along, going so far as to call Yuki out of the clubhouse to corroborate the story. Yes, Yuki says, Yoshi told him Taylor's bat was too heavy weeks ago. Great. No one told Taylor, but I'm glad everyone else agreed. Then again, it might not have mattered. Using the lighter bat, Taylor goes 0-for-3 and looks no less perplexed.

Just when we think the Stompers are stable, they have another hemorrhage. With less than a week left to go in the season, the RailCats reach out again, the Grim Roster Reaper returning for future consider-ations. This time, they ask for Matt Hibbert, our best remaining hitter, runner, and fielder. Hib got Metzger a spot with the Stompers, and now, it seems, his friend is returning the favor. For the first time, we actually agonize over letting a player leave. "A little late, isn't it?" Sam says to Theo. His indignation grows when he checks the American Association standings. "Gary's not even going to the playoffs!" The RailCats are thirty games out of first place and twelve behind the wild card leader. (Metzger, who hits .184 and slugs .287, hasn't helped.) Worse, their season ends six days after ours, so Hibbert would barely be getting any extra baseball.

At the start of the season, Theo told Hibbert he'd do whatever he could to get him a promotion, and Hibbert has earned the chance. But we also have a team to take care of, a team that's trying to win a title and doesn't have a Plan B if Hibbert leaves. Conflicted, Theo consults Ray Serrano, the Stompers' 2014 manager. Ray tells him he has to let Hib go: It's a midlevel indy league's lot in life to feed talent to other teams. Even if it's only two weeks, maybe someone will like him enough to bring him back next year. Maybe he'll have a chance. Once Hibbert leaves, the majority of the hitters from our Opening Day lineup are playing someplace else.

This isn't the way Sam and I have envisioned the stretch run. Good teams are supposed to get better after the break, upgrading wher-ever they're thin. We were a good team, but now we're going backward, growing weaker by the day. The cavalry is *leaving*, and Sam's texts are turning morbid.

Sam Miller

> Just listened to a tape of you on Day 1 of camp, saying Hibbs told you how much this already felt like a Team, a Brotherhood

Theo Fightmaster

A man is as loyal as his options.

Sam Miller

The hardest lesson these guys all learn is that the higher league they're trying to reach doesn't mean shit.

Theo Fightmaster

Grass is often greener.

Sam Miller

And it all turns brown and dies

In ten games for Gary, Hibbert goes 4-for-26.

While some of our players are being picked up, others are walking away from their posts, mostly because they have other obligations but partly because it's depressing to play poorly for a cratering team. T. J.'s last game is August 16: He's going to school in Florida to study strength and conditioning. We're being blown out by San Rafael, so he takes the mound just for the hell of it, our first position-player pitcher. Because baseball is cruel, he pitches two scoreless innings, striking out Matt Chavez (who's already homered in the game off Eric Schwieger) with low-70s sinkers and low-60s curves. Taylor Eads, with one year left at Spring Hill, returns to Slidell on the twenty-sixth.

The pitching staff is also evaporating. Paul Hvozdovic pitches for the last time on August 13, then goes back to school to start coaching. "I needed to know what would have happened if I'd gotten a shot," he tells Sam on his last night. "I got my answer." Ten days later, Jon Rand gives up six runs in an ugly inning against the Admirals, who rarely score six in a game. Afterward, he waits for the rest of the team to leave the clubhouse, then releases himself, cleaning out his locker and disappearing without a word to anyone. In retrospect, I realize that the happy-go-lucky lefty from the first half has been missing for some time. The higher his ERA rose, the less he laughed, the longer his goatee grew, and the darker he dyed it, a physical manifestation of his mood. All around us, dreams are dying. The four departed players, all twenty-five years old or younger, will probably never again play professionally. When they cross the clubhouse threshold, they leave their identities as athletes behind.

I can't blame the lefties for leaving. Every southpaw who starts the season with us—Conley, Rand, Hvozdovic, Schwieger, Godsey—eventually crashes and burns. Godsey got released after a drunken altercation at Steiners—"care of wild animals," the police report cryptically said—and his season may have been the biggest success. Paul's ERA rises to 4.92, and his is the best of the rest. We did whatever we could to turn their seasons around. Rand told us that watching his footage and warming up while wearing an mThrow sleeve helped him throw harder, and it did seem as if *something* had: His four-seamer sat at 81 in his first outing, but it climbed to 85 (on average) a month later. Then it slowly sank back down, the *Flowers for Algernon* fastball. Paul was also a video devotee, and he told us our work helped him find flaws in his timing and balance. One day, he experimented with his slider and asked to see the results on a PITCHf/x plot. Sure enough, the difference stood out: Slider 2.0 was a little slower and sank much more, which we had hoped would add variety to his arsenal. But new pitch or not, he had answers only for the Admirals. In six starts, he gave up two runs in 12 innings against Vallejo, but he allowed a combined 22 runs in 17 2/3 innings against Pittsburg (once) and San Rafael (three times), as the Pacifics pounded him with their right-handed heart of the order. Conley, meanwhile, we moved to the bullpen. We told him to work quickly without holding anything back, and we hoped he'd have another gear, like so many unsuccessful starters who've gone on to lead long lives in the bullpen. When he threw his first fastballs in relief, we held our breath and stared at the radar gun—and then exhaled, disappointed, when we saw the same low-to-mid-80s as always, coupled with the same long pauses and shaky control. With nothing else to try, we reluctantly released him, the only spreadsheet signee who officially failed.

Too late, we come to suspect that our lefties' struggles aren't a coincidence. More likely, they have been done in by a lurking variable that stared us in the face all season but had gone undetected despite all our scouting and stat-mining. It finally dawns on us after Isaac leaves, at which point we wonder: Hey, where are all the left-handed hitters?

Answer: not in the Pacific Association, and especially not on the Pacific Association's three non-Stompers teams.

Level	% Plate Appearances by LHH (Including Switch-Hitters)
2015 MLB	42.6
2014 Stompers	39.1
2014 Stompers Opponents	30.3
2015 Stompers	38.5
2015 Stompers Opponents	18.9

That number on the bottom right, 18.9 percent, might be the most surprising stat of the season, even more shocking than Chavez's slash line. It reminds me of a question one of our podcast listeners sent us to poke fun at our tendency to talk about crazy hypothetical questions, like what would happen if players ran the bases clockwise, or a team planted a tree between the mound and home plate, or baseball's defenders adopted cricket's "silly position," so named because it requires standing so close to the batsman that someone would have to be silly (if not suicidal) to try it. "If baseball were different, how different would it be?" he asked. "Would it only be slightly different or VERY different?" As always, we answered it seriously, concluding that the answer was usually "slightly," because baseball's time-tested equilibrium is difficult to disrupt.

When Sam and I embedded in indy ball, we expected baseball to be slightly different. We figured, and confirmed, that players would be worse in certain ways, and that their shortcomings would mean that some strategies made more or less sense than they did in the majors. What we didn't expect was a league without left-handed hitters. Even that was only slightly different, from a spectator's perspective: We watched games for weeks without noticing anything was amiss. But it was *very* different—career-killingly different—for the left-handed pitchers on the Stompers' staff.

In the major leagues in 2015, there were 277 pitchers who faced at least 250 batters. Only 6 of those 277 faced left-handers in fewer than 20 percent of their matchups, with Marlins reliever Adam Conley—a lefty, unfortunately for him—the low man at 15.7 percent. Compare that to the percentages of left-handed hitters faced by our four most-used left-handed pitchers:

Pitcher	% of PA by LHH
Schwieger	9.9
Hvozdovic	11.0
Rand	11.0
Conley	8.6

Jeff Conley faced thirteen lefties, who batted and slugged .200 against him. If he'd faced lefties three or four times as often—which in the majors would have put him right in line with the rest of the league—he might have done well enough to stay in Sonoma all season. For weeks, Sam and I wondered why the spreadsheet had worked so well with our right-handed recruits but had been so disastrous with Conley and so disappointing with Paul. We wondered why Schwieg, who looked good, who'd *been* good in 2014 (when he'd faced 25 percent southpaws), who'd pitched so well in college that he qualified for our spreadsheet before our spreadsheet existed, kept giving up run after run after run. The truth was that the deck was stacked against our lefties to a degree that was unheard of everywhere else in professional baseball. No other domestic pro league in 2015 had a lower percentage of plate appearances by batters who hit exclusively left-handed than the Pacific Association.

If we'd had perfect foresight, we could have assembled a staff full of right-handed pitchers that was tailored to take advantage of the unique conditions in the Pacific Association, and then the book you're reading would probably be called *We Were Right!* or *I Know, Right?* or *Right of Way: Our Wild Experiment Discriminating Against Southpaws*. But, based on 2014 data, there was no way to anticipate that we would play in such an outlier league for left-handers. As it was, our pitching staff was roughly as left-handed as those of the other teams in our league, even though we were facing far fewer left-handed hitters.

But there is a silver lining: If we'd come to our senses sooner and put a strict righties-only policy in place, we wouldn't have signed Dylan Stoops. I find Dylan when I dive back into the spreadsheet of 2015 seniors, inspired by Santos's success and our need for another arm. Stoops, a 6-foot-3 lefty from Pennsylvania, is a control guy who struck out 75 and walked only 15 in 71 innings as a senior swingman for Richmond, a D1 school. His stats have some blemishes: eight home runs allowed as a senior, and shaky peripherals as a junior. But he has a convincing "why": As a junior, he pitched through loose cartilage in his knee, and he was still rehabbing from postseason surgery when his senior year started. He even has an answer when I ask about the homers, explaining, "When our field was being worked on this spring we played at a park that was 280 down the line." I'm too jaded to fall for the neat narrative, but Stoops is easy to talk to and I'm tired of having a terrible bullpen. I offer him a job.

He takes a day or two to think, then sends me the same Dear John text I've gotten so many times this summer:

> I talked with my parents again and I think with it being such short notice and a short stint out there that I just can't afford to do it financially right now. I also have my grad school classes starting in August and I waited a long time hoping something came up baseball wise but I had to go ahead and pay for them already. I wanted to thank you for considering me and I'm sorry it can't work out. You guys were really helpful throughout this and I won't forget that. If it's possible I'd love to be a part of this next year, if this was my only opportunity I totally understand. Thanks again and good luck the rest of the way!

I almost resign myself to starting from scratch with another free agent. But it's late in the season, and I'm sick of the search. I offer Dylan round-trip travel, not caring if I have to cover the cost. My largesse (by the Pacific Association's pitiful standards) seals the deal.

The Stompers still owe me the airfare, but Stoops is money well spent. After a shaky, trial-by-fire first outing, in which he enters with the bases loaded and lets all three runners score, he's almost unhittable. Only once does he come in for less than two innings: He gets a save with 3 2/3 innings scoreless in a 1-0 win, shuts down the Pacifics for three innings four days later, even picks up a start and goes seven. He's the left-handed weapon we've wanted all year, and he's happy to work in any role save for lefty specialist, which he labels "beyond aggravating." Lefties can't touch him (.243/.310/.270), but the few righties he faces have trouble too (.200/.333/.300), probably because he pitches with no discernible pattern, throws his off-speed stuff for strikes in every count, and relies on a more righty-proof curve, as opposed to Schwieg's righty-susceptible slider. "I was blessed with two above-average breaking balls paired with my fastball," he says, when I ask him why righties can't hit him. "[They] allow me to work differently than other left-handed pitchers. With the movement on my curveball and slider I am able to throw pitches inside that can end up off the plate or under a right-handed hitter's hands." Hitters say Stoops is deceptive, and when he does throw his slider, batters miss it on half of their swings. He's second on the Stompers in strikeout rate and second in getting grounders. No one takes him deep.

Stoops, who won a title in the prospect-rich Cape Cod League and was heavily scouted as a junior, is a first for us, a semi-legitimate prospect who slipped through the cracks not because he's atypical, but because he got hurt at precisely the wrong time. I look for a right-handed counterpart on the spreadsheet and settle on Cole Warren, a righty from Southern New Hampshire University. His stuff impresses Yoshi, but he develops a sore arm *after* we sign him, which wasn't the idea.

Unlike Stoops, most of our replacement players aren't special: They're freely available talent that's unclaimed for good reasons. While I'm away at a wedding, the Stompers sign Peter Bowles, a college teammate of Andrew Parker's at Towson University. "Yoshi was comfortable, Theo was comfortable, I was comfortable, the players were comfortable, Parker vouched for him, and he plays all seven positions," Sam explains. I'm not comfortable, but after Taylor Eads, I can't claim that my methods work any better. Bowles goes 8-for-50 with one extra-base hit and, appropriately, is listed as "Peter Bowels" on Pointstreak for a significant portion of his time with the team. Yoshi says he's *terrible*, and for once I agree. Also *terrible*, according to Yoshi, is Connor Jones, a Villanova grad Sam and I liked at the March tryout and kept in mind for just the sort of emergency we're experiencing. After Matt Hibbert leaves, Jones plays center for a few games because he's the best of our below-average options. Soon he gives way to Chad Bunting, an outfielder from Vallejo who's traded to *us* for future considerations. Bunting has a bad ankle, but right now no injury is a deal breaker unless there's visible bone. Sam and I want to trade for an Admirals infielder, Aaron Brill, but we learn that our clubhouse hates him because he once bunted when the Stompers were up big and because he wears stirrups and sunglasses and goes overboard on EvoShield. It's a fatal combination of bush league and big league that earns him the nickname "Johnny JuCo." Everything seems different from the other dugout: Bad calls look better if they don't go against you, and pitchers who throw off-speed stuff in hitter's counts are gutless if you're playing against them but savvy if they're on the same side. Brill would probably be best friends with everyone on the Stompers if we'd signed him in the spring.

We do sign Eddie Mora-Loera, a small, spunky infielder whose college stats make me cringe. And we add Keith Kandel, a small, spunky outfielder from the amateur Intercounty Baseball League, because Yoshi says "he steals the bases." Sam sends eight emails listing the various reasons why it makes no sense to sign Kandel, such as "stole 10 bases in a league where a 5-10, 200 pound catcher stole 18," and "eight errors in 26 games, which is about 1.4 times as many errors per game as Moch has made," and "a 40-year-old first baseman hit .444 in the IBL this year." Sam concludes, "The only way to think that Keith could be good here is if you believe that the IBL is actually considerably BETTER than the Pacific Association." We don't believe that, but we sign Keith anyway. The only alternative is an Arnold Field groundskeeper, who plays in a men's league on weekends and keeps offering to fill in.

Two players come and go so quickly that I don't have time to introduce myself. The first is Aritz Garcia, the Stompers' Spanish shortstop from 2014. Garcia, a popular player and a strong defender who had a .400-plus OBP, had to quit last year after twenty-one games because of a visa issue, which he now says is straightened out. With great relief, we move Moch to second and install Aritz at short. He gets into *one* game before his immigration attorney tells him that playing for the Stompers could jeopardize not only his visa request, but also his chances of citizenship. That's the end of Aritz. The second one-and-done player is Eric Mozeika, a Yoshi find who walked more men than he struck out during his college career. He gets good movement, and we're so desperate for right-handed relief that Sam and I are happy to have him. But on the same day he debuts for the Stompers, Mozeika gets a call from Bridgeport, the Atlantic League team to which we tried to trade Feh. Just like that, he leaves.

I try to slow the revolving door in our time-honored way: with a spreadsheet. I ask Hans Van Slooten, a developer at Baseball-Reference .com, for a list of players who have been active this season in leagues above ours but who haven't played recently, hoping to find an unemployed local with upper-level experience. (It's too late in the season to convince players to travel.) Most of the listed players are injured, but some were released, and a few aren't far away. I narrow the search to Brett Krill, a twenty-six-year-old outfielder who played twenty-nine games in Triple-A for the Giants in 2014. He hasn't hit well since A ball, but if he made it one step from the majors, there's a limit to how bad he could be. He wants $1,000, which would cover his mileage costs plus two weeks of salary. It's not an unreasonable request, but it's crazy money by Stompers standards. I try to talk him down, but he won't budge. Eventually, Theo and I convince Eric to approve the expense. I text Krill to tell him to get on the road—and after all of my efforts he says he's made other plans that preclude his playing for us. The spreadsheet won't help here. Another crisis arises when Moch—perhaps sensing some vulnerability—asks Theo for more money with weeks left to go, claiming that he can't afford to keep playing without the share of Feh's salary that he used to receive. Fortunately, his host family foots the bill.

In the waning days of the season, the clubhouse feels like a foreign place. After two months, I could have stuck all our happiness surveys in the right lockers without looking. But as the influx of warm bodies fills the empty spots once assigned to other Stompers, rookies cramming two to a cubby so the veterans can have slightly more space in a cramped, run-down room that smells of sweaty male no matter where one sits, I have to depend on the nameplates to tell me where (and who) everyone is. The newcomers are nice enough, and they give us their all, but I barely consider them Stompers: They wear the uniform, but they don't have the history, and while most of them make it into the team picture they're missing from our mental images. A few months after the season, Sam texts me, "What was Pete's last name? Pete on our team."

• • •

Baseball is a game that likes to take breaks. To stay sane in the dug-out, one has to find distractions. This isn't easy when you've seen the same four teams play dozens of times: By the last third of the season, we've heard every ad, memorized every walk-up song, made a mental picture of every player, and watched every way in which a fan could collapse during the dizzy-bat race. Players pass the time by staring at pretty girls, picking out anatomical details one wouldn't believe some-one could see at the grandstand-to-dugout distance, especially through a backstop screen. (It's just as impressive as picking up the spin on a slider.) I stare at sunflower-seed shells. Not the ones that get passed from player to player in big plastic packets, but the ones that have already been crushed and spat out. There's a desert of spent shells in front of each dugout, where they've accumulated over months, maybe years. It's impossible to pinpoint the place where shell ends and dirt begins; wait long enough, and the distinction disappears. Each shell was expelled from the mouth of a young man who wanted to make the majors, but who *had* to know that just by being at that field, leaning over that railing, and using his tongue to propel that shell as far from the fence as possible, he was doomed to fall short. Inning after inning, game after game, each piece joins the countless fragments spit from the mouths of other young men, carrying with it some excess saliva that in turn carries the nucleotides that make up the polynucleotides that wind together in ways that in almost all people say, "Nope, not good enough."

Somewhere in those piles, there are Joel shells, and Isaac shells, and Metzger shells, and Hibbert shells, all in unmarked graves. There are Sean shells, also, and this is unacceptable. We don't want Sean to sink into a mass of other unremarkable baseball players until no one knows who he was. We want him to rise to the top.

Sean has set six goals for himself in 2015, none of which was "bring back the fireman model of bullpen management." We've probably pre-vented him from achieving more of these goals than we've helped him check off.

- Have a permanent residence.
- Go to a minor league baseball tryout.
- Master a song on guitar, and record it in one take.
- Have an income.
- Stick with a healthy routine; sleep, diet, exercise.
- Get my guitar.

We haven't helped his income, unless $400 per month (for three months) counts. A host family is the most transient residence imaginable. And although his whole season is a kind of audition, he can't attend an actual tryout when he's stuck in Sonoma. So we try to bring the tryout to him. For weeks, we've watched passively as other teams took our players. Now we want to take an active role and give someone away with some say in where he goes.

If any major league team will keep an open mind about Sean, it's the one that employs Pat Venditte, an ambidextrous switch-pitcher who throws no harder than Sean. So Sam emails the Oakland Athletics—specifically David Forst, who's a few months away from being named GM of the team after a decade as Billy Beane's assistant. Sam sends Forst a four-page primer on Sean: his stats, his splits, his spray chart, his PITCHf/x comparisons, and a study on how the Pacific Association stacks up to affiliated. ("In our estimation, a player who performs above average in our league is probably suited to something a little higher than short-season ball, but lower than high-A," Sam says.) Forst decides Sean is worthy of being scouted, a victory in itself. He promises to dispatch a scout to an upcoming start.

Sam and I are like proud parents fussing before their kid's college interview. We want Sean to look perfect for his big day. "Conroy shaved beard and got haircut," Sam texts me two weeks before the scout is due to arrive. "Looks 15. Has the bad face."

"Tell him to grow it back before the A's come," I answer.

When the appointed day comes—August 25, a home game against Pittsburg—I anxiously scan the spectators. The scout stands out immediately: young guy, looks like a player, equipped with polo shirt and radar gun. Sam is in the dugout, so I scout the scout. He alternates

between watching Sean and checking his phone, lackadaisically raising the gun on (almost) every pitch. I know he's seeing whatever he
needs to, but I still want to *Clockwork Orange* his eyes so he won't miss
a crucial moment that might show that Sean is minor league material.
Sean's stuff has looked sharper, but he doesn't disappoint, rebounding
from his worst start of the year to go six scoreless, allowing four hits
with no walks and five strikeouts. It's all the more impressive because
he's aware he's being watched. (We warned him in advance.)

Before the outing is over (a bad sign), I see the scout stand and
head for the exit. I intercept him and introduce myself, fishing for his
thoughts. He says Sean pitched well and looks like he knows what he's
doing, and that he's sending Forst an email about him right now. He
doesn't disclose what the message will say. We can guess, though, when
we hear from Forst nine days later. "We're not going to be able to do
anything at this time," he says. "As we look towards our rosters and
depth chart for 2016 we'll keep him in mind, but adding someone right
now is not something we're able to do."

It's the story of Sean's career: pitch well in games, fare poorly in tryouts. This time he did both on the same day.

Even as we bleed players, the Pacifics surge, and we struggle to stay
over .500 for the second half, I take heart in some successes. Santos,
after four more relief outings as impressive as his first one, makes
a start against the Admirals and goes seven shutout innings with nine
strikeouts. After that, he's entrenched in the rotation, although we
still use him out of the pen on his throw day between starts, extract-
ing every quality inning we can. Baps, the throwback who bats with
bare hands and applies eyeblack with charcoal, misses time with a
hamstring strain that seems to sap his power, but he still gets his singles
when he returns to the lineup. At midseason, I send for some samples
of Axe bats, a new brand with an axe-shaped handle instead of a knob.
The redesigned grip is supposed to protect the hitter's hamate bone
and improve bat speed and control, and it's found its way to a few

early adopters in the major leagues. Not everyone wants to try the new bat—Taylor Eads's "stick with what's worked" attitude is the norm among athletes—but Baps embraces it. Shortly before hurting the hammy, he hit the hardest ball HITf/x tracks all season, a 102.4 mph bomb that dies in Arnold's outfield like every center-field fly. Only three other hitters touch triple digits all year. "Must be nice to be strong," Tommy Lyons says, seeing Baps get jammed and muscle a single regardless.

But it's not enough. Here's something else Taylor told us, long before he left: "The best teams don't need managers. And I feel like we've kinda got one of those teams here." We did at the time, but we don't anymore. The departures take their toll: Our overpowering offense from the first two months of the season shrivels and dies down the stretch.

Team	June/July							August						
	P/PA	BB%	K%	AVG	OBP	SLG	wRC+	P/PA	BB%	K%	AVG	OBP	SLG	wRC+
Sonoma	4.06	10.6	17.7	.299	.390	.434	127	4.24	10.8	22.0	.257	.356	.360	91
San Rafael	3.53	9.0	16.5	.285	.357	.412	108	3.70	8.0	16.8	.306	.369	.449	119
Pittsburg	3.52	8.6	17.9	.269	.339	.381	101	3.78	18.8	9.4	.284	.357	.376	98
Vallejo	4.02	8.2	24.6	.234	.309	.330	78	4.09	8.2	22.0	.249	.321	.332	80

The Admirals still suck, the Diamonds are still about average, and the Pacifics are still good. By far the biggest difference is the Stompers' Icarus act. In June and July we so outclassed the competition that Chris emailed me to say, "You guys need to move up a league." In August, we're much worse than San Rafael and somewhat worse than the Diamonds, whom Yoshi pronounced *terrible* in mid-June (before they signed Scott David). We're still taking pitches and walks. But our OBP is empty, because we can't hit. Compounding the problem, we have terrible timing when we do get the bat on the ball. Not only are we worse overall, but we're also *way* worse with runners in scoring position, when offense matters the most.

Half	Pitching (wOBA Allowed)			Hitting (wOBA)		
	Non-RISP	w/RISP	Diff	Non-RISP	w/RISP	Diff
First	.307	.332	+.025	.369	.363	-.006
Second	.326	.378	+.052	.351	.332	-.019

The problem crops up on both sides of the ball: We can't seem to stop stranding our runners or stop our opponents from plating theirs. There's probably no deeper significance to this trend: In the majors, it's routine for teams composed of mostly the same players to go from "clutch" to "unclutch" in consecutive seasons through chance alone, depending on when their hits happen to come. In half of a seventy-eight-game season, unclutchness is even less likely to signify some weakness of character or mental malaise. Nonetheless, our batters' inability to get big hits and our pitchers' inability to prevent them reinforce the deepening sense that we've entered the darkest Stompers timeline.

Like a mourner who's recently lost a relative, I comfort and torment myself by retreating to my memory and replaying scenes from the heady days of June: Feh asking our dugout, "Who wants to face us?!"; Rand gloating that a battered opposing pitcher would "sleep like a baby tonight"; Moch describing our lineup as a "never-ending merry-go-round"; Tommy Lyons coaching at first, his arms and legs so covered in the shin guards and elbow guards worn by Stompers hitters who've reached base that Isaac says he looks like the first robot base coach, and Tommy obliges with a brief robot dance; Kristian saying we were so used to mundane doubles and singles that "we only get hyped for home runs now." I recall another rally from a game we won, back when we never stopped scoring. "Pretty sure this guy knows it's only a matter of time," Feh had said, referring to Pacifics starter Nick Hudson, who had held the Stompers scoreless through three. "The clock is ticking." Later, after we'd knocked Hudson out on a Hibbert single and a Serge sac fly, Feh dusted off one of his signature sayings: "Sands of time, boys. Saaaands of time." And after a two-out run in the same game, Isaac added, "Welcome to the gauntlet, baby. You might get through two of us, but you ain't getting through all of us."

Serge, Feh, Joel, Isaac, Hibbert. All gone, ghosts from a first half when if we weren't coming back it was only because we were never behind. Saaaands of time: The grains are still slipping away, but the hourglass has turned over and time has switched sides.

14

BURN THE SHIPS

Ben Lindbergh

> Any suggestions for how to motivate a team that appears to have lost its spark with a week or so to go, possibly in part because some of its best players have left for higher leagues?

Russell Carleton

> Burn the ships. Obviously.

Baseball is a game of failure, the cliché goes. Baseball is also a game of clichés—most of them clichés because they're true, but this one sucks. Baseball is not a game of failure. That line about failing seven out of ten times and still making the Hall of Fame? Not if you're a pitcher, in which case you can *succeed* six out of ten times and you'll probably get released. Not if you're a fielder, when if you succeed only nine times out of ten they'll make you a DH. Not if you're a manager, and failing fifty-one times out of one hundred means a losing season. Baseball is a game of zero sums, every loss corresponding to another's victory. Hitters fail more often than not, but baseball is a perfect .500.

There's a relatively new cliché about failure in baseball that I like a lot more: The other guy lives in a big house, too. Not all failure corresponds to a lack of effort. Or a lack of desire. Or a lack of preparation. Or a lack of skill. We lose, sometimes, because the other guy is also really good.

I hear that one a lot—though not much around the Pacific Association, where nobody lives in a big house—but not as much as I hear the latest sports cliché: *Burn the ships.* The story goes that the Spanish explorer Hernán Cortés ordered all his ships burned upon reaching the New World so that his men would have no choice but to conquer and colonize. The legend has lately taken over clubhouse motivational speeches: In Los Angeles, former GM Ned Colletti told it in two separate spring training speeches. (The second time, he attributed the bold decision to Alexander the Great, which, according to Molly Knight, the author of *The Best Team Money Can Buy*, inspired the batting practice T-shirts the Dodgers wore that season to mock Colletti: "Burn The Ships" on the front, "ATG"—for Alexander the Great—on the back.) In Kansas City, the veteran outfielder Raúl Ibañez told the story to fire up the team in September 2014. It was such a hit that Royals pitcher Jeremy Guthrie went to a crafts store and bought four wooden boats; the team was going to burn them—start actual fires!—in the clubhouse after each postseason game. (The scheme was scrapped, not for fire-safety reasons but because the celebration after the Royals' first postseason win was so frenzied that Guthrie's plans got overwhelmed.) Our podcast listeners send us new "Burn the ships" references almost weekly: T-shirts for sale with the slogan, football clubhouses that have stenciled it on the walls.

The legend is mostly not true—Cortés scuttled many of his ships, but left some—and often misinterpreted. (Guthrie thought the lesson was "to burn the boats so no one can come and grab us from behind," while Colletti thought the point was "scaring the Aztecs.") It is also, perhaps most embarrassingly, recycled from the 1990 film *The Hunt for Red October*. No matter! I think about ships on fire a lot as we pile up losses in August.

- We lose two out of three at home to Pittsburg to start the month.
- Then, after winning five of six against Vallejo, we lose five of six to San Rafael.
- Then, after edging Pittsburg in two of three, we get swept by Vallejo.

The losses go down easily at first. We have already locked up a spot in the league's one-game championship, and we won the first half by such a runaway that we've all but locked up home field for that game, which goes to the team with the better overall record. (Our lead is so big that at one point Eric Gullotta sincerely proposes forfeiting an entire series against Pittsburg so he can take the whole team to Reno.) It's probably not a coincidence that, in 1981, when a midseason strike caused MLB to implement similar rules—first-half division winners were guaranteed a playoff spot—none of the four first-half champs also won the second half. Urgency is a hell of a drug.

The only reason the second half would matter to us is that we can clinch the league championship—and avoid the championship game— by winning both halves. Secretly, though, a lot of us are looking forward to that game. Especially because we're sure it will be in Sonoma.

Except that we look up in mid-August and realize we are in danger of blowing home-field advantage. It will take an epic collapse on our part, and a furious charge on San Rafael's. The Pacifics are doing their part.

Before we play San Rafael in the second week of August, I get to their field about four hours before game time. As I sit in the bleachers, preparing a scouting report and waiting for the Stompers' van to roll up, Matt Kavanaugh gathers his team behind home plate. I think I'm going to have an opportunity to eavesdrop on a speech. By this point, I hate Kavanaugh, who helped incite the fight between Mochizuki and Schwieger, as much as the rest of the Stompers do; we think he's a phony, that he complains too much, that he's the sort of jackass who withholds peanut butter and bread from our clubhouse because he thinks it'll help him win. We call him Captain Try-Hard, and he always seems anxious to try even harder. We are all pretty sure his team hates him, too; we hear stories that half his guys want to play for us next year, that he is always criticizing Matt Chavez over tiny things and that Chavez hates him, that he's almost been fired, that he's lost the clubhouse. He bugs us all. I can't wait to hear this speech.

But instead of addressing the team, Kavanaugh takes a seat behind home plate and cheers San Rafael's rookies through some truly brutal karaoke. Jake Taylor, who's 6-foot-5, built like Jose Canseco, and tearing through our league in his first week of play, sings every range-stretching movement of "Bohemian Rhapsody," then dances and struts through a voice-cracking performance of the Four Seasons' "December, 1963 (Oh, What a Night)." They're having so much fun. They're also winning— after losing a late-July series to us, the Pacifics go 22-5 in the next month, while every other team in the league has a losing record. As we've struggled with the loss of so many of our stars, picking up spare parts based on who would pay for their own flights, the Pacifics' front office has been building a powerhouse. Not only have the Pacifics done a better job of retaining their talent—or, depending on your perspective, a suspiciously poor job of promoting it—but they've also beaten us at our own game, aggressively upgrading at weak positions by working their deep connections and willingness to spend, while we either dragged our feet or found that spreadsheet players were unwilling or unprepared to travel cross country with weeks left in the season. As our lack of contacts has come back to bite us in the second half, the Pacifics have added:

- Jake Taylor, signed out of the Pecos League; he hits .361/.413/.708 for San Rafael;
- Jordan Brower, signed out of a collegiate summer league; he hits .391/.440/.478;
- Chase Tucker, cut by the Frontier League; he hits .328/.345/.455;

- Celson Polanco, a ten-year veteran with affiliated experience; he posts a 3.30 ERA as a starter for San Rafael;
- Guadalupe Barrera, signed out of the Pecos League; he becomes the Pacifics' closer, with a 1.00 ERA;
- J. R. Bunda, a college graduate making his pro debut. He has a 2.95 ERA as a starter for San Rafael.

Many of whom are now singing rambunctious karaoke in front of their entire team—and me. I watch Kavanaugh clap and cheer, and I realize that all the stories we've been telling each other about him are propaganda. We needed an enemy and he had the stripes. I watch him and I realize he is so obviously a good guy. He and his whole team are content, and I am jealous of what he's built: a happy group in August.

One day, I walk into the clubhouse and everybody looks so serious. Somebody makes big "be scared" eyes at me, so I walk right back out. I piece the story together afterward.

A couple of weeks earlier, Matt Walker lost his wallet. Thought it might've fallen out of his pocket in Eric Schwieger's car. Called Schwieg that night to ask if he could look for it. "Sure," Schwieg said, but shit, he didn't want to go all the way out and look, so he just texted back, "couldn't find it." Couple days later Schwieg does find it; tells himself, cool, gotta remember to give this back to Walker. Tosses it into the center console. Forgets. In the meantime, Walker's worried. His Canadian passport's in that wallet. One day, Santos Saldivar, whose locker is next to Walker's, says, "Hey, ever find your passport?" Walker: "Nah." Santos: "Bummer." Walker thinks, *Huh. Suspicious.* Thinks he remembers Santos snooping around his locker, maybe. Starts telling people he thinks Santos took it. Confronts Santos about it. Accuses Santos. Santos says, "Fuck off." The next day, by coincidence, Santos takes Walker's spot in the rotation. Bad timing. So a "veteran" on our team is telling people that a rookie stole his wallet, which isn't great.

The day before the reckoning, Moch is in Schwieg's car, looking for

something in the center console, finds the wallet. Tells Walker. Gets
Walker fired up. Tells Walker, "There was $80 in it when you lost it,"
which Walker doesn't remember but Moch somehow does. Gets Walker
more fired up. The next morning, Walker's telling his teammates he's
going to kick Schwieg's ass. Goes into the clubhouse, calls a mandatory
team meeting. Talks in veiled language that makes it seem like Schwieg
stole from him. Screams at him, trying to provoke him. ("There are no
dickheads on our team," Walker had once told Ben.) Everybody on the
team is horrified that Walker is making such a big deal over something
that should have been handled privately. "Call a team meeting" becomes
a punch line for every small slight. Schwieger accepts a couple days' suspension, convinced by now that he actually has done something awful.
He's heartbroken, and I'm heartbroken for him.

"My iPhone just autocorrected Stompers to stoners," Theo texts me
soon after. "Siri is on top of her shit."

At about this time we're at Steiners, me and Theo and Andrew Parker
and Erik Gonsalves, and the R. Kelly song "Ignition (Remix)" comes on.
It's a party song, but with the honeyed groove of more intimate pre- and
postparty moments, when the circle around you is self-selected instead
of all-inclusive. It's also preloaded with irony, so that white people can
love it and sing it and bounce, bounce to it without embarrassment. It's
the most satisfying pop song of the past quarter century. As always happens when "Ignition (Remix)" comes on, the mood of the bar gets three
levels happier—"toot toot; beep beep," we bunch of losers sing. As always
happens, we all discover that it's not just our favorite song, but also
everyone else's.

That night, we decide to make it everybody's walk-up song for
one game. These days have become so repetitive for the Stompers:
the same routines before every game, the same walk-up songs for the
same nine batters, the same dispiriting early deficits and lackluster
comeback attempts, the same postgame spreads and leftover hot dogs,
the same late nights at Steiners flirting with the same four town girls,

the same hangovers in the morning. Plus, Connor Jones, our newest right fielder, went hitless in his first two games as a Stomper and is blaming his walk-up music. So, the idea goes, we're going to make this one game about the team, not the individuals. When a batter walks up to the plate, he's not going to hear *his* song; he's going to hear *our* song. He's not Connor Jones walking up there looking to get a hit; he's a Stomper going up there looking to represent a city.

It's a stretch. When I try to claim this idea as part of our sabermetric approach to running a team, Ben looks at me with a sort of sad sniffle, that this is what I've resorted to in my quest to add meaning. I get it.

But lately I've been sitting in silence on the drives to and from Sonoma, dispirited and trying to figure out what the stakes of these games are. I've won plenty in my life—board games, Ping-Pong tournaments, hands of poker, etc.—and so I know how little winning changes anything. Winning doesn't end the quest to win. Winning doesn't relieve the pressure to win. Winning is fun, and then it's over. If we win this season—if we finish first in a four-team race for the championship of the fifth-highest independent league—the world will not stop and applaud every time we enter the room. "Oh, you're the guy who won!" nobody will say. If we win, I will drive home afterward and be as broken and flimsy as I ever was. I will struggle not to eat junk food, I will be a jerk to my family sometimes, I will get angry at people who say bad things about my work, I will get nervous about this cough that won't go away, and when I remember that I'm going to die and that so are my parents and so is my wife and so is my daughter I'll survive the existential dread only by convincing myself that none of it really matters, all of it is an illusion. Winning, especially, is an illusion, or at least an exaggeration.

But then what is losing? Losing is the sad inverse of winning, and yet not so easily disregarded as an illusion; losing is ruining me. Why does losing cost me so much more happiness than winning provides? Because, I come to realize, losing is not only the absence of victory but also the expenditure of an opportunity for victory. This feeling gets stronger every day, every time Theo says "summer camp is almost ending." Ben and I will go home after this and probably never again get the chance to affect our favorite sports team. The Stompers as a franchise may never get another chance to win: The Pacific Association, like all indy leagues, is perpetually on the verge of collapse, and a series of owner meetings in August has caused a panic over the state of next year's finances.

Meanwhile, we're watching players *retire*, right in front of us. We're watching guys give up. We're trying to talk them into staying, telling Taylor Eads to cancel his flight back home to Louisiana because *this is it, pal*, this is the chance. He hangs on for one extra week, gets to play third base in professional baseball's first five-man infield, has a few hits and eats some gumbo, but he still hasn't done what he came here for. He still hasn't hit a home run. So when he steps up to bat in his final game, in the bottom of the ninth with the Stompers trying to rally for a win, and he gets his pitch, a 1-2 fastball dick-high that he absolutely crushes, and the dugout levitates, and . . . his fly ball dies at the warning track in our 435-foot center field, he turns right and collapses onto the dugout bench. He buries his face in his hands for fifteen minutes while the team packs up around him, a few guys patting him on his shoulder: his last lotto ticket, scratched. "I'm proud of you," I tell him, and he doesn't move.

Andrew Parker watches over Taylor in the dugout, and Parker is livid at Moch. In the top of the ninth, Moch had half-assed a ground ball into an error, which led to two runs and might have cost us the game. This doesn't make sense to Parker: Taylor is playing what might be the last game of his life. The last time he'll have this view. The last time he'll ever have twenty-one peers waiting after whatever he does to give him five or pat him on the shoulder and tell him they're proud of him. He's leaving everything on the field. You can't run faster than you run on the last ball you hit as a professional baseball player. And then here's this other guy on your team who looks like he doesn't give a shit. How can you know that your teammates' careers are all in the process of dying, that your own career is in the process of dying, and not hustle? At the very least, why not that?

This is why losing is different. There's a variable here besides the outcome of the game: time. Say you could monetize happiness, perfectly. How much would the happiness of winning a championship go for? Let's say . . . $1,800. It'd be pretty excellent to win a championship, to celebrate first on the field and later at Steiners, to collect mementos from the victory, balls signed by the entire team, pictures with the fans, the scorecard you sneak from the dugout, the newspaper with the team on the front page, the handshake concession from Kavanaugh. That's all worth $1,800. You'd trade a flat-screen TV for it, but not your car for it. Fair?

So now how about the happiness of losing a championship? Why, that'd be $0. I wouldn't pay a cent for that. That sounds awful. So the difference between the two is $1,800. But there's another variable in this equation:

$$\text{Outcome} + \text{Opportunity Cost} = \text{Net}$$

And how much is the opportunity cost? How much would you pay to have this summer back? In twenty-seven years, when you're tumbling toward the earth in a skydive gone wrong, how much would you pay for those ninety days of health and happiness and relative youth and the chance to win that celebration on the field? All the money in the world. Everything you ever earned, for the chance to do it again.

If you win, the opportunity cost feels like nothing. You came to do something and you did it. If you had that opportunity back, you couldn't do better than you did; it doesn't feel like a lost opportunity at all. But if you lose, it means you came to do something and did nothing. You could have done so much more with that opportunity. So we now have:

$$\$0 - \infty = -\infty$$

The value of a lost summer is negative infinity. This is the math I settle on. Baseball *is* a game of failure. Every game fails to forestall death.

Which is why, at the very least, I want these days to be memorable.

Which is why I'm proud of "Ignition (Remix)" Day, a day that pro-
gressed, based on my observation of our players, from amusement (two
batters in) to confusion (three batters in) to annoyance (eight batters in)
to boredom (twelve batters in) back to amusement (twenty batters in) to
joy (postgame, when the song was played over the loudspeakers in
full). We won that game. Connor Jones hit a home run. I remember it.
Toot, toot.

"Action feels good," Theo says after that win.

"So good," I respond. "I can't think of a single thing we've actually
done this year that I regret. Only the things I haven't done."

"We should do things."

"We should do things."

So we try. Anything to make tomorrow different from today.

We call a mandatory team meeting at Town Square. A year earlier,
the manager, Ray Serrano, had "called" a "team meeting" at the bar to
celebrate Captain's birthday. The night was ludicrous; Theo ended up
sleeping in Serrano's garage. This year, Theo stopped by the bar on
Captain's birthday, and it was just Captain, alone. It was too depressing
to bear. So, team meeting. Theo spends $200 on cinnamon whiskey
shots. We all cheer. A day to remember.

We write letters to every player. Tim writes some, Ben and I write
some, and Theo writes some, and Theo prints them out, signs them,
puts them in envelopes, and delivers them to each player's locker
before he arrives. We want everybody to remember how good they
were—which, by implication, is how good they actually are—so we
remind them.

Baps,

In your first season of pro baseball, you're the best hitter on the best
team in the league. You have played in 48 games and you have hits
in 41 of them. You're hitting .357 against lefties, which might be the
craziest stat of the entire league; lefties don't hit .357 against lefties
unless they're named Gwynn, Bonds, or Baptista.

This game is humbling for everybody, and there have been times this year we've been humbled to find out that we didn't know as much as we thought we did. But the flip side, and what keeps us going, is remembering that morning in March when we saw you move, saw you hold a glove and grip a bat, and we knew before we even got to see you take a cut that you were a player. It was obvious then, and it's undeniable now: You're a great ballplayer. And we're a great ballclub. Our record is 40-24.

Let's finish this, Baps.

Sincerely,
Theo

Yoshi,

You took over a team in July that was disoriented, that had no momentum and was losing control of itself. We had gone 3-7 over the final 10 games before you became manager. But when you took your seat in the dugout, everything changed about the way we viewed ourselves, and in those 32 games that you have managed we have gone 19-13. We have the league's best on-base percentage and the best OPS; we have the league's most effective base-stealing team, and we have allowed the fewest unearned runs. Our pitchers have walked the fewest batters, and our hitters have drawn the most walks. We have thrown the fewest wild pitches, and we have committed the fewest errors. We have the most doubles, the most triples, and the second-most home runs, and we have scored the most runs. More importantly, we have the league's best manager, the only manager that makes the best decisions based on evidence and isn't afraid to make the right move, even if it's unusual. This team is, top to bottom, the best in the league, and we are fortunate to have you running it for us. We are 40-24.

Let's finish this, Yoshi.

Sincerely,
Theo

Moch,

You're an on-base machine with an intelligent, adaptable approach at the plate. You've walked in 15.5 percent of your plate appearances, the second-highest rate in the league for a full-season player. You've taken a ton of pitches, and you've rarely struck out. You hit the ball where it's pitched. You're leading the Stompers in RBI, and we can always count on you to consider the situation and make advancing the runner a priority. When you've come to the plate with a runner on 3rd and less than 2 outs, you've driven him in exactly two-thirds of the time, which is the best rate of any Stompers regular. And you've done this while spending most of the season at the most challenging position on the field, where you've made some spectacular plays.

Remember that you belong to the best-hitting team in the league. Not the best-hitting team in June or July, but the best-hitting team today. Even excluding Joel, Isaac, and the other hitters who've left for other leagues, the Stompers in the dugout today have by far the best on-base percentage in the Pacific Association, and you're a big reason why.

We won the first half, and now it's time to finish what we started. Our record is 40-24.

Sincerely,
Theo

Mr. Sean Conroy,

In your first season of pro baseball, you're 4-1 with a 1.98 ERA. You pitched a shutout in your first career start. You have 10 saves, which is the second most in the league despite 10 fewer appearances out of the bullpen than the league leader.

Opponents are hitting .182 off you. You're allowing less than a hit and a walk per inning. You also made history with a courageous step forward that will forever help change the landscape of American pro sports.

We are the best team in the league. Our record is 40-24.

You're really good. So are we. Let's finish this.

Sincerely,

Theo

We win that day, too. For the first time in weeks, our team's self-reported happiness levels spike, to their highest point in a month. "Theo gave me a great letter," Erik Gonsalves scrawls on his survey, circling the maximum mood rating.

But mostly we keep losing. It's the series in Vallejo that really tests us: We enter the series 20-4 against the Admirals, who are 21-48 overall. Eric Schwieger starts game 1. Schwieger is trying anything to salvage his season: He's been aiming for so long to get his ERA under 5, and in his previous start he was hit so hard (ten runs, three innings) that there is no chance; indeed, he's now trying to avoid an ERA over 7. This despite our assurances that he has pitched far better than his ERA, and that sometimes baseball's luck takes a long time to even out. Our assurances get weaker every day. He allows six runs in five innings, his ERA rises to 7.16, and everything is awful. We lose 9-3.

Santos Saldivar starts game 2. He's been the best pitcher in the league since he joined us—Sean with better stuff. He cruises through five innings, up 4-0, but in the sixth he allows two hits off our fielders' gloves and another hit on a pop-up that Santos thinks would have been caught had the right fielder been positioned properly. That brings in four runs, and our bullpen allows five more. The more troubling thing is how fatalistic Santos is in the bullpen afterward, almost amused that he is pitching for a team this bad, a team that (in his view) made him get six outs in an inning. We lose 9-4.

Gregory Paulino starts game 3. He's capable of dominance, with two complete-game shutouts under his belt, but occasionally he shows up with his mechanics off (or, we suspect, his elbow sore), lacking his usual high-80s velocity. The bad days are always identifiable in the first inning. In this first inning he allows three runs. He leaves the game down 7-3. Jon Rand, relieving for the last time, allows six more. We lose 13-4. We've been swept by the cellar dwellers. This is our team. Oh, what a night.

A time-lapse photo montage of me through this season would show the following:

1. I gradually get fifteen pounds fatter.
2. My hair and beard grow unreasonably long.
3. I change my pants twice.

If Ben's weird quirk is that he eats cold beans out of a can, mine is that I don't change my clothes. For the first month of the season, I wear the rust-brown corduroys from spring training and a black Stompers hoodie. The zipper breaks on the corduroys, so for the second month of the season I wear the gray Target chinos that I had to buy for our San Quentin visit and a black Stompers hoodie. The chinos get stained by a broken pen in my pocket, so for the last month of the season I wear beige corduroys and the black Stompers hoodie. I haven't shaved since spring training, nor have I cut my hair.

"Why?" Ben asks me one day.

I relate an encounter I had with the movie director Wes Anderson, who told me at a press junket that he keeps his characters in the same clothes day after day so that it becomes a sort of a uniform, signifying the roles they are playing. When they change clothes, then, it becomes a moment of intention and impact, a shift in plot or emotion. My pants give me power.

If this sounds entirely too cute, fine, but we learn it's how baseball thinks, too. All season, we observe the subtextual meaning of a shave. Early in the year, when Jeff Conley was struggling to live up to his pre-season "I'm the ace of the Stompers" pickup line, he shaved his beard but left a goofy mustache. The team loved it, and big-bearded Isaac and

I briefly fantasized about getting everybody with a beard to match him. Jeff pitched his best game of the year that night. The 'stache was a star! (Nobody else followed suit. He looked really goofy.) Schwieger, struggling in July, showed up with a close-cropped haircut and smooth face. Sean Conroy, after a bad outing in early August, shaved his beard down, exposing cheeks bright enough to light a room. He called this "enacting positive change" (or something like that). And, when we're in the middle of our August swoon, somebody arranges for a barber to come and give everybody shape-ups. When Gonzo misses his window with the barber, he downgrades his happiness survey that day to a 3, just as he did the time he ate too much Taco Bell.

Hair matters. Change matters. Two days after we're swept by Vallejo, I get my hair cut short and shave my beard, leaving a creepy mustache as a callback to the Conley start. We're going to San Rafael for a three-game weekend series to end the regular season. We're in a virtual tie with the Pacifics, so whoever wins two out of three in this series is going to win best overall record and host the championship game.

I'm trying to create a moment of intention and impact, a shift in plot or emotion. I want it to be striking, because Theo and I have decided that I'm going to deliver a "Burn the ships" speech. As I practice it over and over again in front of the mirror, I can't help but notice how stupid I look.

I pause before I speak. I make eye contact with the players I trust the most. They settle me. I breathe deep, then pause one more time and start.

"There's a story," *I say*, "that major league managers all tell their players these days." *I go slowly. I speak too fast when I speak in front of people. I spoke way too fast in spring training, and during all the pre-game shift speeches. But I'm going slow now. After every clause. I take a pause. To hit my marks. To keep my meter.*

"It goes like this: When the explorer Hernán Cortés landed in Mexico, with plans to defeat the Aztecs and colonize the New World, he ordered his ships be burnt. This way his men would have no way to flee. The only direction they could go was forward. The only option was victory. History says it worked, but I hate this story. This is a story about a leader who didn't trust his men, didn't think they would be loyal and fight on their own, couldn't do the job unless some manager at the top took away their agency.

"Cortés was selfish as fuck.

"Cortés, to me, is the Pacifics, telling other leagues' managers that their players aren't good enough to move up, keeping them all stuck here.

"That's not us. That's not our team.

"We want to do everything we can to get you guys out of here, and we pay for that. We've lost a lot of good players because of it. But we're not going to be Cortés. Cortés was a bad guy.

"There's a different story I like a lot more. It's about a guy named Hugh Glass.

"Hugh Glass was a frontiersman in the 1800s, before the West had been settled. He went to the coldest parts of the country, to North Dakota and Montana, where the Indians were violent and the winters were cruel and the grizzly bears were everywhere. In 1823, he surprised one of those grizzly bears, and she charged at him, threw him to the ground, mauled him, and left him near death. The party he was with was sure he would die, so they left him. Only two men stayed behind, to dig his grave, and to bury him. But after they were attacked by Indians they fled, too. They took his rifle, his knife, and all his supplies. Hugh Glass woke up abandoned. He had no food or supplies. His wounds were festering. They were so deep you could see his exposed ribs. He was two hundred miles from another American.

"Glass could have given up. Instead, he looked around and said fuck it, because Glass knew one thing: There is no such thing as almost dead. There is dead, and there is alive, and if you're alive you *have a chance*.

"He set his own broken leg and began crawling. To prevent gangrene, he laid his wounded back on a rotting log and let maggots eat away his dead flesh. With no weapons, he still managed to drive two wolves from a dead bison and ate the meat. He fixed his eyes on an isolated mountain far off in the distance and crawled toward it. It took him six weeks. He survived mostly on roots.

"We know this story because he lived. And we know it because people remember. Records get left and stories get told. Your story will get told. Baseball men in major league front offices will know it and scouts will know it. People you know will know it, and people you meet in the future will find out about it. Everything the world remembers about you as baseball players is happening right now.

"Right now, we get to decide whether they're going to remember a team that got frustrated, that felt abandoned, that gave up and let San Rafael be the heroes; or whether they're going to remember a team that said *Fuck no*, patched themselves up, and made themselves the heroes.

"There's always a part where the hero looks defeated. Always. Every story has it. Where you guys are now is not new and it's not unusual; it's the starting point for every third-act turnaround that this world has ever known.

"A couple days ago, I was listening to a tape recording of our dugout during the third game of the season. That was the game when we fell behind five runs in the first, and then we were down 9-2 in the fifth. The amazing thing about that recording was how loud our dugout was; we were talking, we were encouraging, we were rattling the other team. We sounded like a team that knew it was going to win. You might be thinking, yeah, we had Feh in the dugout, and Feh brought that energy. And it was Feh that I heard on that tape. But it was also Baps. It was Gonzo. It was Schwieger. It was Sean Conroy. It was Kristian. It was Moch. And even though I didn't hear him, I'm sure that Hurley was there doing his death stare the whole time, freaking Pittsburg out with how intense he was. It was Hurley who singled in the tenth, stole third, and scored on a wild pitch to win that game 10-9.

"You guys have this in you. I swear to you, I see it, Theo sees it, Yoshi sees it, and everybody's going to see it. When you go out there today, you just need to see it yourself. I want to hear that dugout that's confident, that never stops talking. I don't care if you're a rookie, I don't care if you're new, I don't care if you're hitting .200, I don't care if you're scared: I need to hear you today, and every day for the rest of this season. Don't worry if you sound stupid. The only rule is it has to work. So let's do this."

This: Win two out of three in San Rafael. Just two out of three. Anybody can beat anybody two out of three, and I feel good about how this series lines up. Game 1, on Friday, will be Schwieg, who enters with that 7.18 ERA. But something has changed in Schwieg. He has spent the whole season trying to shave down that awful ERA—if he could just go 2.00 from here on out then it would get under 5, then 4, and so on—but every time a runner got on base or came home to score it was like a punch in his gut; the frustration of falling short of each new goal had turned him sour. Today, finally, he doesn't have to think about that ERA. It isn't going to be salvaged. There is no incremental goal, no pace he has to stay on. He's a boxer who has lost all eleven rounds but can still win this with a knockout. He's calm in a way I haven't seen since spring training.

I believe in Schwieg.

Game 2, on Saturday, will be Paulino, who has two modes: shutout or disaster. His last start was a disaster, but in six of his fifteen starts he's allowed one run or no runs. We don't have the offense to score six against the Pacifics, who will be starting their ace in that game, but we can score two.

Game 3, on Sunday, if best overall record is still in play, will be Sean. The Pacifics will be using their worst starter, who is recovering from mono to boot. If we get there, Sean against that guy is a massive mismatch.

So we need Zen Schwieger or Ace Paulino to show up. Just one. We've mastered shiftwork: I now simply write out the opposing lineup on an index card and assign a number to each batter: 0 means no shift; 1 means a strong shade; 2 means a heavy shift; and 3 means the full, extreme shift, where we give up as much of the opposite side of the infield as we possibly can. I give that card to Tommy Lyons, and before every batter he walks in front of the dugout and holds up a finger. The whole infield sees it and moves. If they don't move enough, Tommy calls out to them. Everybody listens to Tommy, who has feel.

We're even shifting in the outfield. Jeremy Williams, who sprays grounders everywhere, almost never pulls a fly ball but has big power to right field, so we move all the outfielders thirty feet to their left. Maikel Jova has power to left but only dunks bloopers into right, so the right fielder moves in an extra thirty feet. And then there's Jake Taylor, who has a special shift designated for him: a four-man outfield. If the five-man infield worked so well, we figure, we might as well try the reverse. Taylor pulls every ground ball to the left side, and typically for a hitter like that we would pull everybody over that way, with the second baseman right up the middle. But Taylor doesn't even hit balls up the middle; it's *all* pull. And with two men on that side of the infield, defenses have had no problem getting him out when he does: He is hitting .133 on grounders, with none of those outs going to the second baseman. If two infielders and a first baseman are essentially holding him to a .133 average on grounders, we can gamble by moving the last infielder to the outfield, where Taylor's power makes it hard to cover the entire field.

Yes, we know he might simply poke a little single almost anywhere on the infield, but by this point everybody is content with that possibility. Taylor is crushing us, and we have come to appreciate that any player trying to beat the shift usually looks bad for a couple at-bats, then gets frustrated and gives up. If Taylor tries, we'll consider it a win. We will do it only in situations where an extra-base hit is far more damaging than a single: with nobody on base with one out in the inning, or with nobody in scoring position and two outs in the inning.

Our scouting reports on opposing hitters have found a balance between stupid simple and wordy. We've spent three months hearing how our guys talk about opposing hitters—what sorts of things they find noteworthy—and observing which of our reports get ignored and which get implemented. The report I tuck into the lockers of all our pitchers and catchers before the series shows the Pacifics' hitters ranked by strength against fastballs vs. strength against off-speed pitches; by how aggressive they are, as measured by overall swing rate and out-of-zone swing rate; and by tendency to pull the ball.

As for our own offense, we're pessimistic, though in retrospect it's not obvious why: In the ten games after Isaac Wenrich left, we averaged 5.7 runs, and in the four games between Matt Hibbert's last game and the first game of the final series, we averaged 7.5. Maybe we're worried about the same things everyone else is—our lack of an obvious power source, a lineup almost completely cored since Opening Day—or maybe we are intimidated by San Rafael's pitching staff, which has reloaded in the season's final month. For that, though, we also have a plan: The Pacifics' Friday and Saturday night starters are extremely predictable on the first pitch or when behind in the count—the former has thrown seventy-five consecutive fastballs in such situations—but extremely scary when ahead in the count, with putaway sliders that send front hips spinning. We also know that they know that we are the most patient team in the league, working walks and hit-by-pitches and getting into the other team's bullpen. The latter accomplishment will be worthless in this series, as San Rafael has a deep, well-rested, and all-hands-on-deck pen. So we are going to go up to the plate and ambush every good fastball we see. For a team that our managers have kept grounded in such counts all season, this is like getting the keys to Dad's car.

After midnight Thursday, I tweet, "We need to win two out of three to win best record in the regular season. We're going to sweep." Two minutes later, I follow up with another: "But I know how baseball works, so I'm going to delete that prediction now." I do.

Schwieger pitches beautifully in game 1, throwing fastballs down and in to right-handed batters with so much movement that Andrew Parker struggles to glove them. He allows a run in the second on a double and a couple of productive outs, then holds the Pacifics scoreless through the next five innings. He comes into the dugout after each half inning fired up, and screams encouragement to the offense. I'm there with him. After months of keeping quiet and knowing my place, I'm done caring whether I look silly. The team needs to hear from its dugout, and I am in its dugout, so I scream on every pitch. "Aaaaaat-a-boyyy!" I blend in nicely: The dugout is louder than it has been in any game since Fehlandt was still here.

It doesn't matter. We have a shot in the first inning, when the Pacifics' starter, J. R. Bunda, is wild. We get a walk, and then on a 3-1 pitch Baps smokes one to left field. But it's just a lineout to the left fielder, and after that Bunda settles in with a frustratingly predictable mix: fastballs just off the plate away for (grrrrr) called strikes, then sliders for swinging strikes. Contrary to our plan, we don't swing at a first pitch until the seventh inning. This used to kill me, when I'd write out a scouting report and we'd lose because the thing I said would happen if you do X happened when they did X. But gradually I understood that (a) execution is really hard and (b) sometimes you have to do X. Just because the guy doesn't hit changeups well doesn't mean you can throw him thirty changeups in a row. No matter the scouting report, in every game some baseball happens.

We have our shot in the seventh when we put two on with nobody out, trailing 1-0. Then we send up Kristian Gayday to bat against a right-handed pitcher, instead of pinch-hitting with a lefty. Kristian crushes lefties and has hit .188/.289/.268 against righties. In another simulation of this season, we might have spent six weeks fighting with our manager over how many at-bats he got against righties, but we had other things to worry about, and for the most part Yoshi platooned him in the second half. But what Yoshi hasn't done much of is pinch-hitting, and here Kristian gets to bat in the biggest spot of the game against a pitcher he has no chance against. He strikes out looking, and the Pacifics put it away with two in the eighth. Ball game.

Schwieger was ferocious. He landed the twelfth-round knockout punch, but the other guy didn't go down. The other guy lives in a big house, too.

Baseball is a game of failure.

In game 2, which is now a must-win for us if we want home-field advantage, the Pacifics start Nick DeBarr, their best remaining pitcher (and also their pitching coach), who has carried a nasty 'stache like mine on his face for the entire damn year. He leads the league in strike-outs. A former Tampa Bay Rays draft pick, he reached Triple-A in the Dodgers system six years back and has been in indy ball ever since.

The Stompers' starter is Gregory Paulino, who deserves to be the hero of his own baseball book. Since he showed up on this team, he has been pitifully alone. Before Paulino's previous start against the Pacifics, Paul Hvozdovic asked if he could help him with anything. Gregory said no, then reconsidered and said, "You could get my family from the Domin-ican." After the season we see that on his happiness surveys, he never marked his mood as more than a four out of seven. Spanish-speakers have come and gone, but never native and never Dominican. The only time all year that we've seen him interact with somebody from his native country was inside San Quentin, when a prisoner tracked down a Dominican convict and introduced the two. (Gregory looked so happy.) But that's not the primary cultural gap between him and the rest of the team. Gregory is religious. Lots of guys on the team are religious— chapel is well attended—but Gregory is the one player who lives it. When we talk about the team's preferred methods of partying, we refer to the smokers, the drinkers, and Gregory. His idea of a good time is taking the bus to the mall on a Saturday, staying all day, and taking the bus back. His idea of a *really* good time is when his host mom cooks him a bunch of waffles. That's as good as professional baseball gets for Gregory: Somebody makes you unlimited waffles.

Our team loves Gregory, loves him even though he refuses to wear the pink thong that the best player of the previous game is required to wear under his uniform, loves him even though he was the one guy who skipped our mandatory team meeting at Town Square because he *doesn't go to bars*. But for those reasons, too, he has never been part of the team in the same way. And I admire him more for that. About 5 percent of the reason guys are out here is to make some money. About 10 percent is because they want to win some baseball games.

About 40 percent is that maybe they're going to make the majors, and this is how. But the rest is camaraderie. Being on a baseball team is an invitation to a cool group of guys who will love you, fuck with you, drink with you, teach you, learn from you, remember you, and five years later when they're on a team that needs a shortstop say, "I played with a guy in Sonoma who I could call." By staying true to his faith, Gregory gave up that part of the experience. Every game, while the rest of the team was stretching together and making ball talk, Gregory was jogging by himself around the warning track, back and forth, lap after lap, being a baseball player, being devotional, being alone.

Now the team needs him, and, from his first pitch, we can see that we've gotten the good Gregory. On the days when he's bad, his right leg doesn't kick all the way around on his follow-through, and he relies so much on his arm that the 89s on the radar gun become 84s, and the sliders spin slowly. Today he has the full punctuation kick. He and DeBarr both go six scoreless innings, neither pitching through more than one or two threats.

In the seventh, we have our chance: Baps singles to lead off the inning. Moch, aggressive on the first pitch, singles right after. Then it's time for Yoshi to be the genius. Almost every time the Stompers are in an obvious bunt situation, Yoshi calls for the same thing: a fake bunt on the first pitch, then swing away on the second. It's a small ploy, but without advance scouts taking notes on every game, as we have, no other team has figured this out yet. Every time, the third baseman responds by coming way in. The rest of the infield adjusts its positioning as necessary. The pitcher grooves a fastball. And our hitter whacks it, often past the drawn-in infield. And so it is that Mark Hurley shows bunt on the first pitch and pulls it back for a called strike one. Then he shows bunt early, and I can't help but yell, "The Yoshi!" The pitch comes in and Hurley whacks it, past the drawn-in infield. Baps scores with a slide and we take the lead.

We still have runners on first and second. Chad Bunting pops out. Kristian Gayday, again left in to face a right-hander, pops out. Matt Rubino, the catcher we got in "trade" for Isaac Wenrich, grounds to the first baseman. DeBarr goes over to cover, and the throw is wild! It's off his glove! Mochizuki charges around third, he's going to score easily, when . . .

. . . the catcher has the ball and tags him out. It's the most improbable moment of our season: The ball deflected off DeBarr's glove at a 110-degree angle straight to the catcher at home, so directly and with so much momentum that he didn't have to chase it, didn't have to corral it, didn't even have to leave his position, as if the first baseman had called "bank" and sunk the ball in the corner pocket. Moch, in shock, tries to scissor out of the way, but he's helpless. The inning is over, the rally is dead, the lead is one run.

Paulino keeps his shutout going. Through seven, through eight. He goes to the ninth, and we leave him in. We discuss bringing in Dylan Stoops. We stay with the guy throwing the shutout, the right-hander to face the right-handed heart of San Rafael's order.

The first batter is Jake Taylor. His sleeves are too short. His muscles are imposing. He can't hit fastballs. Gregory has thrown him fastballs all game, and he has been popping balls to right field, or fouling balls off toward the first-base side, or swinging and missing, or taking strike three. Paulino throws him a first-pitch slider. His leg doesn't kick on the follow-through.

When that slider reaches the middle of the zone, Taylor squares it up and hits a fly ball to deep left field. Gregory leaps up before he even turns around to watch. Then he turns around to watch. He puts his hands on his knees and he grits his teeth, hoping that something might somehow get in the way of a baseball that has a clear path to Nevada. As it clears the fence, he puts his hands on his head. Behind him, in perfect synchronization, the catcher, Rubino, drops his arms to his sides. Tie game.

Erik Gonsalves comes in to relieve him. It probably should be Stoops, but what happens next has nothing to do with that decision. Gonzo gets the first batter, Jeremy Williams, to hit a ground ball right to second base. The bat breaks, and the eyes of our second baseman, Yuki Yasuda, track the bat instead of the ball. He doesn't move at first, then suddenly sees it, too late. The runner is on first.

And then Chase Tucker squares to bunt, and he pushes one toward first. Gonzo jumps off the mound to field it, but just as he reaches down, the ball takes an odd hop and goes past him; he scrambles, picks it up, and throws to first, but too late and too wildly. The runners advance to second and third.

After an intentional walk to load the bases, Gonzo throws a pitch eight inches off the ground and about two inches off the plate. A good pitch. Almost a strike. With that hard, two-seam movement that makes Gonzo so hard to hit on his good days and, according to his catchers, so hard to catch, too. Rubino has never caught Gonzo. The pitch hits off the thumb of his glove, goes to the backstop, and the winning run scores. We will not be returning to Arnold Field this season.

The day of my prepracticed speech, before the weekend series, I picked up Dylan Stoops at the airport. He'd flown home for a funeral. I had to honk to get him to my car—he didn't recognize me without the beard or the shaggy hair. His flight had landed late, and as we drove up from the city we checked the clocks on our phones and rooted for smooth traffic. I was scheduled to speak in the clubhouse at 5:00 p.m. We got through the city and onto the Golden Gate Bridge (the first choke point), and then down past San Rafael (the second choke point), and onto the side highways that lead into Sonoma Valley. We cheered each pass. But the last threat was the scariest, a four-mile stretch that gets backed up daily behind a stoplight where the road to Sonoma and the road to San Rafael and the road to Vallejo all meet. I'd been in this four-mile stretch for ninety minutes on the worst days. But as we came over the hill that drops down toward the choke point, we saw clear black asphalt all the way. We were going to make it.

I texted Theo: "37." (The highway we were on.) "Probably 35 minutes out." It was 4:12 p.m.

Theo replied: "Yoshi and I addressed the team." Yoshi had misunderstood and called everybody together at two. When I wasn't there, Captain started agitating for Theo and Yoshi to say something instead.

"These guys need to hear something," he said. "You can't make them wait." So they spoke. Everybody, including Theo, agreed it was ... restrained. A few days later, while walking for pizza at 2:00 a.m., I deliver the speech to Theo. He's the only Stomper who ever hears it, though four months later the rest of the team can see Leonardo DiCaprio playing Hugh Glass in *The Revenant*.

15

IT IS HIGH, IT IS FAR . . .

If momentum is a real force in sports, the Stompers might as well forfeit the title game and save themselves a trip to San Rafael. The Pacifics couldn't be coming in hotter: They've won seven in a row and seventeen of their last twenty, including eight of their last nine against us. The Stompers couldn't be coming in colder: We've lost three in a row and seven of our last nine.

Our players believe in momentum. In the same June game against the Pacifics when Isaac called our lineup "the gauntlet," Jon Rand asked me, "Can you feel the momentum? It's a good feeling." And I *could* feel it—how could I not, when our team was in the midst of starting the season 18-3?—but I didn't trust what I felt, not even when we came back to win. Russell Carleton's *Baseball Prospectus* studies show that momentum depends on selective memory, on forgetting games like a 14-13 loss to San Rafael on July 22, when Mike Jackson followed a string of strong starts with a complete ERA killer, allowing eleven runs in four innings. (It was a hard-luck eleven-run outing, if there is such a thing.) Halfway through, the Stompers were trailing 13-6. But we scored one in the fifth, two in the sixth, and four in the seventh, and suddenly we were tied, with the entire bench believing there was no way we could lose. But we did, by one run, when Maikel Jova singled off Santos and drove in the go-ahead run in the top of the ninth, and the Stompers stranded the tying run in the bottom of the inning. The Pacifics had the momentum, and then we had the momentum, and then they took it again. And if it switches sides that easily, it's probably not worth worrying about.

The Stompers had more momentum in the first half than we knew how to handle. Objects in motion tend to stay in motion unless acted on by an external force, but baseball teams are always acted on by external forces: their opponents and, in our case, the higher independent leagues who poached many of our best players. But if baseball supplies the belief in momentum, it also supplies the response: Earl Weaver's old saying "Momentum is the next day's starting pitcher." The next day's starting pitchers are the reason why, when Sam asks for my thoughts on the title game, I tell him I think we're slightly favored to win, even on the road, even after a spirit-crushing sweep.

My moderate optimism stems almost as much from who *isn't* starting for the Pacifics as it does from who's starting for the Stompers. Max Beatty, the best pitcher in the Pacific Association, is not on San Rafael's roster, and it's all because we've done something a major league general manager would never dream of doing. For weeks, Sam and I have been corresponding with Kevin Hooper, manager of the Wichita Wingnuts of the American Association, who reached out to Yoshi for player recommendations in late July. We've tried to persuade him to sign some of our pitchers, but we've also sent him extensive evidences about Beatty and Matt Chavez, hoping he'd get them out of the league. At first, Hooper wouldn't bite, but on August 24 he sends Sam an email asking about the best available Pacific Association starters. Sam, who's already sent Hooper a scouting report on Beatty that was much more glowing than the one on the whiteboard Joel Carranza erased, now tells him that Beatty is "a mile better than everybody else available in this league," going so far as to give Hooper the phone numbers for Mike Shapiro and Matt Kavanaugh. When Sam follows up the next day, Hooper tells him, "We got Beatty! Thanks for all your help." Oh, nothing in it for us, Hoop. Just a couple of selfless citizens hoping to help out a young man who just happens to pitch for the team we're about to play in a winner-take-all title game.

After this exchange, Sam and I are certain we've seen the last of Beatty, so we get the scare of the season before Sunday's regular-season finale when the Albert Park PA man announces that "El Diablo, Max Beatty" is throwing out the first pitch. It's a nickname, and a surprise entrance, worthy of a professional wrestler: My expression mirrors the stunned disbelief on Kane's face when The Undertaker's gong sounded unexpectedly at Royal Rumble 2004. But the gong was a fake-out, and so is Beatty's return. Like Santos in River City, Beatty was signed to substitute for an injured pitcher, made one ineffective start, and was released when the pitcher he'd replaced decided to make a comeback. The Pacific Association's rosters are frozen, and because Beatty left the league, he's no longer eligible to pitch for the Pacifics—although I still worry that they'll find a loophole and somehow sneak him in.

Celson Polanco is scheduled to start instead. Yoshi, Sam, and I agree that the Pacifics have done us a favor: We're relieved that they've already burned Nick DeBarr, whom our stats had neck and neck with Beatty. But Polanco, a Dominican righty, isn't an easy assignment: He had a shaky first start against Pittsburg on August 4, but since then he's gone at least seven innings in four consecutive starts, including a nine-inning, thirteen-strikeout performance in his title-game tune-up (against the Admirals, but still). Polanco has an imposing mound presence—earringed and dreadlocked, he's listed at (and looks) 6-foot-4, 250, and he releases the ball from 6.6 feet off the ground, the highest of anyone in our database—but he's more of a soft tosser than his stature would suggest. The Pacifics picked him up on a tip from Maikel Jova, who played against him in the North American League in 2012. (I try not to be bitter about the fact that the best tip we got from *our* players in August gave us .160-batting Peter Bowles.) At thirty-one, Polanco is in his tenth pro season and his sixth independent league, after four years in the Houston Astros and Toronto Blue Jays systems.

There's zero debate about who's starting for the Stompers: Santos. In mid-August, we almost lost Santos to the same enemy that took T. J., Taylor, and Paul: higher education. Although his last semester at Southern University doesn't start until after the championship game, he had to enroll in person, and the deadline was during our season. Rather than lose his remaining starts—especially this one—the Stompers paid to fly him to Louisiana and bring him back to Sonoma the following week. This is why: Since July 15, the day Santos debuted, the four best pitchers in the Pacific Association (minimum 20 innings pitched) by wOBA allowed have been Santos, Beatty, DeBarr, and Dylan Stoops. (The worst: our Opening Day starter, Matt Walker, who allowed a home run to Pacifics *reliever* Cory Bostjancic—making his first professional plate appearance—in his swan song on Sunday.)

Beatty and DeBarr aren't available, so advantage Sonoma (although Polanco—who outdueled Santos, Dylan, *and* Sean Conroy in a game on August 15—would rank sixth on the list). Other than Santos and Dylan, there are only two Stompers pitchers who could conceivably pitch again: Sean Conroy and Mike Jackson, who last started five days ago but hasn't worked out of the bullpen since the first half of the season. Whatever else Sam and I may have failed to do right this season—and there's a long list of failures—we'll always have this: We signed the three Stompers pitchers most likely to appear in the championship game, and we talked another team into signing the stud who would have started for the Pacifics. Since the playoff will decide the champion of the Pacific Association's season, any swing in the odds of winning this single game has a huge impact on our championship probability. The upgrade from whoever would have started for the Stompers in the absence of Santos, Dylan, and Sean and the drop-off from Beatty to Polanco have to be worth a big bump in win expectancy, so I'm mentally awarding myself and Sam some fraction of a championship regardless of whether we win. Process matters more than results, right?

For analytical purposes, probably: This game won't tell us much about which of these two teams is better, let alone which was better before we had to fill holes with whomever we had on hand. The problem with "process" is that whatever we might tell ourselves about the analytical insignificance of a single game, our emotional state and sense of self-worth hinge on this one win. Before the weekend series in San Rafael started, Sam told me he didn't care about the championship; he just wanted to finish with the best record in the league, since that would be a more meaningful achievement. I understand the sentiment, but I want the title. And so does Sam, now that it's what we have left. Theo, who may want to win more than we do, suggests that we collect the players' ring sizes to remind them what's at stake. I borrow a ring sizer from a local jeweler, but the plan feels too hokey to put into practice. Plus, this is the Pacific Association: Even if we won, we could only pay for Ring Pops.

The night before the game, I stay up late with my laptop and hard drive cutting together clips, the Thelma Schoonmaker of the Pacific Association. I make videos of Santos, Dylan, Sean, and Mike facing current Pacifics hitters, upload them to YouTube, and send them around. "You guys are great," I write. "Go make more highlights." Then I make videos of every probable Pacifics pitcher from games against the Stompers, upload those, and send them to our hitters. "Know your enemies," I add. The only response to either email I receive from a Stomper, other than a "Thanks Ben!!" from Yoshi, comes *after* the game, when Keith Kandel contacts me to ask if I can make a highlight video of Keith Kandel. Later, Moch also mentions that he wants one of himself.

I expected as much. My time in the clubhouse has taught me that players at this level are lukewarm on preparing for opponents. When they're watching video of themselves, though, they're like the dudes on *CSI* who frown at satellite footage and ask the nerds next to them, "Can we clean that up at all?" So in the spirit of making every moment memorable, and in the interest of distracting our players from how much apparent momentum San Rafael has, and also because Yoshi asked me to, I make the mother of all highlight packages, a six-minute, season-spanning reel of every uplifting moment the still-active Stompers have had against the Pacifics all season. I set up the TV from my living room in the tiny visitors' clubhouse in San Rafael, connect it to my computer, and crank up the volume. Yoshi calls the team together just before the players take the field to warm up, and I press PLAY.

The sweet sounds of "Ignition (Remix)" fill the room, and instantly everyone in the standing-room-only crowd is smiling, very much in the mood to watch themselves be good at baseball. The hitter clips play first, solid swing after solid swing, drawing oohs and ahhs and whistles and insults. Then the pitchers are up, throwing pitch after pitch past Pacifics bats, each whiff generating jeers like it's the end of a round in a rap battle. The reel wraps up, after two times through "Ignition," with a view from center of Mark Hurley's walk-off homer against Pittsburg on July 8, the whole team waiting for him at home plate, holding each other back, and finally enveloping him. If it's not *quite* as inspirational as the "important moment" montage you've seen at every stadium, with Bluto yelling in *Animal House* and Howard Beale yelling in *Network* and Rocky running up the steps, it's pretty darn close—and maybe better, because it's *us* on the screen, and after all those mistake pitches and weak swings the Pacifics seem *terrible*. The players thank me and stream out to the field. Sam says "nice job," and his smile dissolves any lingering friction between us caused by the difficult decisions we've made (or not made) about a baseball team neither of us had heard of a year ago. We haven't always agreed on how to get here, but we both desperately want to win tonight.

We'll have to do it with a lineup that includes four newcomers— Kandel, Bunting, Rubino, and Mora-Loera—who've combined for 83 plate appearances as Stompers.

Sonoma Stompers			San Rafael Pacifics		
Name	Bats	Position	Name	Bats	Position
Yuki Yasuda	R	2B	Zack Pace	L	CF
Keith Kandel	R	RF	Danny Gonzalez	R	SS
Daniel Baptista	L	1B	Maikel Jova	R	RF
Chad Bunting	R	CF	Jake Taylor	R	1B
Gered Mochizuki	L	SS	Jeremy Williams	R	LF

Mark Hurley	R	LF	Chase Tucker	R	2B
Andrew Parker	R	C	Ricky Gingras	L	C
Matt Rubino	L	DH	Johnny Bekakis	R	DH
Eddie Mora-Loera	R	3B	David Kiriakos	R	3B

Kandel batting second in a must-win game is like something out of Sam's and my nightmares: He's the old-school idea of a number-two hitter, the speedy, slappy type, not the Hurley or Baps who belongs there (as we've been trying to impress upon Yoshi all year). But Kandel is hitting .385/.467/.692 in his four games for Sonoma, and he supposedly "steals the bases," so second hitter he is. The one consolation is that the Pacifics also have a singles hitter, Danny Gonzalez, in that spot. Matt Chavez, He Who Must Not Be Pitched To, has belatedly left the league, signed by the San Diego Padres in late August and assigned to their high-A affiliate in Lake Elsinore, where he's three and a half years older than the league-average player. He's the first Pacific Association product plucked directly out of the league by an MLB team.

We'd love to take credit for this signing, too: We've been complaining to Chris Long about Chavez for months, and Chris has been talking to the Padres, his former employers. But the Padres' assistant general manager, Josh Stein, bursts that bubble, telling me that the team pursued Chavez because of a recommendation from a former big leaguer, the late Tony Phillips (who played eight games for Pittsburg at age fifty-six), and a childhood connection between Matt Kavanaugh and Padres area scout Sam Ray. "Sam went and watched him for a couple games, saw raw power in BP, saw him get pitched around a lot in games, spent some time with Matt and thought he merited a shot," Stein says. "We discussed it internally and felt like we could find enough PA's in the Cal League to give it a real shot for the rest of this year and then we'll see where it takes us."

I'm content with where it's already taken Chavez: away from San Rafael. (I'm also happy to hear that being pitched around was a point in Chavez's favor, since Kavanaugh tried to pressure Yoshi into pitching to him by telling him the intentional walks we were issuing would hurt him.) Chavez finished with a 216 wRC+, which means he created 116 percent more runs than a league-average player would have in the same number of plate appearances. To put that into perspective: Barry Bonds's wRC+ was 220 from 2000 to 2004, when he hit 258 homers, drew 306 intentional walks, and won four MVP awards (plus one runner-up finish). The self-confidence (or self-delusion) of professional athletes is a powerful force: To the last plate appearance, and the last long home run, our pitchers were confident that they could get Chavez out the *next* time, despite our instructions to pitch around him or put him on. But against the Stompers, specifically, he was far better than Bonds in his best season, doing more damage against us than he did against Pittsburg and Vallejo combined.

Opponent	PA	HR	AVG	OBP	SLG	K%	BB%	wRAA	wOBA	wRC+
vs. Stompers	107	17	.412	.533	1.059	15.0	15.9	26.8	.594	278
vs. Non-Stompers	201	14	.367	.433	.667	20.0	9.5	23.8	.455	183

Factoring in playing time, Chavez's offense was about 2.5 times more valuable than anyone else in our league, even though he missed the last 15 percent of the schedule. Yet the Barry Bonds of the Pacific Association was considered a borderline candidate for high-A, which is three levels below the big leagues. Baseball is hard.

We're not the Stompers of old, but neither are they the peak Pacifics. We've lost roughly a third of our roster, and the Pacifics have lost their two best players. I'd like to make this matchup sound like an epic, last-gasp showdown between two teetering giants, Superman and Doomsday punching each other to pieces. But it's less glamorous than that. We're more like watches that haven't been wound—still ticking, but too slowly. It's the last evening in August, and unless this game goes to extras, neither team will live to see September. *Saaaands of time.*

· · ·

Before the season started, when Sam and I still dreamed big, we wondered whether we could win games by telling our hitters not to swing once they were ahead in the count by two balls, on the theory that Pacific Association pitchers wouldn't be able to throw strikes often enough not to walk them. Even in the majors, pitchers' control is less pinpoint than you think. Since 2009, on 3-0 counts with opposing pitchers at the plate, major league pitchers have thrown the ball in the strike zone only 68.0 percent of the time (520 times out of 765). Think about that: These were situations in which there was no chance that the batter would swing, even on a lollipop directly down the middle, and yet pitchers threw the ball in the zone barely more than two-thirds of the time. Granted, that's a skewed sample, because control artists aren't likely to fall behind a pitcher 3-0 in the first place. But it's backed up by COMMANDf/x data that shows that MLB fastballs miss their targets by roughly eleven inches, on average, only half a foot less than the width of the plate.

We abandoned the idea of the "stop swinging" strategy when we got data from Sportvision that showed that low–minor league pitchers aren't that much worse than big leaguers at throwing strikes when they have to—and also when we thought about how much our hitters would hate us if we told them always to take on 2-0 and 3-1. But the Stompers still have the league's lowest swing rate (41.1 percent, with the three other teams clustered between 47.2 and 48.4), and that could come in handy tonight, since Celson Polanco tends to nibble against lefties and almost always throws his breaking balls outside the strike zone.

On his first four pitches, Polanco misses his spots by feet, not inches. Yuki, who has the league's lowest swing rate, doesn't offer at any of them, and forty seconds into the game the Stompers have a runner on first. After two more balls to start Kandel's at-bat, Ricky Gingras, the Pacifics' catcher, calls time and goes out to talk to Polanco, who looks frustrated and fusses with the resin bag. In the first-base coach's box, Tommy Lyons thinks, "Wow, we have it. They're giving it to us." Maybe Polanco will never throw a strike. Just more balls and more walks, loading the bases and forcing in runs, until Kavanaugh has no choice but to take him out. But whatever Gingras says seems to settle Polanco down, and he throws two called strikes to Kandel, who then pops out.

The outfield flags are hanging limp. There's no wind, which is almost unheard of during night games in San Rafael, where our camera in center often blows over. It will stay upright tonight. Baps, the third batter, swings his new pink bat (which he calls "the Pink Panther") and wallops the first pitch to left-center, but Zack Pace, as always, gets a good jump and tracks it down, having covered a wide swath of the outfield without looking as if the outcome was ever in doubt. Baps tells us later that he thought he'd hit a homer, but the ball isn't carrying. Polanco gets Chad Bunting to ground out, and now it's Santos's turn. Polanco threw eleven fastballs in twelve pitches in the first, because he was never ahead in the count, but Santos, who knows he has Sean and Dylan behind him, doesn't keep any of his arsenal in reserve. He starts Pace with a changeup, then switches to the sinker, then fires two fastballs at 90. Pace grounds out, and Andrew Parker—who's using hand signals instead of his fingers, which Santos can't see—calls for a first-pitch curveball and a second-pitch slider to Danny Gonzalez, who lines a shot that Santos spears as he falls off the mound to the first-base side. Maikel Jova swings at a high fastball, another 90, and pops the Pacifics out of the inning.

Both sides go quietly in the second, but in the third inning the Stompers apply pressure. Leading off, Matt Rubino drills a line drive to deep right-center. Pace's pistoning feet kick up dust on Albert Park's outfield diamond, making it look as if he's being strafed by a pursuing fighter. But he's timed his sprint perfectly, and he snags this one, too. Polanco loses the zone again with Eddie Mora-Loera up, falling behind 3-0 and walking him on a way-wide 3-1 pitch. Then he throws away a pickoff attempt, allowing Eddie to advance to second. Yuki pushes a bunt past Polanco to make it first and third with one out, then steals second without a throw on the first pitch to Kandel. Keith reaches out and slices the second pitch to shallow right, where Jova makes a shoe-string catch. It's not a surefire sac fly, but it's deep enough to try, so Eddie tags and breaks for the plate. He stops on the way home, as if surprised that Jova has unleashed an Ichiro, but the throw from the normally strong-armed right fielder is actually weak, wayward, and cut off by first baseman Jake Taylor. Now Eddie seems surprised that Jova *hasn't* unleashed an Ichiro, but Taylor is running right at him and throwing to Chase, so Eddie takes off for the plate again. Tucker at third throws the ball home, and Gingras goes ten feet up the line to catch it and apply the tag to Eddie, who tries in vain to scurry around him. In fifteen seconds, the Stompers have gone from a rally with an expected payoff of roughly 1.3 runs to an inning-ending double play. And they owe it to what Baseball Twitter would call a TOOTBLAN, "Thrown Out on the Bases Like a Nincompoop."

In the bottom of the third, Santos is fully armed and operational. Johnny Bekakis K's on three pitches, taking a called strike on a slider and then waving weakly at a curve and another slider in the dirt. David Kiriakos singles, Pace strikes out—a rare occurrence—on a fastball up, and Gonzalez goes down swinging on another nasty slider down and away. Santos, who threw a curve at 68 and a fastball at 90, slaps his chest on his way off the mound, with five strikeouts through three innings.

In the fourth, he walks Jova, which is even harder to do than striking out Pace: The San Rafael right fielder entered the game with only 13 walks in 354 plate appearances, the league's second-lowest rate. The second pitch to Jake Taylor, a fastball in the dirt, gets by Andrew Parker and goes to the backstop, and now Santos is in trouble, down 2-0 to the Pacifics' best hitter with no outs and a runner in scoring position. The next pitch is almost the worst-case scenario: It's a hanging slider, waist-high for the 6-foot-5 first baseman, and Taylor puts his whole behemoth body into the swing. The slider doesn't do anything except sit on a tee at 76, but there's a corollary to the principle that pitchers can't always throw strikes: Hitters can't always hit hanging sliders, and Taylor swings through this one. The next pitch is lower and slower, coming in at 70 mph and corkscrewing inside, and Taylor whiffs again. After that, there's a fastball up and away at 88, and Taylor is called out on a check-swing by home-plate umpire Dean Poteet, the only ump who earns regular compliments from Pacific Association players. It's Santos's sixth consecutive out via the strikeout, only the second time a Pacific Association pitcher has done that in the same game this season. (Beatty did it in June.)

But then Jeremy Williams singles to left, and Mark Hurley makes a mental mistake, throwing to third even though Jova is already there. Williams takes second on the throw as Yuki, the master of fundamentals, stands in front of the base and lifts up his arms in exasperation. The next batter, Chase Tucker, reaches out for a 2-2 slider away and pulls it softly through the same hole, the weakest possible single. Jova scores, and this time Hurley holds the ball, triple-pumping as if he's afraid to throw to the wrong base again and decides that the safest course is not throwing it anywhere. Williams scores standing up, and Tucker advances to second the same way Williams did, as the ball eventually comes in to Eddie at third base.

Two runs have scored on a walk, two Hurley mental mistakes, and a lousy excuse for a single, and even that small lead, which wouldn't have made me nervous in June, now seems almost insurmountable. The Stompers haven't had a come-from-behind victory since August 7, and that was a 1-0 deficit after the top of the first, which they erased in the bottom half. The last time they won a game they were trailing at the *end* of an inning was July 30, which was before eight of our current twenty-two players joined the team. To make matters worse, it's a weekday. Over the past two seasons, Pacific Association teams have slugged 43 points higher on Saturday and Sunday than they have from Monday through Friday. We think we know why. Weekday games start later, which makes them colder, darker, and more hostile to hitters— hardly the ideal conditions for the comeback we now need.

With one out in the top of the fifth, Rubino lines a solid single to center, and with Mora-Loera up Polanco loses the plate again, walking him on four pitches, the last of which almost goes over the head of his catcher. "He can't throw strikes to short guys," I say to Sam, and sure enough, Polanco walks Yuki, who now has two more walks than strikeouts on the season. That loads the bases for Keith Kandel; he just needs to hit a fly ball somewhere to score a run. Instead, he strikes out half-swinging at a fastball over the plate, and I'm angry about the batting order all over again. Baps strikes out, too—but not before an 0-1 fastball inside crosses up Gingras and glances off his glove to the backstop, allowing Rubino to come in from third. We're back within one.

The reduced deficit lasts seven minutes. Santos gets two easy flies for outs in the fifth, but then walks Danny Gonzalez, another aggressive hitter who usually has to hit his way on. Walking a nonwalker comes back to bite him again. Santos gets Jova to swing through a slider low and away, and Parker wants another slider in the same place. But Santos misses inside, and Jova, who rarely misses bad breaking balls, drives a double to left. Gonzalez scores, and we're down two again, this time with three fewer outs remaining.

As Chad Bunting leads off the next inning for the Stompers, Sean Conroy gets up in the pen; Santos's season is over. Sean hasn't pitched since his audition for the A's, so if needed he's fully prepared for another fireman appearance like his late-July triumphs over San Rafael. Bunting sees ten pitches, fouling off seven, before striking out. Moch walks, another free pass for a short guy, and takes a big lead off first. For most of the season, stolen bases were a weapon for the Stompers, who entered this game with by far the league's best stolen-base success rate and stolen-base run total.

Team	SB	CS	SB%	SB Runs
Stompers	88	28	75.9	10.3
Admirals	127	53	70.6	8.5
Pacifics	34	19	64.2	1.2
Diamonds	56	34	62.2	−0.5

Much of that success, though, had come from Hibbert and Feh: Moch has attempted only three steals all season. Nonetheless, he takes off on 1-2. In this league, Gingras is an average-throwing catcher, with a 2.05 pop time and a 35 percent caught-stealing rate (average is 32). Moch picks a changeup, but it's high and out over the plate, giving Gingras an easy release. Moch slides in too late, a precious runner erased. The next pitch hits Hurley high on the back, which would've advanced Moch anyway, assuming Polanco had thrown the same pitch.

"I don't think Hurley's going to be stealing here," Tim says on the radio broadcast. "Parker can definitely run into one." But Hurley *does* take off, on the very first pitch, and he's thrown out, too. We're down two runs, and we've run into three outs on the bases. This isn't like us. "I didn't like that he stole while I was hitting," Parker says after the game. "Just in case I hit one, 'cause that would be a tied ball game. I understand them moving shit, but . . ."

"Desperate," Sam says.

"Yeah," Parker replies. "Like almost a panic. Like, we're not doing shit, but . . . blink and a blast away from a tie ball game."

I assume this is a counterproductive Yoshi attempt to manufacture runs; weeks earlier, he'd told me that he wanted someone who could steal the bases if we needed to scratch out runs in the title game. According to Tommy Lyons, though, the steal sign wasn't on. Moch and Hurley acted on their own.

Sean, who lied and circled two sevens on his pregame happiness survey because it worked so well on Pride Night, comes into the game and sets down the Pacifics in the sixth, aided by Moch, who ranges far up the middle to snare a Williams bouncer, spin, and fire to Baps, who scoops it. Eddie (short guy!) walks *again* in the top of the seventh, but that's all the Stompers muster. Sean works around a Gonzalez walk to post another zero in the bottom half. Just before Jova makes the final out of the inning, the Pacifics' PA man announces that the concession stands will be selling beer beyond the seventh inning. "We have not yet had last call," he says. I hope that also applies to our offense.

Polanco's at 109 pitches (and on his fourth trip through the lineup) as the eighth inning begins, and if Sam and I were in the Pacifics' dugout, we'd be screaming for a reliever. Patrick Conroy, a lefty, is up in the Pacifics' pen for the fourth time, and closer Guadalupe Barrera is stretching. Soon, another lefty, Chris Lovejoy, joins them. But Polanco is still going strong. Keith leads off with a strikeout, and Williams makes a running catch on a Baps fly to left that almost falls in. We're down to four outs.

After going down 1-2, Bunting—possibly reaping the benefits of making Polanco work extra hard in his previous at-bat—gets hit in the rib area, a painful place where Jon Rand once told me he likes to throw at hitters because "no one works out lats in baseball." That brings up Moch, the lefty, and Kavanaugh heads to the mound for what seems like a certain call to the pen for one of the two lefty relievers he has waiting. Polanco has thrown 120 pitches, and Moch has been a much better hitter against right-handers (138 wRC+ vs. righties, 93 wRC+ vs. lefties). He's also a short guy, Polanco's apparent kryptonite. But Kavanaugh opts to stay with Polanco, who receives a round of motivational butt slaps as his teammates leave the mound. The first pitch is low and in for ball one. Pitch two is low and even farther in. Pitch three is high and away, and pitch four is low. Moch drops his bat and trots to first, and Polanco turns to our center-field camera and drops a beautifully framed F-bomb.

Now Kavanaugh comes and gets Polanco, and brings in the lefty Lovejoy to face the right-handed Hurley. Hurley has a 153 wRC+ vs. lefties, and a 112 wRC+ vs. righties; Lovejoy has allowed a .222 wOBA to lefties and a .303 wOBA to righties. This might be the worst managerial move ever made.

"What the hell is he doing?" I ask Sam.

"Shut up shut up shut up," Sam answers.

Since Sam isn't feeling social and I don't want to be in the dugout if this doesn't work out, I decide that I'd like a change of scenery (for non-superstitious reasons, I swear). With no other games going on, we have a second camera set up in the stands directly behind home plate, where our entire scouting staff is assembled to see the last act of the summer. When I join them, they give me anxious smiles and speak in hushed tones, as if they're afraid any additional stress might make me snap.

Hurley takes a called strike, then gets an 82 mph fastball that floats over the middle. He swings and grounds the ball into left field, the twin of Tucker's run-scoring single in the fourth. Bunting scores. Moch almost gets back-picked at second by the throw in from Williams but dives back to the bag safely.

Next up is Andrew Parker, who kills left-handed pitching. Actually, "kills" is an understatement. Here are Parker's 2014–15 platoon splits:

Split	PA	HR	AVG	OBP	SLG	wOBA
vs. LHP	250	18	.255	.384	.569	.392
vs. RHP	359	8	.162	.351	.279	.316

The only thing Parker does better against right-handers is get hit by the ball, which he sometimes tries to do intentionally by placing his meaty arm in the path of the pitch. All of his prodigious power, built by squats and bench presses and protein shakes and four dumps a day, manifests against southpaws. Barrera, the Pacifics' closer, is ready, or about to be, and he's held righties to a .163/.179/.163 line. Barrera vs. Parker would be the worst matchup imaginable for the Stompers, yet Kavanaugh stays put. The closer is the closer because he's the closer, and closers don't come into the game in the eighth. I revise my earlier statement: *This* is the worst managerial move ever made.

Lovejoy starts Parker with a fastball inside at 84, and Parker checks his swing but can't prevent himself from fouling it off. Then he swings through a fastball on the outside corner, a vicious hack, and the Pacifics are one strike away from escaping with a 3-2 lead. But for some reason, our bench senses something big.

"Everybody was like, '0–2, he's gonna fucking ambush one,'" Sam tells me later.

"Why?" I ask.

"No idea," he says.

Aside from the auspicious matchup, there's no reason to be optimistic about this pitch. Parker has a slightly below-average swing rate on

0–2, so it's not as if he's known for trying to do damage when he's down in the count. Worse, he hasn't gotten a hit *all season* after starting a plate appearance 0–2: He's 0-for-22, with two walks and a hit-by-pitch. Expecting Parker to get a hit here is the opposite of playing the percentages. Then again, so is using a lefty specialist to face a lefty-killer.

Parker crouches in his open stance, bat bouncing on his shoulder. Lovejoy whips his arm around, and the ball is on its way, headed not for Gingras's glove, which is well off the outside corner, but for the plate and the fat part of Parker's bat. (Pitchers, remember, routinely miss their spots.) There's the freeze-frame moment before Parker starts his swing . . .

And then there's pandemonium, hot team and cold team combining to cause a storm. It's a high, arcing shot to left-center. Parker, who despite his bulk has by far the fastest home run trot in the league, drops his bat and starts sprinting. With two outs, the runners are off on contact, Moch from second and Hurley from first. Williams and Pace converge in the outfield just as Moch rounds third and Hurley rounds second, running with the short strides and tucked-in arms that the players say make him look like a velociraptor. Williams pulls up, and Pace, still reaching up with his glove, slides feet-first just before he hits the wall, rebounding off its base to fall flat on his back. The infield umpire signals home run as he jogs toward the play: It's a three-run homer, and a 5-3 Stompers lead. Tim is screaming so loud that no font size could do his decibel level justice.

Moch is leaping, skipping, and raising his hands as he heads home with high, dainty steps. He stomps on home plate with both feet. Hurley hits the plate seconds later and slaps Moch's butt. The rest of the team, including Sam, spills onto the field, and Moch hugs Parker and hops a few feet at his side, as if the two are in a tandem sack race. I hug Jessie. I hug our scouts. I sprint back down to the dugout. Whatever chemical cocktail my brain releases feels too good to be legal, producing a blinding, slow-motion moment of nonsexual ecstasy. At least I *think* it's nonsexual. It's pretty hard to tell.

The euphoria lasts about six seconds, though it seems longer. An instant later, everything changes. At Pace's urging, the ump reverses his call: He's now calling Parker's hit a ground rule double.

It feels like the moment when you wake from a wonderful dream, and you fight to stay inside of it but can't stop it from slipping away. Already, Parker is heading to first to give his elbow guard to Tommy before he goes back to second base, and Hurley is returning to third. Then the team clears the field and it's back to baseball, a tie game instead of one in which we have a two-run lead. Two minutes ago, a tie game would have made me elated. Now I'm numb and wondering why this had to be the one windless night in San Rafael history, and why we hadn't won enough to get the game to Sonoma, where a drive like Parker's would have cleared the wall without any confusion.

I have a dirty secret to confess: I didn't think it was a homer. I thought I'd seen it bounce inside the fence, although I couldn't tell where it went after that, and when everyone celebrated and the ump said it was gone, I was happy to defer. Tim, who was watching from his radio table on the first-base side, says he'll take it to his grave that the ball bounced off the concrete on the other side of the wall. To a man, the Stompers swear it was gone. It hopped, they insist, and balls don't hop like that on the soft warning track in San Rafael. Theo makes the convincing case that Pace didn't catch it, and because Pace catches everything playable, it had to be out of play. Months later, Theo asks Pace about the play. Pace says he slid, and the ball hit the ground three inches from his glove and bounced over the wall. He was mad at himself for missing it. "Definitely on the warning track," he says. "I don't slide if it's not in play."

On August 13, we lost a game in San Rafael that ended on a similarly perplexing play. We were down by two, with two outs and Isaac on first, and Hurley lifted a fly to right that Bekakis tried to catch. He dove, tumbled, and had his back to the field for a few seconds, but the umpire never ran out: He just waited for Bekakis to raise his glove with the ball inside, quite possibly after picking it up and putting it in there himself. He was probably telling the truth, and Pace probably is also, both because he has no real reason not to and because with Williams as a witness, and the way teammates talk (to each other at first, and eventually to their opponents), a cover-up would be a difficult secret to keep. Sam still thinks it was gone. But we don't know, and we'll never know, because the only source we have is someone else's word. It's odd not to know, a throwback to an earlier era: Major League Baseball has been using video replay to review boundary calls since 2008, and TV broadcasts have done so for decades. But in the Pacific Association, there's no replay ump to appeal to, and on our zoomed-out, behind-home-plate video the fielders and the ball are too blurry to tell. Even those *CSI* guys couldn't enhance the image enough to prove it was a double beyond a reasonable doubt.

When the game resumes, Kristian Gayday pinch-hits for Rubino, and Kavanaugh finally takes out Lovejoy and brings in in Barrera, who gets Kristian to pop out to shallow left to end the inning. On his way back to the dugout, Hurley steps on the plate for the second time in the inning. Like the last time he touched it, the scoreboard stays the same.

Sean is back out for the bottom of the eighth, which he starts by hitting Jake Taylor. "Stoops should get up for Gingras," I say, and Sam says it's a good idea. He tells Tommy, and Tommy tells Yoshi, and on the other end of our human bullpen phone Stoops starts throwing. But Sean bears down, getting Williams and Tucker to strike out swinging with identical sliders. Time is called, and everyone meets on the mound. Stoops is close to ready, but Yoshi leaves Sean in to face the lefty-hitting catcher. After two fouls, Gingras sends a weak grounder to second, and Yuki flips to Moch for the last out of the inning. Sean pumps his fist, a show of emotion he reserves for Super Smash Bros. and fireman games against San Rafael.

Leading off the ninth, Eddie works the count to 3-1, then unloads on an 85 mph meatball from Barrera. It's going, going, and not gone, because there's still no wind to propel it a few feet farther, and it falls into Pace's glove right in front of the wall in right-center. Yuki also flies out to Pace, and Keith grounds to short.

It's now the bottom of the ninth, and the game is still tied. Sean has thrown 51 pitches, but he's a starter in disguise, and his season high out of the bullpen is 74. The bottom of the order is due up, Bekakis and Kiriakos, so he comes back out for inning four.

He starts Bekakis with a strike, then just misses off the outside corner with a slider. He releases the 1-1 pitch too late and it also goes wide, and then he tries an over-the-top curveball that ends up in the dirt. The 3-1 pitch is right down the middle, with Bekakis taking all the way, but the 3-2 fastball bends too far inside. The Pacifics' leadoff man is on. Kiriakos drops down a predictable sac bunt, advancing Bekakis to second. Sam motions the outfielders in.

This would be the time to use Stoops, with the left-handed Pace up and Sean facing hitters for the second time. It's not a no-brainer—definitely not a Polanco/Lovejoy/Barrera debacle—but maybe, if we could forget how hard we fought to get Sean into this role, and how he finished off the Pacifics in two relief appearances just like this one, and how we've seen him hold hitters to a .170/.211/.283 line with runners in scoring position this season, we would see more clearly that replacing him is the right move. Yoshi doesn't pull him, and we don't protest, because leaving Sean in has always worked before. This time, though, he misses outside, misses outside again, misses low, and throws an intentional fourth ball, bringing Gonzalez to the plate. Now Yoshi walks to the mound, and Sam and I, standing side by side, are chanting under our breath, "leave him in, leave him in." Gonzalez is 3-for-6 against Sean on the season, with two walks, but we believe the big-sample stats that say Sean is great against righties. The double play is in order, and getting grounders is Sean's specialty. Yoshi leaves him in, and Sam and I exhale.

With the speedy Bekakis leading from second, Sean delivers to Gonzalez, who waits in his closed, pigeon-toed stance. During a game in early July, as the Stompers tattooed Pacifics starter Wander Beras, Feh said, "Too many sliders, too early. Only Conroy can do that." Normally, Conroy can, but this first-pitch slider is down the middle, too high and too flat. Tim Livingston narrates the end of the Stompers' season. "And the first pitch—swing and a lined shot, left-center field, a base hit," he says. "Coming in to score will be Bekakis, and the San Rafael Pacifics are the champions of the Pacific Association." Sean doesn't see the ball fall. He glances back to gauge where it will land, starts to back up home, and realizes there's no need. He trudges off the field, with the sprinting, celebrating Pacifics collapsing in a happy pile behind him.

"You were lethal," Sam tells Sean in the clubhouse moments later. "You can get away with fifty mistakes, or you can lose on one. And we got away with none."

"If there are two things I would have done differently," Sean says, "it's the 2-1 curveball to the leadoff guy [Bekakis], and staying in after I walked him. The last pitch was a mistake, but it's not a regret, because I threw it hard."

When I walk across the grass to retrieve our tripod—still standing in the stagnant air—I pause for one last look at the field through the chain-link in the outfield. For the first time, I notice a dead spider sitting in the center of its web, which is attached to the top of the fence. It's been there for some time, a husk that looks deceptively like a living thing. I empathize.

"Hey," Moch says in the downcast clubhouse after the game. "Fuck it. Keep our heads up. Let's not hang our heads too long." It's been about four minutes since the season ended in agonizing fashion, so some amount of head-hanging seems acceptable to us. Sam and Theo don't take his words to heart.

SAM: Well that was a stupid idea.

THEO: Playing a baseball game?

SAM: Coming and trying to run a baseball team.

THEO: Yeah. Bad idea.

SAM: Let's not do that again.

THEO: Better to be lucky than not very good.

SAM: Better to be Kavanaugh than us.

THEO: You see how fucking dumb this is? Coming down to
　　something like that.

SAM: Yup. A lot of dumb things.

THEO: All of the things are dumb.

"Fucking Pacifics," Sam says to Andrew Parker. "Did it have to be
the Pacifics? Pittsburg couldn't have gotten hot?"

"Are they the Yankees?" says Parker, with *Moneyball* on his mind.
"And are we the A's? Is that how this turned out?"

"Yeah," Sam says. "Three aces, couldn't get it done."

Mac, the clubhouse attendant, gives a profane speech with three false
endings, each almost-conclusion followed by another torrent of swear
words. "We all fuckin' did a lot of shit this year," he says. "You guys
gave me the fuckin' best summer of my fuckin' life." Even in defeat, the
Stompers evidently exude a powerful appeal: In the midst of the Pacifics' celebrations, Zack Pace, who just helped beat us, asks Theo if he can
manage the Stompers in 2016.

Gradually, the players drift toward their rides. I watch their reced-
ing backs for the last time this year—in some cases, very likely the last
time ever.

During the drive to Sonoma in Tommy's truck, Parker breaks the
silence. "I thought I did something special for a second," he says.

Two days later, Sam sends me three responses to my pregame email,
the one in which I'd sent the Stompers' hitters links to my videos of the
Pacifics' pitchers.

"Almost nobody watched these," he says, citing the single-digit
views. "Hate our team."

One minute later: "At least two or three clicks on each is me, at
least one on each is Theo, and about eight or ten of Polanco's are me.
Hate."

Seconds later: "Also, are you really going to make a highlight video
for Moch?"

. . .

I had the hero's ending in mind by the time Parker passed second. Plucky sabermetric upstarts build a baseball team full of rookies and rejects. Trust a short righty who didn't get drafted, and a D3 sidearmer who tops out in the mid-80s, because we judge them by their actions, not their appearances. Defeat the favorites, and their 6-foot-4 veteran with affiliated experience, because although they were bigger, they weren't as smart. Goliath got complacent, leaving his starter in too long and bringing his closer in too late, while *we* pulled our starter early, having spent the whole season grooming a fireman for this moment.

That story would've worked, but it's not the one we got. We have to wear this one. And we did some things well in our last stand, particularly being patient against Polanco, who walked seven Stompers. We also did some things poorly: bad base running and defensive decisions. Yoshi, playing to type, blames the mistakes on our reliance on rookies, who are known to be *terrible* in big games. The irony is that Hurley lost his rookie status as soon as Bekakis scored. With his first pro season officially over, he's been elevated to veteran, which means he's no longer liable to make mental mistakes. If only he'd known two hours ago whatever it is he knows now.

Sam and I lost our rookie status at the same time. Unlike Hurley's, our baseball careers might be over. But if we were to continue, we could point to our prior experience. And as much as we've mocked baseball's bias against rookies, we *would* be better, just by virtue of having been there before. We would still make mistakes, but fewer that were driven by bad process, the front-office equivalent of throwing the ball to the wrong base. The next time, we'd know not to hire someone with whom we wouldn't work well. We'd know not to rely only on our powers of persuasion to the total exclusion of our power to put our foot down. We'd know that our spreadsheets are probably more predictive for pitchers than for position players. We haven't lost our belief that data can help people build better baseball teams. We've just gained a greater appreciation for how hard it can be to collect and communicate.

It's not easy to motivate in an industry that's older than all of us. But once we'd survived our first stumbles, the game got slower. In time, maybe we would get meaner, more aggressive, quicker to cut bait. "That may be the lesson I learned (or hope I learned) from this year," Theo tells me months after our last loss. "I really wish I could go back in time to release Walker. Probably never even let him make the team." None of us wanted Walker, but we didn't have the words to say why, or the faith in ourselves to insist, or the heart to tell him.

Even with all of our too-late starts and too-long leashes, we might have won a title had the wind cooperated, or had there been a bump on the warning track where Parker's ball (probably) touched down, or had someone gotten a glove on it but failed to hold on. Instead, we lost a one-run game in a one-game series, the ultimate unpredictive event. And Matt Kavanaugh, who made the craziest of all managerial moves—worse than any of the clunkers that cost me sleep this season— took his team to a title. I wish I could say he didn't deserve it, but the Pacifics completed a heck of a comeback. Somebody should write a book about it.

EPILOGUE

San Carlos, California
December 15, 2015

Dear Theo,

If I had to name my five favorite moments from this summer, the list would end up about seventy deep. Definitely one of those seventy, and maybe one of the true top five, would be when, two nights after the season ended, you offered me the Stompers' 2016 managerial job. I was drowning in melancholy up to that point, not just because we had lost—not, actually, at all because we had lost; I have never in my life felt happier than in those six seconds when we thought Parker had homered, and to experience those six seconds, to know the highest emotion one can feel in baseball, is strangely satisfying enough—but because it was over, "it" the season and "It" the whole thing. Like an idiot, I had been looking forward to It being over. I had been fantasizing about finally replacing my dusty, sole-holed dugout shoes, about finally washing all the dust off myself and seeing what my daughter looked like these days. And then It ended Monday night, and I drove home Tuesday morning, and about thirty-five miles out of town, when I was descending toward the bridge, I felt the longing for It to keep being. Your offer felt like a lifeline.

I also thought you were joking, or at least nuts, until we talked deep into that night with Parker and Gonzo and Tommy and Sean and they told me, yeah, of course they'd play on a team I was managing. Ben and I went into this season with the assumption that, as non-ex-player statheads, we might never have a place in the dugout. These guys I respected most were telling me that we had broken through. That I could contribute to this sport at a different level than I'd ever dreamed of.

I've had three months to think about it. It has been a struggle. Eventually I turned to that old standby: the pro/con list. The pros were longer, but the cons were weightier. I remain mired.

I guess the first thing to decide is whether I'd be good at it. That's such a complicated question—I don't really know whether most managers are good even after I've had twenty years to watch them— but in a very narrow, literal sense, did I even prove that I was "smart"? Ben and I weren't very good at projecting performance. Before Opening Day, we each predicted our players' slash lines or ERAs. We had seen their stats in previous years and knew their baseball histories. We had spreadsheet data on a bunch of them, and we had spent more than a week watching them in spring training and discussing their strengths and weaknesses with you and Fehlandt. If Ben and I are smart, we should have been pretty good at projecting their performance. We were not!

Name	Predicted OPS	Actual OPS
Lentini	.896	.804
Wenrich	.888	.846
Gayday	.868	.658

Carranza	.858	.981
Parker	.858	.747
Hibbert	.833	.833
Baptista	.770	.811
Miranda	.708	.747
Hurley	.700	.828
Gavlik	.683	.645
Mochizuki	.671	.835

Name	Predicted ERA	Actual ERA
Paulino	2.50	3.76
Hvozdovic	2.88	4.92
Conroy	3.18	2.70
Schwieger	3.38	6.62
Conley	3.55	6.46
Godsey	4.03	2.53
Jackson	4.10	4.72
Walker	4.50	6.40
Rand	4.53	5.87
Gonsalves	5.05	4.95

Nailed Hibby! Missed more or less across the board on everybody else. We thought Kristian would be better than Joel! We thought Conroy would fall somewhere between Hvozdovic and Conley. You know a little about correlations, right? A correlation of 0 means no relationship, a correlation of 1.0 means a perfect relationship. The correlation between our projections and the actual stats was .24—what statisticians would call "a weak positive correlation." In fact, if we'd had to fill out the opening lineup with the same nine guys that Fehlandt did, but in the batting order we thought was best, we would have barely outscored Feh's lineup—5.79 runs per game to 5.73—and only because we wouldn't have buried Hibbert in the ninth spot for crazy "second leadoff hitter" reasons. If we'd filled out the lineup using *anybody* on our Opening Day roster, based on our projections, we would have had Parker playing instead of Baptista and Gavlik instead of Mochizuki. Knowing what we do now about everybody's performance, that lineup would have been significantly *worse* than Fehlandt's, scoring 5.43 runs. Yuuuup. We were worse than Fehlandt. Happy now?

Our spreadsheet was smarter than we were. Our six spreadsheet-signed pitchers allowed 4.39 runs per nine innings. The rest of the staff allowed 6.29. It is not a stretch to say that the spreadsheet might have kept us out of last place—if you and Fehlandt could only get a 6.29 ERA from your first choices, I don't want to imagine your second-tier choices.

But our spreadsheet hitters flopped. Among guys with more than 50 at-bats, Taylor was our second-worst hitter. Kristian was our third worst. And even when we had had weeks, even months, of observing our guys in games, we still misevaluated them. Ben wanted to cut Hurley, right before he turned into one of the league's best hitters. We fought to get Moch dropped to lower in the lineup, and we finally succeeded around the end of July. He hit .389/.494/.597 in August, easily the best performance on our team. Remember when I sent T. J. an encouraging email in August, where I used HITf/x data to show how hard he was hitting the ball—that bad luck was making his numbers look worse than he was? "As you play your final eight games with us," I wrote, "keep doing what you're doing. You're hitting like a beast, and you're going to have a big final eight days."

He hit .174/.321/.174 the rest of the way.

It's easy to remember the good moves—that we saw Baps and Hurley and identified them as what they turned out to be, the two best players in a 100-person tryout; that we signed Santos, Stoops, and Sean sight unseen and got three aces playing for almost the minimum—and blame the misses on small samples. It's easy to make the world look just the way you want it to. But I've spent the months since August wondering how far Fehlandt might have taken this team. Fehlandt was smart, too.

Now, I don't know how much it matters to you how good I'd be; I'm not sure how much it matters to me. Your goals as GM of the Stompers, near as I could tell, were, in order,

1. Do right by these players; don't get in the way of careers that might still go somewhere.
2. Protect the existence of the team and league by producing an entertaining experience at sustainable expenses.
3. Win.

My priorities would be slightly different, but we agree on number 1. That was a revelation, actually. When this project was conceived, a little more than three years ago, we were going to take over a team and make them do all our crazy experimental stuff so we could see if it worked. True lab-mice conditions. The players were chum for our curiosity and ambitions. Over the years, we came to realize that no experiment would be useful if the conditions didn't mirror real life. If we took away the players' agency they wouldn't perform, or to the degree they did perform it would all be polluted by resentment, mistrust, confusion, etc. So we could do the lab thing, but we had to do it in a way that was respectful.

But once we started signing players and getting to know them, and especially once we saw them in spring training, we realized that they were not in our story so much as we were in theirs. They were the ones who were putting everything on the line to chase this dream, and if we didn't respect those dreams—not just pretend to, but truly respect them—we wouldn't be able to live with ourselves. So "do crazy stuff to see if it worked" changed to "do crazy stuff once we were confident it would work."

I don't think this season answered the question of whether we're good at this, but it did answer the question of whether, within the "their story, not ours" framework, we could do it at all—whether there exists a path for putting statistically derived unorthodoxy onto professional fields.

Before this started, I was so afraid of asking the players to do anything new. But it wasn't just me, you know? Fehlandt was afraid too. He was afraid that changing pitching roles would upset or discombobulate usage patterns. And Yoshi was afraid that the club would crumble if veterans weren't treated with deference and rookies with a sort of paternalistic distance. That's why he decided to bench Taylor Eads that one day, even though Taylor was our hottest hitter, and even though Taylor was the one I was most worried would lose confidence if he was benched for the new veteran outfielder. For goodness' sake, Yoshi was worried every time we walked into his office that we were making him look "weak" in front of the team, that they would think statheads, not the manager, were making moves. But none of those fears—Feh's, or Yoshi's, or ours—were ever justified, and nothing we worried was one step too far ever led us off a cliff. The players even filled out their happiness surveys, hundreds of them deposited obediently into the lockbox. It's funny, because statheads are the ones who get the reputation for treating players like number-generating cogs, for not respecting them all as individuals, but the old-school notions of how they had to be used seemed even more reductive: Sean couldn't come into the seventh because the closer is the closer because he's the closer, but isn't he really just Sean? Isn't *the best way to use Sean* the best way to use Sean?

Paul just texted me, by the way. I had asked him if we were good, Ben and I. He said, "It was awesome learning the new ideas in the game we have been playing our whole lives. U guys were the smartest people in the dugout." Man, I love Paul.

Look, I'm never going to be the fair and impartial judge of my own performance. Maybe we were the worst. But yes, I believe we can be good for these players' careers, just by being open to everything they can do. I believe we were good for their careers. Sean, Stoops, and Santos: They were *retired*, playing weekend rec leagues for fun. Now they're prospects. You told me in August that the lesson from all of this may be that one person—or, between you, me, and Ben, three people—ultimately just can't do that much, no matter how good their data. A baseball team is too complex an organism, and the center will always hold. In the standings, I think you're right. But we did a lot, the three of us. It never felt wasted.

Of course, a small but stubborn part of me wants to resist your premise about not being able to do much in the standings. Yoshi was a great manager, Theo. He wanted to see our data, he wanted to listen to our arguments, and he wanted to engage with new viewpoints. What made the second half so frustrating, and what makes it so tempting to take Yoshi's job, is that ultimately the last stage of every decision—even data-driven decisions—is the gut. Our data could get us only so far, and even we knew that to get from a spreadsheet to the decision on the field meant weighing the situation and taking a leap. Ben and I could look at the same data and come to two different conclusions; so, too, could Yoshi. Our guts diverged. When you show somebody data and they still do something you disagree with, it's maddening. It feeds the appetite for more power. I want my gut to run things. My gut tells me my gut could add ten more wins.

But was my gut any better? I can't help thinking of Josh McCauley, the pitcher I signed three days into the season. I'd heard about Josh months earlier, when I was trying to recruit Paul. They had gone to the same college, and the coach there told me Paul probably wouldn't sign with me but this other kid, Josh, was the one I wanted anyway. Big dude. Pitcher's body. 6-foot-5, muscular, thick calves, threw in the mid-90s with a hammer curve. He'd been a D1 pitcher until an assistant messed up his class schedule and enrolled Josh for a class that Josh never knew he was in. At the end of the semester, an F landed on his transcript. It made him academically ineligible, and he'd gone to little Shepherd University just so he could get seen by scouts. Naturally, he found out later that that wasn't allowed, either, and he had to sit out most of the year—but the scouts came anyway, watching him pitch before games that he was ineligible to pitch in. That's how attractive Josh McCauley was. That's how attractive all Josh McCauleys are.

The Cubs took him in the twenty-first round. He went to Arizona to take a physical and sign the paperwork that would make him a professional ballplayer, but he failed that physical. The Cubs sent him home, unsigned. He had Tommy John surgery—his insurance, not the Cubs', paid for it—and now he was trying to make his way back. He had signed with an upstart league in Oregon, but that league had fizzled just weeks into the season. That's when Josh finally returned our calls. I talked to his manager in Oregon City, who assured me Josh was already throwing in the low-90s and was only getting stronger. But I looked at his stats in college and they weren't very good. I looked at his stats in Oregon City and they weren't very good, either. I should have stayed true to what we were doing, but my gut kept saying "big right-hander, big stuff," and I chased that. Josh was awful. He pitched twice for us and threw nowhere near the low-90s. My gut had been gullible and disregarded the data.

So now I get an offer not to do more with data—Yoshi heard the data, and was always open to it—but to do more with my gut. I'm not sure that's a worthwhile goal. It feels like learning to accept that other people are going to make different decisions than I would is a far greater goal than pursuing absolute power so I can impose my own.

Maybe that's weird. Remember Vallejo's bench coach? There was a day when he showed up in our dugout about an hour before a game between us and Pittsburg. I'd heard he was looking for a new job, even though he was still with Vallejo. So we're making small talk and he asks me, "Hey, how far back in the standings are we now?" I tell him, "Vallejo? I think you guys are seven back in the second half." And he says "I'm not with Vallejo anymore." Oh, okay so—he'd been hired by Pittsburg? "Nah," he says, "I'm with y'all now."

Well, I mean, no, he wasn't. I knew that he hadn't been hired by us, that he wouldn't be hired by us, and that if somehow he had been hired by us I'd know about it. But there he was, just declaring it so. And it worked! He stayed in our dugout that entire game, our new bench coach by sheer will alone. Top-five moment of the year, Theo. And then the next day he decided Vallejo wasn't so bad after all, and he went back there. So weird, *so weird*, but all year I saw how this attribute—show up and just declare you belong—makes indy ball go 'round. Like Matt Walker, showing up and declaring he belonged. Like that kid we didn't draft at the tryout, the one who lied about his college stats and may have made up a suspicious sick grandma to try to get us to sign him—and who ended up getting a job with Vallejo and playing professional baseball for most of the year. This sport is for people who see an opening and take it and don't ask whether they're qualified or welcome. As you and Ben saw all year, I just don't have the gumption to do that. Two paragraphs up, I was second-guessing hypothetical decisions I haven't even made yet. I'm probably just not built for a baseball dugout.

I don't know, Theo. I keep going back to a conversation I had with McCauley on the third night of our season. I'd just picked him up at SFO after our wild, extra-innings win over Pittsburg, and we were eating In-N-Out just around midnight. Did I ever tell you about his order? He'd never been to In-N-Out, so I recommended the grilled onions. He tells me thanks, but "I don't eat anything healthy." Onions caramelized in oil was too healthy. He got a cheeseburger with no tomato, lettuce, or onion. Man, I loved McCauley.

Anyway, while we're eating I tell him what the Pacific Association is like. "There are some good prospects," I say. "And there are some older guys. What I've learned is that there are two kinds of players in this league. There are the guys who are here because it's just fun to play baseball, to be around baseball, and if somebody is willing to pay you to do it then why not? The economy sucks for job-hunting anyway, and they're probably not giving anything up to be out here. Have fun, be recognized, party, play ball.

"Then there are the guys who are here because they actually have a chance of making it, and this is what they need to do to get that chance. You're one of those guys. Paul is one of those guys. The baseball world, for whatever reason, didn't give you guys the chance you deserved, but you're as good as a lot of the players it did. So you keep going until you get that chance.

"But the hardest part for me is that a lot of the guys who should be in the first group think they're in the second. They're so stressed about every bad at-bat. They're so hurt by every non-promotion. If they knew they were in the first group, I'd be so happy that they're out there, having fun and living life. But they don't, so instead it just makes me sad, that they're chasing something that just doesn't exist and getting their hearts repeatedly stepped on for it."

Last summer, Theo, I was the first type. I had the best summer of my life. I love those twenty-two ballplayers more than just a fan ever can. I'm inspired by what they do for the game, by what you do for the game. I wish I could live in that space forever. I can't, though, not for first-type reasons. I'm old. My daughter's first day of kindergarten would be during our final week of the season, and if I take the job I'll miss it. My wife is going to be looking for a new teaching job, and if I do this I won't be able to provide the support she'll need. A baseball team feels like a family, but my family *is* my family, and I can't leave them behind for another summer just because it's fun. To take this job, I'd have to convince myself I'm the second type.

It hurt too much to watch so many young men this summer convince themselves they were the second type. Thank you, Theo. However, with a heavy heart, I decline.

But I hope you keep doing this forever.

Sincerely,

Sam

AFTERWORD TO THE PAPERBACK EDITION

In the early morning hours of March 29, 2016—about seven months after Andrew Parker's, um, extra-base hit—I saw a scary tweet from @SonomaStompers. "Sending thoughts, prayers, energy, good vibes and absolutely anything else we can think of to Isaac and his family," it read, followed by a screenshot of a Facebook status that explained the situation: Isaac Wenrich, the former Stompers catcher and team leader who'd left for the Florence Freedom as part of the second-half offensive exodus, had suffered a "major" heart attack in Glendale, Arizona. He was twenty-six, and he'd been about to leave for his first Frontier League spring training.

Over the next few days, as Isaac lingered in an ICU in a medically induced coma, Sam and I emailed, tweeted, and texted with others in Isaac's orbit, piecing together what had happened. Like many poorly paid independent-league players, Isaac made money during the off-season by applying the only marketable skill one acquires while playing professional baseball: teaching other people to play baseball. On the day he almost died, he was due to give a lesson to a thirteen-year-old pupil named Nate Boyer.

As Nate later recounted to the media, the session stopped being about baseball when Isaac silently toppled from his seat atop a bucket of balls. At first, Nate assumed that Isaac was playing a prank, as he liked to do, but then he noticed that his instructor, who'd earlier complained about chest pains that he'd dismissed as indigestion, was breathing erratically. Isaac had been holding his smartphone, and when Nate picked it up, it was still unlocked. He dialed 911. "I don't think he's breathing," he told the dispatcher, sounding short of breath himself.

The kid knew some CPR, thanks to his days as a boy scout, and that training returned to him as the dispatcher talked him through the chest compressions. Isaac lucked out in two other ways: At this high-leverage moment, a group of firemen was a few blocks away, and a nearby medical facility was well equipped to treat him. Surgery saved his life, clearing a complete blockage of his heart's main artery that was caused by ruptured plaque. It was a "widow-maker" heart attack, the kind that can kill the muscle's whole front wall with one catastrophic occlusion. Had the phone not been unlocked, had Nate not kept his head (and had training), had the firefighters not been nearby, and had the hospital he needed not been so well situated, Isaac would have died. Instead, he was one of the 5 percent who survive.

When we were telling the Stompers' story, I'd allowed myself to daydream about an updated edition decades down the line, the kind that comes with a "Where are they now?" section. The italicized text would spoil the ending of every career, summing up each Stomper's life in a sentence or two: *So-and-so topped out in Triple-A; So-and-so became a banker; So-and-so settled in [insert small town] and passed away peacefully in 2065.* I knew that one by one, the stars of our summer would be swept from the board—first as players, and then as people. But this felt too soon for that process to start. Before we got the good news that Isaac had pulled through, I felt guilty for having thought (and written) that he was probably wasting his time doing drills all winter. Now I wanted nothing more than for him to keep blocking balls and running up stadium stairs, whether or not it ever brought him to the big leagues.

On May 27, only two months after his heart attack, Isaac returned to Florence's lineup, catching and batting sixth. He went 2-for-2 with a walk and scored a run. Two weeks later, on June 10, his host parents flew in Nate Boyer to throw out the first pitch before a game against Evansville. They kept Nate's presence a surprise, just as his host family in Sonoma had kept it a surprise when Isaac's visiting girlfriend, Katy, had hidden herself inside the Stompers' Rawhide costume, raced around the bases between innings, and then removed the mascot's head to kiss the shocked catcher at home plate. This time, as Nate walked to the mound in full uniform, an unsuspecting Isaac trudged from the dugout to the plate without looking at his obligatory batterymate, ready to play his pro-forma part in the ceremony—corral a too-low, too-slow throw, hand the ball back to the civilian, smile, maybe pose for a picture.

The PA announcer interrupted the routine. "Isaac, if you'd turn around for just one second . . ." the booming voice said, and Isaac complied. Still facing sideways, he recognized Nate and let out a wild whoop. Hollering, he leaped and hopped and skipped to the mound, where for ten seconds solid he hugged Nate, the teenager who'd recorded a bigger save than all of Sean Conroy's combined.

In that day's game, Isaac went 1-for-3, which *lowered* his average. Eleven games into his season, he was happy and healthy and hitting .382.

Isaac's near-death experience was the first of three news stories in 2016 that helped catapult the team to an outsized national footprint for a low-level indy league franchise, just as Sean's Pride Night start had the previous year. The second story, like Sean's, concerned finds from our spreadsheet.

On May 16, Sam and I got an email from Dan Turkenkopf, the director of research and development for the Milwaukee Brewers, one of several team executives who had recently been hired away from sabermetric standard bearers such as the Houston Astros and Tampa Bay Rays. Like Sam and me, Dan was a former writer for *Baseball Prospectus,* and he wanted to tell us that he'd enjoyed reading the book. I responded in the same "very little to lose" spirit that made me semi-seriously tell Dan Evans that we'd take one team and, later, ask Sportvision to install its high-tech system at our backward ballpark. I wrote back to Dan, saying that maybe in lieu of posting a glowing online review, he could recommend that the Brewers sign Santos Saldivar.

I wasn't expecting anything more than a good-natured "no." Dan had read our raves about Santos, and he hadn't asked for more info. But for whatever reason—doing his due diligence, humoring me, or just satisfying his curiosity about what pitchers' stuff would look like numerically so far from the majors—he asked to see Santos's PITCHf/x data. "I doubt we'd have a place for him anywhere and wouldn't want to get hopes up," he wrote back, "but you painted an interesting enough picture that I'd love to see the plots."

I sent him everything we'd collected: the advanced performance metrics on The Grapevine, the video of Santos's cartoonish stuff collecting a series of swinging strikes, and the PITCHf/x treasure trove, which contained the trajectory and speed of every pitch Santos had thrown at Arnold Field. Dan asked a couple of technical questions, and then the thread went dormant. I thought the exchange would end there, until two days later, a one-line email arrived: "Can you get me Santos's contact info?"

Impressed (just as we were) by Santos's tight curveball and wide array of offerings, Dan had already talked to the Brewers' farm director, who'd looked past Santos's short stature to the breaking ball beyond. The next day, Theo Fightmaster told me that the Brewers had called him twice to nail down a deal. He didn't drive a hard bargain. The Brewers bought Santos's rights for $3,000—a vanishingly small sum by big league standards, but still about $600 more than the Stompers would have paid Santos for a full second season in Sonoma. When I told Sam that the Brewers had reached out to Theo, he wrote back, "yesssssssssss." And when I told him the deal was done, he added three extra s's: "yesssssssssssssss."

The next day, we saw a congratulatory tweet sent by Jose De Leon, the top prospect who had been Santos's teammate at Southern University—

and who was himself less than four months away from his September debut with the Los Angeles Dodgers. "What a journey!" De Leon's message said. That journey had taken two more turns since Santos's start in the Pacific Association title game. In March, he'd received a spring-training invitation from the Acereros de Monclova, a Mexican League club. "I pitched as good as I've ever pitched," Santos told me and Sam on a podcast in May. But before he could secure a roster spot, a former Acereros pitcher was released from affiliated ball, and his old team chose the familiar face. "They picked him up, and they told me I didn't have the experience," Santos said. It was a spot-on reenactment of his rude introduction to pro ball, when the River City Rascals had released him in favor of a returning arm (even though that arm was injured). Santos was stalled on the same M. C. Escher–esque staircase as many other entry-level employees, attempting to acquire experience despite repeatedly being turned down because of a lack of experience.

Following the Acereros setback, Santos had nearly re-retired from baseball, but after further reflection he decided to re-sign with the Stompers, who'd (sort of) sweetened their pitch with an offer of an internship at owner Eric Gullotta's office. He was on his way to Sonoma when the Brewers' call came. "I was literally getting off the plane in San Francisco, and they gave me the call that the Brewers were interested in signing me," Santos said. "Fifteen minutes before I got to Sonoma, I got the offer, and they told me I was headed [to the Brewers]." When Yoshi met his erstwhile ace at the park to tell him how happy he was to have him back, Santos had to break the news that he'd be leaving the next morning for Brewers extended spring training in Glendale, Arizona— the same Phoenix suburb where Isaac had suffered his heart attack. There, the Brewers Sorting Hat assigned him to their Rookie League affiliate in Helena, Montana. For the second time in ten months, Santos's career had been resurrected by someone who'd never seen him pitch in person. He was now a made man.

On August 16, history repeated itself in a wonderful way. This time, the inquiry came from San Diego Padres assistant general manager Josh Stein, who wanted to know what we could tell him about our other lights-out late-season find, Dylan Stoops. Stoops had spent most of the 2016 season in the Frontier League with the Traverse City Beach Bums, and he'd done us proud, posting the highest strikeout rate and the second-lowest ERA among the team's regular starters. I sent Stein a letter of recommendation I'd already written, along with the same PITCHf/x and video data we'd dumped on the Brewers. It was "way more" information than Stein had expected to receive about a pitcher's performance in the Pacific Association.

Days later, at the end of what Dylan described as a "long, losing season," the offer arrived. Like Santos, he'd gotten his college degree, and he was prepared to retire at the end of the summer until the Padres threw his athletic career a lifeline. "A lot of emotions flooded me at that point," Dylan told Sam and me. "When I finally got the confirmation, it was everything from laughing and then tears when I called my parents, because they were just out of control. My mom dropped the phone, and she was bawling. It was a great feeling. Everything had come together at a time I had least expected it."

Sam had preexisting plans to watch the Lake Elsinore Storm, the Padres' High-A affiliate, play on August 24. It was the only minor league game he'd attend all season. In the most serendipitous Stompers-related rendezvous since Sean and Isaac had met by coincidence in Cooperstown, the Storm's starting pitcher that day was Dylan Stoops, making his non-indy debut as a professional pitcher. In five innings, he allowed only one run, striking out eight without any walks. "More of that, please," Stein emailed me.

No Brewers scout had ever written an amateur report on Santos, and no Padres scout had ever written an amateur report on Dylan. Each pitcher had at least one serious strike against him from a scouting perspective—for Santos, his height, and for Dylan, his injury history. In an earlier era, neither one would have gotten the chance to come from behind in the count. Just as we'd used Chris Long's spreadsheet to compare the pair's college stats in context, the Brewers and Padres had used the PITCHf/x stats we supplied to compare their indy ball performance to that of pitchers inside the minor leagues' gated community, without being blinded by distance, appearance, or quality of competition. Objective metrics had made the world smaller, and maybe fairer. As Dan Turkenkopf told us, "having the full combination of the PFX, video, and stats is really helpful—especially since I doubt we'd get eyes on [Santos] otherwise."

Baseball's barriers to entry are falling fast. A company called Rapsodo is releasing a portable camera/radar system that stands on a single stalk behind home plate and aims to measure more than our more expensive, pre-installed PITCHf/x system. MLB's Statcast system, coupled with cognitive testing and wearable tech, is making it easy to assess and optimize players' true talent in ever-smaller samples. And Santos, who told us he'd gotten so good because he'd "YouTubed and Googled how to work with pitches," was now a prospect because a team had You-Tubed him. "It didn't take just me to strike out a couple guys to get looked at," Santos said. "If it wasn't for the videos, if it wasn't for the PITCHf/x, I would probably be at home right now." Or as Dylan put it, "I thought it was over, and then all of a sudden, you guys sent me a message on Twitter and my world changed." So did ours.

If Sam and I could have traded in the Santos and Stoops signings to bring back the original "home run" ruling on Parker's hit, we wouldn't have done it. All summer, Sam and I worried that we weren't doing enough with our eyes in the sky, but the true value in our constant record-keeping came later, when we used it to help two players prove they'd earned promotions. As Santos texted me, "Just sucks this couldn't be in the book." Santos, I've got good news.

"I wrote a book about a baseball season and regret how utterly it fails the Bechdel test," Sam observed in an essay he wrote for ESPN after the 2016 World Series, referring to the often-unmet standard that a film ought to include two female characters who talk to each other about something other than a man. Much as we would have liked it to be otherwise, we had to face the fact that our story was a sausage fest. When our only overture to a female pitcher didn't pan out, we let the idea drop, in part because we were overwhelmed by the work ahead of us (we had a tough enough time finding men), and in part because we were supposed to be the data guys, and there wasn't much data to support the idea that women would be the best available arms. In other respects—statheads in the dugout, an openly gay pitcher, a Japanese-born manager—our belief in performance over propriety had the happy byproduct of lowering baseball's boundaries. It didn't do the same where women were concerned.

In 2016, the Stompers went much further than a phone call. Backed by funding from the film director Francis Ford Coppola, who owns a winery near Sonoma, they committed to fielding a truly coed team. Plenty of pro teams (including the 2015 Pacifics) had rostered one woman, often for one game, but the Stompers set out to be the first to have multiple women on the field since a 1950s Negro League club, the Indianapolis Clowns. They envisioned the women's participation as an open-ended engagement, rather than a one-day only stunt done largely for publicity's sake.

Of course, it's impossible to untangle the Stompers' purer motivations from the less high-minded ways in which the team stood to benefit from the unorthodox arrangement, just as it was when they welcomed Sam and me: Coppola's sponsorship, increased attendance, and national name awareness were at stake. Nonetheless, the idea was driven by a desire for inclusiveness, and it took effect while the season was still in full swing; the Stompers announced the signings in late June, which signaled that a coed team took precedence over any potential impact on the pennant race. Lastly, they took time—a precious commodity during the lead-up to Opening Day—to make multiple scouting trips in search of the perfect players.

A recommendation from Justine Siegal, the first female major league coach, led Theo to Kelsie Whitmore, a seventeen-year-old out-fielder/pitcher who had accepted a softball scholarship at Cal State Fullerton, where she would be enrolling in the fall. And a trip to the U.S. Women's National Team tryouts in North Carolina yielded Stacy

Piagno, a twenty-five-year-old pitcher/infielder. (Because women's baseball is much smaller and less well established than the men's game, two-way players are quite common.) Both women were slated to play for Team USA in the Women's Baseball World Cup, which would take place in South Korea in September.

The publicity blast was stronger than both women had anticipated. On the day they debuted—with Whitmore in left field and Piagno pitching—a *BuzzFeed* headline proclaimed, "This Pro Baseball Team Signed Its First Women Players and People Are Super Excited."

"Going into it, we had no idea that any of this would be as big of a thing as it was," Piagno later told me. "We just heard about this opportunity to go play out in Sonoma, and we were like, 'An opportunity to play baseball? Of course, why wouldn't we take it?' So we just went out and we were going to go play, and we heard, 'Oh, you guys have an interview on this day,' and then one interview turned into like five, and then ten, and then there's cameras, and then it just like really took storm and became a big thing."

Whitmore and Piagno each spent more than a month with the Stompers. (For one day, they were also joined by catcher Anna Kimbrell, another Team USA member who paired with Piagno to form the first all-female battery in pro ball.) Both women had the competitive natures to deal with the doubts and the skeptics. "It's fun to play against people who doubt you or who view you visually, and then you get to prove yourself against that," Piagno said.

That external pressure would have been harder to weather if they'd had trouble within their own team. Whitmore, who arrived first, said, "There were a couple guys when I first got there, they looked at me, and they just gave me that look where it was like, 'Man, I don't think they're going to like me.'" In the end, though, neither player reported any problems fitting in. "We had a great group of guys," Piagno said. "Everybody, at least in my experience, was very accepting." And just as had been the case with Sean Conroy, acceptance often translated to not tiptoeing around touchy subjects—with one exception. "I overheard a couple of them talking, that there were times . . . they'd almost slap us in the butt on accident, but they would hold themselves back," Whitmore said. "It was just a habit."

Piagno added, "I totally felt like they were some of the most respectful guys ever. But at the same time, while they were respectful of us, they were definitely still themselves, as far as things that they said or the way that they joked. . . . That's what we want. We want to be treated just like any of the guys. And it was a blast."

Here's the part where all three of these feel-good stories hit the same snag. Isaac, Santos and Dylan, and Kelsie and Stacy all beat long odds to be where they were in the summer of 2016. They were all easy to root for, inspirations as both players and people. On a purely statistical level, though, they all looked a little out of their league.

After Isaac's reunion with Nate, he went 31-for-162, a .191 average. He finished the season with a .702 OPS—not *bad* for a Frontier League catcher, but more than 150 points worse than his 2014–15 production in the Pacific Association, and not good enough to attract higher-level attention, especially since he was already old for the league. In 2015, Isaac had helped Florence push into the playoffs; in 2016, the Freedom finished 46–49. Wherever he plays in 2017, he'll be twenty-seven, historically regarded by statheads as the typical player's peak age. He'll still be far from the majors, and no closer to affiliated ball.

Santos and Dylan had mixed minor league records, at best. Santos had hoped to advance to A-ball, but he spent the whole season in the Rookie League, where he posted a 5.73 ERA in nineteen games out of the bullpen. That's not as bad as it sounds: For one thing, much of the league was at altitude—"Every park had a mountain in the background," Santos said—and for another, the team took his two-seamer away to force him to throw his four-seamer for strikes. At that level, baseball is about development, not stats, and the rest of Helena's staff had a 5.96 ERA. Still, given Santos's dominance in Sonoma, both we and he had expected more. We no longer had access to pitch-tracking data that might have told a different story, so we could only obsess over the best and the worst of the stats we saw: a strikeout per inning, but also too many homers and too many walks allowed.

Dylan's affiliated adventure hit the skids in his second start. Even in his strong first start, he was sitting at 84 mph, missing bats by spinning sliders and curves in the 60s and 70s, which worked well once but wasn't a sustainable strategy. In his second start, bad command and bad bounces came back to bite him, and he faced only nine batters, seven of whom reached base. He finished his three-game stint in Lake Elsinore with a 7.94 ERA, albeit with nine strikeouts for every walk. "My arm and my body were shot toward the end of the experience," Dylan said. "It had just been a long summer for me, and without the guidance and the lifting and the running, they weren't surprised that my body was falling apart."

A confident Santos had told us in the spring, "If I make it to that level, that means I can compete against them." For the first time, that truth was in doubt for both players. "If you leave a ball just a little bit up, it's gonna be hit on a line, it's gonna be hit hard," Dylan said. "There's no room for error."

Kelsie and Stacy soon made the same discovery. Most media reports tended to skim past their stats; "The Women Succeeding in a Men's Professional Baseball League," read the headline on a *New Yorker* "Sporting Scene" story, which made no mention of how the women were doing aside from a vague sentence that said "both contributed to the Stompers' success on the field." Those contributions were undeniably limited: At the plate, Whitmore went 1-for-13, with a walk and eight strikeouts, while Piagno went 1-for-5 and Kimbrell went 0-for-3. (Both "1's" were singles.) On the mound, Whitmore allowed six runs in one two-inning outing, while Piagno allowed sixteen runs in twelve innings. The increased quality of competition forced both players to alter their game plans. "I kind of became like an off-speed pitcher versus more of a power pitcher with the women," Piagno said.

The struggles of all of these players were no more demoralizing than mine and Sam's the previous year. Like them, we had been out of our element, trying to prove we belonged at a level where we hadn't demonstrated our skills. And like them, we had often fallen short, not only of our ultimate goal (a Pacific Association title) but also of the way we wanted to conduct ourselves from day to day. And yet, hidden among our failures were the seeds of successes that didn't need much time to take root.

Oh, yeah: I've probably buried the lede. The year after Sam and I tried to build a new kind of baseball team, the Stompers won the Pacific Association championship.

As I followed the team's progress from New York and Sam monitored their wins and losses from his new home in Long Beach, the Stompers went 47–31, winning both halves of the season and finishing six games ahead of the second-place Pacifics. They completed a polar-opposite stretch run with eight consecutive victories against the Pacifics in August, and they clinched the crown in San Rafael on August 26, the earliest date yet for a Pacific Association champion. Even that underplayed their performance: The Stompers outscored their opponents by 127 runs, while each of the other three teams ran a negative run differential. I asked Theo how it felt to get payback against the Pacifics. "Better than it should," he said.

The timing of the Stompers' first title lends itself to one of two interpretations: that Sam and I had been holding the team back, or that Sam and I had set up the team for its subsequent success. I'm not sure there's that much truth to either. The Stompers' website still lists us as "special assistants to the GM," but in most ways, this wasn't our team.

In several small ways, though, it was. Sean Conroy started on Opening Day and threw another three-hit gem on Pride Night, although a sore shoulder hampered him for much of the year. Daniel Baptista overcame injuries to record the second-most at-bats on the team, with the second-highest batting average. Taylor Thurber, a spreadsheet missed connection I couldn't keep away from the Frontier League in 2015, signed with the Stompers in 2016, led the team in innings (with a 2.95 ERA), and finished third in the league's Pitcher of the Year voting. In the second game of the season, Thurber entered in the fifth inning and went 4 1/3 frames to finish off a one-run win. The Stompers still used firemen, and they led the league in three-inning-plus saves. Maybe they started something: Not long after the Stompers' season ended, the Cleveland Indians rode a fireman, Andrew Miller, to an unexpected pennant.

Yoshi, who was named Manager of the Year, continued to ask for evidences, which were often supplied by an updated version of The Grapevine or by Michael Conlan, a member of our Corduroy Crew who returned for a second season. The Stompers didn't suffer a second-half decline because they were always prepared to replace players, having learned from our passivity the previous year. And when they did drop or pick up players, they always adhered to an analytical mindset. As Tim Livingston, elevated to assistant general manager in 2016, told us, "The philosophy of going further than just feel on guys was pretty strong with us this year and was a direct influence from you guys."

So no, Isaac's off-season workouts probably won't get him to the big leagues, but they may have made him strong enough to survive his close call with mortality. And in becoming the first player to jump directly from the Stompers to a major league organization, Santos gave hope to every Pacific Association player who follows him. "It opens up their eyes that it is possible to get picked up from this league," he said. It also helps the Stompers, whose recruiting efforts have benefited both from the book and from the breakthroughs of Saldivar and Stoops. When I asked Theo not long after Santos's signing how many times he'd incorporated the news into his pitch to potential players, he said, "about a dozen times so far."

As for Kelsie and Stacy, they hope that their high-profile summer with the Stompers—who intend to keep pulling players from the female 51 percent of the population—will keep changing minds. Although the two women were surrounded by cheering girls after every game, they haven't forgotten the male minds they changed. "When you see a little boy come up to you and ask for your autograph, that's super cool," Whitmore said. "He doesn't know what it's like for a girl to be playing baseball. He's not judging us at the moment. He's just looking at us as a ballplayer." They had the same effect on the older boys who suited up for the Stompers. "Their mentality of girls in baseball totally changed," Piagno said. "They respect it, and they accept it, and they look at it differently. They understand what we go through and what we've accomplished."

For now, there's nowhere to go but the national team; with no all-female league in existence, the two women often hear "Oh, you mean softball" when they tell people they play baseball. But by proving it was possible to win a championship with a coed clubhouse, they hope they'll make that question less common. "The more society sees that [women love playing baseball], it will become more of a normal thing, which will be great for us," Piagno said. And as a step in this direction, the Baseball Hall of Fame recognized the women's achievement—and, for the second consecutive year, the previously obscure Stompers—by including Kelsie's bat and a ball signed by Kelsie, Stacy, and Anna Kimbrell in the "Today's Game" exhibit, which also features David Ortiz's spikes and Ichiro Suzuki's memorabilia from his 3,000th major league hit.

As I write this, Isaac's dream, and Santos's and Dylan's dreams, and Kelsie's and Stacy's dreams, are still alive. And when in time they do leave baseball behind, it will be because their performance told them to, not because the door was barred to begin with. Yes, the only rule is it has to work. But in order to work, it first has to have the freedom to fail.

THE SONOMA STOMPERS
FINAL TEAM STATISTICS

First-Half Standings				
Team	W	L	PCT	GB
Sonoma Stompers	26	11	.703	—
San Rafael Pacifics	19	19	.500	7.5
Pittsburg Diamonds	18	20	.474	8.5
Vallejo Admirals	13	26	.333	14

Second-Half Standings				
Team	W	L	PCT	GB
San Rafael Pacifics	29	11	.725	—
Pittsburg Diamonds	20	19	.513	8.5
Sonoma Stompers	18	22	.450	11
Vallejo Admirals	12	27	.308	16.5

Overall Standings				
Team	W	L	PCT	GB
San Rafael Pacifics	48	30	.615	—
Sonoma Stompers	44	33	.571	3.5
Pittsburg Diamonds	38	39	.494	9.5
Vallejo Admirals	25	53	.321	23

STOMPERS HITTERS

Name	G	PA	H	HR	SB	BB%	K%	AVG	OBP	SLG	OPS	wRC+
Mark Hurley	74	326	90	9	11	5.2	17.8	.302	.362	.466	.828	128
Gered Mochizuki	69	314	77	5	2	15.9	17.5	.303	.414	.421	.835	122
Matt Hibbert	68	311	79	4	32	10.6	15.4	.306	.418	.415	.833	138
Daniel Baptista	65	280	81	6	0	7.9	19.3	.321	.386	.425	.811	115
Isaac Wenrich	58	260	69	10	4	9.2	24.6	.296	.365	.481	.846	117
Yuki Yasuda	57	252	61	0	16	15.9	15.1	.307	.448	.367	.815	139
Kristian Gayday	57	227	47	3	0	10.6	22.5	.237	.330	.328	.658	91
T. J. Gavlik	50	188	38	3	4	10.6	13.3	.235	.324	.321	.645	67
Joel Carranza	44	197	64	10	0	6.6	19.3	.358	.406	.575	.981	156
Andrew Parker	33	125	21	5	0	13.6	29.6	.206	.344	.382	.726	102
Fehlandt Lentini	32	148	39	5	6	4.7	14.2	.289	.345	.459	.804	119
Taylor Eads	29	113	18	0	3	17.7	30.1	.205	.345	.307	.652	79
Sergio Miranda	25	114	25	0	1	16.7	10.5	.281	.421	.326	.747	125
Brennan Metzger	18	86	31	1	5	12.8	17.4	.292	.407	.389	.796	141
Peter Bowles	17	54	8	0	0	5.6	29.6	.160	.222	.180	.402	9
Eddie Mora-Loera	9	37	6	0	1	18.9	24.3	.214	.405	.250	.655	88
Connor Jones	9	34	7	2	0	8.8	44.1	.226	.294	.419	.713	61
Chad Bunting	7	26	5	0	3	0.0	11.5	.200	.231	.240	.471	16
Matt Rubino	6	17	4	0	0	17.7	11.8	.308	.471	.308	.779	115
Keith Kandel	5	20	5	1	1	10.0	15.0	.278	.350	.500	.850	111
Jose Canseco	2	8	2	1	0	0.0	12.5	.250	.250	.625	.875	95
Tommy Lyons	1	5	2	0	0	0.0	20.0	.500	.600	.500	1.100	195
Jon Rand Jr.	1	1	0	0	0	0.0	0.0	.000	.000	.000	.000	−113
Aritz Garcia	1	4	0	0	0	25.0	25.0	.000	.250	.000	.250	133

STOMPERS PITCHERS

Name	IP	G	GS	BF	BB%	K%	BABIP	ERA	WHIP	K/BB	FIP
Gregory Paulino	93.3	16	15	383	6.3	22.7	.279	3.76	1.19	3.48	3.78
Eric Schwieger	89.7	15	15	394	6.6	17.3	.319	6.63	1.46	2.62	4.35
Mike Jackson Jr.	82.0	16	14	360	6.4	20.0	.380	4.72	1.56	3.13	3.41
Matt Walker	64.7	15	10	300	10.0	12.7	.321	6.40	1.75	1.27	5.75
Sean Conroy	60.0	22	4	244	4.9	21.3	.237	2.70	0.95	3.47	3.00
Paul Hvozdovic	49.3	17	6	218	5.5	16.5	.321	4.93	1.43	3.00	3.98
Santos Saldivar	48.3	13	5	201	8.5	28.9	.353	2.05	1.27	3.41	2.23
Erik Gonsalves	40.0	22	0	198	11.1	16.7	.370	4.95	1.85	1.43	3.99
Jon Rand Jr.	38.3	20	0	181	8.8	14.4	.333	5.87	1.71	1.63	4.84
Jeff Conley	32.0	7	6	152	10.5	16.4	.346	6.47	1.84	1.56	4.74
Dylan Stoops	23.0	7	0	96	9.4	30.2	.351	3.13	1.30	2.90	1.97
Ryusuke Kikusawa	17.0	8	1	79	15.2	17.7	.346	7.94	1.88	1.17	5.07
Cole Warren	13.3	7	0	61	14.8	19.7	.333	6.08	1.77	1.33	4.37
Jerome Godsey	10.7	7	0	42	9.5	16.7	.241	2.53	1.20	1.75	4.42
Josh McCauley	3.7	2	0	23	13.0	8.7	.471	12.27	4.00	0.67	7.65
Eric Mozeika	2.0	1	0	8	0.0	25.0	.200	4.50	1.00	—	6.74
T. J. Gavlik	2.0	1	0	9	0.0	22.2	.429	0.00	1.50	—	1.64

For more statistics, photos, and videos from the Sonoma Stompers' 2015 season, visit the book's official website at www.theonlyruleisithas towork.com.

END-OF-SEASON AWARDS

MOST VALUABLE PLAYER

Matt Chavez, Pacifics

PITCHER OF THE YEAR

Max Beatty, Pacifics

ROOKIE OF THE YEAR

Mark Hurley, Stompers

RELIEF PITCHER OF THE YEAR

Sean Conroy, Stompers

MANAGER OF THE YEAR

Aaron Miles, Diamonds

DEFENSIVE PLAYERS OF THE YEAR

P: Sean Conroy, Stompers

C: Isaac Wenrich, Stompers

1B: Daniel Baptista, Stompers

2B: Yuki Yasuda, Stompers

3B: T. J. Gavlik, Stompers

SS: Danny Gonzalez, Pacifics

LF: Mark Hurley, Stompers

CF: Zack Pace, Pacifics

RF: Matt Hibbert, Stompers

ACKNOWLEDGMENTS

It took a lot of people saying yes to convince us to take this fantasy seriously: Dan Evans was the first, followed by Joe Hamrahi, Theo Fightmaster, Eugene Lupario, Jonah Keri, Sydelle Kramer, Eric Gullotta, and our editor, Paul Golob.

Once we got to that point, it took a lot of people's help to make us sometimes seem smart. Chris Long gave us big league credibility (and a big league spreadsheet), and knew the mistakes we were going to make way before we did. John Choiniere brought order to our data. Ryan Zander and Graham Goldbeck at Sportvision made our PITCHf/x dreams come true, and Harry Pavlidis and Dan Brooks made those dreams useful. Ben Schroeder at Sydex Sports Software, and Zepp, Motus, Axe Bats, and Ultimeyes gave our players the equipment and resources to feel like big leaguers for a summer.

Our scouts—Leland Bailey, Noah Clark, Michael Conlan, Brett Handerson, Kortney Hebert, Tom Keown, Mark Reynolds, and Spencer Silva—spent as many hours watching bad baseball as we did. Each brought something irreplaceable to the Corduroy Crew, and the only thing more valuable than their scouting was their ever-cheerful company.

Zak Welsh and Michael Rosen were part of our team when we needed them most.

We relied on the intelligence and counsel of so many baseball friends, among them Russell Carleton, Bradley Ankrom, Chris Carminucci, Hans Van Slooten, and Mitchel Lichtman. Ken Maeda, Scott Kramer, and everybody at Banished to the Pen made the project feel special, which some nights we needed. Everybody associated with the Stompers was generous with time, insight, and encouragement: Jack and Andy Burkam, Mac Sweeney, Sean Boisson, Tommy Lyons, and the Stompers' host families. Commissioner David Alioto was a great ally. Chris Prete was a great landlord.

Thanks to Mallory Rubin and Dan Fierman at *Grantland*, and Jim Walsh, Stephen Reichert, and Sean Neugebauer at *Baseball Prospectus*, for letting us disappear for the summer. Jason Wojciechowski, Bret Sayre, and Patrick Dubuque cleaned up the mess Sam left behind at *BP*. Thanks also to Daniel Mahan, Alex Rubin, Steven Goldman, Gary Kershner, Jim Hinch, Eric Marsh, and Rod Miller.

Fehlandt Lentini and Takashi Miyoshi let us onto their turf and, on balance, both were open, supportive, and great to be around. It was a privilege to learn from them. Tim Livingston let us onto his turf, too. His invitation to come out to the park is the best email our little podcast ever got. Tim, Feh, and Yoshi get such different things out of baseball, but watching them all summer made it obvious that there's no wrong way to love the game.

Lastly, thanks to our families: to Betty and Jit Fong and Jane, and to Doris and Sam and Jessie.

ABOUT THE AUTHORS

BEN LINDBERGH is a staff writer for *The Ringer* and the cohost, with Sam Miller, of the podcast *Effectively Wild*. He is a former staff writer for *FiveThirtyEight* and *Grantland* and a former editor in chief of *Baseball Prospectus*. He lives in New York City.

SAM MILLER is a national baseball columnist and feature writer for ESPN. He is a former editor in chief of *Baseball Prospectus* and coedited three editions of *Baseball Prospectus*'s annual guidebook. He lives with his family in California.